Janet Wallach's own interest and expertise in Arab politics and history led her to the life of Gertrude Bell. A contributor to the *Washington Post* and other publications, Janet Wallach is the co-author, with her husband, John Wallach, of two books about the Middle East: *Still Small Voices: The Real Heroes of the Arab–Israeli Conflict* and *Arafat: In the Eye of the Beholder*. She lives in New York City.

BY JANET WALLACH

Still Small Voices:
The Real Heroes of the Arab-Israeli Conflict
(WITH JOHN WALLACH)

Arafat: In the Eye of the Beholder
(WITH JOHN WALLACH)

THE EXTRAORDINARY LIFE

OF

GERTRUDE BELL

Adventurer, Adviser to Kings,

Ally of Lawrence of Arabia

DESERT QUEEN

Janet Wallach

Weidenfeld & Nicolson
LONDON

A PHOENIX GIANT PAPERBACK

First published in Great Britain by
Weidenfeld & Nicolson in 1996
This paperback edition published in 1997 by Phoenix,
a division of Orion Books Ltd,
Orion House, 5 Upper St Martin's Lane,
London WC2H 9EA

Third impression 1999

First published in the USA in 1996 by
Nan A. Talese
an imprint of Doubleday
a division of Bantam Doubleday Dell Publishing Group, Inc.
1540 Broadway, New York, New York 10036

A CIP catalogue record for this book is available
from the British Library.

ISBN: 0 75380 247 3

Printed and bound in Great Britain by
Clays Ltd, St Ives plc

Contents

∞

To John, David and Michael,
who surround me with love

Acknowledgments

∞

Gertrude Bell first came to my attention more than twenty years ago when, reading one of her books on the Middle East, I was struck by the courage of this bold Victorian woman. As I was about to travel to that part of the world for the first time, any fears that I had were diminished; indeed, my curiosity was piqued by her descriptions of journeying alone in the early 1900s, surrounded only by Arab men, speaking almost no English, sleeping in tents, riding camel or horse through dangerous regions, risking robbery and even death. I put the book back on the shelf, but the spirit of that intrepid traveler stayed with me.

It wasn't until the Gulf War in 1991 that references to Gertrude Bell popped up in newspapers, books and periodicals. Seeing her name reminded me of her book and my admiration for her. Learning of her importance to the modern Middle East, and in particular her crucial role in Iraq, she seemed to me an ideal subject for a biography. Little did I know just how marvelous a subject she would be.

Gertrude Bell was keenly aware of the importance of her work, often reminding her parents that her letters were a record of history. Thousands of those letters and diary entries are now preserved in the Robinson Library of the University of Newcastle, where I did much of my research. I have tried to be as true to them as possible; where I used conversation and dialogue in *Desert Queen*, the quotes were taken directly from that material or from the letters and memoirs of Gertrude Bell's family, friends and colleagues. Any changes in spelling, particularly of Arabic words, were done to make the book more unified and the reading a little easier.

One of the bonuses of writing about Gertrude Bell was the opportunity to travel in her footsteps. I spent time with the Bedouin in the desert and with archaeologists, diplomats, writers and historians in England, Cairo, Damascus, Jerusalem, Amman and, most intriguing of all, Baghdad. I spoke to dozens of people who had heard about her from family and friends and to at least a dozen people who had actually known her themselves (including one who claimed to have been her lover). Some could still recall the authority of her voice, the severeness of her gaze, the exuberance of her dress. Others I spoke with helped me understand the mood of the places, the attitudes of the Arabs, the position of the British, the importance of the tribes, the impact of oil, the role of India. I am grateful to the many people who were so generous with their time, their memories and their knowledge.

I could not have gone to Baghdad without the enormous help of Ambassadors Nizar Hamdoon and Sadoon Zubaidi. Bahnam Abu al Souf, an ebullient archaeologist, and Mohammed Ghani Hikmat, Abdul Razaq Al Hassani, Muayad Sayid Damevji, Esman Gailani, Yousif al Gailani, Amin al Mummayiz and Ali Salah all gave me rare glimpses into Iraqi culture and history.

In Amman, I was fortunate to meet with Prince Raad, Souleiman Moussa, Talal al Patchachi, Abdul Aziz el Dhourie and Qais al Askari, who all had thoughtful insights into the monarchy and the tribes. Marwan Murwasha was, as always, a generous friend. In Cairo, Leila Mohanng helped me find old photographs. In Jerusalem, Val Vester recalled not only "Auntie Gertrude" but Hugh Bell, Florence Bell and Valentine "Domnul" Chirol. Amatzia Baram of Haifa University is an enthusiastic teacher who, undaunted, ploughed through hundreds of pages of manuscript and willingly shared his enormous knowledge.

In London, Roger Hardy of the BBC, Lamya Gailani, Renee Kabir, Nazha Akraui, Salma Sati el Husari and Naha Rahdi were a great help in reconstructing Baghdadi life. My thanks to Caroline Barron for permission to use the papers of her grandfather David Hogarth and at St. Anthony's College at Oxford, my special thanks to Lady Plowden and to the Trustees of the Trevelyan Family Papers. In Newcastle, Lesley Gordon helped with the Bell papers in the Special Collection of the Robinson Library at the university; Jim Crow steered me through the six thousand photographs taken by Gertrude Bell. Lynn Ritchie gave me excellent advice and Robin Gard kindly served as guide around Newcastle. Jane Hogan helped me in the Palace Green Section of the Durham University Library. At the Oriental Institute at Oxford, Jeremy Johns answered dozens of questions on archaeology and more. Sally Chilton talked fascinatingly about her father, Philip Graves.

In New York my thanks to Selma Rahdi for her help with archaeology and to Linda Fritzinger, a soul mate and scholar on Valentine Chirol. In Boston, Suhair Raad al Mummayiz helped me locate people to interview. In Washington, D.C., Christine Rourke and Betsy Folkins of the Middle East Institute were always willing to search for obscure facts and books; Nancy Wood did marvelous research on mountain climbing. Edmond Ghareeb and Nameer Jawdat were patient readers and teachers. My great thanks to Simon Serfaty, a good friend and wise counselor; Ghida Askari offered good cheer and vivid memories of her grandfather; Tamara Weisberg was always ready to listen; Sue Glaser added her psychologist's insights on childhood; Amos Perlmutter gave me his ebullient advice on the great British personalities; and Geoffrey Kemp helped me understand the role of India and oil. Christine Helms and Clovis Maksoud both led me to invaluable sources. Tania Hanna was a willing and able research assistant.

Ron Goldfarb and Linda Michaels, my literary agents, were enthusiastic believers from the beginning. My thanks to Jesse Cohen for his patience with endless details. I am indebted to Nan Talese for her encouragement, inspiration and attentive care to this project. Most of all, my thanks to my husband John, whose understanding and love made it possible to write this book.

Janet Wallach
NEW YORK, FEBRUARY 1996

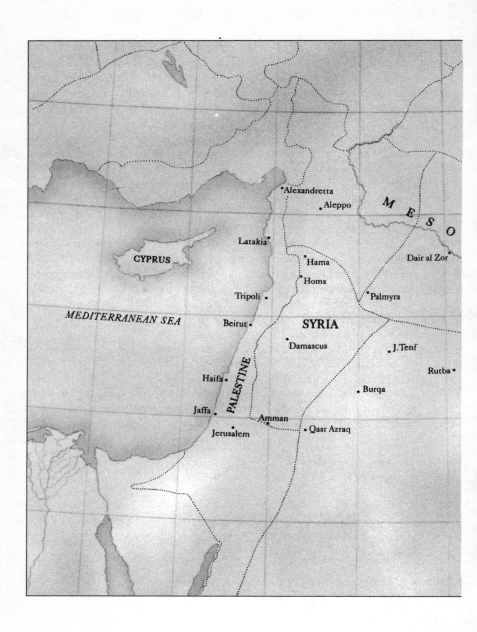

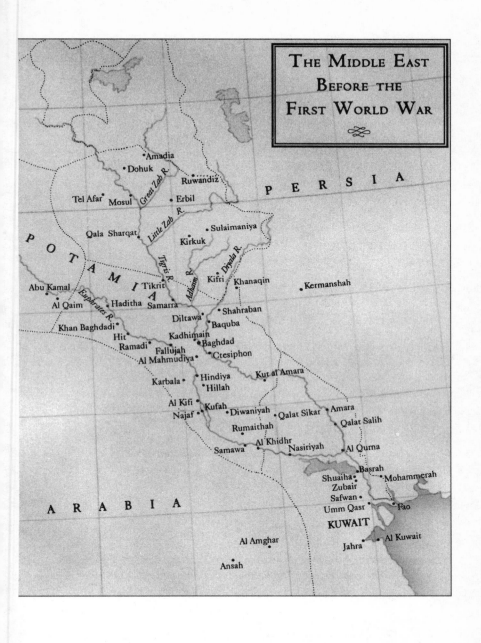

THE MIDDLE EAST
BEFORE THE
FIRST WORLD WAR

PERSIA

• Amadia
• Dohuk
• Ruwandiz
Tel Afar• Mosul   • Erbil
Great Zab R.
Little Zab R.
Qala Sharqat•   • Sulaimaniya
• Kirkuk
Tigris R.   Diyala R.
Adhaim R.
Abu Kamal•   • Kifri   • Khanaqin   • Kermanshah
Al Qaim•   • Tikrit
• Haditha   A• Samarra
Euphrates R.
Khan Baghdadi•   • Diltawa   • Shahraban
Hit•   • Kadhimain   • Baquba
Ramadi•   • Fallujah   • Baghdad
Al Mahmudiya•   • Ctesiphon
Karbala•   • Hindiya   • Kut al Amara
• Hillah
Al Kifi•   • Kufah
Najaf•   • Diwaniyah   • Qalat Sikar   • Amara
Rumaithah•   • Qalat Salih
Samawa•   • Al Khidhr   • Nasiriyah   • Al Qurna
Basrah•
Shuaiha•   • Mohammerah
Zubair•
Safwan•
Umm Qasr•   • Pao
KUWAIT

ARABIA

Al Amghar•   • Al Kuwait
Jahra•
Ansah•

POTAMIA

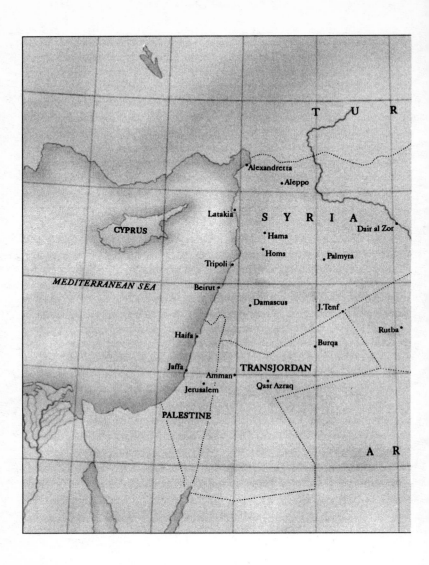

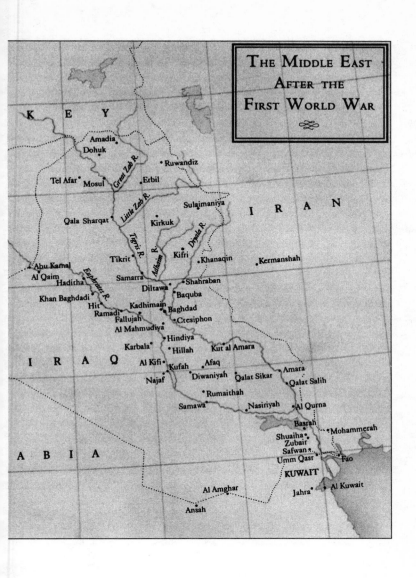

THE MIDDLE EAST
AFTER THE
FIRST WORLD WAR

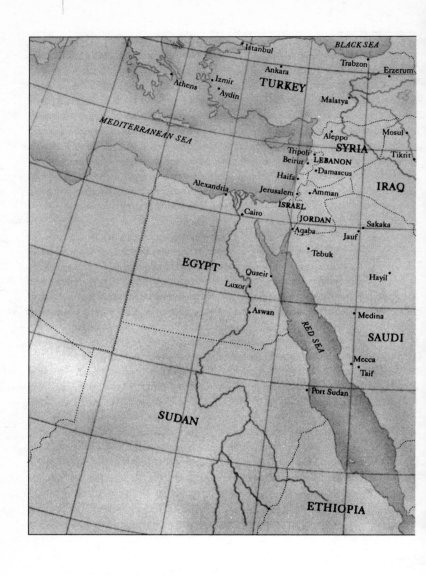

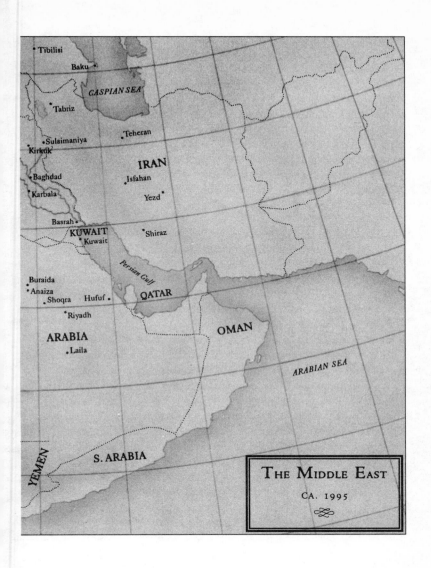

THE MIDDLE EAST

CA. 1995

Prologue

∞

She was always surrounded by men: rich men, powerful men, diplomats, sheikhs,* lovers and mentors. To picture her you had only to
envision a red-haired Victorian woman with ramrod posture, piercing
green eyes, a long pointed nose and a fragile figure fashionably dressed,
and, whether in London, Cairo, Baghdad or the desert, always at the
center of a circle of men. So it was only natural that on the drizzly
evening of April 4, 1927, less than a year after her death, those who
gathered at London's Royal Geographical Society to pay her tribute
were mostly men. Resplendent in white tie and tails, beribboned medals
flanking their chests, they marched through the halls recounting their
explorations and hers.

"Gertrude Bell," "Gertrude Bell," the name flew around the
room. She had been, they seemed to agree, the most powerful woman
in the British Empire in the years after World War I. Hushed voices
called her "the uncrowned queen of Iraq." They whispered that she
was the brains behind Lawrence of Arabia, and a few knowingly

---

* For the meaning of this term and other Arabic words used in the book, please refer to
the Glossary, starting on page 381.

ventured that she had drawn the lines in the sand for Winston Churchill.

Some said she had been arrogant, imperious and ruthlessly ambitious, but others knew that flowers and children could melt her heart, and that what she had desperately wanted, more than anything else, was to have been a wife and mother. They had heard she was engaged to be married once, and that later there had been a painful love affair, but they wondered why she had never wed.

A handful of men acknowledged she had achieved nothing less than a miracle by creating the modern state of Iraq; many grumbled that she had given in to the whims of the Arabs, causing the British no end of trouble and expense. A few even believed that she, the exuberant Englishwoman, had fallen in love with Faisal, the melancholy Arab prince, and that she had lost her head like a schoolgirl, but none could deny her achievements: the first woman to earn a first-class degree in Modern History at Oxford; the author of seven books, scores of articles in publications that ranged from academic journals to the pages of *The Times*, and a White Paper considered to be a masterpiece by the British Government. She was the only woman to earn the grade of Political Officer during the Great War and the only woman after the war to be named to the high post of Oriental Secretary; the winner of the gold medal of the Royal Geographical Society; the honorary director of antiquities at the Baghdad museum; and the recipient of a Commander of the Order of the British Empire.

The members of the Royal Geographical Society reminisced about her life before the Great War: a lone Englishwoman in the male, Muslim world of the Middle East, a famous author who wrote about the Arabs, an acknowledged archaeologist, a courageous traveler who dined with china and crystal, dressed in extravagant clothes, rode on camel and horse and penetrated dangerous regions of the Arabian desert. They had heard she was a spy who went behind enemy lines to gather information for the British during World War I. They remembered the way Vita Sackville-West had described her "irrepressible vitality" and her "gift of making every one feel suddenly eager; of making you feel that life was full and rich and exciting." And yet, on that same visit to Iraq in 1926, Vita had noticed how frail and ill her friend looked. Gertrude Bell's life had ended tragically only a few months after that, two days shy of her fifty-eighth birthday.

At the gathering in her honor, her father addressed the distinguished group. Sir Hugh, in his eighties, affirmed the unique relationship of which so many had known. "I think," he said, "there never were father and daughter who stood in such intimate relations as she and I did to one another." But it was her mentor David Hogarth, President of the Royal Geographical Society, who spoke that evening about her Arabian adventure, of which "[T. E.] Lawrence, relying on her reports, made signal use in the Arab campaigns of 1917 and 1918." That trip through the desert was only one of the many milestones that marked the journey of her life.

DESERT QUEEN

P<small>ART</small> O<small>NE</small>

A Victorian

CHAPTER ONE

Of Great and Honored Stock

∞

Great persons, like great empires, leave their mark on history. The greatest empire of all time, the one that stretched over a greater amount of ocean, covered a greater amount of land, contained a greater number of people than any before it, was the British Empire of Queen Victoria. Her superpower left its mark on continents and subcontinents, from Europe to Australia to India to America to Africa to Asia, from Adelaide to Wellington, Bombay to Rangoon, Ottawa to the Virgin Islands, Alexandria to Zanzibar, Aden to Singapore. The British navy ruled the seas, British coal fueled the ships and industries, British bankers financed the businesses, British merchants ran the trade, British food fed the stomachs and British factories clothed the bodies of one fourth of all human beings who lived and worked and played in every corner of the world.

Nothing better exemplified Britain's place at the center of the universe than the very first world's fair, the Great Exhibition of 1851, held in London. Along with Queen Victoria (who visited it forty times), half a million people—entrepreneurs, industrialists, landed aristocrats, diplomats, professionals, tradesmen and workers—came on opening day to see the "Great Exhibition of the Works of Industry of All Nations" at the new Crystal Palace in Hyde Park. Six million more people followed, most of them arriving by railway, to walk under the domed glass and along the carpeted hallways, to see goods from countries as nearby as France, Germany, Italy and Spain and from as far away as Russia, Persia, Turkey and China. They saw every imaginable product and some that were unimaginable: fabrics, raw hides, machine looms, jewelry, china, chocolates, coffee, tea, carpets, automatic revolvers, hydraulic presses, mechanical wood saws, wheat-grinding machines, gold quartz mills, high-pressure steam engines, a twenty-four-ton chunk of coal and a machine that sent messages by telegraph. The point of the exhibition, said Prince Albert, who had conceived it, was to show how far mankind had come and to give a direction for future development. No nation had come farther than Britain, the pioneer of the Industrial Revolution, "the workshop of the world." Its citizens had the highest per capita income and its workers contributed more than half of the fourteen thousand exhibitions at the Crystal Palace. In addition to the products of its colonies, the British booths displayed English cottons from Lancashire, sturdy woolens from Yorkshire, linens from Scotland, edged tools and fancy silver from Birmingham, glass and cutlery from Sheffield and huge machinery from Northumbria.

Nowhere did Britain's workshops toil harder than in Northumbria. In this remote region of northeast England, gray clouds still hover like withering ghosts, reminders of the black smoke of the furnaces that once choked its air and filled its skies. Northumbria. Its very name rumbles with the grimness of murky towns, desolate moors and dark seas. From its plants and factories came ships and railroads and enough iron and steel to help Britain fill forty percent of the world's supply. From beneath its surface came vast amounts of salt, lead, alum and iron ore and enough coal to help Britain provide two thirds of the world's needs. To and from its coastline came and went massive steamships carrying goods and keeping Northumbrians in touch with every outpost of the Empire.

If Northumbria was England's industrial country, Middlesbrough was its model town. Built out of bleak salt marshes, it began in 1801 with twenty-five people, but after railway lines were laid and ironworks started, it exploded into a booming town with a population of 7,431 in 1851, 19,416 in 1861 and more than 90,000 at the end of the nineteenth century. Its collieries that mined coal and converted it into coke (by 1840 Middlesbrough was mining one and a half million tons of coal annually), its blast factories that smelted iron ore into iron (by 1873 it was producing five and a half million tons of iron ore), its foundries that combined the silvery iron with the refined coke to manufacture steel (by 1879 it was producing over 85,000 tons of steel), its railroad lines, its factories, its potteries, its mills, its ships, its docks and its warehouses drew workers from all over Britain. Young men and women eager for jobs in the miserable pits or the hellish foundries came from the West Midlands, Wales, Scotland, Ireland, the East Indies, even the United States, and stared in awe at the night sky lit up with the brilliant flames of the steel furnaces or watched in amazement as locomotives steamed out of town hauling railroad cars filled with coal, iron, steel and pottery for every major city in England. The people who came for jobs crammed into the sooty rows of brown brick houses and breathed in the smutty air, cheering their mayor when he told the Prince of Wales that Middlesbrough took pride in its smoke. "The smoke is an indication of plenty of work . . . an indication of prosperous times, an indication that all classes of workpeople are being employed. . . . Therefore we are proud of our smoke."

The men and women who prospered most—industrialists, merchants, barristers, physicians, and their wives—would sometimes celebrate a special birthday or an anniversary by traveling the thirty miles north to Newcastle. The big city on the River Tyne was the capital of northern England, a commercial center, a bustling port, the place to go for an evening of theater, a day of shopping, a fine meal at a fancy inn.

If Middlesbrough was a booming town without a past, Newcastle was an ancient city rich with history. Residents of Newcastle who yearned for a bit of fresh country air could ride out to Wallsend and examine remnants of the Emperor Hadrian's Wall, built to defend Roman soldiers against Celtic warriors; or they could explore the moors and coastline where Englishmen once battled Scotsmen from the north, Anglo-Saxons from Germany, Vikings from Denmark and Normans from France. Back in town, a nineteenth-century man could still climb the castle keep built by William the Conqueror's son in 1080 or wander through the Guildhall, where craftsmen once met to set the wages of young apprentices. Men who disagreed over land or debts no longer argued at the Moot Hall, but they still held meetings at the County Hall, celebrated special occasions in the Merchant Adventurers' Court and prayed together at the five-hundred-year-old Saint Nicholas's Church.

Their work, too, was part of Newcastle's long history. As far back as the sixteenth century, its collieries had supplied 163,000 tons of coal to London, and its shipbuilding industry had built seafaring vessels— first, sailboats of wood, then, after 1838, steamships of iron and, later, massive ships of steel. Its old dock had been turned into a bustling quayside, harboring cargo ships bound for ports throughout the Empire. Twenty-four hours a day, three hundred and sixty-five days a year, British vessels that had set off from Newcastle plunged into the great North Sea to places like Eskimo Point or Cape Town or Karachi, bringing out finished goods from Britain and bringing home food and raw materials. Racing across the distant waters, they carried coal to fuel the navy, iron to lay the railroads, machine tools for the factories, armaments to defend the lands, carriages to transport the people and clothing to dress them; and they brought back, to name just a few things, silk, cotton, rubber, rice and tea from India; fish and furs from Canada; cocoa and ivory from Africa; gold and mutton from Australia; diamonds, pineapples and bananas from South Africa; tea from Ceylon; spices from Arabia; sugar, lime and turtles (for turtle soup) from the Caribbean.

If Middlesbrough was cramped and grimy, cosmopolitan Newcastle was the pride of its city planners, a spacious, orderly town with busy thoroughfares, open squares and an elegant avenue called Grey Street, considered one of the most graceful in all of Europe. The city was hailed for its Classical-style buildings, its stately houses, its first-class Theatre Royal. Its lively commercial center offered an enterprising fellow the chance to borrow money from a bank or try to make his fortune on the local stock market housed in the domed Central Exchange. Its shops boasted goods from around the world: shawls from Kashmir and sealskin muffs from the Yukon; diamonds from South Africa and rubies from India; tea from China, wine from France; and its bookstores sold guides to, among other places, Syria, Egypt and India.

India, of course, was where everyone had a family member or a friend or a friend of a friend. Almost twenty thousand British controlled the lives of two hundred and fifty million Indians, mostly Hindus and Muslims, whose exports of agriculture and raw materials and whose imports of nearly everything else from British soil made India the jewel in the crown of the British Empire. Back and forth the British traveled, a grueling four-month trip by ship around Cape of Good Hope, until the year 1869, when the great opening of the Suez Canal shortened the sea voyage to only three weeks, making it even easier to bring more goods to the shops in Newcastle.

The city's merchants prospered from millionaires who came to buy. One of those who came regularly to cosmopolitan Newcastle to purchase shirts of imported Egyptian cotton or to surprise his wife with a necklace of African ivory beads was the grandfather of Gertrude Bell, the prominent industrialist Isaac Lowthian Bell.

❧ ❧ ❧

Lowthian Bell, as he liked to be called, was a perfect man for his time, possessing a rare combination of scientific learning and manufacturing genius. Born in 1816, he had studied physics, chemistry and metallurgy in Germany, Denmark, at the University of Edinburgh, at the Sorbonne and in Marseilles and, at the age of twenty-four, joined his father's ironworks at Newcastle. Within a short period he pioneered the use of blast furnaces for smelting iron ore and introduced the first plant in England for the manufacture of aluminum. In 1844 he and his two brothers established Bell Brothers, a company that eventually included ironstone mines, collieries, limestone quarries and steel mills. Driven mostly by Lowthian Bell's extraordinary energy and vision, the firm was the northeast's largest and most important ironworks and colliery in the 1870s. It employed more than forty-seven thousand men and supplied one third of all the iron used in England.

Heads bowed when Lowthian Bell came into a room. He knew more about Northumbria's iron and coal than anyone else and could answer any question, either on statistics or the scientific side. Far better educated than any of his peers (entrepreneurs were not noted for their learning), he was the spokesman for Northumbrian industry, a director of the North-Eastern Railway and president of five different chemical and engineering institutions. Highly regarded as a scientist, he was a Fellow of the Royal Society, the country's most prestigious group of scientists, and had won the first Bessemer gold medal, along with other medals for his work in the arts, engineering and industry. He published numerous papers and authored two books, *The Chemical Phenomena of Iron Smelting* and *The Principles of Iron and Steel Manufacture*, important contributions on the manufacture of iron and steel.

A man who took a keen interest in his community, he was elected twice to be mayor of Newcastle, served as sheriff of County Durham, and held a Liberal seat in Parliament for five years. As deep as his interest was in Northumbria, however, he was always restless, traveled constantly and kept a sharp eye on the competition, especially in America, where he was even made an honorary member of the American Philosophical Institution. He was a man of the world and a man with a sense of his own place in it. Lowthian Bell not only earned the reputation as the world's greatest ironmaster; he made enormous contributions to the British Empire and created one of Britain's greatest fortunes. In time, his granddaughter Gertrude Bell would inherit his money, his brilliant mind, his inquisitive nature and his exuberance for life.

In 1842 Lowthian Bell had married Margaret Pattinson, daughter of a chemical manufacturer, and a few years later, in partnership with his father-in-law, opened a chemical works at Washington, a few miles from Newcastle. Down the road from the medieval ancestral home of George Washington, the young couple built an imposing Gothic house, complete with stained glass windows, terra cotta gargoyles and a large square tower. The red brick structure had enough rooms to accommodate an endless stream of guests and enough domestic servants to care for the five babies who soon arrived. Margaret gave birth to three girls and two boys; their elder son, born on February 10, 1844, was a handsome, carrot-haired, blue-eyed lad. Thomas Hugh Bell would be Hugh to all who knew him and father to Gertrude Bell.

The Bell household bubbled with activity. Visitors constantly came and went, and young Hugh was allowed into the drawing room to meet his father's friends. The boy listened as Charles Darwin and Thomas Huxley expounded their ideas on evolution, and John Ruskin, the art critic and social reformer, and William Morris, the aesthetic socialist, discussed their revolutionary ideas of how man should not just improve industry but how industry should improve the life of man. It was radical talk in the home of an industrial magnate, but Lowthian Bell was no ordinary man. He was an adventurer who believed in a solid foundation of learning and a dedication to society.

The year of the Great Exhibition, when Hugh Bell was eleven, he was sent to school in Edinburgh. Four years later he traveled to France to study chemistry at the Sorbonne and then to Germany to study organic chemistry and mathematics. Reluctantly, at the age of eighteen he returned to England to join his father's business. As energetic as his father, and equally curious, he would someday be considered by *The Times* "a great authority on all questions connected with the coal and iron trades." But Hugh had a broader intellect. First assigned to the head office of Bell Brothers Ironworks at Newcastle, he was soon made director of the company branch at Middlesbrough and would go on to run the entire business. But he spent much of his time promoting secondary education. He founded the Middlesbrough High School, was chairman of the Free Library Committee and chairman of the School Board. An effective speaker, he delivered speeches around the country on public education, public health and military reform and proudly pushed through a bill protecting children from dangerous work.

Vivacious and good-humored, Hugh delighted his friends with amusing stories in English, French and German and tickled his guests with his latest pun. He would sometimes come down to breakfast with a piece of paper in his hand; from the conversation the evening before, he had elaborated on an irony or sharpened a satirical story. He loved to read, enjoyed engaging in any area of conversation and could quote contemporary thinkers as easily as he could tell an original joke. A boisterous man with a generous heart, he had the charming ways and courteous manner of a true Victorian gentleman. But he was, he admitted, a "bitter free-trader," and almost as bitterly opposed to Home Rule for the Irish; if pushed too hard, he could be mercilessly blunt. He had no fear of physical challenges, loved to ride to the hounds and climb to precipitous heights, and said frequently, "obstacles are made to be overcome." Brilliant and incisive, he gave the impression of polished steel.

But the tall, handsome bachelor, who had an eye for the ladies, met Miss Mary Shield. A fragile-looking young woman with a gentle face, large, sensitive, wide-set eyes and a finely shaped mouth, the daughter of an important Newcastle food merchant, she married Hugh in 1867. After their wedding at the parish church near her family's summer house in the Scottish isles, they returned to Washington, where the Lowthian Bells had added on several new rooms, including a fashionable Turkish bath, and by Christmas Mary was pregnant.

∞ ∞ ∞

Arrived, on July 14, 1868, the London *Times* announced: Gertrude Margaret Lowthian Bell. The first-born of Hugh Bell and Mary Shield Bell had reddish hair and piercing blue-green eyes, her mother's bow-shaped lips and rounded chin, her father's oval face and pointed nose. Of honored stock and Northumbrian heartiness, she had inherited too, from her paternal side, the energy and intellect, the drive and determination that made the Bell males so outstanding.

Under the watchful eye of her nanny, Miss Ogle, Gertrude was soon dressed in bloomers, petticoats and cotton frocks, fed her porridge, made to eat her vegetables and encouraged to play outdoors. She was reminded to obey her parents (and Miss Ogle), sit up straight, hold her knife and fork properly and speak to adults only when spoken to. The country's greatest role model, Queen Victoria, she was taught, was "a good wife, a good mother, and a good woman . . . due, under God, to the training she had in childhood and girlhood." The Queen was dedicated to her princely husband, her children and her Empire, and she set the highest example of morality, self-discipline and hard work.

It was appropriate that the Bells' family fortune was earned through industry and toil. Britain's great strength, after all, came from its navy, its trade, its coal and iron. Few men contributed more than the Bells. They worked not only to enhance their own communities, but to maintain Britain's place in the sun. They took pride in the British Empire and in its role as custodian of the universe. Whether in their huge and all-important colony of India or on some tiny island in the Caribbean, the British believed it was their duty to protect the natives, uphold the trade, spread morality and defend the territory. If the British did not do it, they assumed, someone else would, and no one— not the Germans, not the French, certainly not the Russians (who lusted after India)—could ever do it as well. Theirs was a world run by men of initiative, courage and conviction. It was a world graced by women who, in their domesticity, were no less than the guardians of the English race.

Like other young women of her class, as she grew older Gertrude would be expected to stay at home (unlike her brother, who would be sent off to Eton), be taught by governesses and have accomplishments. In the prevailing belief that a healthy body was as important as a healthy mind, she would learn to ride, to swim and to play tennis; to be fluent in at least two foreign languages, preferably German and French; to be well versed in literature and knowledgeable in music and art; to be good at fancy needlework, dabble in painting and know how to play a musical instrument. Most of all, it was thought, she would aspire to be a good wife and mother. But unlike other young women of her class, Gertrude had ambitions that would go far beyond the home. Like her father and grandfather, she would be driven to reach for intellectual challenges. She would attend university, travel widely and take up more than one successful career. Like her father and grandfather, she would help the Empire sustain its greatness and even expand its rule. Like her father and grandfather, she would penetrate the unknown and explore the frontier. But unlike Hugh and Lowthian Bell, she would have no desire to make her world in Northumbria. Her world would be in the East, in Arabia, in Egypt, in Syria and, most of all, in Iraq, where she would make her mark on history.

❧   ❧   ❧

At the age of two Gertrude was brought to Red Barns, her parents' huge new mansion near Middlesbrough. From the tall case- ment windows in the children's wing of the house, she kept track of her favorite gardens, her little one next to Papa's, blooming with butter- cups, hyacinths and roses. On most days she ran across the fields, climbed trees or raced to the family stables for riding lessons. Beyond the great expanse of green lawn lay the racquet court, the bicycle house and the pond, and beyond even that lay a more rugged landscape. Red Barns, in the seaside town of Redcar, was close to the rough North Sea, which crashed against the English coastline. With her crisply dressed nanny beside her, Gertrude stood at the edge of the sea and wriggled her toes in the briny waves, watching the great steamships sailing off to faraway ports. Like Kipling, she could ask:

> *"Oh, where are you going to, all you Big Steamers,*
>   *With England's own coal up and down the salt seas?"*
> *"We are going to fetch you your bread and your butter,*
>   *Your beef, pork and mutton, eggs, apples and cheese."*

Indoors, from the nursery Gertrude wandered through the house's fourteen bedrooms, paid calls to the kitchen to chat with the cook or peeked into the conservatories, but the best activity was visiting with her mother. Snuggled on Mary's lap, she nestled in the rustling layers of her taffeta dress, enfolding herself in her mother's special scent. Secure and protected, Gertrude's life seemed to be as smooth as her cashmere blanket. But sorrow would soon snag its pretty design.

✤   ✤   ✤

Nearly three weeks had gone by since her mother took to bed in the winter of 1871. At first, great excitement filled the house with the announcement of the arrival of a baby boy. But the bleak March skies of northern England darkened over Red Barns as the little girl waited in the nursery, eager to return to her mother's loving arms, curious to see the infant, Maurice. Her brother's cries were not the only strange new sounds in the house; hushed whispers blew like an evil wind outside her mother's door. The frail Mary Bell was too ill to leave her bed, and the physician who attended arrived more often now; the clomp of the doctor's steps came faster and heavier, but instead of improving, the patient was growing weaker. It was not long before pneumonia set in, and then, as quickly as they had come, the doctor's footsteps disappeared. The little girl, watching anxiously for her mother's return, saw her hopes snatched as suddenly as a raven seizes its prey.

Gertrude was not yet three when her family dressed her in black to mourn her mother's death. Mary was buried in the fields at Rounton Grange, a new estate being built by Lowthian Bell, and for several years after, young Gertrude re-enacted the funeral. Each time a favorite cat or other animal died, she grieved with a heavy heart, and with much fanfare led an imposing procession to bury her pet in a cemetery in the garden.

In a photograph taken the year her mother died, the curly-haired child shows a furrowed brow that forms an arch over her troubled soul. Her haunted eyes peer restlessly for answers, and the distant expression, seen in every photograph of her from childhood to womanhood, fore-shadows a life spent searching. But, as she leans her foot on a stool, defiantly looking as if she were about to jump on it or kick it over, her firm expression gives hint of her strong will and resolution.

Anger, betrayal, a sense of abandonment; these are the feelings that surge in a child who has lost a parent. But Gertrude was also fortunate to be enveloped by her father's love. Few can deny the powerful affec-tion of a three-year-old girl for her father; even more, he became her role model. He would be the person she most patterned herself after, the one whose stamp of approval she always sought. From him she gained enormous confidence and the attitude for overcoming obstacles.

Distraught over his wife's death, Hugh was able to take solace in his daughter's love and to share with her the pleasures of long walks and rock-climbing, riding horses, raising rabbits and cultivating flower gardens. For her birthday he gave Gertrude a watering can; she reported to him that wild roses bloomed abundantly in the garden. On another occasion she announced that she had gathered a nosegay, proudly not-ing that the roses had come from *her* garden. As an adolescent she sent him descriptions of a neighbor's garden: bright scarlet dahlias, yellow-brown acacia, tall, thin chrysanthemums grew there, she wrote, but "I like the way we grow ours better." Even as an adult living in Baghdad she shared with him the progress of her garden, wishing sometimes he would come and help. Flowers were but a small part of the powerful bond she nurtured with her father; all her life she rejoiced in his admiration and regarded him as an unending source of wisdom, under-standing and love.

∞ ∞ ∞

Her brother, Maurice, became her closest playmate and perfect foil. Fearful of her sharp tongue and her reprimands, he followed her like an awkward puppy. When she led him to the top of a nine-foot wall and ordered him to jump, the little boy heeded and fell flat on his face, but she landed gracefully on her feet. Climbing treacherously to the roof of the greenhouse, Maurice went crashing through the glass, but Gertrude scampered safely across the panes. At the beach, when their nurse wasn't looking, the children slipped from her side and Gertrude dashed with her brother from one cove to another or hid in the boats moored on the shore. In bad weather they played inside, pasting pictures in their scrapbooks, watching magic lantern slides, playing with their trains and dolls.

Until Gertrude was eight, the distraught widower Hugh, when not at work, spent most of his time at home. Despite the urging of his sisters, Hugh refused to think of marrying again. But on a vacation in Scotland in the summer of 1874 he was introduced to a friend of his sisters named Florence Olliffe. The twenty-four-year-old playwright had lived in France, where her father, a prominent physician and social-ite, had created the seaside resort of Deauville. In Paris she had known diplomats and literary figures and counted among her family friends the writers Charles Dickens and Henry James. After her father's death she and her mother had moved to England, where she impressed those she met with her sophisticated style; Hugh was struck by her elegant manners and her intense blue eyes. Florence noticed not only Hugh's courtly ways, but when she saw him for the first time, standing at the end of a rose-covered path, she recognized how beautiful he was and how very sad.

For two years their relationship continued, and in the spring of 1876, when it turned more serious, Florence wrote a note to Gertrude. "My Dear Miss Olliffe," Gertrude carefully penned in response, an-swering questions about her flowers and a pair of ominous ravens, "Thank you very much for your letter. The ravens are tamer and very nice. I think you will like the garden very much, the flowers are all coming out." She signed the letter, "Your aff'ate Gertrude."

That June in London, at the Harley Street home of Lady Stanley, a staging was held of an opera that Florence had written. The enlight-ened Lady Stanley, grandmother of Bertrand Russell and mother-in-law of Hugh's sister, made the event a sparkling occasion. At the end of the evening, when Hugh escorted Florence back to her mother's flat at 95 Sloane Street, he asked for her hand in marriage. "Lady Olliffe," he announced, "I have brought your daughter home, and I have come to ask if I may take her away again."

They were married two months later, on August 10, 1876, at a small church on Sloane Street. It seems so odd now, and even somewhat cruel, but the children were not included in the wedding. Instead, Gertrude sent a note: "My dear Miss Olliffe. I write this letter for you to have on your wedding day to send you and Papa our best love and many kisses. Thank you for the doll's frock which fits beautifully . . .

From your loving Gertrude." For their honeymoon the couple went off to America, where Florence's sister and brother-in-law, Mary and Frank Lascelles, were posted at the British Embassy in Washington, and the next time Gertrude wrote to Florence, thanking her for a locket, she addressed her with a new title: "My Dear Mother."

Even before the wedding, Florence had tried to win the little girl's heart, sending her clothes for her dolls and gifts for herself. Eager for the attention, Gertrude was troubled, nevertheless, by this new woman who took so much of her father's time. While her parents were on their honeymoon, she wrote to them with some concern about their safety, told them she dreamed of dead ravens and wished that her parents were with her. By autumn, Florence and Hugh were back at Red Barns, and life returned to some of its old rhythm. A portrait done by Edward Poynter shows eight-year-old Gertrude seated on her father's lap, his arm around her, their fingers entwined, their faces glowing with love and affection. In its essence, it was a picture that could have been drawn at almost any point in their lives.

When Hugh and his new wife went off to London the following April, Gertrude was almost in despair. "Dear dear Mamy," she wrote to Florence, "I am very very sorry you cannot come home. . . . I send love to Papa and all. I am dear dear dear Mamy your loving Gertrude." A short while later, she received news that her parents were returning: "Dear Mamy, I am so very very very very very very glad you are coming home. . . . Do get me a doll. I have got none. . . . Dear dear dear dear dear dear Mamy, you don't know how glad I am you are coming home. From your very very very loving Gertrude."

Eager for Florence's love, the little girl struggled to please. Florence opened up an exciting world of books, theater, art and interesting people. As a child Gertrude liked nothing so much as to sit at her side, listening to her read from Lewis Carroll's *Alice In Wonderland* or the tales of Ali Baba, Sinbad the Sailor and Aladdin and his Magic Lamp from the *Arabian Nights*. As Gertrude grew older, she found much in Florence to admire: her talent as a writer, her efforts at social justice, her accomplishments as a hostess, her literary friends, her stylishness and fashion sense. Even more, she was grateful for the friendship and family life that Florence provided.

But her stepmother's impatience with anything less than perfection prickled Gertrude like a spiky thorn. A photograph, taken when Gertrude was nine, reveals some of the tension between them. Florence, resplendent in a rich velvet dress trimmed with fur, is seated in front of a leaded glass window, her expression forbidding as she looks down at a large book in her hands. On one side stands Maurice, in his buttoned-up suit, on the other, Gertrude, in a plain wool dress, but as close as they are placed to her, the children seem miles away. There is no contact: no physical touching, no emotional bond. While little Maurice seems to be biting his lip to stop himself from crying, Gertrude looks soulful, her eyes off somewhere in the distance. If tears could fill the chasm between them, there would be enough to plug an ocean.

Gertrude's willfulness had caused a string of nannies to quit their job. Florence, too, had little tolerance for Gertrude's "highly spirited" ways. As soon as she began having her own children (there would be three in all: Elsa, Molly and Hugo), Gertrude, aged ten, was sent on long visits to her cousins (her favorite was Horace Marshall) or to her grandparents' new house at Rounton Grange. More than once reports came back to Florence about Gertrude's naughtiness, her dangerous climbs on steep rocks, the risky adventures that often scared the relatives.

Wherever Gertrude was, she escaped through her books. They were her magic carpet, but anything she read had to be approved by Florence. At the age of eleven she glided through John Richard Green's long *History of the English People*. At fourteen, she asked her cousin Horace if he had read Browning's new book of poetry. "I suppose not," she answered with resignation. But, she boasted to him, in one week she had galloped through volumes of letters and biographies of Mozart, Macaulay and Mrs. Carlyle. At sixteen, she dashed through George Eliot's *Silas Marner*, and then asked meekly, "What other book of hers may I read now?" Even at the age of twenty-three, after ordering a best-selling novel about the seduction of a maid, she wrote apologetically to Florence, telling her to return it: "Naturally I should have asked you about it before I read it."

No matter how bright they were, girls of Gertrude's class rarely were sent away to school; instead, they were tutored at home and, at the age of seventeen, were presented at court and introduced to society. Within three seasons of coming out, each was expected to find a husband. But Gertrude had shown an exceptional mind, too keen to be kept at home. Florence and Hugh, progressive thinkers both, took the radical step of sending her to a girls' school in London. It would calm the energy level in the household and, at the same time, feed Gertrude's hungry intellect. Queen's College, a girls' school on Harley Street, was started in 1848 as a series of Lectures for Ladies.

It was a total change from the protected world of Red Barns and Rounton Grange. For one thing, her classmates were all girls. For another, the rules were stricter in London than they had been at home. Intellectually, she had little concern. Her first-term grades marked her as an outstanding student: first in her class in English History; second in English Grammar, third in Geography, fourth in French and Ancient History. When a subject was too easy, she asked to be transferred to a more advanced class and welcomed the extra load of work. But eager as she was to learn, and as good a scholar as she was, the sixteen-year-old found the experience at Queen's College lonely and painful. "I was horribly miserable yesterday," she wrote after she returned for a new semester; "the first few days are the worst." Torn from the comforts of home, she missed her male companions—her brother Maurice, her cousin Horace and her father—and disliked the company of other young women. She found them "uninteresting," affected and not up to her speed. Nevertheless, the privileged young lady, whose grandfather had just been made a baronet, discovered that she did not always stand above the crowd: "It's a very disagreeable process, finding out that one is no better than the common run of people. I've gone through rather a hard course of it since I came to College and I don't like it at all." She dreaded the "great flat stretch of weeks with nothing to look forward to," and filled her days with extra school assignments. History was her favorite subject, and as she studied the English monarchy she began to comprehend Britain's powerful role in the world.

City life did not please her; London was a quick flirtation, an evening of laughter followed by a lonely night of tears. For Gertrude, the countryside was constant love; it embraced her with arms full of roses and caressed her with blossoms and trees. "I wish I were at home," she wrote wistfully in the fall. "There must be such a delicious autumn smell in the country, and then crackly yellow and red leaves, oh it makes me quite discontented to think of it." Knowing how much she loved the outdoors, Florence made sure there were always fresh flowers in her room at school. When she slipped up once, Gertrude chided, "You didn't send me any flowers this week! Did you forget?"

In the loneliness of her schooldays, she sought company through her letters. Her wooden pen with steel-tipped nib, a bottle of ink and paper became her constant companions. Throughout her life she would keep them by her side, and sometimes, when there was no one else, she used them to talk for hours to her family. Over the years, she wrote to her stepmother partly as duty, partly in friendship, partly as a journal of her experiences. Often her parents were apart and she wrote to them both. Her arm never tired; the words seemed to push the pen onto the paper without her body's exerting any effort. She told everything there was to know; and later, when the British needed to know the terrain of the desert, she could tell them almost every grain of sand she had traversed, and when they asked about any man she had met, she could describe the birthmarks on his face and the warts on his character.

In spite of the separation at school, Florence kept a firm watch, scrutinizing Gertrude's manners and supervising her social life. Gertrude was required to ask permission before visiting anyone outside Florence's circle, and like all young, unmarried women from proper families, she was not allowed on the street without a chaperone. She found the rules for her gender terribly frustrating. Even a visit to a museum required an escort: "I wish I could go to the National, but you see there is no one to take me. If I were a boy, I should go to that incomparable place every week, but being a girl to see lovely things is denied me!"

At times she seemed perfectly willing to accept her mother's control, and, indeed, all her life she acted with obedience toward her parents. She wished that Florence would come to London and visit and was delighted when Florence arranged for friends to invite her to tea. At their homes she met, among others, Mrs. Humphrey Ward, the well-known novelist; Mrs. Green, widow of the historian; Anne Ritchie, the daughter of William Thackeray; Richmond Ritchie, her husband and an influential diplomat; Jenny Lind, the Swedish soprano; Fanny Kemble, the actress and, later, Henry James and the poet Robert Browning.

At other times, when Florence was very critical, Gertrude dipped her pen in anger. After receiving three excoriating pages, she wrote back to tell Florence they were "quite horrid," and announced gleefully that she had avenged herself by promptly burning them. Her mother constantly reprimanded her for spelling errors and grammatical shortcuts, and after one particularly critical letter, Gertrude complained about Florence's "priggish" style. "Would you have me say when talking of the sovereign, 'The Queen of England, Scotland, Ireland, Empress of India, Defender of the Faith'?" the sixteen-year-old asked. "My life is not long enough to give everything its full title." Another time she complained, "You've told me all those things so often that I know them by heart. . . . I don't think it's any use your telling me over again. Generally, I think I could write out your letters before I open them and come pretty close to the original withal!" How different were her comments to her father. "You don't scold me nearly enough," she told him, "but I'm much sorrier when you don't scold me than when you do."

In her letters to Hugh, Gertrude solicited his help on freeing her from the dreaded piano lessons Florence insisted she have; she asked his advice on schoolwork, offered her views on history and sought her father's opinions on free trade, Home Rule for the Irish, the fate of Prime Minister William Gladstone and the Liberal Party. She divided her writing between Florence's interests in literature, fashion and the arts and Hugh's interests in politics and world affairs. But slowly her own interests were developing in all of these areas. She wrote to Hugh that history might become her career (at least, although she did not say so, until she married), and in her last semester, at the suggestion of her teacher, she approached her father gingerly and asked permission to continue her studies at Oxford. If Hugh agreed to send her to university, it would be another radical step. Instead of a world of domesticity, she would be entering the realm of the elite and the powerful, a world ruled and peopled almost completely by men. "My only fear," she wrote to her father, "is if I once go there you will never be able to get me away!"

Chapter Two

A Man's World

∞

Gray stone walls enclosed the University of Oxford, barriers warding off the prosaic and welcoming the privileged to its rarefied air. An assemblage of chosen people lived within, the intellectuals and the high-born, supporting one another's sense of superiority, reinforcing each other's sense of distinction. Gertrude's acceptance bolstered her already strong self-esteem. As unhappy as she had been at Queen's College, confined to a middling female world, she had proven herself an outstanding scholar. Now, in a far more appealing atmosphere, with the Bells' drive and determination, she would rise to the highest levels.

Since the twelfth century, clergymen, kings, prime ministers, diplomats, philosophers, scientists and academics had secluded themselves behind the Oxford walls to breathe the fresh air of thoughts and sample a feast of ideas. Each college hall, each cobbled path, echoed with the footsteps of powerful leaders and pioneer thinkers. Men like Roger Bacon argued in the thirteenth century for experimental methods of inquiry. In the sixteenth century Sir Thomas More defended the Catholic Church over the will of Henry VIII, and in the seventeenth century Oliver Cromwell, the country's leader, served as Chancellor. There were scientists like Edmund Halley, who discovered a new comet, and, in the nineteenth century, Thomas Huxley, who brilliantly defended Darwin's ideas of evolution. There were architects like Christopher Wren, who designed the Sheldonian Theatre and, later, artists like William Morris and Edward Burne-Jones, whose stained glass windows lit up Christ Church Cathedral; poets like Matthew Arnold, who immortalized the school's spires; philosophers like John Ruskin, whose books could be found on the shelves of the Radcliffe reading room. From the rule of the Plantagenets until the reign of Queen Victoria, the brightest young men, but only men, had entered Oxford; in exchange for the freedom to think, they cloistered themselves in austere surroundings, clothed themselves in simple robes, and undertook a life of celibacy. But the tone of Oxford changed in 1874, when male students were allowed to marry. And it changed even more dramatically in 1879, when Miss Elizabeth Wordsworth, grandniece of the poet, became the first principal of Lady Margaret Hall, for young women. Only a few years later, in 1886, LMH would serve as home for Gertrude.

As principal of the women's school, Miss Wordsworth felt her first priority was to see that her students married. She was convinced that God intended woman to be "Adam's helpmate," and to fill that role properly, she insisted, a young woman must develop the "minor graces" of "neat handwriting," "skillful needlework," and "the ways of opening and shutting doors." Her girls were allowed to sit in on lectures and to have their own tutors, but the pursuit of intellectual ideas was still considered questionable, not just for women but for the country. As the contemporary philosopher Herbert Spencer put it, thinking was dangerous for females; "the overtaxing of their brains," he declared, would lead to "the deficiency of reproductive power." When Gertrude arrived, the halls of New College Chapel still reverberated with the recent sermon of Dean John Burgon: "Inferior to us God made you, and inferior to the end of time you will remain." But Gertrude Bell hardly felt inferior: at eighteen, she was already sure that she was the equal of any male, and if anyone doubted her word, she had her father to back her up.

∞ ∞ ∞

O*xford!*, she exclaimed at the top of her first letter home, in May 1886, and she reveled in being one of only a handful of girls in the company of hundreds of men. Round-faced and chubby, exuberant and ebullient, she arrived "half child, half woman," her new friend Janet Hogarth said, "rather untidy, with vivid auburn hair, greenish eyes, a brilliant complexion, and a curiously long and pointed nose." Notably she added, Gertrude had "a most engaging way of saying, 'Well you know, my father says so and so' as a final opinion on every question under discussion."

On the first day of class, Gertrude walked hurriedly with Mary Talbot, a colleague in the History program, and their requisite but doting escort, Miss Wordsworth. Dressed in their long, loose black gowns and black laced boots, square black caps firmly planted on their heads, the young women chatted in nervous anticipation, stepping briskly across the old stone walks. Like Alices in Wonderland, they had to "fly" from the farthest outposts of Oxford, where they lived at LMH, through the grassy University Parks, to arrive in time for their History lecture in Balliol.

Climbing the stairs, they reached the alabaster hall and saw before them, perpendicular to the lecturer's platform, rows of long, green baize tables and, seated at them, some two hundred men. No space was reserved for the two young women, however, and no one showed any inclination to make some room. Instead, they were led to the platform, where the professor presided. Sliding into their seats, the women listened intently while the tall, gaunt Mr. Lodge lectured on English History. "We felt it was a great event!" Gertrude wrote to her parents. Not even the thrill of her first class, however, nor the lecture by the well-known teacher could dull her sharp tongue; all that he said was straight out of his book, she scoffed. It "would have been said much better if he had read us the first few chapters."

It was a strange segregation of females and males, as though the women's very presence would poison the atmosphere. But to Gertrude the separate table on the platform added to the awesome prestige of being privy to an Oxford lecture. And when Mr. Bright, who taught History, had them sit in the room with their backs to him, it made her laugh. The problem was his, she believed. Certainly she did not mind sitting "cheek by jowl" with a roomful of men.

❧   ❧   ❧

She enjoyed the routine of lectures in the morning, lunch at LMH, reading at the Radcliffe library and private tutorials on Saturdays. Together with Mary Talbot, she penetrated the male-filled halls of the Bodleian and hunted out books under the glaring eyes of the librarian. After receiving the requested books, she wrote her parents, they felt they "really *were* members of the University." Earlier, when she had first arrived and did not yet have her student pass, she had been rebuffed at the Radcliffe reading room. It had come as a shock to the young woman who got almost everything she wanted. But now she was comfortably secure. The tall, dark-eyed Mary Talbot, a niece of Prime Minister William Gladstone, soon became Gertrude's closest comrade. Edith Langridge, who lived in the room next door and was an earlier graduate of Queen's College, looked after her. Janet Hogarth, whose older brother David was an Oxford scholar and an archaeologist doing work in the East, would also become a lifelong friend.

She appreciated the care of the "very nice" Miss Wordsworth, although it must be noted that the principal thought Gertrude was not a woman one could count on. "Would she be the sort of person to have in one's bedroom if one were ill?" Miss Wordsworth asked. In fact, except for her father, Gertrude had little patience with other people's problems. She did enjoy the respect of her tutor, Professor Hassall, who praised her work, and she was fortunate to have the company of her childhood companion Horace Marshall. Her cousin was at Trinity College at Oxford, and Gertrude received permission from Miss Wordsworth to go alone with him on "discreet little walks." Other young men had also come into her life, and although one of her friends from home had announced her engagement, and another had already wed, for Gertrude these flirtations marked the first stirrings of her sexual awakening. She wrote to Florence about her "good friend" Mr. Raper, who took her skating, and the "fascinating" Mr. Cockerel, who invited her to his rooms for tea (always with a chaperone, of course); and on visits to London she enjoyed the company of her handsome cousin-by-marriage Billy Lascelles.

She was thriving at Oxford and, as Horace's mother noticed, she was even "a shade thinner." Her posture was not yet up to par, and her shoulders were curved from her stooping. But half an hour's walk every day with a back board would help, her aunt suggested, assuring Florence: "Every time I see the child I think her more charming. I am sure Oxford is doing much for her."

Oxford made her more self-reliant than she had ever been. "One goes as one likes," Gertrude announced enthusiastically, clearly flourishing on her own. If it was a distant cry from today's universities, where coed dormitories and shared bathrooms are the norm, it was still a far different atmosphere from the stuffy world of Queen's College, where women were constrained by rigid Victorian customs. At Oxford it was a man's world and the rules for men were far more lenient; Gertrude could accommodate herself to them.

She still wrote to her family every few days, and although she suffered mood swings, sometimes ecstatically happy, sometimes inexplicably depressed, she rarely talked of being homesick. Instead, her letters were filled with reports of her classes and her success at extracurricular activities: playing tennis against Somerville, Oxford's only other women's college; arguing at the Debating Society, where her team won the case for women's right to vote (only a few years later she would fight against the suffragettes); swimming, rowing, playing hockey, acting, dancing and, though she was never religious, attending church. Her younger half-sister Elsa noted later that a sense of security pervaded Gertrude's letters: "There is no vestige of anxiety about the future. Why should there be? Gertrude's experience of life had been that she had only to want something in order to get it."

She still asked Florence for advice on fiction and consulted her more and more about clothes. "I wish you would tell me what to have for a best dress this summer," she begged. "It must be very smart." As Gertrude came into her own, her tense relationship with Florence eased. She praised Florence as a mother and told her, after a country weekend with the family of a friend: "I'm very glad you aren't like Mrs. Kynston. She never takes any interest *at all* in what her daughters are doing."

While Florence was in London, working on the production of one of her plays, Gertrude wrote to Hugh, engaging in long discussions about history, philosophy and politics. "Will you disinherit me when I tell you that I don't believe in competition at all?" she teased the great industrialist. "No, you will crush me by pointing out that my knowledge of political economy is exactly three weeks old!" When Hugh's mother died, Gertrude penned him a note of sympathy, but carelessly forgot to mail it. Her father was hurt, and she answered endearingly: "You must know, whether you get letters or not, that anything that makes you sorry makes me sorry too and that I care very much for whatever you care for." Only a few months later, when a manager of the coal mines died, Hugh was upset that he had not been with the man. "Your just being too late to see him is bitterly sad," Gertrude wrote prophetically. "Oh you dear father, I know so well what it would be to have to die without you there, and never to see you again."

❦   ❦   ❦

As school continued, the work piled up: in one week, in addition to a dozen lectures to attend and six essays to write for her tutor, she was assigned to read a biography of Richard III, a two-volume biography of Henry VIII and Stubbs's history from Edward IV to Edward V. "Now I ask you, is that possible?" she moaned, but her tone revealed that she could easily handle the load. "Don't think I don't like it," she told her mother. She could hardly have liked it more; it confirmed her superior intelligence and reinforced her confidence; and if anyone doubted her opinion, she would cut him off with her favorite retort: "Well, you know, my father says so." Janet Hogarth commented later that Gertrude "was always an odd mixture of maturity and childishness, grown-up in her judgments of men and affairs, child-like in her certainties, and most engaging in her entire belief in her father and the vivid intellectual world in which she had been brought up."

By the end of her second year, and twelve months ahead of schedule, she prepared eagerly for Schools, her last written examinations at Oxford. "It's wildly exciting," she wrote to her parents. "I feel like a kind of gambler who is staking his last sixpence!" On the first day of exams, she waited anxiously with the others in the entry hall until an electric bell gonged and a voice rang out: "Gentlemen for the History school, North School; to the left, Gentlemen." As the men went off, Gertrude kept a discreet distance from them and rushed up a back staircase. She made her way to the women's table in the last row of the room and promptly opened the exam book. Most of the questions were "delightful," she announced later to her parents, noting that she had had no problem finishing her tests and even had time afterward for tennis and afternoon tea.

Escorted by her cousin Horace, she attended a week of parties and dances to celebrate the end of exams. The highlight of the academic ceremonies was Encaenia, the last remnant of medieval practice, when all of the scholars marched in their colorful robes. Gertrude, who had started out at Oxford careless of her appearance, now had a passion for clothes. Long before the ceremonies, she had gone shopping for something to wear and, returning to Lady Margaret Hall, had burst into Janet Hogarth's room: "I've got a hat, Janet, but a hat! Come see it." At the Wednesday lunch, her straw hat, its brim drenched in roses, nearly hid her face. "Her outfits for commemoration week had been one of our great interests," Janet Hogarth later recalled. "She certainly had the dress-sense."

Still whirling from the festivities, Gertrude now had to confront the orals, the most difficult part of the examinations. On the day of her oral exams, wearing a smart new dress and fashionable brown shoes, she sat calmly at the table, a picture of self-assurance. Like most parents, Florence and Hugh had come to Oxford for the event, and with them behind her, she coolly faced the battalion of male professors. First came the distinguished historian S. R. Gardiner, who started the *viva voce* with a question about Charles I. As her parents listened anxiously, Gertrude began her reply: "I am afraid I must differ from your estimate of Charles I." Horrified, the famous don stopped his questioning and turned the baton over to the next man down the row. The interrogation continued on a quieter note until another professor asked her about a German town, noting it was on the left bank of the Rhine. But Gertrude had visited the village the year before. Without hesitation, she replied: "I am sorry, but it is on the right. I know, I have been there." The room gasped.

Despite her audacity, however, when the results came back, she learned she had received a First in Modern History, the first woman to do so. The announcement appeared in *The Times*, and along with accolades from her family, she received a flood of congratulatory letters from friends. Her triumph confirmed her predilection to say what was on her mind and declare what she knew was right. Florence called it "her entire honesty and independence of judgement." Invigorating to some, tactless to others, her assertiveness would exhilarate many and intimidate many more. It opened doors that otherwise would have stayed shut, but it also earned her a reputation for arrogance.

She was brash and immature, and in spite of her dazzling scholastic achievements, Gertrude had failed the most important test of all. Unlike her two friends from home, she had had no one ask for her hand in marriage. She was twenty years old, a snob, a bluestocking, a woman with an "attitude"; her haughtiness and self-importance hardly appealed to eligible young men, and those who dared to court her were soon dismissed. The few she had dated disappeared by the end of school. Mr. Raper's name melted away with the winter ice, and Bob Cockerel was written off as very nice to talk to and dance with, "but that's quite all." As for her cousin Billy Lascelles, whose mother, Mary, was Florence's sister, she found him amusing but abhorred his "offhand" way.

The time had come to take matters in hand, Billy's mother advised Florence. The Lascelleses were living in Bucharest, where Mary's husband, Frank, was the British Minister to Romania. A winter season with foreign diplomats, it was agreed, might help Gertrude "get rid of her Oxfordy manner."

Chapter Three

An Ill-Fated Marriage

∞

As Oxford had been a school for her mind, Romania would be a school for her manners. As Oxford had allowed her into the world of diplomas, Romania would allow her into the world of diplomacy. Or so it was hoped. With these goals, Gertrude was sent to Bucharest, and although at the Paris train station she bade farewell bravely to her father, she left with fear and trepidation. "I felt very sad at leaving you," she wrote Hugh the next day, "and hoped you missed me a little."

Accompanied on the train by her cousin Billy, she arrived in Bucharest in time for Christmas and the winter season. Until now she had defined herself as a student, and if her agenda included parties, they were secondary to her work. But her role had changed; she was now available for marriage and her primary task was to find a mate. As Florence and Hugh Bell's daughter, she was expected to make an excellent match. And if there wasn't one here, at least she would learn how to conduct herself for the chase.

The social season in Bucharest followed on the heels of New Year's Eve: lavish dinners, concerts, theater, balls followed by suppers that lasted till sunrise, an endless round of parties in a city with little else to do. For three hundred years, until 1829, Romania had been a vassal state in the Ottoman Empire and, for half a century after that, a protectorate of Russia. Only in 1881, seven years before Gertrude's arrival, did it receive its independence, and the young country had yet to exert its influence on the world. But its geographical position, next door to Russia and across the Black Sea from Turkey, made it an excellent listening post, while its resources of agriculture and oil gave it excellent potential as a friend. For the diplomat Frank Lascelles, Romania was a propitious assignment. From here he could develop strong contacts in both the East and the West.

Invitations arrived nonstop at the British Embassy, and along with her uncle and aunt and Billy, Gertrude took part in a whirlwind of events. Mary Lascelles had proven to be far more relaxed than her sister, and under "Auntie Mary's" wing, Gertrude gained a graceful air. Corseted in whalebone and steel, pushed and pulled into an elaborate *décolleté* gown, she learned how to flirt with her ostrich fan, puff on her cigarette and dine on caviar and champagne, to refrain from biting her nails (a family habit) and from twirling her bangs around her finger, and to keep from blurting out everything that came into her mind. With all of this, her aunt hoped, she would change from a snobbish intellectual into a polished *ingénue*.

But Gertrude continued to comment snidely on events. Of the guests at one dinner, she wrote home, Mr. Mawe was "very conceited," and M. Demos, an elderly diplomat, was so tiny and bent "no country could possibly take the trouble to claim him." Of the food at another dinner she wrote, "The fish we smelt the moment [it] left the kitchen, the meat was the consistency of cork." And in the company of a group of diplomats she announced to a distinguished French statesman that he had no understanding at all of the German people. Her aunt was appalled, and Gertrude learned her lesson. When, a few weeks later, a British diplomat came to stay with the Lascelleses, she was "very discreet!"

Bucharest gave Gertrude her first real taste of society, but more than that, it gave Gertrude her first real taste of the world. A world that went beyond British boundaries. At the palace, she met King Carol, a Hohenzollern by birth, and chatted lengthily with his mystic wife, Elizabeth, known as the poet Carmen Sylva. She was introduced to Count von Bülow, who would become the Chancellor of Germany, and to Count Goluchowski, who would become the Chancellor of Austria. She dined with European aristocrats and Asian envoys, and spent a day with the British diplomat Charles Hardinge (later the Viceroy of India), whose enormous knowledge about the East and the Ottoman Empire opened her eyes to problems she knew little about.

She spent weeks with Valentine Chirol, a close friend of the Lascel-

leses who was also visiting them in Bucharest. Now a foreign correspondent for *The Times*, the thirty-seven-year-old Chirol, born in Paris
to English parents, brought up Catholic and educated mainly in France,
had graduated from the Sorbonne, trained in the Foreign Office and
traveled (with no apparent assignment) for sixteen years throughout the
Continent and the East. Highly intelligent and well informed, he spoke
a dozen languages, made impressive contacts and provided information
to Whitehall. No one called him a spy, but he served his government
well. The portly five-foot-ten, red-haired, red-bearded Chirol, who
loved good food and good wine, was nicknamed Domnul during his
stay in Romania, and would become one of Gertrude's closest friends.

For four months during the winter of 1889 Gertrude laughed,
danced and flirted her way through Bucharest, and although no one
asked for her hand in marriage, she was pleased by the attention she
received. And almost always near her side was the blue-eyed Billy Lascelles, a good dancer but a bit too aloof for her liking. "He rarely
confesses himself amused," she complained in a letter home. "As for
me I dance from the beginning of any ball to the end and I am
genuinely amused all the time." Nevertheless, the two were becoming
close. As the winter snows melted, their friendship warmed. Then, at
the end of April, with the well-traveled Domnul leading the way, they
left Romania for a visit to Constantinople.

⤟   ⤟   ⤟

East across the Byzantine Empire in Asia Minor and west into the
Balkan peninsula of Europe, the Ottoman Turks had advanced, ex-
panding from a thirteenth-century Turkish state, with Constantinople
at its head, into a sixteenth-century empire that stretched from the
Euphrates in Iraq to the Danube in Austria. Under Suleiman the Magnificent, the Ottomans controlled Egypt, Arabia, Mesopotamia, Syria,
Persia and Turkey in the East and Hungary and the Balkans—Bulgaria,
Albania, Bosnia, Herzegovina, Serbia, Greece and Romania—in the
West. For hundreds of years the Ottoman Empire had served as a
stabilizing force, balancing the Russian power in the East with the
British and French in the West. For Britain and France it provided
protection against Arab attacks on Western traders conducting lucra-
tive commerce: the British in the sheikhdoms of the Arabian Gulf and
Mesopotamia, the French in Syria.

But by the nineteenth century, weakened by corruption, greed and
too loose a management style, the Ottoman Empire had diminished
and decayed. The loss of Egypt and Greece, along with a depleted

economy, had forced the Sublime Porte (as the Ottoman Government was called) to rely more on the West. When the Russians marched toward Constantinople in 1878 in search of a warm-water port, the Turks, aided by Britain and France, were able to hold them off. But the Turks had fought a costly war. And when a surge of nationalism swept through the Balkans, the Turks lost Bulgaria and Romania, Bosnia and Herzegovina. To the West the Ottoman Empire had become "the Sick Man of Europe"; its fate in the Balkans, the critical "Eastern Question."

What worried the British most was that Russia would once again menace Constantinople, a threat England could not afford. Turkish protection was essential along the route to India, and an Ottoman defeat by the Russians could doom the jewel in the British crown. And thus the British held out a generous hand of financing to prop up the Turks.

∞ ∞ ∞

But the Eastern Question mattered little to Gertrude, at least for now. Her curiosity centered on Constantinople, the cosmopolitan city that straddled Europe and Asia; the splendid city on the Bosporus, ancient capital of Byzantium, seat of the Muslim Caliphate and symbol of Ottoman strength. In Bucharest, she had sampled a soupçon of Turkish flavoring; here, in Istanbul, she could savor an Oriental feast. A banquet of gorgeous colors and exotic shapes unfolded before her, "perfectly delicious" she wrote, as the low sun glittered on the water, bringing color back to the faded Turkish flags, "turning each white minaret in Stamboul into a dazzling marble pillar." She watched the Sultan Caliph, putative leader of the Muslim forces that had swept through East and West, emerge in all his glory on a rare trip from his palace to his mosque. She eyed the spires of the Seraglio, a place at once luxurious and licentious, bringing to life Mozart's opera *The Abduction from the Seraglio*; and she saw the flat dome of Saint Sophia, a miracle of Byzantium.

She and Billy took a *caique* and rowed slowly up the waters of the Golden Horn; they climbed the snows of Mount Olympus and looked out on the dazzling Sea of Marmara; they mounted donkeys and bumped along the narrow passages of the bazaars. She loved seeing the people dressed in Turkish clothes, the men in turbans and loose-fitting pants, the women in silks, their faces covered with veils. She liked the closely latticed Turkish houses, the Turkish restaurants with strange foods, and she liked drinking Turkish coffee while Billy smoked a *narghile*, a water pipe. Swept up in the exotic romance of it all, by the end of the trip she and Billy were nearly engaged. The two set off for home, splendidly content, on the Orient Express. This was, observed her sister Elsa, "the last chapter of absolute happiness in Gertrude's life. She was twenty, she was brilliant, she was charming, she had an attentive cavalier. . . . The future with all its possibilities lay before them."

∞ ∞ ∞

Billy Lascelles fit all the requirements: son of a diplomat, grandson of a famous physician, rakish and rich, educated at Sandhurst and about to begin his military career, he was the ideal candidate for marriage. In London, where Gertrude stayed after they returned in the summer of 1889, he flattered her with his advances. They took afternoon tea together, dined together and sat together in the moonlit garden, talking and playing bezique, their favorite card game, till two in the morning. But Billy offered neither the mental stimulation nor the emotional exuberance she needed. He was too limited in his outlook and too blasé in his approach to life. She was used to the depth and daring, the intelligence and adventurousness of the Bell men. Even on her return to London from Constantinople, she had longed for her father's company. "Dear, dearest Father," she had written, "I do wish you were here. I half hoped you might be. *Do* come soon." As for Billy, after a few months her interest strayed.

In July she turned twenty-one, a coming-of-age that tremored with meaning. She was now three years older than most young women who had entered British society; her introduction could no longer be postponed. She had smiled her way through Bucharest's balls, but it was time for her official coming-out. A presentation at court and a formal party by her parents announced to the world that she had been transformed from an accomplished young girl into an eligible young woman. For the 1890 season, and for the two that would follow, Gertrude waltzed through the marriage market, from one ball to another, escorted by either Florence or an aunt. Pink-cheeked and fleshy-bosomed, she joined the line of other young women standing in front of their chaperones, waiting until young men asked them to dance. She smiled, she laughed, she looked deliciously indifferent, and she inspected the men even more carefully than they inspected her. For Gertrude, this was a difficult time. Few of the men were as brilliant as she. Few had attended Oxford or Cambridge. Few had traveled as far as the East. Few had her curiosity or her knowledge or her bluntness or her audacity. Few could match the standards set by her father and grandfather, and, most painful of all, few would desire her.

One of the few was Bertie Crackenthorpe. For at least a week he was in hot pursuit, inviting her to dine at his parents' house and paying her unending attention, even to his father's chagrin. "I do like him," Gertrude wrote to Florence, assuring her that she had been well behaved. Bertie begged to see her, but Gertrude played coy, refusing to say she would be at home if he called, but crossing her fingers about the future. "We shall see how everything happens," she said wistfully. Yet less than a week later, when she and Bertie were both invited to visit a friend, she hoped he would not go. Bertie already bored her.

In the autumn she returned to Red Barns, a damp retreat, cold and dull. Pretending to be happy, she was often admittedly "miserable," with little to do. She tutored the younger Bell girls (Hugo was off at school), did social work with the wives of the colliery workers and read voraciously. At least her imagination could take flights of fancy. She lapped up biographies of Browning, Wordsworth and Mary Shelley, followed the explorations of Livingstone in Africa, recited Kipling's poetry of the Empire and savored FitzGerald's 1859 translation of *The Rubáiyát of Omar Khayyám*:

> *Dreaming when dawn's left hand was in the sky*
> *I heard a voice within the tavern cry,*
> *"Awake, my little ones, and fill the cup*
> *"Before life's liquor in its cup be dry."*

When spring arrived and unmarried women were once again in season, she returned to her family's London flat. To fill the time, she took fencing lessons at MacPhersons' gym, shopped at Harvey's and on the Brompton Road and, to her mother's horror, took the underground to see Mary Talbot doing welfare work in Whitechapel. Florence was "beside herself," Elsa wrote later, that Gertrude had gone on such an "orgy of independence." More to her mother's liking, she went to art exhibits with the family maid and, similarly chaperoned, paid calls on friends: Caroline Grosvenor, an artist; Norman Grosvenor, her husband; and Flora Russell, daughter of Lord and Lady Arthur Russell. The Russells' at-homes were the envy of London. Their Mayfair drawing room on Audley Square (where the windows were washed, extravagantly, once a week) attracted such well-known figures as Leslie Stephen and his daughters, Virginia and Vanessa; Mrs. Humphrey Ward; and Henry James, who sometimes brought along his friend, the controversial painter of "Madame X," John Singer Sargent. But aside from an interesting conversation here and there, the days seemed to pass, she noted, "without much to show for them."

∞ ∞ ∞

Three seasons were all that a young lady was allotted to find a husband. Gertrude had used up her time. No one had asked her to marry him, nor was there someone she wished to wed. Not that she did not enjoy the company of young men; she did. But her sharp tongue sliced through their egos and her intellectual thirst quickly soaked up what drops of knowledge they shed. She refused to bow to them in her behavior: to be servile or silent or not argue, but rather agree with everything they said. She refused to change her personality to suit another's. And if she did not meet their expectations, so be it. No tight-lipped male would be her lord and master.

Three years of the mating game had made her miserable, yet the prospect of a life alone seemed worse. At the end of an evening at the Russells', she wrote despondently to Florence: "It is so flat and horrid without you. I hope you find your husband a consolation to you, you see I haven't one to console me." Fearful of living her life as a spinster, she ended her letter: "Mother dearest, three score years and ten is very long, isn't it?"

Travel seemed the only solution; Persia the place she had always longed to see. At the age of twenty-three, having spent the winter months learning to speak the language, Gertrude waved goodbye to damp, cold England and left with her aunt Mary Lascelles for the East. Traveling on the Orient Express from Paris to Constantinople, and from there by boat to Persia, she arrived in Teheran on May 7, 1892, to visit Frank Lascelles, recently appointed the British envoy to Shah Nasiraddin. In her first letter home, she rejoiced: Persia was "Paradise."

∞ ∞ ∞

The legation grounds were like "the Garden of Eden," Gertrude exclaimed to her parents. "You can't think how lovely it all is—outside trees and trees and trees making a thick shade from our house to the garden walls, beneath them a froth of pink monthly roses, climbing masses of briers, yellow and white and scarlet, beds of dark red cabbage roses and hedges of great golden blooms. It's like the Beast's garden, a perfect nightmare of roses." She stepped inside the rambling, pale stone house and walked through long hallways, where liveried servants bowed as she passed. Peeking around, she discovered capacious dining rooms, drawing rooms and billiard rooms, countless sitting rooms and bedrooms for family and guests, and everywhere she could smell the scent of roses and hear the songs of nightingales.

The month-long journey to Teheran earned a welcome from the entire Embassy: counselors, military attachés, telegraph coders, first, second and even third secretaries turned out to greet her, including one who seemed to catch her interest. "Mr. Cadogan, tall and red and very thin, agreeable, intelligent, a great tennis player, a great billiard player, an enthusiast about Bezique, devoted to riding though he can't ride in the least I'm told, smart, clean, well-dressed, looking upon us as his special property to be looked after and amused. I like him," she wrote at once to her family.

She met others too, in Teheran, whom she liked, particularly the German chargé d'affaires, Friedrich Rosen, and his wife, Nina. Mrs. Rosen, the daughter of friends of her stepmother's, was intelligent and amusing; Dr. Rosen, a charming man and an Oriental scholar, who soon taught her about Persian culture and stirred her interest in the Arabs as well. The Rosens would become close friends, and when later they were assigned to Jerusalem, she would make her first trip to that city, visiting them while she studied Arabic.

But one man in Teheran stood out from the rest. A week after she arrived, she wrote home again: "Mr. Cadogan is the real treasure; it certainly is unexpected and undeserved to have come all the way to Tehran and to find someone so delightful at the end. Florence [the Lascelleses' daughter] and I like him immensely; he rides with us, he arranges plans for us, he brings his dogs to call on us . . . he shows us lovely things from the bazaars, he is always there when we want him and never when we don't." Not only was he charming but highly intelligent, well read in everything worthwhile in French, German and English.

Astride their horses, Mr. Cadogan led her into the desert, and she gasped at the power of its vastness and vacancy, the beauty of its jeweled oases. "Oh the desert round Tehran! miles and miles of it with nothing, *nothing* growing; ringed in with bleak bare mountains snow crowned and furrowed with the deep courses of torrents. I never knew what desert was till I came here; it is a very wonderful thing to see. . . ."

They went riding together, she always sidesaddle, to the Shah's camp, and found a garden filled with wild animals and an *anderun*, a special palace for the royal ladies. When one of the gardeners opened the palace door, they stepped inside and found themselves "in the middle of the Arabian Nights." Thin streams trickled across the tiled floors and reflections of the water danced in the tiny mirrored pieces of the roof, and all the way was roses, roses. "Here that which is me," she wrote, "which womanlike is an empty jar that the passerby fills at pleasure, is filled with such wine as in England I had never heard of."

She was roused by the sensuality of the East and seduced by the attentions of her suitor, handsome, ten years older than she, and worldly. He read her the mysterious lines of the Persian poets and slipped his arms around her. He took her to strange sights, like the whitewashed Tower of Silence, where the Zoroastrians threw their dead, leaving them for birds to devour, and he held her tightly when she shivered in fear. He showed her hawking and they watched together as the servants released quails into the sky and let loose the hawks to pounce on them. He brought her to a garden where they lay in the grass under trees, dangled their toes in a little stream, and kissed, then watched the lights changing on the snowy mountains. From his pocket he pulled out a tiny volume of Catullus and read aloud the lyric pieces of the Roman poet. "It was very delicious," she wrote dreamily. A few days later they spent an afternoon in a garden tent, and in between their kisses they read the voluptuous quatrains of *The Rubáiyát*:

> *With me along the strip of herbage strown*
> *That just divides the desert from the sown.*
> *Where name of slave and sultan is forgot,*
> *And peace to Mahmud on his golden throne!* . . .

> *A book of verses underneath the bough,*
> *A jug of wine, a loaf of bread—and thou*
> *Beside me singing in the wilderness*
> *Oh, wilderness were paradise enow!*

While a cholera epidemic raged through the country, killing thousands, she and Cadogan celebrated life. They recited the poems of Browning and Kipling and read the short stories of Henry James. They played tennis, they rode into the mountains, they took walks, and on one August afternoon, they strolled two miles down the River Lar to a place where Mr. Cadogan's servant had spread a regal tea. Hungry and wet from a sudden shower, they hid under waterproof sheets and munched on bread and butter and raspberry jam. After tea they wandered along the stream, Cadogan fishing, she talking, until they walked home together. "It was the loveliest afternoon," she purred.

By now they were speaking of their future, spending hours blissfully planning their life together: as a diplomat, he could be posted anywhere in the world; he had been to South America and did not like it, and they both hoped he would stay in the Middle East. It was easy to imagine herself like her aunt Mary, the charming, admired wife of an influential ambassador, with her Parisian wardrobe, traveling in luxury on steamer ships and sumptuous trains, meeting interesting people like prime ministers and kings, living in exotic places like Damascus and Baghdad. Her days were like dreams floating out of Oriental fables.

They had both composed letters to her parents, he to ask Hugh Bell's permission to marry Gertrude, she to tell them of the news. After two weeks, when her parents did not respond, she wrote again, knowing for certain that her father would want to check her young man's credentials. She guessed that the long wait did not augur well; her father was extremely particular about whom she could marry, and Mr. Cadogan did not really fit the bill. Hugh Bell expected a rich husband for his daughter, one who had a good income and good prospects for the future. Henry Cadogan was the eldest son of the Honorable Frederick Cadogan and the grandson of the third Earl Cadogan, but he had not inherited any family fortune. His salary as a junior diplomat was insufficient to support Gertrude, and to make matters worse, he was a gambler who had mounted up significant debts. He was well read and worldly, but as Hugh Bell learned when he contacted family and friends in Teheran, Cadogan was also arbitrary, strong willed, and intolerant of any interference with his wishes.

Even before her father's reply arrived, Gertrude wrote to her mother that if Hugh refused to give his permission, the only thing Cadogan could do would be to stay in Persia and hope for a promotion. If he received an ambassadorship or something similarly remunerative, then the wait would have been worthwhile. "The consolation is that people really do get on in this profession and make enough to live on before so many years. But then," she acknowledged, "the kind of life is rather expensive of course."

At last in September her father's letter came. With a quickened pulse, she opened the envelope, but her deepest fears turned out to be true. Hugh Bell refused to give his consent. He hoped that a separation would make Gertrude change her mind. She was heartbroken. She wrote to her stepmother for solace: "I care more than I can say and I'm not afraid of being poor or even of having to wait, though waiting is harder than I thought it would be at first. For one doesn't realize at first how one will long for the constant companionship and the blessed security of being married, but now that I am going away I realise it wildly . . . our position is very difficult and we are very unhappy."

In spite of their passion, they respected the social rules. They saw less of each other, feeling they no longer had the right to meet. Still she begged her mother to understand Henry Cadogan as she did. She could not bear that her parents think of him as anything less than "noble and gentle and good." This was the loving side he had shown her. "Everything I think and write brings us back to things we have spoken of together, sentences of his that come flashing like sharp swords; you see for the last three months nothing I have done or thought has not had him in it, the essence of it all."

She would choose to do it all over again, she assured them, despite the current pain and the awful separation that was coming. It was worth it all, she told them, "more than worth it. Some people live all their lives and never have this wonderful thing; at least I have known it and have seen life's possibilities suddenly open in front of me—only one may cry just a little when one has to turn away and take up the old narrow life again. . . . Oh Mother, Mother," she wailed.

∞　∞　∞

On the boat journey home she wrote to her trustworthy friend Domnul Chirol, revealing her pain and confusion. "I think you know vaguely about my affairs—*vaguely* is all I know about them myself at present, but I fear they look very bad. It's a threatening, stormy vagueness, not a hopeful one. Mr. Cadogan is very poor, his father I believe to be practically bankrupt and mine, though he is an angel and would do anything in the world for me, is absolutely unable to run another household besides his own, which is, it seems to me, what we are asking him to do." She and her father had not yet had a chance to discuss the situation, but she hoped he would see Henry Cadogan's father and arrive at some sort of decision. In the meanwhile, she and Cadogan were not allowed to consider themselves engaged and the possibility of their marriage remained in the distant future. "I write sensibly about it, don't I, but I'm not sensible at all in my heart, only it's all too desperate to cry over—there comes a moment in very evil days when they are too evil for anything but silence."

She arrived in London in late October and, after the long absence, embraced her waiting mother. To her father, who was in Yorskshire, she wrote that, as unimaginable as it once had seemed, this experience had brought her even closer to him. Perhaps it was because she had known real love, she explained, that she could appreciate her father's love even more. When finally Hugh appeared in London a few days later, she poured out her hopes and fears, her doubts and desires, while he listened quietly. As she had allowed to Domnul, somewhere deep inside her she knew her father was right; for the time being, at least, Cadogan was not an acceptable husband. Yet she yearned to be his wife, and she would wait; she would wait as long as she had to.

Then, for eight months, she endured, existing from day to day, and with Florence's encouragement she worked on *Persian Pictures*, a book about her experiences in the East. In August 1893 she and her mother visited Kirby Thore in Yorkshire. It was there that she was reading aloud to Florence about the cholera epidemic, from the chapter she had called "Shadow of Death," when, like some sort of Persian sorcery, the shadow stepped out from the pages of her book. A telegram arrived from Teheran. Excited and unknowing, Gertrude unfolded the paper and began to read the message: Henry Cadogan had been trout fishing when he slipped into the icy waters of the River Lar—whether by accident or intention it did not say—and, chilled to the bone, was stricken with pneumonia. They were sorry to inform her that Cadogan was dead.

∞   ∞   ∞

That year Gertrude published a translation of the poems of Hafiz; her interpretation of the Persian poet's writings is still considered one of the best:

> Songs of dead laughter, songs of love once hot,
> Songs of a cup once flushed rose-red with wine,
> Songs of a rose whose beauty is forgot,
> A nightingale that piped hushed lays divine:
> And still a graver music runs beneath
> The tender love notes of those songs of thine,
> Oh, Seeker of the keys of Life and Death!

CHAPTER FOUR

Flight

∞

Gertrude had lost more than a lover; she had lost her hopes, lost hold of an entire life. For nearly a year she had been in limbo; fearful that her father's demands would force her plans to unravel, she continued to weave her dreams. Now, at the age of twenty-five, she faced the cold reality that her future was shredded to bits. Henry was dead. The only panacea was work and travel. For the next five years she would rush around the globe, making frequent trips to France and Italy and Switzerland, making longer journeys circling the world, as if the very act of fleeing would force her to forget. But haunted by his memory, she saw Cadogan everywhere: in the blissful faces of newlyweds on the train in France, in the perfect figure of the *David* in Florence, in the pots of pomegranates lined up outside a Swiss hotel. Always restless and easily bored, she felt her nervous energy reach a new level. Throwing herself into her work, she studied Persian and feverishly did research for another book, trying to release the ghosts, yet continually reconnecting herself to Cadogan. The language and the writing only reinforced her sorrow.

"Life! life! the bountiful, the magnificent!" she had rejoiced in *Persian Pictures*, published in the spring of 1894. But she had written the words while she was still in Persia, Cadogan still at her side.

Death had come too soon. No longer able to experience joy, she sought consolation, and she found it in Billy Lascelles. Friendship substituted for their former romance; empathy took the place of passion. He visited her on Sloane Street, and as Florence looked stonily on, wishing perhaps that they had married years before, the two young people went off for a private talk. Gertrude poured out her heart, comforted by his listening.

On a family holiday in the Alps, she shared her pain with Friedrich and Nina Rosen, her friends from Teheran. With Dr. Rosen she discussed *Persian Pictures* and Persian literature and her Persian days with Cadogan; and at night, alone in her room under the duvet, she read the letters of Jonathan Swift and his love, Vanessa. She doubted that any man could appreciate the emotions expressed by Vanessa and felt certain that no woman could fail to understand them. "Swift did not care for her," Gertrude observed; "that's how a man writes who does not care. And how it maims and hurts the woman! One ought to pray every night not to write letters like that—or at least not to send them." She had known the words of a man who cared so much, and on this, the first anniversary of Henry Cadogan's death, they scorched her memory. "I thought of him much last night, and of all he had been to me, and is still." It would be many years before she would know such fervor again, and the letters that were to come would shake the depths of her body and soul.

∞ ∞ ∞

Of all the Persian writers that she and Cadogan had read together, it was the passionate poet Hafiz who was the most complex. His mystical lyrics are still read out loud in Teheran tea rooms and salons, his allegories discussed and interpreted for hours on end. His words require the most sophisticated understanding of the language; his intricate message demands analysis that few can convey; yet eager to plunge into work, Gertrude took up the challenge to translate his poems.

For most of the next two years, she worked on the translations of Hafiz, completing them in 1896. The following year, with the addition of her definitive essay comparing the thirteenth-century Hafiz to Western poets such as Dante and the more contemporary Goethe, the book was published. It won rave reviews. As recently as 1974, a noted scholar, A. J. Arberry, commented, "Though some twenty hands have put Hafiz into English, her rendering remains the best!" With the image of Cadogan still vivid in her mind, she could easily relate to the poet's wrenching heartbreak over the death of his son, expressed in his poem the *Divan of Hafiz*:

> *Light of mine eyes and harvest of my heart,*
> *And mine at least in changeless memory!*
> *Ah! when he found it easy to depart,*
> *He left the harder pilgrimage to me!*
> *Oh Camel-driver, though the cordage start,*
> *For God's sake help me lift my fallen load,*
> *And Pity be my comrade of the road!*
>
> *He sought a lodging in the grave—too soon!*
> *I had not castled, and the time is gone.*
> *What shall I play? Upon the chequered floor*
> *Of Night and Day, Death won the game—forlorn*
> *And careless now, Hafiz can lose no more.*

Still savoring the taste of life in the East, and at the suggestion of Friedrich Rosen (who had learned the language as a child in Jerusalem), Gertrude was now studying Arabic. She found it easy at first, and during the days, reading the tales, she relived her romance with Cadogan. On spare afternoons and evenings, alone in London, she dined with her well-placed friends the Grosvenors, the Stanleys and the Ritchies, made calls on the Portsmouths and on Mrs. Green and Mrs. Ward at their smart at-homes on Russell Square. Momentarily, at least, she could bask in the limelight of the reviews of *Persian Pictures*.

Yet in spite of her achievements as an author, in spite of her success in society, and in spite of the fact that she was now twenty-eight years old, she still faced the constraints of Victorian England. "I didn't go to Lady Pollock's on Tuesday," she complained; "I had promised to go to a party at Audley Square and I couldn't combine the two unchaperoned."

Only marriage could save her from the shackles of chaperones and escorts. In the middle of the season of 1896, her Oxford colleague Mary Talbot was liberated when she married the Reverend Winfrid Burrows. Mary was thirty-four, soon pregnant, and "radiant," Gertrude reported to Janet Hogarth when they met at a tea in London. Janet's brother David Hogarth, an archaeologist, had just published *A Wandering Scholar in the Levant*, his first important book, and the two women had a delicious afternoon, comparing notes on friends, on writing, on travel in the East.

Mary Talbot had been Gertrude's closest female companion. They had spent endless hours together in London, had traveled together to Italy, and now, taking the train to Yorkshire, Gertrude visited her friend in Leeds. She watched the newlywed couple setting up house in the English countryside and recalled the image of marriage that she and Henry Cadogan had sketched. The future might provide other suitors, but few could fulfill the dream she had shared with him, a life so different from Mary's, a life of exotic adventure in the East. Still, she held on to the hope of marriage.

But there were no eligible men in her life. Instead, she fled with her father to Italy, where she walked through the narrow streets of Padua and nearly cried when she entered the square of Saint Mark's. "The band played," she wrote in her diary, "and the Piazetta was full of people, and it seemed too silly, but the whole place was full of Henry Cadogan, and too lovely not to be sad."

Back in England, months later, she came face to face with her dreary plight. Her younger sisters used to watch in awe as maids helped Gertrude prepare for a ball, hooking her corsets, lacing up her petticoats, fastening her wasp-waisted gown, smoothing on her long white gloves. But now Elsa and Molly were old enough to be invited to their own balls; Gertrude helped choose their dresses, but it was they, not she, who waltzed at the parties. "I sat on a bench and watched them dancing round and knew just what you felt like at Oxford," Gertrude wrote to Florence. Of course, after being her chaperone at the Oxford balls, Florence had gone home to Hugh. Gertrude went home to an empty house.

When Mary and Frank Lascelles invited her to their embassy home in Berlin, she jumped at the chance to escape. Like people all over Europe, the Germans were celebrating the Diamond Jubilee of Queen Victoria. The enormously popular Queen, grandmother of both Kaiser Wilhelm II of Germany and Czarina Alexandra of Russia, related by marriage to the monarchs of Romania, Denmark and Greece, was viewed as the embodiment of England and the symbol of the Empire; 1897, her sixtieth year on the throne, was commemorated throughout the Continent. At home in England, officials were brought in from every part of the world; dignitaries partied, troops paraded, rich men gloated over brandy and cigars, and everyone congratulated himself on being part of the world's largest and richest Empire.

In Germany, Gertrude enjoyed the round of balls, banquets, concerts and operas in celebration of the Queen's Jubilee, but despite the royal ties, the British were viewed with some doubt. In South Africa, the two countries were fighting the Boer War; in the East, Germany lusted after India and hungered for the remains of the collapsing Ottoman Empire; and in Europe, Germany and England vied for commerce and communications.

When, as a guest of the court, Gertrude attended a play with her Aunt Mary and Uncle Frank, she watched as a sheaf of telegrams was delivered to the Emperor. A heated conversation ensued between the German ruler and her uncle, the British Ambassador. Gertrude caught scraps of the Emperor's remarks: "Crete," "Bulgaria," "Serbia," "mobilizing"; he was convinced that Europe was on the brink of war. The Russians, the French and the Germans were all eager to grab the spoils that would come with the break-up of the Ottoman Empire. When war came, the Germans and the British would fight on opposite sides.

Talk of war sent a shiver of excitement through Gertrude, but the rest of her stay in Germany was boring, and by the beginning of March she was glad to be back in England. Four weeks later she learned, to her dismay, that Mary Lascelles, her favorite aunt, the one who had brought her to Persia and enabled her to meet Henry Cadogan, had died. Gertrude's emotions rocked like a seesaw when good news followed: Mary Talbot, her closest friend, had given birth to twins. Then came word that, after suffering from complications of childbirth, Mary Talbot was dead.

It was overwhelming: the deaths, the sorrow, the grieving; a dark cloud showering her with tears. Save for the Queen's Jubilee, which put an eerie glow on her sadness, there was little reason to stay in England. By autumn, when the sun had stopped baking the London streets, and the brisk winds returned with her gloom, she could hardly help fleeing. Yet, still a traditional woman, she took the traditional course: she and her brother Maurice signed up for a Cook's tour around the world. They left in December 1897 on a steamship voyage that was more a rest period than an adventure.

They sailed from Southampton across the Atlantic, wrote home from Guatemala and sailed the Pacific Ocean. They docked in Tokyo and Hong Kong, and on the way home she stopped in the French Alps for mountain climbing. The physical challenge of the climb itself, the test of endurance and strength, the quest of conquering something new and difficult attracted her. "Obstacles were made to be overcome," her father had often said, and she believed him. After six months away from home, she came back to England in early summer.

Life was vacuous, a series of parties and fittings for clothes; and once in a while, using lantern slides, she gave a lecture on Persia. She celebrated her thirtieth birthday at home with her family; no prospects of marriage seemed near. She yearned to bury her pain with serious work, yet she could not let go of Cadogan and, seeking his spirit in the East, for most of the following year she studied Persian and Arabic. She hoped to visit Friedrich Rosen, now consul to Jerusalem. But studies took up only so much time; she filled her empty hours in London drawing rooms, where the gossip was laced with talk of the Dreyfus Affair, the case of the Jewish officer court-martialed for treason in France.

Now for Gertrude life was little more than a round of social calls. In Rome she visited Mrs. Humphrey Ward; in Athens she joined her father and watched while David Hogarth worked at a dig, extracting six-thousand-year-old vessels from the earth. She met a colleague of his, the handsome Mr. Dorpfield, and hung on his words as the archaeologist re-created the ancient world from his excavations: with pots and shards pulled from the earth, and with rocks strewn on the ground, he brought antiquity to life. It made her "brain reel," she exclaimed, as the seeds of her interest in archaeology were planted. She returned home through Constantinople and Prague and then Berlin, where her uncle was still the ambassador and the "endlessly cheerful" Domnul Chirol was based as correspondent for *The Times*. She listened to Domnul, who had been living in Berlin for five years, argue against the German Government and its aggressive young emperor, Kaiser Wilhelm II; she confided in him about her loneliness, and she heard his cautionary words as she talked enthusiastically of her newest interest, mountain climbing.

From Germany she went to France to climb the Meije, 13,081 feet, her first big mountain and an undertaking far more difficult than she had imagined. By November 1899, she was off to Jerusalem; she would greet the new century in the part of the world where many people believed that life itself had begun, and where, despite the ghost of Cadogan, her own life would begin again.

CHAPTER FIVE

First Steps in the Desert

∞

Jerusalem. To Christians it was the way to God, the site of Christ's Crucifixion and Ascension, the scene of the Last Supper, the Via Dolorosa and the Stations of the Cross, close to Bethlehem, where Christ was born. To Muslims it was the opening to Allah, the third holiest city in Islam, the place where Muhammad was carried from Mecca on his legendary steed and where he rose mystically to heaven. To Jews it was the symbol of their homeland, the capital of ancient Israel, created by King David when he united the Hebrew tribes, and the resting place of the Ark of the Law, their covenant with God. To some people, such as sixteenth-century German mapmakers, it was the center of the world. To the Ottoman Empire, which ruled it now, it was a prized possession.

She arrived in Jerusalem to study Arabic, her goal to enter the Arab world. She had come to Palestine by ship, sailing from Marseilles with her steamer trunks, a new fur coat and a camera, docking first at Athens, where a friend of David Hogarth's escorted her to the Acropolis and dined with her at the Grande Bretagne Hotel, then on to Smyrna, where dependable Domnul Chirol had notified the British Consul, Mr. Cumberbatch, to smooth her way past Turkish customs. She had booked herself, the only passenger with a cabin, on a dirty

Russian boat crossing to Beirut, and looked on with amazement at three hundred peasants of the Czar camped out on the deck, the women huddled in wadded coats and high boots, babushkas wrapped around their heads, the men in thick coats and boots, their heads topped with astrakhan hats. Like tens of thousands of others—Russian Orthodox, Greek Orthodox, Roman Catholics, Episcopalians, Baptists, Lutherans, Sunnis, Shiites and Jews—they were making a pilgrimage to Jerusalem to expiate their sins. She, an atheist, had faith only in her family and the British Empire. Her doctrine lay in the righteous destiny of England, her conviction in the belief that the British were chosen to lead the world. At thirty-one, she was seeking a purpose for her life.

Gertrude rented a suite with a verandah at the Hotel Jerusalem, two minutes' walk from the German Colony, where Friedrich Rosen now served as the Consul. Her plan was to stay four months, until April 1899. The Rosens—Friedrich, Nina and their two young sons—welcomed her as a member of the family, and each day she shuttled back and forth to their house for lunch and dinner.

Almost as soon as she arrived, Gertrude rearranged the furniture in her suite, removing an extra cot from the bedroom, realigning the sitting room to hold two armchairs, a big writing desk and a table that she piled with books; on the walls she hung an enormous Kiepert map of Palestine and pinned up photographs of her family. A carpet covered the tiled floors, a small wood stove nestled in a corner of the sitting room, and all in all, she wrote home, the place was "cozy." The only things that she needed were a horse, which she quickly found, and a teacher, whom she engaged.

Arabic, which had seemed to come easily at first, now stymied her. "I find it awfully difficult," she confessed to her family. She could converse comfortably at a dinner party in French, Italian, German, Persian and even Turkish, switching back and forth animatedly from one to the other, yet Arabic was strange: "The worst I think is a very much aspirated H. I can only say it by holding down my tongue with one finger, but then one can't carry on a conversation with your finger down your throat, can you?"

She hired another teacher and studied Arabic four hours each morning and an hour or two each night, and then, between meals at the Rosens', she sauntered around the city in her straw boater and lace-trimmed white blouse pinched at the waist, lifting her petticoats and long cotton skirts as she leapt gracefully over the mud. Sixty thousand people now lived in Jerusalem, a majority of them Jews, and many were building their homes outside the Old City walls. But it was inside the sixteenth-century Turkish ramparts that Gertrude spent much of her time.

Entering one of the city's eight gates, she saw medieval life as it was still being lived by Christians, Armenians, Muslims and Jews. At the Jaffa Gate, dedicated to Suleiman the Magnificent, who built it in 1527, she marched along the road, newly paved by the Ottoman administrators for Kaiser Wilhelm II on his visit to Jerusalem the year before, in 1898.

Near the Zion Gate she walked through the Jewish Quarter to the Western Wall, following the bearded men as they shuffled along the alleyways, dressed, even in the scorching summer heat, in long black woolen coats and beaver hats. The squalid streets were roughly paved and covered with filth, animal dung and food refuse decaying in cisterns and open holes. Two years earlier, Theodor Herzl, founder of the Zionist movement, had visited the ancient wall, where Jews prayed in front and Muslims prayed at the mosque above, and decried the area for the "hideous, miserable, scrambling beggary pervading the place." For Herzl the ugliness and desecration were heresy. But for Gertrude it was anthropology. She ignored the filth and saw only the customs and the people.

She took it all in, snapping her Kodak as she walked by herself one Sunday from the Church of the Holy Sepulchre to the Mount of Olives, with its view of the Dead Sea and the hills of Moab on one side and, on the other, the city of Jerusalem. As an atheist, she stood apart from the multifarious crowds and watched in amazement as factions fought over inches of holy turf. Turkish soldiers were stationed to keep the Christians from attacking one another. "It is comfort," she said, "to be in a cheerful irreligious family again!"

Despite her scorn, it thrilled her to be there, elated by the sights and the people and even the moon. "Such a moon!" she extolled. "I have not seen the moon shine since I was in Persia."

Perhaps for the first time since being romanced by Henry Cadogan, seven years before, she was content. She concentrated on her studies, losing herself in her work. "I am extremely flourishing, and so wildly interested in Arabic that I think of nothing else," she wrote home. "It's like a good dream to be in a place where one can at last learn Arabic. I only fear I may wake up some morning and find it isn't true." She could now read the story of Aladdin without a dictionary and found it tremendously gratifying to be able to read Dr. Rosen's volume of the *Arabian Nights* "just for fun."

At night, snuggled in her room, a cigarette and a cup of thick Turkish coffee at her side, she munched pistachio nuts and studied. After several weeks, the language that had thwarted her seemed conquerable. The warm days flew by, and she certainly did not miss the bleak English winter. In the middle of January she wrote home delight-edly, "These two days have been as hot as an English June and far brighter." The Middle East weather invigorated her, so unlike the endlessly gray skies and the damp, enervating air at home.

The news from home was hardly cheerful: Maurice had volunteered to fight in the Boer War, the violent struggle between the Afrikaners and the British over diamonds and gold mines. She worried about his going to South Africa to join an army that was untrained and under-supplied. "I have borne the departure of everyone else's brother with perfect equanimity," she noted, "but when it comes to my own, I am full of terrors."

Only briefly, she considered going home, but realized it would do no good to return to England, and knowing, as always, that the more she engaged in her work, the better she felt. "Arabic is a great rock in time of trouble! If it were not for that, I think I should have packed up and come home, but that would have been rather a silly proceeding," she informed her parents. "An absorbing occupation is the best re-source." So, with subscriptions arriving from *The Times* and the *Daily Mail*, a Bible and two dozen rolls of film received from England, and a gray felt hat trimmed with black velvet bows on its way, she stayed in Jerusalem.

The rites and rituals of the pilgrims fascinated her, and on a January day she rode down to the Jordan River to find an enormous crowd of people waiting to be baptized. Desert Arabs, Arab peasants, workers and servants, Turkish soldiers, Greek priests, Russian priests and Russian peasants wearing fur coats and high boots, all standing in the hot sun, wearing chains of beads and crucifixes around their necks. Amazed by their fervor and their ability to ignore the thick garments even in the broiling heat, Gertrude walked among them, photographing as she went. Then, after half an hour, a procession of priests holding lighted candles filed to the water's edge. The crowd of people clam-bered down the muddy river banks and stood in water up to their waists. When the priest laid the cross three times on the water, guns went off, and everyone baptized himself by dipping and rolling over in the water. "It was the strangest sight," she observed.

∞   ∞   ∞

With Friedrich Rosen, who was born and raised in Jerusalem, she planned a series of solitary trips. His tales of adventure whetted her appetite: only the year before, he had crossed the desert and sipped coffee in the tent of the distinguished Anazeh chief and friend of the Turks, Fahad Bey; he had visited Babylon and met the eminent German archaeologist Dr. Koldewey; he had lived in Baghdad and knew the leading sheikhs and notables.

Desert travel itself was not so different in its way from her mountain climbing or even from academia: a test of endurance, it challenged her physical strength, her emotional equilibrium, her linguistic ability, her curiosity and cleverness and, not least of all, her courage. This would be her first real exploration on her own, and from the moment she mounted her horse and galloped across the bare, sweeping hills she felt free. Like a bird in an opened cage, she spread her wings and soared.

Sending ahead her hired cook and two muleteers, she rode alone on the dusty path from Jerusalem, past parades of donkeys laden with tents and supplies, past caravans of British tourists led by Thomas Cook's. Halfway to Jericho, along the route that General Allenby and his forces would follow almost two decades later, her own guide, Tarif, joined her, and together they continued east through the bare valley, their figures like two tiny dots against the sweep of brown barren mountains. Exhausted, they made their camp. A hot soak in her canvas bath, followed by dinner prepared by her cook, and she crawled into bed, pleased with her independence and protected by a wisp of mosquito netting.

The following morning after breakfast, she mounted her horse and, crossing the wooden bridge that spanned the narrow Jordan River, rode into the Jordan Valley. The landscape had changed: where brown mountains had been before, the hillsides now sprouted grass, and the arid wilderness came alive with colorful fields. She gasped at the sight of the brilliant flowers, and later, in her letter home, she noted "the sheets and sheets of varied and exquisite color": yellow daisies, sweet-scented mauve wild stock, splendid dark purple onions, white garlic, purple mallow, tiny blue iris, red anemone and scarlet ranunculus burst upon the scene.

On a grassy plateau her servants pitched camp, and her tent was quickly surrounded by a group of Arab women, their faces tattooed with indigo, their heads and bodies covered in blue cotton gowns. Unveiled and curious, they sold her a hen and some sour milk—yogurt—called *laban*. Hanna, the cook, served her afternoon tea, and that evening, after dining on soup made of rice and olive oil ("very good!"), an Irish stew and raisins, she jotted down the day's events, adding gaily, "Isn't it a joke being able to talk Arabic!" She not only enjoyed the language; she loved the way of life.

In order to continue her journey, she needed permission from the local Turkish authority, and after some haggling, a tall middle-aged Turk appeared. She invited him into her tent and with a great show of politeness offered him cigarettes ("You see a bad habit may have its merits!") while her cook scurried to bring him a cup of thick, sweetened coffee. But the bribe did not work.

Determined to wait until the cigarettes and the coffee had relaxed him, she turned the conversation to other matters, speaking as best she could in her most diplomatic way. Seeing her camera, he confessed that his greatest wish was to be photographed with his soldiers. She jumped at the news, offered to take his picture and promised to send him copies the absolute minute she had developed them. Before he departed, he too had a gift for her. *"For you,"* he said, he would send a soldier the next day. "I think it's rather a triumph to have conducted so successful a piece of diplomacy in Arabic, don't you?" she beamed in her letter home.

The soldier escort arrived the next morning, a handsome, cheerful Circassian, red-haired and freckled, riding a strong white horse. She set off with him across the steppe on the way to visit the ruins of Mashetta. They passed flocks of storks munching on locusts and came upon scores of black tents of the Beni Sakhr, one of the most formidable Arab tribes and the last to submit to Ottoman rule. When they reached Mashetta, an uncompleted Persian palace, she found its beauty "quite past words . . . a thing one will never forget as long as one lives."

But the image was jarred when, as Gertrude and her Turkish escort turned to go home, three of the Beni Sakhr came riding toward them, "armed to the teeth, black browed and most menacing." Terrified, she could only wait and watch. She was in luck. Seeing the Turkish soldier, the Arabs quickly changed their attitude, salaamed the group and went on their way. Had she not had the soldier escort, she was sure, the meeting would have come to a different end. Her Turkish soldier threw back his head and laughed at the Bedouin. "That was Sheikh Faiz," he sniggered, "the son of Talal," head of the Beni Sakhr. "Like sheep, *wallah!!* Like sheep they are when they meet one of us."

At her flowering campsite the next evening she bathed in a stream and watched her men catch fish by filling a basin with bread, weighing it down with heavy stones and covering it with a cloth. The hungry fish swam through the holes in the cloth to eat the bread, but caught in the trap, they couldn't swim out.

She was eager to explore the Roman ruins of Petra, the ancient capital of the Nabateans, and after receiving permission from the Turkish authority, she ventured on. Two days more of travel and she reached the Bab es Sik, a narrow dirt passage 'more than half a mile long and less than ten feet wide, the entryway to Petra. On either side of her she could almost touch the red sandstone rocks and above her she felt their looming presence as they rose one hundred feet and arched over her head. Suddenly, as she rode along the narrow entrance path, she was struck by a spectacular sight. In front of her stood a great temple cut out of the solid pink rock. Corinthian columns soared "upwards to the very top of the cliff in the most exquisite proportions, carved with groups of figures almost as fresh as when the chisel left them—all this in the rose red rock, with the sun just touching it and making it look almost transparent." The hidden city had been at the center of desert trade and was now a necropolis of seven hundred and fifty tombs. That night she camped amid a row of ornate tombs, three stories high, and felt as though she were in a fairy tale city.

By the time she returned to Jerusalem, after days in the glorious sun, her pale skin had turned brown.

✑   ✑   ✑

A short while later she was off once more, this time with the Rosens, venturing north in Palestine through tiny mountain villages. The sun blazed and she wore a coat to keep out the heat, her head protected by her big, ribboned gray hat over which she had wrapped a white *kafeeyah*, a long cotton scarf; a blue veil covered her face, exposing only the slits of her eyes. After long stretches of sitting sidesaddle, her body ached, but Friedrich Rosen came to her rescue and showed her how to ride like a man. "No more feminine saddles for me on a long journey," she announced to her parents. "Never, never again will I travel on anything else; I have never known real ease in riding till now." Her new saddle carried an amusing bonus: "Till I speak the people always think I'm a man and address me as Effendim!" But she reassured her fashion-conscious mother, "You mustn't think I haven't got a most elegant and decent divided skirt, however, but as all men wear skirts of sorts too, that doesn't serve to distinguish me."

Looking like a Bedouin on her masculine saddle, dressed in her *kafeeyah*, coat and skirt, Gertrude parted from the Rosens about one hundred miles to the northeast of Jerusalem. Leaving behind the soft desert soil, she rode off across the bare, volcanic rocks of the Hauran plain, heading toward the mountains of the Druze. She was in uncharted territory, visited in the past by only a handful of Westerners, and never, in many parts, by a European woman. The region, running through the Galilee, Lebanon and southern Syria, was peopled by fierce warriors and was difficult to penetrate.

The Druze, a secret Muslim sect that combined the teachings of Buddhism, Judaism, Christianity and Islam with the tenets of Greek philosophy, the training of Roman fortitude and the trivialities of peasant life, were known to be militant and hostile. For two hundred years they had fought the ruling Ottoman Turks, and four years before Gertrude arrived, the Turks had suffered humiliating defeat: fourteen hundred Turks were dead while only five hundred Druze had been killed, making the Turks suspicious of anyone who wished to travel in Druze territory. In fact, the Turks did everything they could to prevent it.

But Gertrude feared neither Turks nor Druze. Indeed, she relished the adventure and wrote home confidently that she thought her chances of getting up into the Druze hills were pretty good: "I shall make a determined attack and unless the government stops me, I fancy I shall do it. Everyone in Jerusalem and Jericho told me it was quite impossible but, we shall see. I shall dodge the government as much as possible." Her cat-and-mouse game with the Turks had begun.

The town of Bosrah on the Hauran plateau served as the administrative capital for the Turks and the place where they kept a cautious eye on the Druze. "I am deep in intrigues!" Gertrude announced within hours of her arrival at Bosrah. Anyone visiting the Druze roused the suspicion of the local Ottoman authorities, but she had already plotted her strategy. "One has to walk very warily with Orientals," she explained. "They never say no, straight out; you must read between the lines." She arrived in the courtyard of the Mudir, the Arab Governor of Bosrah, and, over coffee with him, she began to negotiate her trip in Arabic.

"Where are you going?" he asked.

"To Damascus," she replied.

"God has made it! There is a fine road to the west," he suggested, "very beautiful," with interesting places.

"Please God I shall see them!" she exclaimed. "But I wish first to look upon Salkhad." This was to the east, in the heart of the Druze country, where the Turks did not want her to go.

"Salkhad!" he answered. "There is nothing there at all, and the road is very dangerous. It cannot happen."

"It must happen."

"There has come a telegram from Damascus," he lied, "to bid me to say the Mutussarif fears for the safety of your presence."

"English women are never afraid," she lied in turn. "I wish to look upon the ruins."

The conversation continued until, finally, she told him she was staying in Bosrah for the day.

"You have honored me!" he said as he left.

"God forbid!" she answered politely and rode off to see the nearby Roman ruins.

She reveled in the challenge of the game. "It's awfully amusing, and my servants fully enter into the fun of the thing," she reported. "If only I could put myself into communication with the Druze, all would be well." If not, she would start early the next morning and make a dash for it. Once she was inside the territory, it would be difficult for the Turks, so afraid of the Druze, to catch her. She and her men felt like conspirators.

Pretending to be asleep, when the Mudir, the Arab Governor, returned to her tent she hid in her bed and listened while he and her servant spoke.

"The lady has been awake since the rising of the sun," said her servant; "all day she has walked and ridden, now she sleeps."

"Does she march tomorrow?" asked the Mudir.

"I couldn't possibly say, Effendim."

"Tell her she must let me know before she goes anywhere," the Mudir ordered.

"At your pleasure, Effendim."

Waiting until two A.M., she rose and dressed hurriedly, shivering in the cold. Under the light of the stars her five servants packed up camp, and, with one of the men trembling in fear of both the Druze and the Turks, they all sneaked out of town. The evasion was a success. "I've slipped through their fingers," she declared.

❧   ❧   ❧

In the heart of the mountains called the Jebel Druze, she rode through one tiny village after another, causing a stir as she passed the white-turbaned, black-robed men. At Miyemir she stopped to water her horse. The veiled women, dressed in their long blue and red robes, were filling their earthenware jugs, dipping them into the pool. Gertrude dismounted, and a young man about nineteen approached; like all the Druze men and women, he had outlined his enormous eyes in black kohl. The beautiful boy took her hands, and, to her surprise, kissed her on both her cheeks. Other men followed, shaking her hand, eager to inspect the stranger.

With the boy as her guide, she continued in the mountains, past scattered ruins, riding through meadows, vineyards and cornfields, salaaming white-turbaned farmers, who saluted her back, and she laughed at the thought of the angry Turks. When they reached the town of Areh, she received a warm welcome from the village men. Druze style, she walked with them hand in hand, pinkies entwined, until they reached the nearest house. "Are you German?" the people asked warily as she entered. "I am English," she replied, and they almost hugged her. They eyed the Germans as suspiciously as they eyed the Turks, fearful that they craved their land. The English had made a better impression; it was known that in Egypt they administered the country but left the local Arabs in control.

At Areh, the villagers quickly made her feel at home. They piled cushions for her to sit on, brought a stool for her feet and filled a pitcher with water so that she could wash her hands. The women were too shy to unveil their faces or to speak, but she drank good coffee with the men and regaled them with her tales of escape from the Turks. They asked questions about the Boer War, showing their knowledge of towns and generals, and when she told them about her brother Maurice, they listened sympathetically. Could she meet their sheikh? she asked finally. She had read about him in *Murray's* guide-book. "Sheikh!" they said. "Yahya Bey is the head of all the Druze in the land; of course you must visit him." He had just been freed after five years of prison, and they warned her that she must treat him with great respect.

She followed them to the top of the little hill where the sheikh lived in his verandahed house. In the carpeted reception room she saw him: "the most perfect type of the Grand Seigneur, a great big man, very handsome and with the most exquisite manners . . . he's a king, you understand, and a very good king too, though his kingdom doesn't happen to be a large one." She stood regally confident before him, her head high, her hair like a reddish crown, her eyes like brilliant jewels. He beckoned her to join his circle, where he sat eating with six or eight other men, and she folded her skirt and crossed her legs on the carpet. With the thin slabs of bread, she scooped up some *laban* and some of the mixture of beans and meat on the big plate, and talking nonstop, she told her tale, again, hoping to gain his permission to travel freely around the Jebel Druze. She took his photograph, and by the time they said goodbye she had won his promise of an escort. Weeks after she left, when inquiring of her whereabouts, he was known to have asked a visitor: "Have you seen a queen traveling?"

∽ ∽ ∽

By May 11, 1900, she had left the Jebel Druze and reached Damascus, the desert capital. In a moment of reflection, she wrote: "It is at times a very odd sensation to be out in the world quite by myself, but mostly I take it as a matter of course now that I'm beginning to be used to it. I don't think I ever feel lonely, though the one person I often wish for is Papa. I think he really would enjoy it. I keep wanting to compare notes with him." She felt differently about her mother: "You, I want to talk to, but not in a tent with earwigs and black beetles around and muddy water to drink! I don't think you would be your true self under such conditions."

With permission from her parents and a fresh supply of money (her yearly allowance and the income from her books had run out), she extended her journey, bought a deep-pocketed khaki jacket made for a man, and hired three Kurdish soldiers, along with a cook and a guide. When they reached the town of Jarad she went to the house of Sheikh Ahmed. "I lay on his cushions, and ate white mulberries and drank coffee," she recalled contentedly. When they pressed a *narghile* on her, she firmly refused. She had tried it once in Jerusalem. "Never again," she said of the water pipe; "it's too nasty."

∽ ∽ ∽

By the following night the grassy plains had disappeared, and in their place stretched thousands of miles of sand. This was her first night to sleep in the silent, endless desert. "The smooth, hard ground makes a beautiful floor to my tent," she wrote. "Shall I tell you my chief impression—the silence. It is like the silence of mountain tops, but more intense, for there you know the sound of wind and far away water and falling ice and stones; there is a sort of echo of sound there, you know it, Father. But here nothing."

The sun scorched the daytime air, so for the next two days she and her five men traveled at night, twelve hours each night, without water for either humans or horses. The ride was long and boring across the endlesss sands, and she almost fell asleep in her saddle, but her men kept her awake, telling her grisly tales of Bedouin raids and rumors of the cruel, unyielding desert emir, Ibn Rashid. Their stories whetted her appetite to visit the Nejd, the terrifyingly vacant desert she had read about in *Arabia Deserta*, a seminal work describing life with the Bedouin by the traveler Charles Doughty.

When they stopped on the third night and she finally could sleep, she climbed into a muslin bag she had made to protect herself from animal bites and sand flies. "I'm very proud of this contrivance," she wrote, "but if we have a *ghazu*, a raid, of Arabs I shall certainly be the last to fly, and my flight will be as one who runs a sack race."

After another day of riding, they reached a spring. She drank the clear, cold water, closing her eyes to avoid seeing the weeds and creatures swimming in it. Her cook made lunch, fried croquettes and a roasted partridge he had killed, and after tea, she climbed into a cave and slept on thistles. A few hours later they were off again, and by sundown the air had turned bitter cold. At the campsite, to keep warm she put on gaiters and a second pair of knickerbockers, and with a covert cloth coat under her thick winter coat, she rolled herself up in a blanket and cape and went to sleep.

The next day she reached the Roman ruins of Palmyra, a "singular landscape . . . a mass of columns, ranged into long avenues, grouped into temples, lying broken on the sand or pointing one long solitary finger to Heaven. Beyond them is the immense Temple of Baal; the modern town is built inside it and its rows of columns rise out of a mass of mud roofs. And beyond all is the desert, sand and white stretches of salt and sand again, with the dust clouds whirling over it and the Euphrates five days away."

She spent two days exploring Palmyra, and then set off in the early morning for her return to Damascus. Outside the ancient city of Palmyra she came across a camp of Agail Arabs, a band of dark-skinned, unkempt Bedouin driving a caravan of camels to the flowering capital. They were led by Sheikh Muhammad, who came from Nejd, the cruel desert of central Arabia. But instead of hiding in fear of the scruffy Bedouin, she took a second breakfast with them: dates, camels' milk and the bitter black coffee of the Arabs ("a peerless drink," she called it), and talked excitedly with two of the men about Baghdad and the desert. "The interesting part of it is that the Agail are some of Ibn Rashid's people," she reported, "and I'm going to lay plans with Sheikh Muhammad as to getting into Nejd next year." But it was 1900, and the trip she hoped to make to Nejd would not take place for another fourteen years.

"Please God, who is great," the Agail sheikh said. He and his men wanted to travel with her; they needed the protection of her soldiers. She agreed, and, looking like a man in her oversized khaki coat, her tanned brown face half hidden in her *kafeeyah*, she took off, surrounded by the pack of burly Bedouin. On the road to Damascus she caught up with two English ladies, neat and tidy, traveling in a carriage across the desert from Jerusalem, a dragoman on top to guide them, a pack of mules trailing behind with their tents. She was pleased to see them. "I liked them and it's pleasant to meet some one in the desert, but I felt rather disreputable with a troop of Agail on their dromedaries round me and no dragoman and no nothing." The women gave her ginger biscuits (for which she blessed them) and made plans to meet her in Damascus. But she hardly looked forward to tea and biscuits with the fair-skinned English ladies; she much preferred the bitter coffee and adventurous company of the bearded Arab men. Their world felt more natural to her; "a daughter of the desert," they had called her.

The following day a large group of the Hassinah tribe pitched their camp near hers, and their twenty-year-old sheikh, Muhammad, appeared at her tent. A "handsome, rather thick lipped, solemn fellow," she judged him, his hair hanging in braids from under his *kafeeyah*, in his hand an enormous silver-sheathed sword. He greeted her and left. Sheikh Muhammad, not one to be sneered at, had hundreds of tents, countless horses and camels and a house in Damascus.

Gertrude paid a return courtesy call at his tent. While she drank coffee, the Hassinah made a circle around her, their half-hidden eyes staring out at her from under their *kafeeyahs*, their bodies dirty and almost naked. A fire fueled by camel dung smoldered in the air, and one of the men took out a single-stringed instrument and played it with a bow, singing "weird, sad," melancholy songs.

After a long while she stood up to leave, but one of her soldiers reprimanded her. The Hassinah had killed a sheep for her and were preparing it for dinner. In the etiquette of the desert, she was supposed to share their food, and in return for the privilege, she should give them a present. "You can give nothing to an Arab but arms and horses," she noted and, back in her own tent, decided to give the sheikh a pistol belonging to one of her men ("net value two pounds").

She returned to the Hassinah later that night and sat down again on the carpets. This time, besides the bitter black coffee, they offered her "white coffee"—hot water, sweetened and flavored with almonds. She talked with an Agaili about Baghdad and about the mysterious Ibn Rashid, the powerful desert ruler whom she yearned to meet. A black slave brought in a water jar, and as they all held out their hands, he poured the water over their fingers. And then at last came dinner: five men carried in an enormous platter heaped with rice and the meat of a whole sheep. They placed it on the ground in front of her, and she and ten men sat around the platter, eating the food and flat bread with the fingers of their right hand. Behind them stood the black slave holding a glass, which he filled with water whenever someone needed it. Her only disappointment was that the men ate so little; she was still hungry when they finished. There was more hand washing, this time with soap, and then she made her bows and left to go to bed. "It was rather an expensive dinner," she noted dryly, "but the experience was worth the pistol."

∞ ∞ ∞

Her adventure to Jerusalem and beyond had come to an end, and before heading home, she picked up some pine cones from the famous cedars of Lebanon. "Shall we try and make them grow at Rounton?" she asked. She had been looking forward to a respite in England. "But you know, dearest Father," she continued, "I shall be back here before long! One doesn't keep away from the East when one has got into it this far." By June she was planting the pine seeds on the lawn at Rounton.

Chapter Six

A Different Challenge

∞

In Yorkshire during the summer of 1900, and for most of the following twelve months, Gertrude spent time with her sisters Elsa and Molly and her brothers Hugo and Maurice, and cared for her father, ill with rheumatism. From time to time she took the train to London, lunched and shopped with various friends, and dined when she could with Domnul Chirol. Recently made the director of the Foreign Department at *The Times*, Domnul was devoted to her and always willing to lend her a fatherly ear. His concern and compassion, along with his dry wit and convivial attitude, made him her favorite companion. He shared her interests in languages, literature and art, understood her loneliness (he too was lonely) and cherished her friendship. He guided her in political affairs, gave her introductions to important people and encouraged her travels, and as she traveled, she reported back to him; he used the information in his editorials and as background for officials. The reports she made from wherever she went—Europe, the East—were highly detailed. Details almost obsessed her, and in her diaries and correspondence with family and friends, she rarely left out a color or a food or a flower or a description of an experience or a person.

But, except for confiding in Domnul, she avoided discussing how she felt about herself, the way her life was turning out or the loneliness that drove her. In the Victorian setting in which she was raised, she was taught not to brood over sadness but to push it away, to busy herself. And thus, in addition to reading history and literature, she wrote letters, articles and books, studied languages, learned about art, architecture and archaeology, took up photography, played tennis and golf, swam, went riding and played bridge, filling every vacant moment by doing *something*. She had proceeded thus after the loss of Cadogan, and so she continued to do, rushing from one exercise to the next, filling in whatever empty moments remained by writing things down in all their minutiae, intentionally leaving no time for introspection or self-analysis.

∞　∞　∞

She found desert travel alluring, but the mountains gnawed at her too, their very existence summoning her to climb them. In 1899, at the age of thirty-one, she had climbed the Meije; the following summer, after her return from Jerusalem and Damascus, she set off for the Swiss Alps and Chamonix to climb peaks that had not yet been scaled. Arriving at her Swiss hotel at the beginning of August 1900, Gertrude settled into her room, unpacked her suitcase and wrote at once to her father: "I don't think there is a more delightful sensation than that of opening an Alpine campaign—meeting one's guide, talking over the great ascents that look so easy on the map; and laying out one's clean new mountain clothes."

After a few days of practice runs, she climbed Chamonix and then made the ascent up the Mer de Glacé, explaining in her letter home that the Sea of Ice was really a great mass of broken ice that continued to break and crack. The tougher the conditions, the more she enjoyed them, and within a week she wired home, "GREPONT TRAVERSED" and, a week later, "DRU TRAVERSED." The weather turned foul, however, and the bigger peaks would have to wait for another visit.

In August 1901, she was off again to Switzerland, stopping first in London for dinner with Domnul, who cast a wary eye on her dangerous mountain climbing. She shrugged off his concerns and arrived at her Alpine hotel; from the window of her room she could see "the great rock of the Engelhorn opposite, the line of snows of the Wetterhorn, Mittelhorn and Rosenhorn—far away, Pilatus and the Jur touched by the sunlight. Phantom armies of light mists walking over the floor of cloud."

At four A.M. the following morning, dressed in a blue climbing suit,

Gertrude set out with her professional guides, Ulrich and Heinrich Fuhrer, two brothers respected for their ability and well known for their knowledge of the mountain peaks. First, hooking themselves to the same rope, the threesome began their ascent, working their way up the boulders, occasionally scaling rocks so smooth they offered no possibility of a foothold: good practice for the difficult peaks on the Engelhorn.

After several days of snowy weather, they launched a climb on the south side of the fifth peak of the Engelhorn, to a point where no one else had ever been. "[It] *may* be impossible, but I don't think it is," Gertrude informed her family. "They say it is, but we know that the experts may be mistaken." She and the guides made their way up an easy buttress, and the Klein Engelhorn came into full view, looking "most unencouraging"; the bottom third was composed of smooth perpendicular rocks, the next section had a steep rock wall with a deep mountain gorge, which "turned out to be quite as difficult as it looked." They climbed over the smooth precipitous rocks, "scrabbled up" a shallow crack and stopped at the bottom of an overhanging rock, difficult because it was so smooth and unprotected.

Then came the test of her daring. Ulrich tried climbing on Heinrich's shoulder but could not reach anything to hold. Gertrude described the experience: "I then clambered up on to Heinrich, Ulrich stood on me and fingered up the rock as high as he could. It wasn't high enough. I lifted myself still a little higher—always with Ulrich on me, mind!—and he began to raise himself by his hands. As his foot left my shoulder I put up a hand, straightened out my arm and made a ledge for him."

Balancing himself on Gertrude's arm, Ulrich called out: "I don't feel at all safe—if you move we are all killed."

"All right," Gertrude assured him. "I can stand here for a week." And with that he climbed up by her shoulder and her hand.

Heinrich stayed behind, but Gertrude and Ulrich continued the climb, struggling to the top, then working their way down. It was seven in the evening when they reached the foot of the peak and joined Heinrich again. After their fifteen-hour trek, the trio slept that night high up in the mountains, in the hayloft of a farm, breakfasting the next morning on a shepherd's milk and coffee, polished off with their own bread and jam. The adventure ended with a pleasant walk home through the woods.

Later, Ulrich confessed that if, when he asked, Gertrude had said she did not feel safe on the rock, he would have fallen and the three of them would have been killed. In truth, Gertrude admitted, she had hardly felt safe at all. Her air of confidence had merely been a cover for her own fear. Indeed, she said, "I thought I was falling when I spoke." But despite the risks, she felt content: "I don't think I have ever had two more delightful Alpine days."

Within a fortnight they tackled two old peaks, seven new peaks, one new saddle ridge between two peaks, and traversed the 9,130-foot Engelhorn. Invigorated by her success, she informed her father that she hoped to climb one new Engelhorn peak and one of the high arêtes, the sharp, narrow ridges of the mountain: "I *would* like to have one of them to my name! It is a silly ambition, isn't it! Still one does like to have the credit one really deserves." Yet only a few weeks later, in mid-September, it was time to leave; sadly, she packed her belongings, but as she said farewell, she felt gratified to know that she was leaving behind a promontory that had already been named "Gertrude's Peak."

∞   ∞   ∞

At the start of the new year, 1902, the East beckoned. Gertrude set sail from Liverpool with her father and her brother Hugo, stopping first in Algiers, where she wrote in her diary: "Even here there is enough of the East to give one the feel of it. I find it catching at my heart again as nothing else can, or ever will I believe, thing or person." At Naples, she parted company from her family and continued on to Malta, where she joined an archaeological dig.

Poking around the Turkish island, she noted determinedly: "Some day, I shall come and travel here with tents, but then I will speak Turkish, which will not be difficult." Most intriguing, however, was what she learned over a lunch at the British consulate: the day she had arrived in Smyrna, an influential uncle of the powerful sheikh Ibn Rashid had passed through town on his way back to Nejd. If only she had known. "I would have given worlds to meet him." She was sowing plans for a trip to Arabia.

With Arabic still a challenge, she left Smyrna in March, sailing on the *Cleopatra* for Haifa, taking up residence on Mount Carmel, near the site of the great Crusader castle. She hired two sheikhs as tutors, one for Persian, which she found "perfectly delightful," one for Arabic, over which she despaired once again: "I am soaked and sodden in it and how anyone can wish to have anything to do with a tongue so difficult when they might be living at ease, I can't imagine. I never stop talking it in this hotel and I think I get a little worse daily."

She visited Jerusalem and filled every day with lessons, excursions and afternoon teas, and as interesting as she found the local notables, they thought her even more intriguing. "I am a Person in this country," she wrote excitedly to her parents. "I am a Person! and one of the first questions everyone seems to ask everyone else is, 'Have you ever met Miss Gertrude Bell?' " But after two months it was time to leave, and by the end of May 1902, she was home in England, if only for a brief stay.

❀   ❀   ❀

Once more the high peaks of Switzerland tempted her, and in little over a month she left for the Oberland, writing home delightedly that she was recognized by a guard on the Brünnig train. Was she *"the* Miss Bell who had climbed the Engelhorn last year?" he had asked. "This is fame," she informed her family.

Soon after registering at the Kurhaus, her hotel in Rosenalui, she wanted to put herself in shape for serious climbs. Walking straight up a hill, she reached the edge of a glacier and sat down, thinking "what a lucky dog" she was to be there.

Dressed for the biting cold, she was off once again with her guides, the brothers Ulrich and Heinrich, making easy ascents up and down some "charming" little rocks of the Oberland. They tackled "the first of the impossibles, the Wellhorn arête," 10,485 feet, running up the beginning of the Vorder Wellhorn, and after hours of climbing the smooth rocks, they came to a terribly dangerous precipice. "My heart sank," she confessed. "I thought we should never do it." Shivering with cold, they faced a rotting knife edge of rock that crumbled in masses as they went along, with steep precipices beneath them that threatened their every step. But with the aid of an iron nail and a double rope they reached the summit, returning happily to the inn to plan the next event.

In the course of her previous visits she and her guides had considered an ascent up the rocky face of the Finsteraarhorn glacier. Serious climbs were a means to stretch her athletic stamina, to prove her physical strength, to compete with her own sex as well as with males and, most important, to test herself. She was determined to achieve the highest possible position, no matter in which field of endeavor; mountain climbing (a popular sport for females) offered clear tasks and, quite literally, a chance to reach the heights. But if she was going to climb a mountain, she would do it the way she did everything else: not by following in other people's footsteps, but by seeking to break new ground. She would find the untried and persevere to overcome it; otherwise, it was hardly worth the doing.

The climb up the face of the Finsteraarhorn was three thousand vertical feet, steeper and higher than almost any place in the Alps, a daring climb that had not yet been tried. "The arête," she explained, "rises from the glacier in a great series of gendarmes [spires], and towers, set at such an angle on the steep face of the mountain that you wonder how they can stand at all and indeed they can scarcely be said to stand, for the great points of them are continually overbalancing and tumbling down into the couloirs [the gaps], between the arêtes and they are all capped with loosely poised stones, jutting onto and hanging over and ready to fall at any moment." The dangers were enormous, the rocks "exceedingly steep" and as they began their ascent at one A.M. on the fateful day of July 31, 1902, black clouds rolled up from the west. But "the game" had begun. Gertrude was determined to slash through the glacier to the peak.

Tied to one another on a rope, she and the guides pushed their way up the arête for several hours, past some of the terribly difficult "chimneys," narrow clefts in the cliff, until, at a thousand feet below the summit, they were in sight of the final two spires. White flakes started to fall, and they sat down to eat a few mouthfuls of snow; refreshed, they crept along the knife edge of a narrow pass. The snow was coming down faster, furious and blinding, swirling in a small avalanche; they could see nothing of the mountainside either to the right or to the left, and the slope was too slippery with the fresh snow. They had had no choice but to turn back. They knew it would be only slightly less precarious than going up.

They reached a sloping rock ledge, but it offered little relief; from there they would have to drop eight feet down onto deep snow. They fixed an extra rope and tumbled down, one after the other, onto the snow. "It felt awful," Gertrude reported; "I shall remember every inch of that rock face for the rest of my life." It was six in the evening, and their goal was to work down to the most difficult of the narrow clefts while it was still layered with only a little snow. But after they toiled for several more hours down the rocks, a furious thunderstorm began. They were completely vulnerable. "We were standing by a great upright on the top of a tower when suddenly it gave a crack and a blue flame sat on it for a second," she wrote. "My ice axe jumped in my hand and I thought the steel felt hot through my woollen glove—was that possible? I didn't take my glove off to see! Before we knew where we were the rock flashed again." They "tumbled down a chimney as hard as ever we could, one on top of the other, buried our ice axe heads in some shale at the bottom of it and hurriedly retreated from them. It's not nice to carry a private lightning conductor in your hand in the thick of a thunderstorm."

There was no way to continue in the dark and no place to take shelter from the storm, but somehow, linked together on their rope,

they squeezed into a tiny crack between the rocks and huddled together. Gertrude sat at the back on a pointed bit of rock, Ulrich sat on
her feet to keep them warm, and Heinrich sat just below him, the
brothers' feet in a knapsack, the snow coming down, the thunder
booming fast behind every strike of lightning. "At first the thunderstorm made things rather exciting," she explained. "The claps followed
the flashes so close that there seemed no interval between them. We
tied ourselves firmly on to the rock above, lest, as Ulrich philosoph-
ically said, one of us should be struck and fall out. The rocks were all
crackling round us and fizzing like damp wood . . . and as there was
no further precaution possible I enjoyed the extraordinary magnificence
of the storm with a free mind: it was worth seeing." She managed to
doze. Gradually the skies cleared, the stars came out, and they talked
about the sunrise. But the sun never rose; gray skies hung over the day.

For sixteen hours, from four A.M. until eight the next evening, they
were on the arête; they carried nothing to drink but two tablespoons of
brandy and a mouthful of wine, and the only food they had was what
was left in their knapsacks: five gingerbread biscuits, two sticks of
chocolate, a slice of bread, a scrap of cheese and a handful of raisins,
doled out during the course of the day. The climb down was slow and
torturous, almost every yard requiring an extra rope: "You can imagine
the labour of finding a rock at every 50 feet round which to sling it,
then of pulling it down behind us and slinging it again."

It snowed all day, and they watched the white sheets whirl down
the precipices, knowing, helplessly, that the snow was likely to start an
avalanche. They tackled the next chimney, the iced rope slipping like
butter through their hands, and then worked their way down an icy
slope of rock covered with four inches of new snow and split by broad
gaps. "The rock was too difficult for me, the stretches too big, I
couldn't reach them. . . . I handed my axe down to Heinrich and told
him I could do nothing but fall, but he couldn't, or at any rate, didn't
secure himself and in a second we were both tumbling head over heels
down the couloir." Somehow Ulrich held them. "But it was a near
thing and I felt rather ashamed of my part in it." She thought then that
it was "on the cards we should not get down alive."

The cold was bitter, the snow had turned to rain, their clothing
was soaked and they shivered all day as they worked their way down,
only to find themselves at nightfall still on the glacier. They had no
matches to light their lantern and no shelter from the driving rain.
Nevertheless, they found a spot in which to sink their axes, and they sat
on them and she slept a bit, thinking how her brother Maurice had
slept through the rain during the war in South Africa.

When morning came they could hardly stand, but they managed to take a few steps, and by six o'clock, they were safe enough to free themselves from the rope. At ten A.M. on August 3, 1902, they reached the hotel. Gertrude's toes had swelled and she had frostbite, but she announced, "I am perfectly absolutely well except for my toes—not so much as a cold in the head. Isn't it remarkable!" She had made the trip despite Domnul's gloomy forebodings, which, she acknowledged, "came very near to being realised, and I am now feeling some satisfaction in the thought that my bones are not lying scattered on the Alpine mountain cold." She had not reached the pinnacle, but in the face of death-defying danger, she had escaped unharmed. Later on, her guide Ulrich would say, "Had she not been full of courage and determination, we must have perished." Of all the amateur climbers he had known, he added—men and women—no one had equaled her "in coolness, bravery and judgement."

CHAPTER SEVEN

The Desert and the Sown

∞

Her toes still swollen, Gertrude returned to the "horrid cold" of London, even in mid-August of 1902. She hired a personal maid, Marie Delaere, resumed her rounds of afternoon calls, and over dinner with Domnul, who was traveling frequently as foreign editor of *The Times*, planned a trip to Delhi. To celebrate Edward VII's accession to the throne as King of England and Emperor of India, Lord Curzon, the Viceroy of India, had announced an imperial durbar, an impressive gathering of notables. Resplendent, sumptuous, spectacular; no words were too profuse to describe the richness of this coming event. The great meeting of dignitaries, potentates and luminaries would regale the most populous subcontinent on earth with the grandeur of Empire. Replete with jewel-laden elephants and dazzling electric lights, the display of wealth and majesty would reinforce the image of British power to the Indian people and justify the notion of imperial possession. A confirmed imperialist herself, Gertrude looked forward to joining the festivities. For her and for her circle, her country's unique position of strength was a noble necessity. The British, with their commerce, courage and conviction of superiority, were clearly meant to take charge of less fortunate souls.

She journeyed to India with her younger brother Hugo, in part for pleasure, in part to dissuade him from taking Holy Orders. Convinced that being a Christian was a foolish waste of time, Gertrude spent much of the seagoing trip engaged in intellectual argument. But to no avail. Hugo was determined to join the church. By the end of December 1902 their boat reached Bombay, and it was with great relief to both that they turned their attention from the religion of Christ to the religion of Empire.

It seemed that "all the world" had come for the brilliant durbar: family, friends, close officials, all installed, like her, in the privileged tents of the Viceroy, in front-row seats at parades, at the best receptions and the most lavish parties. And to her delight, Domnul, who had come by way of the Persian Gulf, introduced her to representatives of the venerable Indian Civil Service, that prestigious club of Oxford and Cambridge graduates that ruled the colony and its outposts, meted out justice, taught the natives how to pour a good wine and made sure that British business interests were always protected. In particular, she met the tall, distinguished-looking British Resident, the presiding British Consul in Muscat, Percy Cox.

Lunching together with trusty Domnul and the knowledgeable Cox, she learned the latest news from Central Arabia, an up-to-date report on the blood feud between the Emir of Nejd, Ibn Rashid, leader of the seminomadic clan of the Shammar tribe, and his powerful rival, Ibn Saud, head of the Bedouin clan that belonged to the Anazeh tribe. Two of the most powerful sheikhs in Arabia, between them they controlled the vast and vacant desert that formed the central plain of the Arabian peninsula, over which their clans had fought for generations. Years of warring had led in 1891 to the defeat of the Saudis by the Rashids; exiled to Kuwait, an emirate allied to the British, the Saudis had allowed their anger to fester with revenge against the Rashids. Now there was talk of Ibn Saud's return.

Gertrude's meeting with Cox was brief but important; it strengthened her determination to penetrate Arabia and marked the start of a long and important relationship with Percy Cox.

∞   ∞   ∞

From India, Gertrude and Hugo continued on to Singapore and Shanghai, Seoul and Tokyo. Crossing the Pacific, they reached Vancouver, where she climbed the Rocky Mountains and admired the beauty of Lake Louise, but as they worked their way down to the United States, she grew weary of the scenery. In Chicago she was overwhelmed "by the horribleness of its outside, the filth of the streets, the noise, the ugliness." A few more days in America, at Niagara Falls and Boston, and she was eager to leave for home. On July 26, 1903, she landed at Liverpool and spent the rest of the year in England.

Once again, she faced the cold reality of spinsterhood. Her sister Molly had, like her, fallen in love with a man whom her father rejected. But a few months later, Gertrude introduced Molly to Charles Trevelyan, and on January 6, 1904, the couple was married. Gertrude ached, watching her younger sister walk down the aisle. The only men who seemed to be attracted to her were "good old things," like Lord Dartrey, who, she had reported, had "fallen in love with her" on the ship to India, and who held no interest for her.

⧜ ⧜ ⧜

By March, when the brutal English snow and frost made her pine for a "nice desert where the sun shines," she dreamed of a visit to Ibn Rashid. But her plans to go to Arabia were still on hold. Ibn Rashid, sponsored by the Turks, was at war and the area too dangerous to visit. Instead, in London, she attended another wedding, this one of her cousin Florence Lascelles to Cecil Spring-Rice, a diplomat; cultivated her social circle of Foreign Office officials; and pursued a friendship with John Singer Sargent. In August 1904 she decided to make another attempt at mountain climbing, at Zermatt. "Yes, as you say, why do people climb?" she wrote her mother, but she left the question open. Her answer lay in her actions. She climbed mountains as much to conquer her loneliness as to scale the heights.

She adored breaking new ground, being the center of attention, with everyone's eyes and ears on her. But, no less fascinated by those whom she deemed of particular interest, she focused her own attention on the way they thought and behaved. At home, however, life had curdled from ennui. The English were too predictable; she could tell in advance what a politician might do or what her dinner partner might say. The one group she had met that was different was the Arabs; they excited her. They stimulated her imagination; they were romantic, exotic, mysterious, unplumbed.

⧜ ⧜ ⧜

By September she was in London, shopping furiously for fur boas and muffs, seeing friends, dining with Domnul. "It's disgusting weather," she told her mother, as she made plans to head for the East. This time, however, she sought another purpose to her travels. Intrigued by architecture and ancient civilizations, she arranged to study with a French archaeologist, Salomon Reinach, the Jewish scholar primarily responsible for the popular notion that civilization began in the East, where it nurtured the great ideas of mankind. Editor of the prestigious *Revue Archéologique*, Reinach also wrote extensively about the Romanesque and Gothic periods in France, and was director of the Saint-Germain Museum in Paris. Married and ten years her senior, "singularly plain, but an angel," he took her under his wing. He taught her about Egyptian, Greek, Roman and Byzantine art and archaeology, treating her like a favored schoolgirl. "Reinach . . . loves me so dearly," she wrote almost wistfully. "He has simply set all his boundless knowledge at my disposal and I have learnt more in these few days than I should have learnt by myself in a year."

The school session soon over, she returned to London to ready herself for adventure. Her friend David Hogarth had just published a new book, *The Penetration of Arabia*, in which he had written about the enormous unknown desert "still in great part withdrawn from western eyes" and expressed the hope that Europeans would "complete the penetration of Arabia" as soon as the atmosphere was amenable. No one was more eager to carry out Hogarth's wish than Gertrude, but as Percy Cox and others had advised her, the time was not yet ripe. Instead, she would retrace her journey of five years earlier, traveling east of the Jordan River "to that delectable region of which Omar Khayyám sings: 'The strip of herbage strown that just divides the desert from the sown.' "

❦   ❦   ❦

On January 4, 1905, Gertrude departed for the East, her interest reinforced by the knowledge she had gained under Reinach's tutelage, her legitimacy strengthened by a scholarly letter she had published in the *Revue Archéologique* on the geometry of the cruciform structure. At Reinach's urging, she aimed to make serious studies of Roman and Byzantine ruins, to weigh the impact of their civilizations on the Orient. In addition, she planned to take extensive notes on the people, make detailed observations of the Bedouin and the Druze. Her goal was to combine all the material—the archaeological and the anthropological, the social and the cultural, the ancient and the modern, along with dozens of photographs she would take—into a book.

She wanted to inform the English of the ways of the East. She would tell them about the Arab world and its culture: its people, Bedouin tribesmen and educated townsmen; its language, flowery and circuitous; its manners, both primitive and polished; its delicate art; its intricate architecture; its history of holy wars and conquests; its literature filled with symbolism and poetry; its politics fraught with internecine rivalries and tribal revenge; its religion of Islam; its wailing music; its food staples of flat bread and yogurt; its commerce of bazaar merchants and international traders; its agriculture of wheat farming and camel grazing; its fertile soil; its oil-rich sand; its terrain of palm trees, incidental water and endless desert.

The volume, she hoped, would establish her reputation as both a writer and a scholar. And, even more, she hoped it would establish her as a Person. She had experienced that status briefly in the East and in Switzerland; perhaps she would become a Person at home.

The SS Ortona left Marseilles and docked a week later at Beirut, in Syria. To her great delight, she found herself once again in the sort of danger that called for evasive action. Along with her books—Charles Doughty's Arabia Deserta (filled with information about the Bedouin) and Hogarth's The Penetration of Arabia—she had packed some highly suspicious articles: a revolver, a rifle and an assortment of maps, all questionable for a British subject to be lugging through Turkish territory. To ease her way through the customs house, she had sent a note to the British Consul in Beirut, asking for a kavass, a servant, to help her. An old friend appeared, a smiling man in a uniform, and they set off for customs, she with the revolver tucked in her pocket. She had "every possible sort of contraband," she warned him, most anxious about her gun. She had packed the rifle, case and all, in her cabin trunk, wrapping it around with her lacy white petticoats. But if the Turks found the gun, they would confiscate it.

At the customs house she quickly engaged the chief officer in a friendly conversation about the weather while the kavass announced to everyone that she was "a very great lady." Of course, he informed them, it was unnecessary to pay strict attention to her baggage. Case after case went by unquestioned. And when they opened a wooden packing crate, they found nothing but camp utensils.

But the next item of interest was her cabin trunk. "It is needless that they should search this very much," she whispered nervously in Arabic to the kavass.

"I have understood, O Lady," he replied. Gingerly, he lifted her gowns, the white petticoats with their lacy edges ("aggressively feminine," she called them) peeking out beneath. Then, just as the men were about to put back the drawer, one of them caught sight of a pile of maps—"very suspicious objects in Turkey"—that covered the end of the gun case. As he stooped down to look at the maps, Gertrude quickly turned to the chief officer and made a remark about the rain.

"By God, O Lady," he answered, "it is as Your Excellency says: God alone knows when the rain will cease." Then, with a brusque show of friendship, he ordered his man to stop.

The *kavass* quickly pushed in the drawer. "Y'allah, o boy!" he said. "Hasten! Shall we wait here till nightfall?" The dangerous wait was over.

With a polite *salaam*, she smiled at the chief. "I go, upon your pleasure," she said.

"Go in peace," he replied.

She had, she reported to her father, pulled off "a marvel of successful fraud." She would give the *kavass* an extra tip.

The streets of Beirut were filled with mud, but the Oriental aroma made her feel at home. Within hours she was "deep in gossip"; and strolling through the bazaars, she felt the pleasure of being in the Levant. "A bazaar is always the epitome of the East, even in a half European town like Beirut," she wrote home.

In talks with British officials she heard that Ibn Rashid had been driven out of his capital, Hayil, by Ibn Saud, but that Turkish troops were coming to help the Rashids. The Ottomans were making handsome payments to Ibn Rashid, ensuring his loyalty to them, while the British, under the rule of Lord Curzon in India and the watchful eye of Percy Cox in Muscat, were keeping Ibn Saud, along with his ally, the Sheikh of Kuwait, content.

At a dinner a few evenings later she was assured that Ibn Rashid was still at Hayil, holding on with his population of thirty thousand Arabs. The emir, her dinner partner said, was "very enterprising, very brave. He lets no foreigner into Nejd, absolutely impossible to enter, but if you could get in, you would never get out." A more tempting dare would have been hard to find. It was not her plan to visit Central Arabia until the following year, but the challenge piqued her interest.

Her current journey, however, required certain arrangements. She bought horses and mules, and hired Muhammad, the Druze who was her former muleteer. He pledged to go with her "to the ends of the earth." They were off, and a few days later she arrived in Jerusalem.

The British Consul, Mr. Dickson, informed her that Sir Mark and Lady Sykes, a most congenial couple, were also in town. It seemed that Gertrude and Mark Sykes had much in common: smart, enthusiastic and equally impatient, they both came from exceptionally rich Yorkshire families; both had been educated at the best British universities; both were able to travel freely; both were interested in the Levant; and both were destined to have an impact on the Middle East.

Although each was highly opinionated and competitive, for all their similarities they differed sharply. Gertrude was an atheist, Sykes a practicing Catholic; Gertrude had gone to Oxford, Sykes to Cambridge; Gertrude was opposed to her family using titles; Sykes was proud to use his; Gertrude was thirty-four, unmarried and not yet well known at home; Sykes was ten years younger, had already traveled throughout Asia and Turkey and had attracted much attention in England with his published accounts. Just as irritating to her, Sykes had only contempt for the people of the desert, while Gertrude held the Arabs in some esteem. A year earlier, in 1904, Sykes had written about the Arabs of Mosul and Damascus: "Eloquent, cunning, excitable and cowardly, they present to my mind the most deplorable pictures one can see in the East." He called them "diseased," "contemptuous," "idle beyond all hope, vicious as far as their feeble bodies will admit," "insolent yet despicable."

Gertrude would soon write empathetically: "The Oriental is like a very old child. . . . He is not practical in our acceptation of the word, any more than a child is practical, and his utility is not ours. On the other hand, his action is guided by traditions of conduct and morality that go back to the beginnings of civilisation, traditions unmodified as yet by any important change in the manner of life to which they apply and out of which they arose. These things apart, he is as we are; human nature does not undergo a complete change east of Suez, nor is it impossible to be on terms of friendship and sympathy with the dwellers in those regions. In some respects it is even easier than in Europe."

∞   ∞   ∞

Gertrude left her calling card with Mark and Edith Sykes in Jerusalem. They received her "with open arms," she reported; and after a good dinner and a merry evening, she declared them "perfectly charming." Like Gertrude, Sykes was planning a visit to the notorious mountain Druze; the two travelers discussed their separate schemes.

However amusing they found each other that evening, within a few weeks Sykes had changed his mind. Writing a long letter to his wife, he denounced Gertrude bitterly, complaining that she had deliberately misled him. She "had taken the very route I told her I hoped to do," he whined, "after she said she was going elsewhere." Blaming Gertrude because the Turks tried to prevent him from traveling to the Druze, Sykes called her a "*Bitch*" and wished "10,000 of my worst bad words on the head of that damned fool. . . . Wherever she went," he told his wife, she caused an "uproar" and was the "terror of the desert." As brilliant as she was to some, to Sykes, Gertrude was a "silly chattering windbag of conceited, gushing, flat-chested, man-woman, globe-trot-ting, rump-wagging, blethering *ass!*"

⚮   ⚮   ⚮

Gertrude had already set forth. "It was a stormy morning, the 5th of February," as she later described the start of her adventure. "The west wind swept up from the Mediterranean, hurried across the plain where the Canaanites waged war with the stubborn hill dwellers of Judaea, and leapt the barrier of mountains to which the kings of Assyria and of Egypt had lain vain siege. It shouted the news of rain to Jerusalem and raced onwards down the barren eastern slopes, cleared the deep bed of Jordan with a bound, and vanished across the hills of Moab into the desert. And all the hounds of the storm followed behind, a yelping pack, coursing eastward and rejoicing as they went.

"No one with life in his body could stay in on such a day, but for me there was little question of choice."

Along with her Christian cook, Mikhail (recommended by Mark Sykes), her party consisted of three muleteers: Ibrahim, an old and toothless Christian Maronite; his son Habib, handsome and broad-shouldered; and Muhammad, the Druze, large, lazy and charming. She was heading east for the Jordan Valley, "alone down the desolate road to Jericho." To reach the Jebel Druze, she chose the route across the Jordan Bridge, "the Gate of the Desert," she called it. She and her men pitched their tents the first night close to the wooden toll bridge and set off again in the morning, encountering a ragged Arab whose only dream was to go to America. "The same story can be heard all over Syria. Hundreds go out every year," she wrote, noting they hoped to make a small fortune in America and then return to the East.

She rode across the frontier, ready to record in her diary any ruin or individual that might be of interest. Her observations would not only help her write her book, they would help her advise her friends in the British Government. Then, as now, archaeologists and writers ventured where others feared to tread. With her keen eye for detail and her ear for gossip, Gertrude provided information that was particularly valuable. Sending lengthy letters to the highly influential Domnul, reporting to diplomats in the Foreign Office and the India Office, she filled them in on the sorry state of Ottoman rule. The hand of the Turk reached down to Syria and Arabia, but its greedy fingers, so busy snatching bribes or spreading corruption, had spent little time administering the Arabs under it.

Eager to find a European sponsor to arm them against the Turks, the Druze considered the British their ally of first choice. By traveling without the requisite Turkish escort, Gertrude could, she hoped, rekindle the trust of the Druze whom she had visited before, gauge the depths of their discontent and the relative strength of their army. She knew that the Druze did "not play the game as it should be played, they go out to slay and they spare no one. While they have a grain of powder in their flasks and strength to pull the trigger, they kill every man, woman and child that they encounter." It was partly such menace that intrigued her, sucking her in as though she were a child standing at the edge of the ocean, drawn to the giant waves.

Heading for danger, she crossed the desert, adding an Arab guide to her party. Namrud, a Christian, knew every sheikh of the area. Riding on days so raw and wet that her horses plunged through seas of mud, she inspected vestiges of the past—tombs, Roman coins, a ruined temple at Khureibet es Suk—and encountered a camp of the Beni Sakhr tribe in an ongoing feud with the Druze. "There is no mercy between them," she observed. "If a Druze meets a Beni Sakhr, one of them kills the other." Her main worry was Muhammad, her muleteer. If the Beni Sakhr, with whom she had camped that night, knew he was Druze, "they would not only kill him, they would burn him alive." It was decided that Muhammad undergo a quick conversion to Christianity.

For the moment, at least, the Beni Sakhr were her friends. Five years earlier they had called her "a daughter of the desert." Now, as she lunched in her tent, enjoying a meal of curry served on fine china, washing it down with a glass of wine, one of the Beni Sakhr joined her, and they sat together, drinking coffee, smoking her Egyptian cigarettes, talking of the bloodthirsty Druze. At nightfall the desert turned cold and wet; she wrapped herself in her fur, slipped a hot water bottle between her sheets and went to bed.

The following evening, having reached the Druze, she was invited to the long black tent of their sheikh. She approached the men's quarters and entered. It never would have occurred to her to enter the women's side of the tent; to her the harem was a curiosity, a place to observe and photograph. She thought of herself as one of the men, expecting equal treatment, as honored a guest as any male. Indeed, the Arabs had dubbed her an "honorary man."

She moved easily between rival tribes and between contrasting cultures, and that night she dined with the Druze sheikh, sitting cross-legged on the floor, using her hand to eat the meat, scooping the yogurt with flaps of bread. Sitting with the men around the fire after dinner, she drank coffee and smoked cigarettes, while her hosts told her tales of the desert and of Turkish oppression. Wide-eyed and eager, she listened to the Druze stories of a recent *ghazu*, a raid, by the Beni Sakhr.

They had swept across the countryside, carrying off five thousand sheep from the flocks of the Druze. A few days later she learned that two thousand Druze were going to retaliate against the Beni Sakhr. At camp that night, she finished dinner, and while debating whether or not it was too cold to write in her diary, she heard the ugly sounds of a war song drumming in the dark. She looked up and, from the castle walls that rimmed the hilltop, saw a huge flame leap into the sky, a beacon to tell the news of the coming raid to the Druze villages scattered below. She asked the Druze soldier sitting guard in her camp if she could join the militia gathering at the bonfire. "There is no refusal; honor us," he answered. They scrambled to the top of the sandy mountain.

On the edge of the castle moat a group of Druze, men and boys, armed with clubs and swords, were singing a brutal chant. She joined them with her guide and listened as over and over again they sang the call to war:

> *O Lord our God! upon them! upon them!*
> *that the foe may fall in swathes before our swords!*
> *Let the child leave his mother's side,*
> *let the young man mount and be gone.*

The singing came to an end and, holding hands, the men created a circle; three young Druze stepped inside. Moving around the circle, they stopped in front of each man and, shaking their bare swords, demanded: "Are you a good man? Are you a true man?"

With the moon lighting their faces, each one shouted in turn: "Ha! ha!" It was a sound of rejoicing for blood and war.

One of the young men noticed Gertrude. He strode up and raised his sword above his head. "Lady!" he cried, "the English and the Druze are one."

"Thank God! We too are a fighting race," she answered, swept up in the passion to kill the enemy.

Then, still holding hands, the men ran down the hill, Gertrude running with them, holding hands, ready to join the raid. Suddenly she realized that if the Turkish Governor of Damascus got wind of her participation, he would hardly believe that the rest of her work was innocent. Turning into the darkness, she ran down to her tent. Somewhat sadly, she wrote, she "became a European again, bent on peaceful pursuits and unacquainted with the naked primitive passions of mankind."

She stayed three weeks in the mountains, some days doing little else but drinking coffee, smoking cigarettes, gossiping with the Turkish officials who patrolled the area. They soon became her friends. She could go where she liked, and no one would do anything but help her.

Two days later she was out of the Druze country, heading toward Damascus. She arrived in the desert capital on Sunday, February 26, 1905. Dust-covered and sunburned, surrounded by her caravan of ragged Bedouin—a wild-looking bunch, with matted hair and bearded faces, their bodies draped with rifles, daggers and clubs—a string of mules and camels behind them, she entered the bustling city of nearly three hundred thousand people, luxuriant, with mountains on three sides, orchards and running water on the fourth. It was said that when the prophet Muhammad arrived in Damascus, he left at once, thinking that he had just seen Paradise; he was afraid to harm his chances of returning after death. As Gertrude rode through the town, the great Ummayad Mosque stood, as it does today, a symbol of Islamic power.

A warm bath and a good rest at a clean hotel, and Gertrude went off to meet the Turkish Governor. He had sent her an anxious note. It seemed the government had been nervous about her stay in the Jebel Druze. They had received telegrams three times a day reporting on her activities, but never knew what she was going to do next. Not only was the governor interested in her; she had become well known in Syria. Wherever she went, crowds of Arabs followed her, through the narrow city streets, into the noisy bazaar. "I have become a Person in Syria!" she declared.

Droves of notables came to visit at her hotel, and every afternoon she held a reception. "Damascus flocks to drink my coffee and converse with me," she reported with delight. During a meeting with one family, the Abdul Kadirs, she discussed her future plans to visit Ibn Rashid, and won a promise that they would help her in her journey. Most important, she learned that the French Orientalist René Dussaud was also planning a trip to Rashid headquarters in Hayil; it stirred her competitive juices. "I must hurry up!" she exclaimed, hoping to beat him there.

But for the moment it was Damascus that intrigued her, "with the desert almost up to its gates, and the breath of it blowing in with every wind, and the spirit of it passing in through the city gates with every Arab camel driver. That is the heart of the whole matter," she wrote.

∽ ∽ ∽

The rest of her trip she spent in Asia Minor visiting Roman and Byzantine churches. At Anavarz, where thousands of mosquitoes and three-foot-long snakes had taken lodging in the ruins, she copied inscriptions, noted archaeological and architectural details and photographed the remains. Her work would be published in a series of articles in the *Revue Archéologique*.

Along the way she hired a Christian servant from Aleppo, a round-faced fellow of medium height and mild temperament. "Fattuh, bless him!" she wrote, soon after the Armenian started working for her. "The best servant I have ever had, ready to cook my dinner or pack a mule or dig out an inscription with equal alacrity . . . and to tell me endless tales of travel as we ride . . . for he began life as a muleteer at the age of ten and knows every inch of ground from Aleppo to Baghdad." He would be at her side through her most dangerous expeditions.

In Konia she met William Ramsay, a famed archaeologist, and his wife, doing excavations in the area. The meeting was fortuitous: she showed him some of the inscriptions she had copied at Bin Bir Kelesse, the Turkish area of a Thousand and One Churches, an important site for archaeologists, and he confirmed her work, laying a path for their future collaboration.

At Constantinople, her final stop, she talked Turkish politics with British officials, and discussed their major concern, the encroaching power of Germany, manifested in the Kaiser's plan for a Berlin-to-Baghdad Railway. The Germans and Turks were becoming closely aligned in a region the British held dear. The alliance foreshadowed the bloody world war to come. But for the moment, all was quiet. By early spring, Gertrude was back in England, at work on her book about Syria and the Druze. She had come away with some strong thoughts on the East:

> Islam is the bond that unites the western and central parts of the continent, as it is the electric current by which the transmission of sentiment is effected, and its potency is increased by the fact that there is little or no sense of territorial nationality to counterbalance it. A Turk or a Persian does not think or speak of "my country" in the way that an Englishman or a Frenchman thinks and speaks; his patriotism is confined to the town of which he is a native, or at most to the district in which that town lies. If you ask him to what nationality he

belongs he will reply: "I am a man of Isfahan," or "I am a man of Konia," as the case may be, just as the Syrian will reply that he is a native of Damascus or Aleppo—I have already indicated that Syria is merely a geographical term corresponding to no national sentiment in the breasts of the inhabitants.

It would take her until the end of December 1906 to complete *The Desert and the Sown*, the book that made it amply clear that not only in the East—in Syria, Arabia, Mesopotamia and Turkey—but in England, too, Miss Gertrude Bell was a Person. For the two years that she worked on the book, Rounton Grange became the center of her life. Both of her grandparents had died, and although Florence Bell was never content in the country (she much preferred London life to the provinces), Hugh had moved his family into the landmark house in Yorkshire. For Gertrude, Rounton was bliss; it had always been her favorite place, and she gave it loving care, nursing her flower beds, creating a huge rock garden that won several awards and working in her study.

She struggled over the book, wrote articles and book reviews for *The Times* and *The Times Literary Supplement*, and did social work in the town of Clarence, helping the wives of the Bell Brothers' ironworkers. A steady stream of house guests kept her from being lonely: socialites such as Lady Russell, who brought the gossip from town, or the American actress Elizabeth (Lisa) Robins, who appeared in Florence's plays; the diplomat Cecil Spring-Rice, posted in Washington; Friedrich Rosen, still a member of the German Foreign Ministry; Sir Alfred Lyall, the British Administrator in India; Sir Frank Swettenham, the High Commissioner of the Malay States. There was the educator Dr. Daniel Bliss, founder of the American University in Beirut; the archaeologist William Ramsay; and the punctilious Domnul, whose political analyses were held in high esteem.

Indoors, in the big Common Room, the guests arranged themselves on the comfortable blue-and-green-patterned sofas designed by William Morris, and, with Gertrude at the center, the heated conversations bounced off the dark, silk-covered walls, jumping to the tiger skin on the floor, to the piano, and out the high arched windows to the sprawling garden. The discussions covered the globe, from Japan's ability to supplant the Europeans in cheap foreign markets, to the hopelessness of the Russian economy and the probability of a revolution against the Czar, and also the danger of the German Kaiser and the economic threat to Britain from the Berlin-to-Baghdad Railway.

At tea in the garden on a lovely summer day, Frank Swettenham revealed one of the secrets of his remarkable career as a diplomat. "Whatever success I have had in life," he told an attentive Gertrude, "I owe to having been willing to accept information from any source. It only meant a little trouble, being nice to people, and polite when they came to me with news, and rewarding them for it when it was worth having. The government offices won't accept information except from official sources. I know hundreds of people in the Far East who could give them the most valuable information, but they won't take it."

Gertrude took careful note of his words. She felt no hesitation in talking to anyone. Whether with shopkeepers, desert sheikhs or British dignitaries, she radiated confidence. Like a skilled diplomat, she could start a conversation with ease and establish her own credentials with lightning speed, ticking off the influential names, reeling out the right tidbits of knowledge, dishing up the latest gossip, sprinkling her sentences with whom she knew and where she had been, imparting generous pieces of information, but cleverly gathering in more than she gave. Her talent was invaluable, whether in formal drawing rooms or flapping desert tents.

∞   ∞   ∞

After two years she was eager to return to the East. On a brief visit with Saloman Reinach to have him go over her writings for the *Revue Archéologique*, she met René Dussaud, who showed her Nabathean and Safaitic inscriptions and discussed what was to be found in the Nejd, the Arabian desert of Ibn Rashid.

But the timing was still not right; the desert was still dangerous, and the British Government would not give her permission to travel there. Instead, she proposed a trip to William Ramsay, boldly offering to pay his expenses if they could work together in Turkey and jointly write a book about their excavations. Although his assistants, ordinarily, were much more experienced than she, Ramsay agreed, and in March 1907 Gertrude went off to meet him in Asia Minor.

She left, basking in the glow of reviews for her newly published book, *The Desert and the Sown*. Its ebullient prose and careful analysis, her extensive photographs, and a color frontispiece, "Bedouins of the Syrian Desert," by John Singer Sargent, made it an immediate success. The work was deemed "among the dozen best books of Eastern travel" by David Hogarth, who placed it in importance alongside *Arabia Deserta*, the now classic work by Charles Doughty. It was called "brilliant" by *The Times* and "fascinating" by *The Times Literary Supplement*, which noted: "Women perhaps make the best travellers, for when they have the true wanderer's spirit they are more enduring and, strange to say, more indifferent to hardship and discomfort than men. They are unquestionably more observant of details and quicker to receive impressions. Their sympathies are more alert, and they get into touch with strangers more readily." The *New York Times* remarked: "The ways of English women are strange. They are probably the greatest slaves to conventionality in the world, but when they break with it, they do it with a vengeance."

If not with vengeance, at least with determination, Gertrude plunged into her work with Ramsay, knowing that collaborating with him would help confirm her reputation as a serious archaeologist.

She arrived at the British consulate in Konia, stopped to pick up her mail and make arrangements, and met Major Charles (Richard) Doughty-Wylie, the British official in residence. Almost at once she wrote to Domnul, "You know there is an English V. Consul here now, a charming young soldier with a quite pleasant little wife. He is the more interesting of the two, a good type of Englishman, wide awake and on the spot, keen to see and learn. Will you tell Willie T. [William Tyrell in the Foreign Office] I congratulate him on the appointment."

After her work with Ramsay was finished, she returned to Konia and stayed with the Doughty-Wylies. Mrs. Wylie, a gracious host, took her to the bazaar to buy kilims and accompanied her to a church to measure the floor plan. But it was back at the consulate villa that Gertrude spent hours pleasuring a burgeoning friendship with the tall, blue-eyed officer in the Royal Welch Fusiliers, Major Doughty-Wylie. The sympathetic vice-consul was the nephew of Charles Doughty, whose *Arabia Deserta* served as Gertrude's bible. Meeting Doughty's nephew was more than just good luck. It was a gift from heaven. The charming fellow—virile, funny, chivalrous—tantalized her with stories of his uncle and entertained her with heroic tales of his own, as both a soldier and statesman. Sitting under the trees in the big garden, they sipped tea and traded thoughts on the Turks, the Arabs and the East. By the time she left Konia, she pronounced the Doughty-Wylies "dears, both of them."

Chapter Eight

Women's Rights

∞

It would seem surprising, even ironic, that Gertrude Bell, an educated, well-read, well-informed woman who continually challenged herself with new experiences, was active in the anti-suffrage movement. And yet, for her and the women of England, the year 1908 marked a watershed.

For more than sixty years English women had been gaining the right to vote: first, for local boards administering money to the poor, then for school boards, municipal leaders, county councils; in effect, choosing the people who represented their interests as wives and mothers. Issues of local scope. That was enough. Demands for universal suffrage were brusquely turned aside. Queen Victoria herself had written in 1870, "This mad, wicked Folly of Women's Rights . . . [is] a subject which makes the Queen so furious that she cannot contain herself."

In fact, a strong female current had been running against the right of women to vote in national elections. Led by Mrs. Humphrey Ward (oddly enough, long active in promoting women's education at Oxford), they stated, in 1889, "The emancipating process has now reached the limit fixed by the physical constitution of women and by the fundamental difference which must always exist between their main occupations and those of men." Women, said Mrs. Ward, can never provide the sound judgment to decide questions of "foreign or colonial policy, or grave constitutional change." Those issues were not within the "necessary and normal experience" of women.

Still, the suffragist movement was gaining momentum. In 1903 Emmeline Goulden Pankhurst formed the Women's Social and Political Union, an organization pushing for universal suffrage. For five years, Mrs. Pankhurst struggled unsuccessfully. Then, in 1908, she tried more militant methods. With the help of her daughter Christabel, Mrs. Pankhurst led violent demonstrations: the suffragists burned more than a hundred buildings, set fires in hotels and churches, smashed store windows, bombed public areas, and besieged Parliament. "Votes for women!" they screamed as they chained themselves to the iron ledge of the Ladies' Gallery.

But their shrieks created a backlash. The suffragists' behavior shocked the public, especially people like Gertrude Bell, who valued tradition. To her, the harassment of public officials was nothing short of heresy. After all, they were among her closest friends and family.

∞ ∞ ∞

The first committee meeting of the Women's Anti-Suffrage League took place in London during the summer of 1908. Gertrude, happy to lend her support, wrote to her mother that "all went well." But demands on her time were not so pleasing. "We have Lady Jersey as chairman," she said, and then went on, "I have been obliged to become honorary secretary which is most horrible."

Nevertheless, she rallied to the cause. If it seemed odd for one who lived such an unconventional life to take such a conventional position, it was not: Gertrude's independence only masked her roots. She was a daughter of the Victorian Age, bred in a world dominated by men concerned with nothing less than aggrandizing the Empire, raised in an era graced by women considered to be no less than the bearers and guardians of the English race. As boldly as she behaved in the East, at home she remained within the boundaries of tradition, and her tradition was that of the upper class, privileged, protected and not to be challenged by the impoverished, uneducated working class.

Gertrude had spent hours with Florence helping the wives and mothers of the Bell Brothers' ironworkers. It only confirmed her view that, though women had the right to work in local government, they were not yet equipped to run the country. In the industrial town of Clarence she had spent mornings reading aloud to members of the magazine club, visiting one or another of the dingy row houses. A knock on the door was often answered by a woman of thirty who looked twice that age, her haggard face lined with years of drudgery, her thick figure ravaged by constant childbirth and miscarriages, her arms filled with infants crying for milk, while screaming toddlers crawled underfoot, the children only a few years away from being sent to work in the coal mines. In the squalor of the crowded flats, the odor of disease clotted the air, and thick soot from the factories coated everything from the bedclothes to the kitchen table. Every day was a struggle to exist. Exhausted and illiterate, these women and tens of thousands like them were in need of education to better their lives at home; they were hardly qualified to make decisions of state, the anti-suffragists said.

Gertrude saw herself as the equal of any man, but most women, she was firmly convinced, were not. Their votes would certainly be questionable; they could even prove to be dangerous. Like her mother Florence, or her father Hugh, or their friends Lord Curzon, Lord Cromer and Lord Robert Cecil, Gertrude argued that the female role was fundamentally different from that of the male: women were meant to rear children; men were meant to run the country. Furthermore, they all believed, only men had the sound judgment to rule the colonies, to determine foreign policy and to decide matters of the constitution; therefore, only men should have the right to cast a ballot. Rare was the woman knowledgeable enough to make a contribution to the affairs of state. Yet even as she promoted the agenda of the Anti-Suffrage League, Gertrude worked on her book about Byzantine Anatolia and yearned to penetrate the mysterious regions of the Arabian desert.

CHAPTER NINE

Lawrence

∞

"There is a moment when one is newly arrived in the East, when one is conscious of the world shrinking at one end and growing at the other till all the perspective of life is changed," Gertrude wrote as she started out, in the winter of 1909, on her first expedition from Syria to Mesopotamia. "Existence suddenly seems to be a very simple matter, and one wonders why we plan and scheme, when all we need do is to live and make sure of a succeeding generation."

Her own ability to contribute to successive generations was becoming more doubtful as the possibility of marriage floated beyond her grasp. But as for planning and scheming, she could hardly resist, riding off onto dangerous paths, plunging into political whirlpools. Almost as soon as she arrived in Syria, she was swirling in local politics, promising to write to Domnul at *The Times* in London and keep him informed of the latest news, which, she hoped, he would publish. (In Constantinople a group of reformers, the Young Turks, were threatening the Sultan with nationalist ideas, and the winds of change were blowing in Syria, too.) But the real reason for her trip was to do research for another book. The success of *The Desert and the Sown* stirred her on.

She had taken time, the previous winter, to study at the Royal Geographical Society, learning how to do surveying, make astronomical observations and apply the techniques of mapmaking. She had hoped to be able to use her knowledge on a trip to Central Arabia, but a meeting with Percy Cox in London had pushed the journey aside. The British Resident in the Gulf had cautioned her that, besides the usual, perilous raids and brazen thievery, war had broken out among the tribes; it was far too dangerous for anyone to cross the desert.

Redirecting her attention, she decided to map the uncharted sands of Mesopotamia. She began her journey in Syria, once again, to study the Roman and Byzantine churches, and to help David Hogarth, who had asked her to take casts of the stones of the Hittites, the ancient iron smelters, progenitors of England's ironmasters. From there she would go on to Iraq.

Her trunk once again packed with pistols and with Maurice's rifle from the Boer War, her saddlebags crammed with books and cameras, the forty-year-old Gertrude laid out a journey from Aleppo, across the Syrian desert to Iraq, then down alongside the Euphrates River, five hundred miles southeast to Baghdad, where she would regroup and travel along the Tigris, northward to Turkey.

In Aleppo she met up with Fattuh, her highly capable Christian servant, and arranged her belongings: her tents, a folding bed, mosquito netting, a canvas bath, a canvas chair, rugs, table, pots and pans, enough provisions to last at least a month, and linens, china, tea service, crystal and silver cutlery for proper dining. They hired seven baggage animals, a dozen horses and three muleteers—Hajj Amr, Selim and Habib. There were two servants, the round-faced Fattuh, in his striped shirt and Turkish pants, and his young brother-in-law Jusef; two soldiers; and herself. Riding dawn till dusk for two full days across the sweeping grassy plains, she thrilled to being in the open, untamed, yawning ocean of desert, unbound by drawing room constraints, free to be, to do, to say, to feel as she wanted. She wrote to Florence that she could "scarcely believe it to be true."

She reached the Euphrates, the narrow, shallow passage that once nursed the cradle of civilization and now divided Syria from Mesopotamia, "the land of two rivers" (Iraq, the Arabs called it). "A noble stream," she pronounced the Euphrates, "as wide as the Thames at Chelsea"; a "turgid liquid," infested with insects, algae, bacteria and ancient dust. She insisted that Fattuh boil her water, and he did, without a protest.

At the river's edge, biblical transport waited to ferry her across: she climbed into one of the narrow, high-bowed boats and watched as the boatman mimicked the ancients, using a long pole to steer the vessel across to the opposite shore. She had reached the region of the Hittites and their city of Carchemish. Finding the mounds of stones that David Hogarth had asked her to inspect, she worked for several hours, her men helping to dig out the boulders with picks and spades. In the late afternoon, after casting the inscriptions, she returned to the mound above the river where her camp was pitched. Fattuh boiled some water and brewed a fresh pot of tea. Relaxing outside her tent, Gertrude sipped the English brace from her china cup and scrawled contentedly to her family: "The broad Euphrates sweeps slowly past the *tel*, and I have just watched the sun set beyond the white cliffs of his other bank. I doubt whether there is anyone in the world so happy."

∞ ∞ ∞

Within several days she had left behind the villages of the plains and entered the empty sands, where treacherous Arab raiders roamed the desert preying upon each other's flocks. "All this country is racked, as it has been for the past four thousand years, by the lawless Arab tribes," she wrote home. No government had ever discovered a way to keep the tribes in check. When she asked her men to accompany her on a nighttime ride, they were so frightened of blood-feud enemies that not a single man would go alone. But if the Bedouin feared each other, she was afraid of no one. Instead, she dove into the wilderness, leading her men through heat that burned the evening air, across land so dry that the oases offered the animals only caked earth in place of drinking water. Her throat was parched and her body was coated with dust.

She had ridden more than four hundred miles toward Baghdad when, in the middle of March, she arrived at the town of Hit, known since ancient times to be a source of petroleum. The Babylonians, Assyrians and others had used its dark sticky fuel to light their lamps and fire their cooking stoves. Hit was an ugly place, the air choked with smoke and the ground pitted with refuse, not unlike the grim industrial English town that housed the Bell Brothers' Ironworks. "Except for the palm groves," she wrote, "there is very little difference between Hit and Clarence." Oil oozed from the earth, and peril menaced the air as she and her men continued on, rifles strapped to their sides, through sink-holes of pitch and across black crusty land.

They rode warily, searching for Arabs to camp with. The rule of the desert prevailed—"Everyone is an enemy till you know him to be a friend"—and they could not risk setting up their tents alone. They could be murdered; robbed at best. But if they found a tribe to camp near, the hosts would protect them as though they were guests. This was the territory of the Dulaim, notorious fighters, but at the sight of their black tents, her men slowed their horses. Approaching carefully, she gave the *salaam*. The Dulaim chief, Sheikh Muhammad el Abdullah, "a handsome creature," invited the Englishwoman inside his tent, and together they sat in front of the fire, drinking the bitter coffee of the Bedouin. A few hours later, inviting him to her tent, she offered him afternoon tea. "The bonds of friendship are firmly knit," she declared in her letter home. At night, after Fattuh cooked her dinner, she rolled herself up in her rugs and fell soundly asleep.

Toward the end of March she wrote home excitedly: she had come upon a spectacular ruin, the most important relic of its period. "As soon as I saw it I decided that this was the opportunity of a lifetime." Not a word had been written about it, and it was hers to shout to the world. The Arabs called it Ukhaidir, meaning a little green place, but it was neither small nor green. A huge stone and wood castle surrounded by round towers set in immense outer walls, inside it had one court after another with domed and vaulted rooms, gorgeously decorated plaster walls, hidden chambers with high columns and round niches. By studying this palace she could learn more about sixth-century Eastern art than in all the books she could read.

She worked steadily, photographing, sketching, drawing the plan of the castle to scale. Dressed in her white cotton shirt, petticoat and long patch-pocketed skirt, black stockings and laced-up shoes, a dark *kafeeyah* wrapped around her sun helmet, she gauged the building, walking around the standing walls, lying down on the hard cold floors to take the measurements. Her men stood by her side, cooperative but on guard against the Bedouin raiders, who were everywhere. "Nothing will induce them to leave their rifles in the tents," she complained. "They are quite intolerably inconvenient; the measuring tape is for ever catching round the barrel or getting caught up in the stock, but I can't persuade them to lay the damnable things down for an instant." One night as she lay awake in her tent, she heard the sounds of gun shots whizzing overhead. Her men went out to chase them, but the invisible attackers disappeared into the dark.

Working at Ukhaidir convinced her that this was an archaeological find that would impress even the most important authorities in the field. "It's the greatest piece of luck that has ever happened to me. I shall publish it in a big monograph all to itself and it will make a flutter in the dovecots," she wrote home. The discovery could secure her reputation as an archaeologist.

On the last day of March 1909 Gertrude left the castle, sneezing and coughing from the drafty halls of Ukhaidir. Traipsing across the windy, dusty, drought-ridden desert, its landscape strewn with dead sheep and goats and with human corpses, she was overwhelmed by a rush of sadness.

∞ ∞ ∞

Her journey took her next to Babylon, where a group of German archaeologists were excavating the site. From the time of the Amorites, in the eighteenth century B.C., until the age of the Chaldeans, twelve hundred years later, the city had risen and fallen like piles of sand in the hands of kings. It had reached its peak in the sixth century B.C., when Nebuchadnezzar made it the capital of his New Babylonian Empire. He had surrounded the city with thick walls, wide enough to race two chariots abreast across the tops, and ordered the construction of grand temples and vast palaces.

It was "the most extraordinary place," Gertrude wrote after viewing the work of Dr. Koldewey and his team. "I have seldom felt the ancient world come so close." The archaeologists had dug out most of Nebuchadnezzar's palace; she could see the "great hall where Belshazzar must have held his feast . . . the remains of the platform in which Nebuchadnezzar used to sit when it was hot . . . his private rooms and the tiny emergency exit by which the king could escape to the river if his enemies pressed on him."

With the help of the Germans, she planned the rest of her trip: from Babylon to Seleucia, and then along the Tigris to Ctesiphon, the ancient Sassanid (Persian) capital that fell in battle to the Arabs. By April 1909 she reached Baghdad. The British Consul, Colonel Ramsay, welcomed her to the Residency, a resplendent symbol of British power: "a palace," she described it, surrounded by a fortress wall, guarded by Indian soldiers, twelve caravans, thirty sepoys, and countless indoor servants. ("I had to tip them all when I left," she later complained.) The consul's wife, she found abhorrent: "a dull dog, a very stiff, narrow and formal Englishwoman, dreadfully afraid of giving herself away or of doing anything not entirely consistent with the duty and dignity of the wife and daughter of Indian officials." Just the sort of woman she would encounter again and again in the East. But the consul himself, wary at first, responded to Gertrude's charms and proceeded to show her his secret reports to Whitehall, the Foreign Office. As a result, she wrote to *The Times* emphasizing the need for a railway line from Basrah to Baghdad, to be financed, most important, by Britain.

Her stay in Baghdad was brief, but with names and letters from

Friedrich Rosen, she managed to see some of the notables and meet the most important Islamic authority in the town. The Naqib, religious leader of the Sunnis, and respected by the Shiites as well, was a crucial link to the rich large Muslim community. She "felt rather anxious," meeting such an authority, she confessed; "our political relations with him are so very delicate, and he is so particularly holy." Beholden to the ruling Turks and a man who rarely spoke with women, he received her nonetheless, robed and turbaned and "with effusion, and talked without stopping for an hour and a half." Still, she managed to interject the right questions. After instructing her on Mesopotamian history, from the time of the biblical flood up until the present, he finished by inviting her to his private family house on the river.

∽   ∽   ∽

Leaving Baghdad, she reached the territory of the Shammar, the great tribe of the north. "They rule this country with a rod of iron," she wrote. "Not a caravan that passes up and down from Tikrit to Mosul, but pays them tribute on every animal, unless, of course, they happen to be under government protection as I am." The Shammar owed some of their strength to the Turks; Humeidi Beg Ibn Farhan, a son of the ruling "sheikh of sheikhs," was "particularly in their favor," she wrote later, "in touch with the Ottoman official world, as a go-between on behalf of the tribe." But now Gertrude entertained the handsome young man in her tent; beguiled by the gentle, indolent sheikh, she talked with him about the desert. At the end of their conversation, the British lady reverted to habit and handed him her visiting card. In return, he offered her welcome to all the Shammar tents. "Someday I shall profit by the invitation," she noted. "I like making the acquaintance of these desert lords, it may always come in useful."

Making her way north she reached Mosul and then rode onward to the land of the Yezdi, the devil worshippers, who offered her a room to sleep in. But the thicket of fleas hopping around sent her back to her tent. In the mountains of the Kurds she rode through luxuriant valleys, wild with olive, pomegranate, mulberry, fig and almond trees, and visited old castles, monasteries and churches. Intrigued by the churches in one particular town, the village of Khakh, she decided to spend an extra day.

In the middle of the night, in her tent, she heard a noise and woke to find a man crouching on the floor. She tore open the mosquito net around her bed and leapt off her cot to jump him, but by the time she untangled the netting, the man had run away. She shouted to her servants—her soldiers, who should have been on guard, were fast asleep—and, still standing in her nightgown, remembered to see if anything had been stolen. Everything that had been lying about was gone. The thief had taken her clothes, her saddlebags, her boots, and all the contents, including her money, of one of her trunks. Worst of all, the saddlebag he had stolen held her notebooks and photographs. He had made a clean sweep of every precious article in her tent. The whole journey, four months' work, was a waste. She was overwhelmed.

"The truth was," she admitted, "we had all grown thoughtless with so much safe travelling through dangerous places, and we needed a lesson. But it was a bitter one." And then, after an anxious week, with the local police and the Turkish Governor and the closest British Consul all alerted, the thief was found. Everything except her money was returned. Embarrassed by her own carelessness, she apologized to the village people for all the trouble she had caused, and left. But most humiliating of all, the tale was published at home in *The Times* and other papers. Publicity was something she always shied away from; it seemed to her to be vulgar, and although she craved recognition, she somehow thought it should come spontaneously from her superiors and peers.

A few weeks later, after trying fruitlessly to see Richard Doughty-Wylie (he was away at Adana, trying heroically to stop a Turkish massacre of Armenians), she came to the end of her seven-month trip. It had proved a great success. "We have reaped a harvest that has surpassed the wildest flights of my imagination. I feel as if I had seen a whole new world, and learnt several new chapters of history," she wrote. But at the very last stop, in Constantinople, her heated excitement was doused with a splash of cold water. As she dined at the French Embassy, she learned that she had been scooped in her discovery of Ukhaidir. Before she had even had a chance to publish her find, the French archaeologist M. Massignon had written about Ukhaidir in the *Gazette des Beaux Arts*. All the fame and the glory that she had dreamed of had been snatched away in the night.

✺   ✺   ✺

For eighteen months after she returned home, Gertrude stayed in England, working on a book about her Mesopotamian journey. *Amurath to Amurath* was a chronicle of the people and the archaeology she had encountered. But Ukhaidir still held out an enticing hand. In spite of the disappointment, of someone's having beaten her story, she was the only one who had drawn the castle's plans. In January 1911, with mixed reviews for *Amurath to Amurath* casting a cloud ("Those who expect brilliant scenes and characteristic dialogue from the author of that fascinating book *The Desert and the Sown* may feel some disappointment in reading her present work," said *The Times*, adding, however, "*Amurath*, in short, is a serious contribution to Mesopotamian exploration"), she set off again for the East.

Riding from Damascus, rifle at her side, she was eager to re-examine the ruins she had discovered two years before. Once more, winding her way across the Syrian desert, she traveled through soft sands and balmy days, through mud and slop and "scuds" of winter rains, across miles of barren wasteland and across plains peopled with raiding horsemen and welcoming sheikhs. Riding her mare in the sharp dry air of February, wrapping her fur coat close to her body, bathing at night in camp, she felt invigorated. "I think every day of the Syrian desert must prolong your life by two years," she rejoiced in a letter home.

By the beginning of March 1911, she reached the palace fortress of Ukhaidir, confirming it as "the finest Sassanian art that ever was." She spent a day measuring, mapping out the plans of the ancient castle, reassuring herself that her earlier work had been accurate. As she left the site the following day she felt a surge of excitement and a wave of sadness. "I wonder whether I shall ever see it again and whether I shall ever again come upon any building as interesting or work at anything with a keener pleasure," she wrote wistfully.

Her Mesopotamian trip progressed: through Najaf, the Shiite holy city where pilgrims came from Persia as well as from Iraq; through Kalat Shergat, where a mound marked the capital of ancient Assyria; through Haran, where the Jewish tribes had lived before they moved on to Canaan. It was the first of May and she was feeling lonely. She longed "for the daffodils and the opening beech leaves at Rounton—it's not all beer and skittles travelling, you know; I still have an overpowering desire to see my family."

She was pleased to have come close to Carchemish, where David Hogarth was still carrying out his excavation of the Hittite site. The remains of the once-thriving city had been discovered more than thirty years earlier, but interest was reawakened when work on the Berlin-to-Baghdad Railway reached this area of the Upper Euphrates. The German-financed train line was a clear threat to British trade and influence in the entire Persian Gulf. With Carchemish less than a quarter of a mile away from where the Germans were building a bridge across the river, it was a convenient watching post for English archaeologists to report back home by letters and photographs. Hogarth was a serious scholar doing work for the British Museum, but like other Englishmen in the region, he carried out observations of the Germans that were valued by the British government.

The night before Gertrude was to visit, the local authorities informed her that Hogarth had left the dig. Nonetheless, they noted, his assistant, Mr. Campbell Thompson, was still working at the site. By now, after four months of travel, she was eager to see almost any English colleague, and was curious to revisit the Hittite ruins she had written about in *Amurath to Amurath*.

At the age of forty-two, preceded by her reputation, and accompanied by her servant Fattuh, Gertrude set out early on the morning of May 19, 1911, dressed in her desert costume: a long divided skirt, linen jacket, and *kafeeyah* draped around the brim of her canvas hat. Carrying a haughty air of self-assurance, she rode to Carchemish and, at their lodgings in the village, came upon two fledgling archaeologists, Thompson "and a young man called Lawrence (an interesting boy, he is going to make a traveller) who had for some time been expecting that I would appear."

Campbell Thompson, Hogarth's assistant at the Ashmolean Museum, was a tall, quiet academic, soon to be married, who taught linguistics and enjoyed deciphering ancient codes. His junior colleague, Thomas Edward Lawrence, destined to be a myth-maker and a legend himself, was a twenty-three-year-old graduate student with a specialty in medieval pottery. Looking him over she saw a short fellow, strongly built, with yellow hair, intense blue eyes, a high forehead and a straight nose. An eccentric dresser fascinated by Oriental things, he favored a gray flannel blazer piped in pink, white flannel shorts, gray stockings and red Arab slippers; around his waist he tied a bright red tasseled Arab belt, which marked him as a bachelor. Since he was obviously eligible, his cause had been taken up by the local villagers, who were eager to find him a wife; hearing of Gertrude's pending arrival, they assumed she was coming to be his bride.

Thompson and Lawrence had not only been expecting her; they had been anxiously awaiting her arrival. She was famous and famously outspoken, and the two men welcomed her warily; this was their first venture in excavating and, having found few antiquities, they knew she was perfectly capable of sending back damaging reports. With studied politeness, they took her into their house, an abandoned licorice warehouse suffering from a leaky roof and damp mud floors, and charmed her, pouring coffee into ancient cups of thin unglazed clay, filling her ears with stories, lamenting the lack of valuable finds; so far they had discovered not much more than a slab of warriors carved with headless captives, a five-foot-high basalt relief and some champagne cups found in the Hittite graves.

After lunch the threesome walked to the *tel* to observe the digging. Gertrude had described the northern mound of Carchemish in *Amurath to Amurath*: "covered with the ruins of the Roman and Byzantine city, columns and moulded bases, foundations of walls set round paved courtyards and the line of a colonnaded street running across the ruin field form the high ridge. . . . It has long been desolate, but there is no mistaking the greatness of the city that was protected by that splendid mound."

As she reached the hill, she saw that trenches had been cut out; below the Roman remains could be seen foundations dating to prehistoric times. Still, she opined, there was "precious little" and the work was "bad." Only a few weeks earlier she had observed the precise excavations and elegant reconstructions of some German archaeologists; now she watched as, under English tutelage, some eighty natives shoveled the earth, hacking away at the remains of ancient civilization, eager to find a treasure and receive a promised bonus. Gertrude was taken aback. "Prehistoric!" she exclaimed, and proceeded to lecture the two young men on the modern techniques of digging.

The young scholars had readied themselves for the challenge.

> And so [Lawrence wrote the next day to his mother], we had to squash her with a display of erudition. She was taken (in 5 minutes) over Byzantine, Crusader, Roman, Hittite and French architecture (my part) and over Greek folk-lore, Assyrian architecture, and Mesopotamian ethnology (by Thompson); prehistoric pottery and telephoto lenses, Bronze Age metal techniques, Meredith, Anatole France and the Octoberists (by me): the Young Turk movement, the construct state in Arabic, the price of riding camels, Assyrian burial-customs, and German methods of excavation with the Baghdad railway (by Thompson). This was a kind of hors d'oeuvre: and when it was over (she was getting more respectful) we settled down each to seven or eight subjects and questioned her upon them. She was quite glad to have tea after an hour and a half, and on going told Thompson that he had done wonders in his digging in the time, and that she thought *we* had got everything out of the place that could possibly have been got: she particularly admired the completeness of our notebooks.
>
> So we did for her. She was really too captious at first, coming straight from the German diggings at Kalat Shirgat. Our digs are I hope more accurate, if less perfect.

They involve no reconstruction, which ruins all these Teutons. So we showed her that and left her limp, but impressed. She is pleasant; about 36, not beautiful (except with a veil on, perhaps). It would have been most annoying if she had denounced our methods in print. I don't think she will.

Gertrude was indeed impressed; the conversation continued animatedly through dinner, and after pleasing Lawrence no end by presenting her hosts with two Meredith novels, which she had already finished, she spent the night at Carchemish. She awakened before dawn and rode out of camp at five-thirty A.M., somewhat bewildered by the villagers who came out to jeer; she had no idea that, in trying to calm them, Lawrence told them she was too plain to marry. Years later she laughed when she found out from Hogarth that Lawrence had given them such an excuse to keep his bachelorhood.

The evening after she left Carchemish, Lawrence sent Hogarth a note, far more sympathetic than the one to his mother: "Thompson has dressed tonight and something of the sadness of the last shirt and collar is overtaking him, for Gerty has gone back to her tents to sleep. She has been a success: and a brave one. She called him prehistoric! (apropos of your digging methods, till she saw their result—an enthusiast . . . young I think)."

At almost the same time, back in her own camp, Gertrude was writing to Florence, giving no hint at all of either the rivalry or the newfound friendship with T. E. Lawrence: "They showed me their diggings and their finds and I spent a pleasant day with them."

CHAPTER TEN

Dick

∞

At home again in England in 1911 and 1912, Gertrude worked on her book about Ukhaidir, taking time out to write articles for academic journals on archaeology and book reviews for *The Times*, attend the coronation of George V in London and make speeches for the Anti-Suffrage League. But now it was Asiatic Turkey that consumed her interest. The Ottoman Government was suffering a quick decline, succumbing at home to the will of the Young Turks (the reformist group that rose against it in the name of nationalism), and in Europe to the fervor of independence of the Balkan states. During the costly Balkan Wars of 1912, the Sultan lost his hold over Serbia, Greece, Bulgaria and Montenegro. What would happen to the Ottoman interests in Asia? Gertrude worried. Syria, Mesopotamia, Arabia would all be up for grabs. "I should not be surprised if we were to see, in the course of the next ten years, the break-up of the empire in Asia also, the rise first of Arab autonomies," she wrote presciently toward the end of 1912 to Domnul, just knighted and traveling in India after his recent retirement from *The Times*.

She had been hearing much about Turkey from Richard Doughty-Wylie, who was now living in Constantinople. They corresponded frequently, she and he and his wife, Judith: Gertrude filling them in on her trips and her books, congratulating him on his heroic efforts to stop the Turkish massacre of Armenians at Adana; they telling her about events in Anatolia and in Constantinople, where he was posted during the Balkan Wars. Gertrude had seen him in England in 1908, when he came home for a brief visit, and again in 1912, when he was called back to London for a change in assignment. But before long, he went off again, in charge of the Red Cross relief effort in Turkey, where the Balkan states were allied and fighting to yank Macedonia away from Turkish rule. On Christmas Day 1912 she received a letter from him from the Turkish capital, and weeks after, in the early spring of 1913, Doughty-Wylie and his wife arrived in London. Gertrude took tea with them on an occasional afternoon, dined with them on an evening, chatted with them about events in the East.

The more she saw of him, the more attracted she was. No one she knew intrigued her like Doughty-Wylie. He was the consummate male of the British Empire, a decorated soldier-statesman, a sensitive, literate scholar who loved to quote poetry, a shrewd political analyst, a lustful man who roused her deepest desires. In July, she invited him to her Yorkshire house, and in a prurient moment when his wife was away, he accepted her invitation and came. It was a daring move for Gertrude. Rounton was home, intimate. She would be bringing him into her most personal world, showing him her most emotional treasures, revealing herself in a way that she never would have done in London.

She introduced him to her family, showed him around the favorite house of her childhood, the flower beds she had nursed, the rock garden she had created, the library where, even as a young girl she had read voraciously. They talked and talked, she, about the loneliness of being unmarried; he, about the loneliness of being unhappily married; she, about the joy she found in solitude; he, about the joy he found in sex. She sensed his profound hunger and felt the thrill of his passion. They stood in her bedroom, close to each other, her heart pounding, her cheeks turning hot, and as his blue eyes burned with desire, he took her in his arms. He wanted her, but she refused.

A few days later he wrote from London to thank her for the visit. It was to be the first of dozens of letters between them, each an intense display of fervor and passion. There were never love letters like these between other couples, she would later tell a friend; never letters of such depth and pain and beauty. In this first round of their new correspondence, Dick told her how he loved seeing her in her "vital setting," surrounded by the people, the house, the gardens that meant so much to her. He loved talking to her, hearing what she cared about most. He had always wanted to be her close friend, he said, ever since they met in Anatolia. "Now I feel as if we had come closer, were really intimate friends. . . . I must write something, something to show you how very proud I am to be your friend. Something to have meaning, even if it cannot be set down, affection, my dear, and gratitude and admiration and confidence, and an urgent desire to see you as much as possible. . . . Yours ever, R."

But as quickly as he roused her hopes, he dashed them. A note came the following day to say that once again he was being posted abroad. She sat in her room at Rounton and wrote, telling him of the pleasure she felt in the early morning hours in her garden, of the joy she felt at being near him. Her letters reached him at his old bachelor quarters in London, where he was staying while Judith was away in Wales.

"While I am alone, let's be alone," he teased in reply. "Ah yes, my dear, it's true enough what I said about solitude, on every hill, in every forest, I have invoked, and welcomed her. . . . And you, too, know the goddess well, for no one but a worshipper could have written what you did about the hush of dawn in the garden. But for all that, we shall meet and say nothing, and go on as before."

But he was troubled, he said, by a recurring dream: "Rounton ghosts visited me the next night also. Is there any history of them? . . . some shadowy figure of a woman, who really quite bothered me, so that I turned on the light. It wasn't your ghost, or anything like you; but something hostile and alarming." He ended the letter, "Dick."

She was a spinster of forty-five, alone, aching for a husband, yearning for children. He was a married man, grounded to a woman of wealth and social position. The situation seemed impossible, ridden with ghosts and guilt. Yet even as he spoke of the hopelessness of it all, her desire grew. When was he leaving? she wanted to know. What would happen to them? Should she still write to him after he left? Should she write only to him or to Judith too?

He informed her calmly that she had better write to them both. Having read her letters before, his wife would find it odd if she were suddenly barred from seeing their correspondence. After all, "on voyages one lives at close quarters—not even with you would I like it, that is, not always, but only when we wanted to. . . . But what's the good of writing like this?" he asked.

He was nearly ready to leave for the Balkans, prepared to say goodbye to Gertrude, taking away any hope of another rendezvous. And yet he continued to rouse her, telling her "we shall still meet in thoughts and fancies," and taunting her with his lust. He ended the letter: "Last night, a poor girl stopped me—the same old story—and I gave her money and sent her home. . . . So many are really like me, or what I used to be, and I'm sorry for them. . . . These desires of the body that are right and natural, that are so often nothing more than any common hunger—they can be the vehicle of the fire of the mind, and as that only are they great; and as that only are they to be satisfied."

And then it was time for him to go. Please write, he begged. She should call him Dick, and he would call her Gertrude, and even if his wife read the letters, their intimacy would seem to be nothing at all. Many people call each other by their first names, he told her. But as for the passionate words she had written over the past few weeks, he vowed: "Tonight I shall destroy your letters—I hate it—but it is right-ful. One might die or something, and they are not for any soul but me. Even though I hide in the silent room, they pursue me. Goodbye, my dear, I kiss your hands."

It had been the most intense, most extraordinary few weeks in her life. Finally she had met a handsome, intelligent, sophisticated man who shared her passions for the East, the desert, the Arabs, ancient worlds, modern politics, poetry, literature, solitude. He, like no one else, understood and loved them as much as she did. Now he was gone, and she was left with anguished memory.

∞   ∞   ∞

She made plans to return to the desert. There was never a year more favorable for a journey into Arabia, or so they said in Damascus. Miss Gertrude Bell arrived in the city on November 27, 1913, eager to hear such news. Looking a bit weary after her voyage—by boat from England to France, a week aboard ship on the Mediterranean, then by rail from Beirut—the slightly agitated, forty-five-year-old Miss Bell stepped impatiently from her carriage, smoothed the wisps of ginger hair peeking out from her feathered hat, straightened her hobble skirt and marched briskly into the lobby of the Damascus Palace Hotel. She preferred this centrally located hotel, although it was first class and not deluxe, for she enjoyed the good rates and the good service, and the solicitous manager, who remembered her, of course; and although he might have forgotten how haunted her green eyes appeared, or how sharply pointed her nose, he recalled at once the commanding tone in her voice and the authority in her bearing. Flustered by the arrival of the famous lady (everyone in Damascus knew of the intrepid English-woman who traveled alone through the desert), he welcomed her with a profusion of bows and *salaams*, and she returned them routinely.

Gertrude signed her name at the register and, as always, with shoulders erect and head held high, proceeded to her room. A string of Arab boys in caftans scuffled behind, struggling to carry the heavy steamer trunk that Marie, her maid, had packed with smart French gowns, pegged skirts, fur coats, tweed jackets, fringed shawls, frilly blouses, plumed hats, parasols and linen riding clothes. One of the servants toted her toiletries case fitted with silver brushes and cut-glass flacons, their polished caps twisted tight to prevent any lotions from spilling. Two more boys bore the suitcase carefully stuffed with lacy corsets and petticoats, a masquerade for her maps, cameras, film, binoculars, theodolite and guns.

The rest of her baggage consisted of crates filled with Wedgwood china, crystal stemware, silver flatware, table linens, rugs, blank notebooks, sets of Shakespeare, archaeology texts by de Vogue and Stryzgowski, history books collected since her student days at Oxford, Doughty's *Arabia Deserta*, Hogarth's *The Penetration of Arabia*, the Blunts' *Pilgrimage to Nejd*, guidebooks, quinine, camphor, boric ointment, a remedy for diarrhea, bandages, soaps and flea powder. It would take two weeks in Damascus to reorganize before moving forward into the desert.

As soon as she settled in her room, simple but adequate, she sent for one of the Arab boys and, handing him some *baksheesh*, some coins, instructed him to deliver her calling cards, not to any Turkish officials, she warned, but to a few European acquaintances like Lütticke, the head of the well-known banking house, and Loytved, the German Consul, and to local Arabs she knew she could trust.

She arranged her clothes as best she could and smiled to herself as she took out her shoes and felt for the bullets inside them. "I need not have hidden the cartridges in my boots!" she wrote home. "We got through customs without having a single box opened." She had foiled the Turks again.

After the sun set over the Syrian hills, she pinned up her hair, changed into a gown and checked to see that her cigarette case was in her evening purse before going downstairs to dinner. She was greeted warmly in the hotel restaurant, where full *pension*, but not wine, was included in the ten-franc daily room rate. The waiters hovered attentively, bringing her food that was reliable if not remarkable, as *Murray's* guidebook had promised. After coffee she excused herself from the Bruntons, an English couple at her table, and went to her room, making a few notes in her leather diary before retiring.

In bed that first night in the city, she could hardly keep from thinking about the journey to Central Arabia that lay ahead. She had cherished the idea of this expedition for more than a dozen years. Time and again she had tried to organize the voyage, but in the past the warnings of friends like Sir Louis Mallet in the Foreign Office or Willie Tyrrell, the Secretary of State, had forestalled her. Four years ago Percy Cox, the British Resident in the Gulf who worked for the Intelligence office of India Civil Service, had cautioned her again; it was far too dangerous for anyone to cross the desert.

But she had never given up her desire to uncover the mystery of Central Arabia. She was well aware that its vast, relentless desert, the Nejd, was fraught with hazards. She knew she might face endless days parched from lack of water, and endless days soaked from floods, as heavy rains drenched the impervious ground. It was winter and there would be weeks when the temperature dropped below freezing at night and weeks when the sun blazed furiously at noon. She knew she would have to fight off hordes of fleas that hovered around the camels, and that she would find snakes and scorpions stalking the sand. And there would be the inevitable sand; sand as far as the eye could see, sometimes bleak black sand, sometimes yawning yellow mounds of sand, sometimes hard, gray, unforgiving sand.

And yet, she loved the desert. For her it meant escape. She had written years before: "To those bred under an elaborate social order few such moments of exhilaration can come as that which stands at the threshold of wild travel. The gates of the enclosed garden are thrown open, the chain at the entrance of the sanctuary is lowered . . . and, like the man in the fairy story, you feel the bands break that were riveted about your heart." Indeed, the bands around her heart were not just the obstacles of English society but the shackles that constrained her love for a married man. Travel would let her break free.

The morning brought good news. Fattuh, the loyal Armenian who had served her on a decade of desert journeys, had arrived from his home in Aleppo. There was much to be done before she could set out from Damascus, and they went off together to see one of the people who could assist her the most, Sheikh Muhammad Bassam, a man she had met in the desert long ago. Rich and well-connected, Bassam shared the friendship of the Bedouin sheikhs as well as the confidence of the notables in town. He could help her hire the most experienced guide, help her find the best and cheapest camels, help her lay out a path in the shifting Arabian sands.

The weather was "heavenly," she wrote home, and with only a jacket to cover her blouse and long skirt, and a felt hat on her head, she hurried along the streets. She reached the seedy façade of sun-dried bricks that formed a wall around Bassam's house, knowing that beyond it lay a large courtyard graced with bubbling fountains and colored stones. Her low heels clicked againt the marble floor of the patio, and she paused for a moment to breathe in the sweet scent of oranges, lemons and pomegranates. Ah, it was good to be back in the East!

Bassam welcomed her, as did his wife (a handsome woman born in the Nejd), to the sitting room, but as soon as the greetings were over, the woman disappeared. A servant arrived, bringing the English guest a coffee that was thick and pleasingly bitter. Gertrude spoke in classical, florid Arabic, moving the conversation as quickly as she could. How was his father? his sons? she asked politely. How were his orchards? his sheep? the friends they had in common? And what about Turkey? What did his friends in Damascus think? How did the desert Arabs feel? she wanted to know. Bassam asked her opinion of the Ottoman state, now in the throes of revolution, and noted that in Basrah, in Mesopotamia, where Great Britain had a stronghold, the people wanted British protection. Finally the conversation reached her plans to penetrate the desert.

She was determined to meet the leaders of two of the greatest Arabian clans: Ibn Rashid and Ibn Saud, the two formidable rival warriors of Central Arabia. With the Ottoman Empire in a weakened state, there was reason to believe that both men would welcome her, each eager for the latest political news. As for her own government, the journey would prove highly significant. If war were to come, the fate of Arabia might hang in the balance. The British would want to know who would be reliable Arab allies against the Turks.

She turned to her host. Among those she had already spoken to, she had heard conflicting comments. Now she asked Bassam's advice. Did he think it was safe to enter Central Arabia? There was no need to worry, Bassam reassured her; it would be perfectly easy to go to the Nejd this year. The atmosphere was calm; fighting had ceased between Sauds and Rashids. She had come at "an exceedingly lucky moment," she wrote later to her mother; "everyone is at peace. Tribes who have been at war for generations have come to terms and the desert is almost preternaturally quiet."

An ivory holder between her fingers, she smoked a cigarette, and as the breeze blew in from the garden, they sketched a route she knew well, east of Damascus, then south to the great Nejd, the vast Arabian desert, remote and rarely traveled, a virtual battleground for Bedouin tribes. Only three or four Europeans had survived the journey, but with skillful guides and the right *rafiqs*—tribal escorts paid to guarantee safe journey through each tribe's territory—Gertrude hoped to avoid the murderous raiders and treacherous thieves who crisscrossed the Nejd. She planned to arrive, first, in Hayil, the nineteenth-century headquarters of the Turkish-supported Ibn Rashid. From there she aimed to go farther south to meet his enemy, Ibn Saud.

She should avoid going near the Hejaz Railway, she and Bassam agreed. With the Ottoman Empire in disarray, the Turks suspected the British would encourage Arabs to revolt. Inquisitive officials and bored police would ask too many questions. What exactly was she doing there? they would demand to know. She could answer truthfully that she was an archaeologist seeking Byzantine ruins, or that she was an author researching a book, but they might not believe her. Indeed, they might even detect some deception in her tone, though she would never let them know it was the pain of a love affair that she was hiding. She had successfully avoided the Turks before, and she felt sure she could outwit them once again. Nevertheless, the thought of the game sent a shiver down her spine.

The servant brought another coffee and she drank it quickly, thanking Bassam for his support. She stamped out her cigarette and said goodbye.

It took ten days for mail to reach home and she could not afford the time. Instead, at the telegraph office near her hotel she wired home to Rounton, asking for extra money, explaining that she had used her next year's income for the trip, promising her father that she would pay him back with earnings from the new book she hoped to write. Hugh Bell was always cautiously frugal, and Gertrude accounted for her spending like an obedient young wife. He had never stopped her before, of course, yet she always asked his permission. In an almost childlike way she wrote to him: "The desert is absolutely tranquil and there should be no difficulty whatever. . . . I hope you will not say No. It is unlikely that you will because you are such a beloved father that you never say No to the most outrageous demands. . . . Dearest beloved Father, don't think me very mad or very unreasonable and remember always that I love you more than words can say."

∞ ∞ ∞

With Bassam's long list of suggested provisions in hand, Gertrude made forays past the great Ummayad Mosque and into the crowded Damascus *souk*. Almost everything she wanted—food, clothing, even camels—was available in the covered bazaar. In a new Parisian suit, and with the amiable Fattuh at her side, she tramped through the dirty passageways, brushing past pashas in gold-embroidered robes; sheikhs in gilt-edged cloaks; Turks covered in long silk coats with colorful turbans wound round their heads; Christians in frock coats, holding rosaries in their hands; Jews with long beards, their heads in turbans, their pants in Turkish style; Armenians and Greeks in colorfully embroidered tunics; old men proudly wearing the green turbans that announced they had made the pilgrimage to Mecca; Bedouin, just in from the desert, in their striped blue *abbas* and *kafeeyahs*; their women tattooed in indigo and veiled in dark blue cloth; and native boys hardly wearing anything at all.

She stepped carefully away from the piles of dung left by camels and mules parading through the labyrinth of alleys. The narrow streets were a storefront for fortune tellers reading palms, public scribes and seal engravers selling their services, vendors everywhere hawking their wares. A cacophony of cries from ragged beggars and sweaty street merchants and wailing muezzins rang in her ears. The sweet smell of Middle Eastern foods drew her on: carts piled high with pistachio nuts, roasted peas, sweet Damascene pastries, licorice, biscuits and all kinds of breads. The brim of her hat was nearly crushed as she dodged sherbet sellers in bright red aprons, butchers carrying carcasses on their shoulders, drink vendors lugging two-handled jars.

At the entrance to the covered lanes, close to the Ummayad Mosque, the aroma of spices wafted from the Souk ali Pasha; she looked in at the tobacco stalls and the coffee stands and she sampled fresh desert dates. She paid a visit to her friend the red-bearded Bahai, who owned a tea shop, and he welcomed her as always with a cup of sweet Persian blend. "Your Excellency is known to us," he had told her years before when she first stopped in. When she had reached for her money he said, "For you there is never anything to pay."

Fattuh headed for the Souk el Jamal, where the caravans came to buy and sell their camels. Paying no attention to the putrid stench, he haggled over the dromedaries, settling happily on an average of thirteen pounds apiece; next door he found the big leather saddles and tapestry saddlebags. Gertrude poked her way through the Souk el Arwam, where Greek merchants sat on the floor of their shops, calling out to her to offer weapons, armor, shawls, carpets and water pipes. She bargained skillfully in the clothing stalls, piling up armloads of cheap cloaks, *kafeeyahs*, cotton cloth and kerchiefs to give as presents along the way. And at the food markets they bought enough bread, butter, meat, eggs, cheese and water to last three or four weeks. Still there was more to be done. Camel drivers were needed, and with Sheikh Bassam's help she hired Muhammad Murawi, an old guide said to have friends among every Arab tribe along the way.

∞∞∞∞∞∞∞∞∞

The desert was thick with robbers. Lacking mercy for those in their own tribes, much less for Europeans, they would steal her money at the slightest chance; she could not risk carrying cash for restocking supplies. With her guide, Muhammad, she rode the electric tram to Maidan, just outside the city, to meet an agent of Ibn Rashid. If she gave the merchant two hundred pounds, he would give her a letter of credit she could draw on in Hayil.

The man was waiting at a native restaurant. A large party was with him, a dozen or so local men and visitors from the south, all curious to meet the lady, El Sitt. Their heads covered in braided cloths, their bodies clothed in robes, they greeted her: "*Salaam Aleikum.*" "*Aleikum salaam,*" she responded, as they made space at one of the wooden tables that filled the familiar-looking room—mosaic patterns on the tile floor, Islamic pictures on the whitewashed walls. A spread of hors d'oeuvres was set before her, plates of *lebeneh*—white cheese—with olive oil and dried mint, *taboule*, olives, *baba ghanoush* and more. Scooping some *humus* onto a leaf of flat bread, she savored the chickpeas and leaned forward to talk. She spoke knowledgeably, discussing antiquities, answering the men's questions about ancient money, showing them how to write the early Sufaitic alphabet.

She had questions of her own: about the disposition of the Turks; about the terrain and oases of the desert; about the *ghazus*, the vicious raids that were the Bedouin's game of life and death; about the politics of the desert tribes; and about the tribal wars. She asked anxiously, her eyes studying their black-bearded faces, searching for truth. One after another their turbaned heads nodded reassuringly, answering that all had become serene; tribes that had been at war for generations had come to terms and peace becalmed the desert.

One of the dark-eyed men murmured that, though there had been a dispute between the tribes of Ibn Rashid and Ibn Saud, all were now at peace. "Are the old enmities to be forgotten? Can you mold the desert sand into shape?" she wondered dubiously. She found it intriguing to watch the strange young man who spoke. Abd al Aziz was the agent of Ibn Rashid; tall and slight, with thin black hairs on his narrow face, his slim frame wrapped in a gold-embroidered cloak, his head covered in a huge camel's hair robe bound in gold. There was something curious about the way he leaned back against the pillows, scarcely moving, hardly lifting his eyes, while his soft voice flowed in slow classical Arabic. Then she noticed his mood change, and gradually he began to stir, waving his thin hands and talking of Hayil and strange jewels that had been brought to the medieval city, about hidden treasures in the mosques at Karbala, about mysterious writings in Central Arabia. The others listened attentively: "Ya Satif! Ya manjud," the men around her murmured. "O Beneficent, O Ever Present," they purred, in admiration of his stories.

His tales left her somewhat skeptical; nevertheless, she paid close attention to the sly-looking Bedouin. This was the man she had come to meet. After a while, when he finished telling his stories, they broke bread to bind their friendship and shared salt as a promise of his tribe's protection. She looked closely at his treacherous face; she could only hope that his word was good.

∞ ∞ ∞

The morning before the journey was to begin, Fattuh complained of feeling ill. His temperature climbed deliriously; the doctor thought it was malaria. Always impatient, Gertrude nevertheless delayed her trip, restlessly filling the time by playing bridge, nervously eating too many helpings of sour curds. "I've grown fat," she wrote home, from "the best food in the world." A few days later she was told that Fattuh had typhoid. The waiting had become too much. She decided to hire a substitute servant and risk traveling along the railway line. In a week Fattuh could take the train and catch up.

At night in her hotel room she wrote feverishly, jotting details in her diary, drawing up descriptive letters to her parents and friends, dashing off a note to her fellow archaeologist T. E. Lawrence, writing that she would see him again at Carchemish on her way back in the spring. Drawing out fresh stationery from her leather case, wooden pen in hand, she dipped the steel tip into the inkwell and wrote another letter. Still desperate and depressed, mired in loneliness, wanting so badly to be with Dick, but knowing too well it was not her fate, she wrote her true feelings to Domnul:

"I want to cut all links with the world, and that is the best and wisest thing to do. Oh, Domnul, if you knew the way I have paced backwards and forwards along the floor of hell for the last few months, you would think me right to try for any way out. I don't know that it is an ultimate way out, but it's worth trying. As I have told you before, it's mostly my fault, but that does not prevent it from being an irretrievable misfortune—for both of us. But I am turning away from it now, and time deadens even the keenest things."

❧   ❧   ❧

A stack of mail arrived from home. She riffled through the envelopes and her eye caught a letter from the Balkans, from Captain Doughty-Wylie. Hastily she slit it open. It was four months since she had seen him! She scanned the pages eagerly, devouring his precious words:

> It's late and I'm all alone, and thinking of those things, of philosophy and love and life—and an evening at Rounton—and what it all meant. I told you then I was a man of the earth, earthy. . . . You are in the desert, I am in the mountains, and in these places much could be said under the clouds. Does it mean that the fence was folly, and that we might have been man and woman as God made us and been happy. . . . But I myself answer to myself that it is a lie. If I had been your man to you, in the bodies we live in, would it change us, surely not. We could not be together long, and there's the afterwards sometimes to be afraid of.
>
> Do you never think like this? I don't know—probably not—as I told you, I am a man of the earth. And still it is a great and splendid thing, the birthright of everyone, for woman as man, only so many of them don't understand the divine simplicity of it. And I always have maintained that this curious, powerful sex attraction is a thing right, natural and to be gratified . . . and if it is not gratified, what then; are we any the worse? I don't know.

That night she could hardly sleep, his words rushing through her mind. She thought of the trip and how she had to break with the world. Her camels were ready, her men and goods were packed; in another day she would be on her way to the Nejd and the vast Arabian unknown.

CHAPTER ELEVEN

Toward Hayil

∞

Gray clouds cloaked the sky as Gertrude set off to the east of Damascus, leaving behind the world of shops and friends and spoken English, riding away without permission from the Turks. It would take three months' time to reach Hayil, headquarters of Ibn Rashid; from there she hoped to visit Ibn Saud, *inshallah*, God willing. "I feel like an Arab sheikh," she wrote, with her caravan of twenty camels laden with goods; three camel drivers—Ali, Abdullah and Fellah; her cook, Selim; her elderly guide, Muhammad Murawi; and her *rafiq*, the paid escort Hamad. Sitting high on the camel saddle, she held the loosely tied halter in her gloved hands and tapped the animal with a switch, sending it to the left or the right as she rode across miles of marshy land. Pockets of truffles lay underfoot, wild fowl occasionally flew overhead, wild boar rushed past, and an hour outside Dumeir, the last outpost of civilization between Damascus to the Euphrates, she stopped to camp.

Her men had never traveled with a European before, and she watched impatiently as they struggled to set up her canvas tents—a small one for her, two larger ones for themselves, and a separate one for the cooking—fumbling with the poles and the furniture. Eventually, they adjusted the wooden dining table and the canvas chairs, stationed the canvas bathtub and the folding bed. It was all so strange to them, compared with the Bedouin tents made of goat hair, furnished with cushions and woven rugs. Without Fattuh, who had packed her belongings, she had difficulty sorting through the boxes, searching for bed linens, pots and pans, and the sponges for her bath. Worse, she discovered, her new cook did not even know how to boil an egg for breakfast.

Nevertheless, the men seemed willing to learn, and dinner that night, with meat from Damascus, she pronounced "quite good."

Relieved finally to be under way, she slept well. But during the night the wind and the rains came. The downpour continued all the next day, making it muddy and impossible for the camels to walk. With little choice, she stayed in the camp and, shivering, wrapped herself in her wool jacket and fur coat. Fleeting thoughts of Turkish authorities trailing from Damascus made her tremble slightly more, and although she tried to concentrate on her last issue of the *Weekly Times* from home, she could not keep her mind from wandering to the Balkans and Dick.

Work was the only cure, she knew, and while the men chopped wood for the fire and straw for the camels, she sewed, as she had been taught by her childhood nanny, diligently stitching cotton bags to hold the provisions. When the skies finally cleared two days later, the ground was so soaked that the camels slipped when they marched, moaning as they fell helplessly in the muck. Within a few hours, however, the caravan had reached the open desert. She rode across the hills of black volcanic earth, contented by the feel of the solid stones crunching beneath her camel's hoofs.

The cook fried tender mushrooms for dinner, and in the afterglow of a brilliant sunset Gertrude joined the men in their tent for coffee and a smoke. Later, when the endless land was eerily quiet, she snuggled in her bed, a hot water bottle warming the sheets, the blankets pulled around her. A candle flickered on the table as she wrote a letter home:

"Already I have dropped back into the desert as if it were my own place; silence and solitude fall round you like an impenetrable veil; there is no reality but the long hours of riding, shivering in the morning and drowsy in the afternoon, the bustle of getting into camp, the talk round Muhammad's coffee fire after dinner, profounder sleep than civilization contrives, and then the road again. And as usual one feels as secure and confident in this lawless country as one does in one's own village." Within five days of the outset, she had been lulled into a soothing routine, reaching her first goal of Jebel Sais, a large, dormant volcano. "Content reigns in my camp and all goes smoothly," she said.

The following morning they moved past the black hills onto the flat and yellow plain, but soon the men caught sight of rising smoke and a camel flock, signs of the Jebel Druze. Gertrude spotted a horseman galloping toward them, firing shots into the air. He wheeled his horse around them, shouting that they were foes and ordering them not to use their guns. With that, he aimed his rifle at Gertrude and demanded that Ali, her helper, hand over his rifle and his fur cloak.

Within seconds, more of the tribesmen appeared. Terrified, Gertrude found herself surrounded by a dozen Druze, shrieking insanely, matted black hair flying in their faces as they leapt into the air, their bodies half-naked except for one, who had no clothes at all. Shouting crazily, one of them grabbed Muhammad's camel, drew the sword hanging behind the saddle, and danced around the group, slashing the air and hitting Gertrude's camel on the neck to make it kneel. As the animal struggled to get up, Gertrude could only watch in silence while the thieves stripped her men of their revolvers, cartridge belts and cloaks.

A week out, and already her hopes were scorched. There was no way they could continue without guns and bullets; they would have to return to Damascus. Suddenly one of the ruffians recognized one of Gertrude's men, and just as abruptly, two sheikhs arrived who knew Muhammad and Ali. With great relief, Gertrude invited the sheikhs to drink coffee in her tent, and after the stolen goods were returned, she paid off the pair with *baksheesh*. The caravan was soon on its way again, but her voyage carried heavier baggage now—the weight of ominous portents.

⤟ ⤟ ⤟

"What sort of Xmas Day have you been spending?" she asked her parents. "I have thought of you all unwrapping presents in the Common Room and playing with the children." She could picture the family at home in Rounton, gathered in the splendid stone house. In the big room with its William Morris furnishings and hand-blocked chintz, a tall tree would be decorated to the brim, and the air would be rich with the smell of pine needles and logs crackling in the fireplace. The little ones, having tiptoed down early from the nursery, would be bubbling with excitement over the goodies they had found in their stockings.

She pictured her father, Sir Hugh, tall, slim, with curly red hair and a straight sharp nose, his gold spectacles rimming his blue-gray eyes and lighting up his handsome bearded face, telling an amusing story about his latest speech for Labour; her mother, Florence, hair piled high, wearing a long black lace gown from Paris, keeping a stern eye on the manners of the grandchildren. Her brother Maurice would be talking of hunting, shooting and fishing, his favorite ways to spend his time; her sisters, Molly and Elsa, as pretty and charming as Virginia Woolf had commented when they were all vying for the same young men, now married and with children of their own; her brother Hugo, foolishly, Gertrude thought, now a minister in the church, was off, living in South Africa.

The six-story house would be filled with guests, as always, making the place lively, the conversation as spirited as Florence enjoyed. There would be diplomats, politicians, journalists, writers and actors; some would be upstairs playing billiards or chatting privately in Hugh's red-carpeted study; others would be outdoors, at the squash courts or taking a brisk walk down the avenue of tall trees.

While the servants prepared dinner, family and friends would walk to the church in the village, some of them singing Christmas carols, some of them talking to Hugh while he pointed out a tree here and flowers newly planted there. Home again for lunch, they would take their places in the dining room, admiring the great tapestry on the wall, *ooh*ing and *aah*ing as the cook sent out the most delicious food: an enormous dinner of roast turkey, warm plum pudding and mince pies. Later that day, masses of cousins would arrive for tea, and while the grown-ups gossiped, Hugh would give out his special presents to the children, a leather case filled with three different sizes of scissors for his granddaughter Valentine (named after Domnul, their good family friend), a scrapbook for this child, a diary for that one; Gertrude still kept her own diaries from childhood.

⊛   ⊛   ⊛

Far away in Burqa, Syria, Gertrude rose early on Christmas Day, and while the mercury edged its way up from 28 degrees Fahrenheit, she breakfasted outdoors next to her tent. At the Byzantine outpost, she spent the day doing archaeological work: finding evidence of Roman occupation, taking rubbings of Greek, Safaitic and Kufic inscriptions, measuring and planning out the ancient fortress, reconstructing it from the rocks that remained. After tea, she returned to the site to photograph the stones and take a latitude for her mapping. "I have had a profitable day," she wrote home. "I have not had time to think whether it has been merry."

The ruined castle at Qasr Azraq was the setting for her New Year's Eve. "Who lived in this site?" she asked her guide Hamad. "We would learn from you. Who knows?" he replied. Instead of attending the formal ball her parents gave at home in England, she sat with her men around the campfire sipping bitter coffee; and while Faris, her new *rafiq*, told tales from the *Arabian Nights*, she looked at the men's faces and saw, in the flickering light of the fire, the dreamy eyes of one man, the laughing face of another, the gleaming white teeth of a third. Her own blue-green eyes were filled with sadness. At last, when she rose to go, they all stood and sent her away to her tent with a blessing. Outside the tent a sliver of moon shone on the camels, lighting the palm trees and the black walls. "So the year ends," she wrote in her diary, "with Arabs, Druze and the shades of Roman emperors and Mamluks. Heaven send a better one."

There was no bathing for the new year of 1914, nor for several days after: the water supply was too low. Her hair and her clothes layered with dust, she felt as though she would never be clean again. But by the end of the first week in January she announced she was pleased with the way the journey had progressed: she had done some good archaeological studies, among them, an important castle at Kharaneh; she had taken bearings for her mapping for the Royal Geographical Society; and by now she had trekked some two hundred miles, coming as far as the railway line at Ziza. When she arrived at Ziza, to her delight, along with a stack of mail from home, she found Fattuh, pale and thin. She greeted him excitedly and welcomed him to her camp; she had "missed him dreadfully," she said. He, too, was happy with the reunion.

Supplies were running short. Hours earlier Gertrude had sent four of her men to town to buy food and water and whatever else was needed. They had not yet returned, and she worried, briefly, but her thoughts were distracted by a delicious lunch brought by Fattuh from Damascus. Afterward, she and Ali rode for an hour to Mashetta to examine the ruins of the seventh-century winter palace built by the Persian King Khosroes II. On the way back, her guide spotted something moving across the empty landscape. "Are those horsemen or camel riders going to our tents?" Ali asked. Gertrude lifted her binoculars and scanned the horizon. "Horsemen," she answered warily, now making out the uniforms of soldiers.

She kicked her camel with her heels to make it go faster, but by the time they reached camp, ten soldiers on horseback were already at her tents. The drunken one in charge told her angrily that the Turkish authorities had been looking for her ever since she left Damascus. They warned her that she had better leave. She listened politely, scowling at herself for being like an ostrich in the sand, not realizing what a fuss there had been about her. "Paf!" she wrote to her parents, annoyed that she'd been caught. "I was an idiot to come in so close to the railway."

As soon as the Turkish soldiers left, she wrote out telegrams to friends—the British Consuls in Beirut and Damascus—and gave them to Abdullah to take to town. But her man was stopped en route, the telegrams snatched, and the fellow sent to prison inside the Ziza castle. A few hours later Fattuh was jailed too. As Gertrude watched helplessly, the returning soldiers ransacked all the baggage, claimed all the weapons, and posted seven men around the tent. Angry and tired, she still refused to concede. "I am not beaten yet," she wrote the next morning, as though it were all a contest. She and her men could go back to Damascus and start over on a different route through Palmyra. Fattuh responded cheerfully: "I spent the first night of the journey in the railway station, and the second in prison, and now where?" Gertrude told her parents, "It's all rather comic," but it wasn't.

There was little laughter in her. The mail had brought letters from Doughty-Wylie telling her he was back in London and planning to see her mother. How she wished she were there with him! In another letter, he spoke tenderly about a diary she had kept and sent to him. "It's perfectly wonderful and I love it and you. I kiss your hands and your feet, dear woman of my heart," he wrote. "I cannot tell you how it moves me to hear you say—not that—to see it—written by you—that you might have married me, have borne my children, have been my wife as well as my heart. Thinking at all points—you yourself and me myself—each free, each independent, each intent to be one—Yes—I've dreamed these things."

"I love you, but I shall never have you,—only always in the real world be your lover, your obedient servant, your loyal friend. . . . And I will try to be more like what your lover might be, and shortwise—but it will be sometimes hard, because I am an ordinary man—and follower of delights."

She was distraught. What might have happened if she had given in to his desires? What if, in that moment of passion, she had let him take her? Would it all be different? Would they be together now? But she refused to let him make love to her as long as he was married to someone else. It was wrong. What's more, she could have become pregnant. In her tent that evening, feeling desperate, she unleashed her feelings to Domnul:

"I have known loneliness in solitude now, for the first time. . . . Sometimes I have gone to bed with a heart so heavy that I thought I could not carry it through the next day. Then comes the dawn . . . and I walk on through the sunlight, comforted . . . taught at least some wisdom by solitude, taught submission, and how to bear pain without crying out."

∞   ∞   ∞

She moved her camp to the nearby town of Amman, once the capital of the Ammonites, later the city the Greeks called Philadelphia and now the home of Circassians—red-haired, fair-skinned Muslims from the north—driven from their mountain homes by the Russians and resettled here by the Turks. For the first time in three weeks she saw grass and green hills and crops growing, and she met friends and notables she had not encountered since her first desert trip, fourteen years before. Her Circassian friends invited her to a wedding and the fifteen Protestant families in town invited her to tea.

But the pleasure would not last. She learned that telegrams had been flying since December 17; Sir Louis Mallet, the British Ambassador to Constantinople, had informed the British Consul in Damascus that the Turkish Government begged that she not travel to Central Arabia. Wired Mallet, "In my private opinion she would be wise to desist from travelling in the countries of Ibn Saud and Ibn Rashid." Mallet informed the Foreign Office in London: "There is considerable unrest among the Arabs. . . . Government have disclaimed all responsibility in the case of Miss Bell." Gertrude was told that if she continued from Amman toward Nejd, her own government would wash its hands of her.

She puffed on a cigarette and read the wire from the Turkish Vali, the Governor, in Damascus. Mallet had informed the Ottomans of her journey, and the Turks insisted she sign a note acknowledging that she traveled at her own risk; they refused to take any responsibility for her safety. Putting pen to paper, she wrote her name cavalierly. But on the last night in Amman she lay in bed sleepless, twisting and turning with the thought that she was an outlaw. "The desert looks terrifying from without," she scrawled in her diary.

The following day she left Amman, riding toward a farm three hours away that belonged to some Christian Arab friends. The last time she had seen them was in 1905, but the men boomed a hearty welcome and invited her to stay the night. Tall and broad-shouldered, they were as big in heart as in body: they slew a sheep to show her hospitality, piled up a platter of rice in her honor, and, since three of her men had quit in fear, they promised to provide her with camel drivers and new *rafiqs* to guarantee her safety from one tribal territory to another. In the warmth of their friendship, her terror disappeared. She had started a new diary for Doughty-Wylie, and in it she wrote: "The desert is clothed once more in abiding serenity. Thus we turn towards Nejd, *inshallah*, renounced by all the powers that be, and the only thread which is not cut is that which runs through this little book, which is the diary of my way kept for you."

☙   ☙   ☙

"You now must make acquaintance with the members of the expedition," Gertrude jotted on Sunday, January 18, 1914, as her caravan headed in the direction of Arabia: first, there was Muhammad Murawi, who had ridden with Ibn Rashid; his nephew Salim, an all-around helper; the affable Fattuh, "the alpha and omega of all, with his eye on everything, although it never appears to be off me." There was Ali, "an idle dog" but "brave as a lion"; Muhammad's nephew, Said, the head camel driver; and under him Meskin, of the Agail tribe; Mustafa, a peasant from Jerusalem; and the black-skinned Fellah, who worked in the men's tent and "has the good word of everyone."

With eight men plus two *rafiqs*, Gertrude left the high ground and rode six to eight hours a day across the Beni Sakhr territory, flint-covered land scattered with herds of camel and flocks of sheep. The trek was wearying, and as they rode her men told tales of bloodthirsty raids—the endless cycle of tribal revenge. In the evening Gertrude sat in her tent composing reassuring letters to her family, jotting notes in her journal, and making longer, more intimate entries in her diary for Dick. She did not mention to her parents that she had seen her first scorpion that day. To Dick she wrote, "I am really beginning to enjoy it all," admitting that she had been so unhappy on the first part of the trip, she had seriously considered turning back. "But when two days ago I cut myself loose from civilization I felt as if I had cast down all binders."

Years earlier a young Arab boy had helped her see beyond the surface of the landscape, to "read the desert." She noted the beds used by Arab boys, hollow squares made with big stones; the half-moon nests in the earth scooped out by camel mothers for their young. She knew the names of the plants and the uses to which they were put: the *utrufan*, used by the Arabs to scent their butter; the prickly *krusa'aneh*, for an excellent salad; the dry sticks of the *billan*, for camels' food; and the *gali*, for making soap.

She stopped at Tubah to photograph the Ummayad Palace; a few days later she measured the castle near Bair. She had now reached the land of the Anazeh, the most powerful of all the Bedouin tribes. The route of her caravan ran close to water wells, making it vulnerable to raiding parties that met at the pools. Her men were afraid to go to sleep at night, but Gertrude brushed off the danger: "I should sleep but little in the next few weeks if I were to be disturbed by such things."

But her men's fears were not without good reason. On the morning of January 21 they discovered a Bedouin's body. "He was killed," her *rafiq* Sayyah observed. Looking down at the corpse she could see that the cotton *kafeeyah* was covered with blood. "Occasionally I wonder whether I shall come out of this adventure alive," she commented, adding despondently to Dick, "But the doubt has no shadow of anxiety in it—I am so profoundly indifferent."

The earth had turned dry and black, thickly strewn with flints; gleaming, yet bare and forbidding. Her thermometer registered the temperature, fluctuating from the freezing point in the morning to seventy degrees in the midafternoon. She spied a lone geranium flowering on the low ground: courageous, she thought. Another day and the caravan was low on water. They had not bathed or washed in days. Then, coming out of a wide valley, they spotted fresh camel footprints in the sand. Ali announced there must be Arabs nearby. "Tonight we shall hear their dogs," he said.

They settled in camp, and Gertrude followed her *rafiqs*, climbing the hills to scout. It reminded her of a game she and Maurice had played when they were young, wandering around the house, up and down the stairs, hiding from the housemaids.

"There is smoke!" Sayyah called out. The black plume curling over the hill was a certain sign of a campsite, probably that of a raiding party. Inspecting the area nervously, she and her men encountered flocks of sheep and some shepherds of the Howeitat tribe. They were known throughout the Euphrates, from Arabia to Syria and Mesopotamia, for their terrifying *ghazus*, campaigns of plunder and warfare that had made them rich and powerful. Every one of their men and boys was called into service for a major raid, and sometimes as many as five thousand camel riders were assembled. Riding for days on end, they rarely slept or ate. Once they reached their destination, they would swoop down on the enemy camp like a whirlwind, screaming war cries and creating wild confusion. Tents were overturned, sheep and goats stampeded and any person who stayed behind was sliced to death.

Gertrude knew there was only one thing to do: ask the Howeitat for protection before they discovered her and made their kill. The following morning she rode her camel into the camp. Finding the largest black tent, she approached the sheikh's home. She kneeled her animal, hitting it on the neck to make it sit, then waited for a servant to invite her inside. She followed him into the tent of Sheikh Harb; inside she saw the carpets on the floor and the camel saddles covered with sheepskin to make them comfortable for leaning. A true Bedouin, Harb welcomed his honored guest, offering coffee poured from a brass pot into tiny cups, inviting her to return later for the evening meal.

At sundown, freshly bathed in water from the Howeitat well, feeling clean for the first time in days, Gertrude donned her dinner gown and returned to the tent with a gift for her host. They sat—she and her guides, Harb and his men—cross-legged in a circle, before them a large copper tray piled high with boiled rice cooked in grease from sheep's milk, topped with a roasted male sheep, slain in her honor, sprinkled with raisins, almonds and onions. Before they began, Gertrude was offered the prize delicacy, the eye of the sheep. Murmuring gratefully for such hospitality, she quickly swallowed the organ, then reached with her hand to take some meat. Later the leftovers would be served to the others.

As dinner went on, another guest arrived: Muhammad Abu Tayyi, cousin of Audah, the greatest sheikh of the Howeitat; "magnificent," Gertrude described him, "tall and big with a flashing look, the Howeitat reputation for dare-devilry written on his face." Like his famous cousin (who kept count of the men he killed) now away raiding the Shammar, Muhammad Abu Tayyi had dark skin, high cheekbones, a black mustache and small goatee. He served as an agent of the Ottomans, in charge of collecting the camel tax, and responsible, too, for a portion of the distant Hejaz Railway.

Together they enjoyed a dessert of dates and buttermilk, but over the coffee, made with cardamom, the conversation turned sour. Had she come with or without Turkish permission? the Turkish agent wanted to know. Feeling uneasy, Gertrude got up to go, leaving her men behind to calm the atmosphere. As she lay in her tent, she could hear shouting and arguing. In the morning she learned it was over some private matter, and she sighed with relief.

In the Bedouin custom she stayed three days with Harb. Then, accompanied by a new *rafiq* and Muhammad Abu Tayyi, she went on to the territory of the Ruwallah tribe. The fierce Muhammad slept in the tents of Gertrude's men and dined with her by candlelight at her gleaming table. He brought her gifts of an ostrich skin and a lamb. "I can scarcely bear the thought of sacrificing it," she wrote of the baby sheep. "Yet I cannot well carry it with me like Byron's goose."

They rode toward the hills of the Jebel Tubaiq and, at Muhammad's suggestion, stopped at a ruin, which she photographed. They reached the camp of Audah Abu Tayyi. He was not there, but Muhammad, an important man on his own, offered her hospitality. She was eager to get on to Hayil, but, intrigued by the great camp, the largest she had ever seen, and allured by his charm, she agreed to stay. He showed her into the harem and introduced her to his wives, their bodies covered in blue cloth, their dark faces tattooed in blue, their lips dyed with indigo. Privately, they complained to Gertrude of "the burden of woman" in nomadic life. The Bedouin women were expected to rise with the early morning light and begin their chores at once: to feed the sheep, milk the camels, bake the bread, repair the tents, spin the sheeps' wool and weave the camels' hair, all the while taking care of their babies. And when it was time to move on, it was their job to strike the tents, pack up the belongings and, babies held tight, march on. Gertrude listened attentively to their woeful stories, photographing their painted faces as they spoke.

In the evenings she dined with Muhammad. Sitting on fine woven rugs spread across the soft sand, she, in her French gown and fur coat, puffed cigarettes through her ivory holder, while he, wrapped in a sheepskin cloak, a white linen *kafeeyah* over his dark brows, smoked a *narghile* between his thick lips. Men of all ages joined them around the big fire, and with pungent smoke filling the air, they talked for hours about the politics of the desert and the daring exploits of Audah Abu Tayyi. As Muhammad's black eyes flashed, he told her romantic adventures of the princes of the Nejd.

Long after sunset, when the *nagas*, the camel mothers, had come home, Muhammad rose, drew his fur cloak around him, went out into the dark night with a huge wooden bowl and filled it to the brim with camel's milk. He brought it to Gertrude, who drank it with relish. "I fancy that when you have drunk the milk of the *naga* over the campfire of Abu Tayyi, you are baptised of the desert and there is no other salvation for you," she wrote to Dick. When she walked back to her tent in the frosty night, a falling star whizzed by.

On the following day it was time to leave; Muhammad Abu Tayyi gave her a gift of half a load of corn, and she gave him a pair of Zeiss binoculars. She had observed him act as a judge before his tribe. "He is a man, and a good fellow; you can lay your head down in his tents, and sleep at night and have no fear," she said. "I learnt much of the desert and its people. The Howeitat are great people." He had showered her with kindness and over the course of three days she and Muhammad had become "great friends." It was a friendship that would be highly valuable later, when she worked with T. E. Lawrence to organize the revolt against the Turks.

∞ ∞ ∞

They were twenty nights from Hayil. The land had turned reddish-gold and sandy, and the gray-green shrubs of the desert blossomed

with pale flowers. Gertrude met up with a rich Shammar family wanting to return to the Nejd. In exchange for acting as her safeguard
against the Shammar, they asked for protection against the local tribes.
Now, along with her own men, her party included Arab aristocrats
with their camels and flocks of sheep, plus members of the Sherarat
tribe; all, she noted, trekking across a world of "incredible desolation,
abandoned of God and man." In her diary to Doughty-Wylie she
wrote:

"I think no one can travel here and come back the same. It sets its
seal upon you, for good or ill. . . . I wish you were here to see this
wide desolate landscape, and breathe an air which is like a breath from
the very fountain of life." This was the real desert, vacillating sand
heaped in long low hills or spilling in shallow valleys: "In spite of the
desolation, and the emptiness, it is beautiful—or is it beautiful partly
because of the emptiness? At any rate I love it, and though the camels
pace so slowly, eating as they go, I feel no impatience, and no desire to
get anywhere."

There were fewer ruins now and less to photograph, but she continued to do her mapping, walking behind the caravan, taking her
bearing with her compass. Traveling on, she heard from a passing
Howeitat that Sheikh Sayah, a well-known ruffian of the Wad Suleiman, was camped a few hours to the east. It was better to approach and
ask for his protection than hide and risk being robbed. She advanced
toward his tent. The one-eyed sheikh received her cordially, offering her
coffee and dates. But when he questioned her reasons for coming there,
Gertrude became suspicious. A short while later he paid a visit to her
camp: any hint of courtesy had disappeared. The rogue rifled through
her belongings, examined all her possessions and demanded each item
for himself. Bristling with anger, she refused; he moved on to the men's
tent. A few minutes later he came back, Muhammad in tow, swearing
angrily that no Christian woman had ever been in this territory before
and had no right to be there. He demanded her binoculars and pistol.
Night was coming, and she yielded, handing over her revolver in exchange for the promise of a *rafiq*.

In the morning he returned, this time threatening to send them
away without an escort if she did not give up her own binoculars. A
bitter wind blew, and as she sat anxiously on the side, shivering in the
cold, her men negotiated the ransom. She could overhear the talk, and
the waiting became more frightening when the one-eyed brute told two
of her men that he planned to kill her. If they helped him, they could
share the spoils. Her servants refused, but in the end she was forced to
give up both her valuable binoculars and her gun. About to leave, she
mounted her camel and glowered down at the thief. He had reverted to

his friendlier ways. "Why do you not say *hal* [how are you]?" he asked with a smile. "I would say no word to you," she snarled. In her diary she wrote, "May God deprive him of the other eye."

∞   ∞   ∞

Still a week away from the Nejd, the harshest desert of all, she now felt perfectly safe. But at the wells of the Haizan, where she stopped to water the camels, she heard bad news. The Emir Ibn Rashid was not at Hayil. He was away in the northern desert, the Nefud, raiding the Shammar. The Emir had informed his men of her imminent arrival, but she would rather have dealt with the leader than with his deputies.

One of her camels refused to stir. Thinking the animal was weary, Gertrude brought it food and tried to coax it up. But the camel was writhing in the agony of death. "She is gone," Muhammad said. "Shall we sacrifice her?" Animals had always meant much to her. Even as a child she had mourned the death of her pets, organizing their funerals, marching in solemn parades to their graves. She quivered at the sight of the dying animal. "It were best," she answered. Muhammad slit the camel's throat.

As they marched now across the empty wasteland of the Nefud, the days were tedious, the nights infinitely lonely. Except for the harrowing stories around the campfire told by her men, there was little conversation. She felt frustrated by the lack of work and isolated by the lack of friendly people. Overwhelmed with the monotony and still nine days away from Hayil, she wrote to Dick that she was suffering from bouts of severe depression. Was the adventure, she wondered:

> worth the candle. Not because of the danger—I don't mind that; but I am beginning to wonder what profit I shall get out of it all. A compass traverse over country which was more or less known, a few names added to the map. . . . The net result is that I think I should be more usefully employed in more civilised countries, where I know what to look for and how to record it. Here, if there is anything to record the probability is that you can't find it or reach it, because a hostile tribe bars the way, or the road is waterless, or something of that kind. . . . I fear, when I come to the end, I shall say: "It was a waste of time." It's done now, and there is no remedy, but I think I was a fool to come. . . .
>
> There is such a long way between me and letters, or

between me and anything, and I don't feel at all like the
daughter of kings, which I am supposed to be. It's a bore
being a woman when you are in Arabia.

The heavens opened up, shaking thunder, pouring hail and rain.
Gertrude sat in her tent reading *Hamlet*, and as she read the tragic story
of greed and deceit in the royal house of Denmark, so much like the
bitter rivalry in the desert, the world came into focus. "Princes and
powers of Arabia stepped down into their true place," she wrote to
Dick, "and there rose up above them the human soul, conscious and
answerable to itself."

A few days' more travel and she reached the end of the Nefud. At
the top of the last sand bank she looked down. The desolate landscape
was terrifying: black lifeless sand whipped by a bitter wind. This was
the Nejd, the threatening desert of Central Arabia. "*Subhan Allah!*" said
one of her men. "We have come to *Jehannum*; we have come to Hell."

Chapter Twelve

Prisoner in Arabia

∞

The Nejd was empty and eerily silent, its flat plains hard and almost interminable. But on Tuesday, February 24, 1914, Gertrude and her men were in sight of Hayil. The ancient city, in medieval times a hub of commerce, had been a stop on the frankincense route between the Arabian Gulf and the Levantine coast. For hundreds of years Persians had paused there on the pilgrimage to Mecca. In the mid-nineteenth century, Hayil had become the headquarters for Ibn Rashid of the Shammar tribe; since then there had been constant strife with Ibn Saud of the Anazeh.

Ten years earlier, Ibn Saud had broken out of the exile imposed on his father by Ibn Rashid, and, with the help of fifteen men, scaled the walls of Riyadh in the dark of night, ready to seize it as soon as the doors were opened in the morning. This daring success had earned him a reputation as a desert warrior. Unbeknownst to Gertrude, as she reached Hayil, the Saudis and their Wahhabi army (Islamic fundamentalists) were on the warpath, carrying out a bloody revenge for their years in exile. As for the Rashids, they had become much weaker, sapped by internecine rivalries so brutal that the present Emir, the oldest surviving member of the ruling Rashid family, was only sixteen years of age.

Gertrude spent the night of February 24 encamped on a granite plain sprinkled with thorny acacia trees and sweet-smelling desert plants. It was safest not to enter the walled town unannounced but to wait while messengers bearing gifts made her arrival known. She rose at sunrise and, clad in her linen costume, brimmed hat covered with a silk *kafeeyah*, rode her camel toward Hayil. On the way she encountered her guide Ali, who reported that he had met Ibrahim; the Emir's uncle was in charge until the ruler returned. Ibrahim had sent three slaves on horseback to escort Gertrude into town.

Flanked by the sword-bearing horsemen and her own gun-toting men, Gertrude rode on camel like a queen in state to the medieval ramparts of Hayil. Then, leaving her camel behind, she skirted the mud walls and entered the city by the south gate. At the doorway of the very first house, she was led up a long ramp to an open court and into an immensely high, columned room. Carpets covered the floors, Islamic writing decorated the walls and divans lined the perimeter. This was the *roshan*, the reception room, of the late Muhammad Ibn Rashid's summer palace. Gertrude was told to wait there with her new slaves.

Spotting a ladder, she climbed to look out upon the town, but before she could see beyond gardens and cornfields, she was forced to come down. Two women had come to call: one, an old widow, served as the caretaker; the other, Turkiyyeh, a lively Circassian veiled in a dark purple cloak, was dressed in brilliant red and purple robes, with ropes of pearls around her neck. She had been sent years ago by the Sultan in Constantinople as a gift to Muhammad Ibn Rashid. Now she was sent to entertain Gertrude.

Turkiyyeh inquired of her plans, and Gertrude admitted she hoped to go farther south to visit Ibn Saud (well known as the enemy of Ibn Rashid). The woman undoubtedly was sent to spy, Gertrude realized. Nonetheless, chattering away, she proved invaluable as she revealed the local gossip: the mud walls of Hayil were thick with conspiracies, secrets and murderous plots. Within the past eight years three Emirs had been assassinated; their slaves and eunuchs slaughtered with them, their bodies all thrown into the palace wells. The palace women were taken as wives, first by one assassin, then by the next, and despite the momentary rule of Ibrahim, it was the Emir's grandmother, Fatima, who was the true power behind the throne.

After lunch, the strong scent of attar of roses wafted into the *roshan*, and a parade of slaves heralded the arrival of the Emir's uncle. Wearing Indian silks and carrying a gold-mounted sword, the perfumed Ibrahim was all smiles as he entered the room. He sat down beside Gertrude on the divan and talked to her about the European adventurers who long ago had visited Hayil. He appeared intelligent and well educated, but his eyes shifted nervously, and Gertrude began to feel uncomfortable as he revealed the series of family murders that had led to the rise of the current Emir. They talked some more, and then, as Ibrahim rose to go to afternoon prayers, he took aside her servant and whispered in his ear: the town's religious leaders were suspicious of Gertrude's motives. She was not to leave the *roshan* until she received permission.

No one else came to call that day and no one else came that night. Nor did anyone come the following two days and two nights. She paced and she sat and she paced and she sat again, waiting for something to happen. But nothing happened. She had been taken prisoner in Hayil.

At last, on the fourth evening, she was allowed to visit Ibrahim. Long after sunset, the only time when the women of Hayil were permitted in the streets, she was escorted by slaves through the dark, silent town. Only a soul or two passed by, creeping close to the hovering walls. As her borrowed mare neared the gates of the fortress palace, she was met by a battery of slaves.

Entering the great colonnaded reception room of the palace, Gertrude marched straight across the polished stone floors toward Ibrahim. He sat with a group of men against the far wall. They rose from the carpets to greet her, and, taking the gifts she offered, her host gestured for her to sit at his right. A slave poured coffee and she leaned against the cushions, relaxing a little, sipping the bitter drink, while they all discussed the history of the Shammar tribe and the Rashids in particular. Before she could even raise the issue of her imprisonment, however, another slave brought in a censer and swung it three times in front of each guest. The breeze of incense was the signal to leave. Later, Ibrahim returned her gifts.

The days went wearily on. Each morning she was awakened by the low wail of her gatekeeper: "*Allahu akhbar, Allahu akhbar*; God is great, God is great. There is no God but God. God is great." Each afternoon she waited to hear about her freedom. But she heard not a word. There was nothing to do, she was nervous and edgy, the silence screamed and the high walls of the *roshan* were closing in on her.

On the sixth morning she was allowed to go riding with an escort in Ibrahim's gardens. The same evening Ibrahim summoned her to a private audience. Bringing the gifts back to him, she explained that she had spent all her money. Except for a few camels she had sold upon her arrival in Hayil, she was now virtually penniless. In addition, the rest of her camels were far away, feeding. Ibrahim listened. She was anxious to go on, she pleaded, but she had no means of transportation and no money to pay for *rafiqs*. She asked to draw on her letter of credit. Finally Ibrahim spoke: the letter of credit could not be cashed until the

Emir returned. When would that be? she asked. At least a month from now, he answered. She grew more frightened and smoked a cigarette.

∞   ∞   ∞

"I had no idea what was in their dark minds concerning me," she wrote. She had told the Rashids she intended to visit their enemy, Ibn Saud. It was a foolish admission, and no doubt they saw her as a traitor, afraid she would give the Sauds useful information. What the Rashids would do with her now was an open question. Her fate was in their hands. "Why, or how it would end, God alone knew." She could do nothing but sit in her room with Turkiyyeh, listening to more harrowing tales of butchery, rape and revenge. The place smelled of killing and the air whispered of death. "In Hayil," she observed, "murder is like the spilling of milk."

She had been inside Hayil for a week when her own men came with talk from the town. The peace promised in Damascus was a lie; war was all around them. The Emir was raiding in the north, and Ibn Saud was mustering his forces. The road was barred, and she could no longer consider going south to pay a visit to Ibn Saud. He was preparing to attack Hayil. If the city was besieged, she had little chance of survival.

She sent a message to Ibrahim, asking anxiously again about her money. The influential chief eunuch, Said, came with the answer: she could not leave Hayil without permission from the Emir. "I have no money and I must go," she begged. "Going and coming are not in our hands," he answered coolly.

That night she was summoned to visit the young mother of the Emir. Once more in the eerie darkness she followed the slaves to the huge palace, and as she entered the harem she found it medieval, "more like the Arabian Nights than ever." In the great columned rooms, the women were dressed in their Indian brocades and jewels, the children were heavily laden with jewels, and slaves and eunuchs stood all around. She listened to the women's tales as they described being passed by the men from hand to hand. "The victor takes them . . . his hands are red with the blood of their husbands and children!" At the end of the evening she was led back to her house. The doors closed behind her and once again she was a prisoner.

Nine days had passed and the silence had grown even deeper and the walls of her room seemed to shift even closer. She begged again for her freedom, but the only outing she was permitted was a visit to the garden of a pair of perfumed princes. Dressed in gold-embroidered robes, the two young men hardly spoke, staring silently, solemnly at her with their kohl-rimmed eyes. Later that day, Said the eunuch returned. He repeated the message that nothing could be done without the Emir's permission. Gertrude had tried everything: she had implored Turkiyyeh and Said, sent messages to Fatima and Ibrahim, but all to no avail.

In the early evening she was called to the men's tent, where Said presided. This time no sweet Oriental phrases passed her lips. Brimming with anger, she demanded her camels and her money. She had to leave Hayil at once, she declared. Defiant, she rose abruptly, leaving the men still seated. She knew this was a brazen act, something done only by the greatest of sheikhs. She was too angry to consider the consequences.

At dusk her camels arrived. After darkness fell, Said came with a bag of gold coins worth two hundred pounds, the amount she had deposited for her letter of credit. He had no explanations and no apologies. She had full permission to go where and when she liked, he told her. "I am much obliged," she replied with great dignity. But, she reminded him, for nearly two weeks she had been imprisoned in Hayil. Boldly, she announced she wished to see the fortress palace and the town by daylight.

The following morning, March 7, she was taken on tour around the city, permitted to photograph whatever she liked—the buildings, the marketplace, the people. Afterward, Turkiyyeh invited her to tea. A crowd of deaf and blind people had assembled at her door and she flung them a bag of copper coins. Then she gathered her men, and when she was comfortable on her camel, she heaved a sigh of relief and turned her back on Hayil.

"And now I will tell you my general idea of Arabian politics," she wrote to Dick. "Hayil gave me a sinister impression. I do not like the rule of women and eunuchs. . . . I think the Rashids are moving towards their close. Not one grown man of their house remains alive— the Emir is only sixteen or seventeen, and all the others are little more than babes, so deadly has been the family strife. I should say that the future lies with Ibn Saud," she noted rightly. "I cannot find it in my heart to wish the Rashids much good. Their history is one long tale of treachery and murder—you shall hear it some day. I do not know what Ibn Saud is like, but worse he cannot be. So there! My next Arabian journey shall be to him. I have laid out all my plans for it."

All hope of traveling south to Ibn Saud had been doused. The quickest route back was through Baghdad, and on March 8 Gertrude set off. Deadly tired from the strain of imprisonment, and sadly disappointed at not being able to complete her trip, she now faced marches of eight to ten hours a day across the Nefud, where dangerous outlaws were on the rampage and Shiite tribes were warring with Turkish troops. Managing to dodge them safely, within three weeks she reached Karbala, the Shiite holy city in the desert, and went directly to see an old acquaintance. They talked for several hours about religion, politics and the future, and he told her he was coming to England to study.

"What will you do with your family?" she asked.

"Oh," he answered, "I shall leave them here, and I shall probably divorce my wife before I leave."

"So," Gertrude wrote, "perhaps he will be in search of a bride when he comes to England. I wish I could find him one—a pleasant one. I like the good little man." Best of all, she noted that March day, they had talked in English, and she hadn't heard English since December 15.

The following day she left Karbala and arrived a few hours later in Baghdad. "The end of an adventure always leaves one with a feeling of disillusion," she told Dick; "just nothing. Dust and ashes in one's hand, dead bones that look as if they would never rise and dance—it's all nothing, and one turns away from it with a sigh, and tries to fix one's eyes on the new thing before one. This adventure hasn't been successful, either. I haven't done what I meant to do. But I have got over that. . . . Now I think I must end this tale."

There was mail waiting for Gertrude in Baghdad at the Residency of the British Consul, stacks of envelopes from friends and family. Her heart beat faster as she opened the letters from Dick, only to discover that he too felt alone and discouraged.

"Where are you? It's like writing to an idea, a dream," he called to her. "Is it that gloom that is so black tonight? Or is it the regret for things lost, great and splendid things I find in your book, your mind and body, and the dear love of you, all lost. . . . would you like me to write you a love letter—to say in some feeble whisper what the mind outside is shouting—to say, my dear, how glad and gratified and humble I am when I think of you." Half taunted, half mesmerized, she folded his letter and tucked it away.

Gertrude had business in the city: camels to sell, local notables to meet, arrangements to make for the remainder of her trip. She found the newly appointed British Consul in Baghdad, Colonel Ramsay, to be not only unhelpful but ignorant, and wrote contemptuously that he slept all morning and played cards in his room after lunch. He spoke no foreign language, not even French, had no understanding of Turkey or Turkish Arabia. "And this is the man who we send here at the moment when the Baghdad Railway on the one hand, our irrigation schemes on the other, are passing from schemes into realities . . . please God!"

But in contrast to the lazy British official, the local Muslim religious leader, the Naqib, was a man of great knowledge and authority and a loyal subject of the Turks. Gertrude had met him before and this time she spent two hours with him, writing afterward that she was "vastly amused, as ever, by his talk."

In between her meetings, she read more letters from Dick. Another of her personal diaries had arrived, he told her, and he had spent the day reading it. "It's perfectly wonderful and I love it and you. I kiss your hands and feet, dear woman of my heart. Let it be for a moment; in many thoughts, and many hours, perhaps in many lives, I'll answer it." He had written about her to his uncle Charles Doughty, and now he passed on to her the famous traveler's good wishes. His note continued, adoringly:

"And the desert has you—you and your splendid courage, my queen of the desert—and my heart is with you. . . . It makes me humble, darling, such a perfect love as that—something that one has dreamt of as one dreams of dim glories, all a wonder. I am not worthy of such a gift. If I was young and free, and a very perfect knight, it would be more fitting to take and kiss you. But I am old and tired and full of a hundred faults. Ah, my dear, my dear, what things you say— they hold the heart—and to my soul you answer."

Again he wrote about his lust: "You are right—not that way for you and me—because we are slaves, not because it is not the right, the natural way—when the passions of the body flame and melt into the passions of the spirit—in those dream ecstacies so rarely found by any human creature, those, as you say, whom God hath *really* joined—In some divine moment we might reach it—the ecstacy. We never shall. But there is left so much. As you say my dear, wise queen—all that there is we will take."

His letters made everything she did seem worthwhile again. He made her feel brave, strong, courageous and, more than anything else, womanly. He had written to her again and again while she was in the desert, telling her of a meeting with her father in London, of his new assignment in Ethiopia, of his passionate love for her and of his joy in reading her special diary for him: "You said in the book you wanted to hear me say I loved you, you wanted it plain to eyes and ears, and in the book for me to lean on, you set it down.

"I love you—does it do any good out there in the desert? Is it less vast, less lonely, like the far edge of life? someday perhaps, in a whisper, in a kiss, I will tell you. . . .

"You give me a new world, Gertrude. I have often loved women as a man like me does love them, well and badly, little and much, as the blood took me, or the time or the invitation, or simply for the adventure—to see what happened. But that is all behind me.

"Where are you now?" he asked in despair. But almost cruelly he went on, "I love to think of you lonely, and wanting me."

She had written to him of her distaste for infidelity and her desire for marriage. "There *is* a real marriage, a fidelity of the mind. Nothing touches that," he answered; "fidelity of the body is a word only, the other is the meaning of it. I do not think anything of the one and the whole world rests on the other. Chastity is not a virtue at all, only if one loves one must say so with every pulse and heartbeat. I don't know why I wrote this. I have come out of my kingdom by it, and can't get back. But I shall never be your lover, my dear, never. I read that beautiful and passionate book, and know it. Never your lover, that is, man to woman, a splendid thing enough after all. But what we have we will keep and cherish. Yes, we will be wise and gentle as you said."

For now she could only read his words and dream of him. Dick had left England for the diplomatic posting in Ethiopia. There was no possibility of their seeing each other.

At the beginning of April 1914, Gertrude bade farewell to Baghdad on her way to Damascus and then to Constantinople, where she hoped to see Ambassador Sir Louis Mallet. Four months earlier he had tried to stop her journey, but she had valuable information for him now about Arabia and Ibn Rashid and Ibn Saud.

Before she left, she wrote to Domnul: "You will find me a savage, for I have seen and heard strange things, and they colour the mind. You must try to civilise me a little, beloved Domnul. I think I am not altered for you, and I know that you will bear with me. But whether I can bear with England—come back to the same things and do them all over again—that is what I sometimes wonder. But they will not be quite the same, since I come back to them with a mind permanently altered. I have gained much, and I will not forget it.

"I don't care to be in London much. . . . I like Baghdad, and I like Iraq. It's the real East, and it is stirring; things are happening here, and the romance of it all touches me and absorbs me."

Chapter Thirteen

Rumblings of War

∞

After three weeks Gertrude left Baghdad and marched west across the desert to Damascus, ignoring the hardships that hinder most travelers. Her caravan was now smaller, easier to move: two small native tents for camping, with only a rug on the ground as her bed, and Fattuh, Sayyah and Fellah as her staff. They were in Anazeh territory, "the real Bedouin," she called these camel people who wandered ceaselessly through the desert. "The others are just Arabs." She was content to be with them, sitting with their sheikhs, drinking their coffee around their fire, although she remembered what one of her *rafiqs* had said around just such a campfire:

"In all the years when we come to this place we shall say: 'Here we came with her, here she camped.' It will be a thing to talk of, your *ghazai*. We shall be asked for news of it, and we shall speak of it, and tell how you came." It made her anxious to think what they would say. "They will judge my whole race by me," she reckoned.

She had no guide to lead her across the Syrian desert, but, she confessed, "it amuses me to run my own show. And so far all has gone well."

They rode quickly, sometimes for eleven hours a day, and for the first time she succeeded in sleeping on her camel. Only a few days out,

however, they saw telltale footprints of a raiding party. It was dangerous to relax. Riding across land that was "flat, flat and flat," they
stopped at a well and learned that the raiders were Shammar who had
stolen forty camels from the local Anazeh tribe. The victims had
pursued the thieves, she was told by a young boy, and had seized ten of
their mares. What's more, they killed one of the leaders. "Did his
companions stay to bury him?" Gertrude asked, suddenly picturing the
corpse in the open desert. "No, *Wallah*," the boy answered; "they left
him to be eaten by the dogs." The image was gruesome. "I could not
get him from my thoughts," she wrote to Dick, "the dead man lying on
the great plains till the dogs came to finish the business."

Half-drawn, half-repelled by a sea of sinister dots in the distance,
she and her men made their way toward the black tents of the Anazeh.
They spent the night on a grassy patch of plain near grazing herds of
camel, and in the sharp cold air of the early morning they saw the
encampment spread out before them. They counted a hundred and fifty
goatskin tents on the plain; as many more lay behind the green ridges
under a giant cliff. Arriving at the heart of the Anazeh camp, Gertrude
rode up to the largest tents, knowing they belonged to the reigning
sheikh. Dismounting, kneeling her camel in front of the Bedouin's
coffee tent, she hid her nervousness and strode confidently into the
quarters of Fahad Bey ibn Hadhdhal, Paramount Chief of the Anazeh.

The formidable leader of the desert's most aristocratic tribe,
Fahad Bey was an old man with a reputation for ruthlessness and the
badges of brutality to prove it. He wore an air of dignity, stemming in
part from his powerful position among the Anazeh, in part from the
palm fields he owned near Karbala and in part from the notable title
his father had won from the Turks. The sheikh was small and slim, his
beard bleached to snow, his face deeply browned from almost seventy
years in the sun. Beneath his robes he bore the wounds of a youthful
raid. A huge hole had been carved in his breast, the work of an enemy
lance that, thrust in his back, went straight through his chest. "No one
but an Arab of the desert could have recovered," Gertrude later wrote.

Spreading fine carpets on the ground, he motioned for her to sit.
She rested against a wooden camel saddle, watched by a falcon perched
behind Fahad Bey and by a greyhound lying beside him. While servants
brought them thick coffee and dates, she and the Arab talked. He asked
if Iraq was quiet and she answered no, describing the uneasiness with
the Turks. They discussed the city of Basrah in southern Iraq and its
well-known politician, the ruthless Sayid Talib. And then Fahad Bey
questioned her more closely. Why did she want to travel? he asked.
"There is lying among Islam," he continued, "but not among the English. Tell me the truth. Why do so many travelers come into the

desert. Is it for profit or for industries?" She told him it was for knowledge and curiosity. He could not believe it, he said. The traveler "might die"; "it was dangerous"; "it was toilsome." But she insisted that the English made no profit from the desert. They did not like to sit at home much; they liked to see the world. *"Sadaq,"* she said, "believe me." *"Sadaq,"* he answered, "I believe you."

He showed her his harem, the long tent where the women stayed, and introduced her to his latest wife and their children. They posed and she took their picture. Later in the day she rallied her servants and went off to take the measure of an ancient site. While they were on the way back to camp, the skies blackened and the heavens poured hail-stones and rain. After the storm passed, Fahad Bey came to her tents, and his servants prepared the best meal she had ever been served by an Arab sheikh. They dined on roast lamb stuffed with curried rice, and on bread, yogurt and meat patties resting on a pile of rice.

Afterward they drank coffee and smoked, and she gave him news of the Naqib and other acquaintances in Baghdad and Basrah and an-swered more of his questions about the mood in the cities and the feelings about the Turks. She filled him with information from the European capitals and tickled him with gossip, from the salons of Constantinople to the palace inside Hayil. When she left the next day he urged her to take an escort. She was touched by his kindness, but she had no idea how important an ally he would become.

∞ ∞ ∞

Only a few days later another fierce storm struck the desert. "Ma-licious scuds of rain" hit the earth, she wrote, and in her diary she asked Dick, "Do you remember Shelley's song to the Spirit of Delight?

> *"I love snow and all those forms of the radiant frost*
> *I love wind and rain storms, anything almost*
> *That is Nature's and may be*
> *Untouched by man's misery."*

On the morning of May 1 she arrived in Damascus, too weary even to celebrate the sight of the vineyards and orchards. She had never felt so tired. She went to sleep early and slept for an hour or two, but her mind was filled with camels marching across her dreams. During her stay in the city she heard frightening news from Hayil. The Emir's uncle, Ibrahim, had been murdered, his throat slit with a sword.

Word came from Constantinople that Sir Louis Mallet welcomed a meeting with her. He would be interested in hearing what she had learned in Arabia.

Taking a boat from Beirut to Constantinople, she arrived four days later, at a time when the capital of the Ottoman Empire was in upheaval. The Young Turks—university students and young men from the military academy who had banded together in 1908 and forced the Sultan, Abdul Hamid, to reinstate the constitution and then to resign—had only recently overthrown the War Ministry and taken control of the government. In addition, the seven-hundred-year-old empire, which once extended over Asia, Europe and Africa, had been greatly diminished.

The Turkish Government, riddled with corruption and bribery, was in dire financial straits. It had borrowed money to fight the Balkan Wars and depended upon loans from European countries to survive. The Germans had been particularly helpful, financing and constructing the important railway line from Berlin to Baghdad. But the aggressive German presence in the Middle East was threatening the British, who had always been concerned with protecting their routes to India.

Now Britain's interest in the region had become even greater. Its unrivaled navy delivered goods around the world and brought home three quarters of England's food supply. To maintain its superiority, in 1911 the First Lord of the Admiralty, Winston Churchill, had ordered a major change, switching the nation's battleships from coal-burning engines to oil. Far superior to the traditional ships, these new oil-burning vessels could travel faster, cover a greater range, and be refueled at sea; what's more, their crews would not be exhausted by having to refuel, and would require less manpower.

Britain had been the world's leading provider of coal, but she had no oil of her own. In 1912 Churchill signed an agreement for a major share in the Anglo-Persian Oil Company, with its oil wells in southern Persia and refineries at Abadan, close to Basrah. It was essential for Britain to protect that vital area, yet with the Ottoman Empire so weakened, the region was highly vulnerable, particularly susceptible to German-sponsored attack.

Gertrude was eager to report her findings on the desert Arabs to the British Ambassador in Constantinople. Despite British hopes that, should war break out, the Turks would remain neutral, suspicions were rife that Turkey might ally itself with Germany. She had seen with her own eyes how loose the Ottoman rule had become over the Arab tribes, and she believed that the British could take advantage of the situation. Well-informed friends had convinced her that the Arabs in Syria were

Gertrude Bell, aged three,
just after the death of
her mother in 1871.
(University of Newcastle)

Gertrude, aged eight, reading to her
bored brother, Maurice.
(University of Newcastle)

Gertrude, aged four, with her adored
father, Hugh Bell. "Obstacles are made
to be overcome," he often told her.
(University of Newcastle)

Gertrude, aged nine, and her brother,
Maurice, with their stepmother,
Florence Bell.
(University of Newcastle)

Gertrude,
aged sixteen,
before going away
to Queen's College
in London.
(University of Newcastle)

Billy Lascelles,
Gertrude's first love.
(University of Newcastle)

Gertrude with family and friends at Rounton after a game of lawn tennis.
Seated center: Gertrude, Hugh Bell. *To their left:* Molly Bell, Maurice Bell, Valentine
"Domnul" Chirol *(wearing sailor's cap)*, Gerald Lascelles, Florence Bell.
(University of Newcastle)

Vice-Consul Dick Doughty-Wylie with his wife,
Judith, in their garden in Konia, Turkey, July 1907.
Dick and Gertrude would become
more than just good friends.
(University of Newcastle)

Dick Doughty-Wylie, 1914.
Soldier, statesman,
poet, adventurer, he was
everything Gertrude
dreamed of in a man.
(University of Newcastle)

Gertrude, dressed in her cotton frock, with her servant Fattuh outside her tent in Turkey, June 1907. *(University of Newcastle)*

Gertrude taking measurements at her major archaeological discovery, Ukhaidir, Iraq, 1909. *(University of Newcastle)*

The high-columned
guest house at Hayil
where Gertrude was
kept prisoner, 1914.
(University of Newcastle)

Gertrude's caravan ready to leave the walled city of Hayil,
headquarters of Ibn Rashid, 1914. *(University of Newcastle)*

Gertrude Bell and Percy Cox give Arabian warrior Ibn Saud a royal tour of Basrah, November 1916. *(University of Newcastle)*

Hugh Bell reading the newspapers in the sitting room of Gertrude's house in Baghdad, 1920. *(University of Newcastle)*

Arnold T. Wilson, 1920.
Gertrude's main
adversary, he made life
difficult for her
in Baghdad.

Sir Percy Cox negotiating with Ibn Saud over
the border between Iraq and Kuwait, 1920.

Gertrude's servants
and her saluki dogs
stand in the walled
garden of her house
in Baghdad, 1920.
(University of Newcastle)

Gertrude
in her feathered hat and fur boa.
(University of Newcastle)

favorably disposed to British rule. She had heard, too, that in Arabia, the increasingly powerful Ibn Saud, who had spent his years in exile in Kuwait, an area friendly to the British, was eager to ally himself with England.

Sir Louis Mallet listened carefully. Intrigued by her story, he immediately wired Sir Edward Grey, the Foreign Secretary. He described her trip, her impressions of Ibn Rashid, what she had heard about Ibn Saud, and the limp rule of the Turks. There was not a shadow of authority, he noted; "the tribes under Ottoman rule were out of hand. Miss Bell's journey, which is in all respects a most remarkable exploit, has naturally excited the greatest interest here."

Rumors of Gertrude's adventures quickly spread around town, and acquaintances from earlier trips were eager to hear her tales. Her stay in Constantinople was brief, but she dined at the home of Philip Graves, a *Times* correspondent (his wife agape as Gertrude puffed away on a cigarette), and saw the newly married young diplomat Harold Nicolson and his pregnant wife, Vita Sackville-West.

But socializing was not Gertrude's desire, and on May 24, 1914, she was back in London, recipient of the prestigious gold medal from the Royal Geographical Society. Returning to Rounton, she sought only tranquillity, recuperating from the emotional and physical exhaustion of her trip. Yet in England, too, she found that life was in a state of flux: society was changing. During her absence, controversial books had been published: Proust had written *Swann's Way*, D. H. Lawrence had brought out *Sons and Lovers* and James Joyce produced *Portrait of the Artist as a Young Man*; George Bernard Shaw's boisterous play *Pygmalion* had opened at His Majesty's Theatre in April 1914, with its shocking line "Not bloodly likely" parroted across the nation. The Suffragists were still battling, but women had already been released from the bondage of whalebone and steel and were enjoying the freedom of elasticized brassieres. On a more somber note, the world was on the edge of turmoil, only two months away from war.

❧   ❧   ❧

While Gertrude rested at home, shattering news arrived in England: the heir to the Austro-Hungarian throne, Archduke Ferdinand, had been assassinated. The murder had taken place on June 28, 1914, in the Serbian capital of Sarajevo; the assassin, a Bosnian sympathetic to the Serbs' demand for independence. The incident, that "damned fool thing in the Balkans," was just the kind of spark that the German

Chancellor Otto von Bismarck, had predicted would inflame the world in war. The stunning event touched off a series of pacts and alliances that had been signed by the leaders of the major European nations.

The Anglo-French Entente of 1904 had allied England and France against the aggressive nation of Germany. It followed on the heels of the Anglo-Russian Convention of 1907, uniting England and Russia, two governments that were highly suspicious of each other but even more fearful of the Germans. And it wasn't just paranoia that made England, France and Russia sign a Triple Entente. War was "a biological necessity," proclaimed General Friedrich von Bernhardi, one of the leading German military thinkers. Germany now had the second most powerful navy in the world (Great Britain still had the first), and German businessmen and politicians licked their lips at the prospect of bigger markets, expanded territory and the possibility, as they saw it, of becoming the world's greatest power. The British, the French and the Russians all feared that war-hungry Germans would march across the Continent, both to the east and to the west, on their way to conquer the world.

The assassination of the Austro-Hungarian archduke brought an immediate reaction. Austria-Hungary, hoping to annex Serbia as she had annexed Bosnia and Herzegovina, declared war on Serbia. But Russia, which considered itself a Slavic nation, expressed outrage at the idea that the Slavic Serbs would be swept up into the Austro-Hungarian Empire. The Russian declaration of war touched off a German promise to come to the aid of Austria-Hungary. German mobilization, German forces pressing against the borders of France, and a German fleet prepared to enter the English Channel produced an angry response: France and England had no choice but to activate their forces and join together in the war against the Germans. By August 1, 1914, guns and cannons boomed across the Continent.

On the Eastern Front, the Turks soon allied themselves with the Germans. The British Government was particularly concerned with protecting both its precious routes to India and its petroleum fields in the Persian Gulf, now susceptible to enemy aggression. Gertrude, once the bane of British officials, became a source of vital information about the East. She was asked for a full report on what she had learned in Syria, Iraq and Arabia, and on September 5, 1914, she sent her assessment to the director of Military Operations in Cairo, who immediately passed it on to Foreign Secretary Sir Edward Grey:

> Syria [she wrote], especially Southern Syria, where Egyptian prosperity is better known, is exceedingly pro-English. I was told last winter by a very clever German

named Loytved, an old friend of mine now at Haifa, that
it would be impossible to exaggerate the genuine desire of
Syria to come under jurisdiction. And I believe it. . . .

On the whole I should say that Iraq would not willingly see Turkey at war with us and would take no active
part in it. But out there, the Turks would probably turn
their attention to Arab chiefs who had received our protection. Such action would be extremely unpopular with
the Arab Unionists who look on Sayid Talib of Basrah,
[the sheikh of] Kuweit, and Ibn Saud, as powerful protag-
onists. Sayid Talib is a rogue, he has had no help from us,
but our people (merchants) have maintained excellent
terms with him. Kuweit depends for his life on our help
and he knows it. Ibn Saud is most anxious to get some
definite recognition from us and would be easy to secure
as an ally. I think we could make it pretty hot for the
Turks in the Gulf.

Her report was studied with deliberation at both the War Office
and the Foreign Office in London and at Military Intelligence in Cairo.
In Europe the battles were already raging; in another few weeks, Britain,
France and Russia would be at war against the Turks. Now, in September 1914, even before the men who ran the government had decided on
their policy toward the Ottomans, Gertrude presented them with a
strong recommendation to organize the Arabs in a revolt against the
Turks. She wanted desperately to be on the scene in the East. But for
more than a year she was refused permission; the area was considered
too dangerous for a female. Being a woman was a major obstacle.

CHAPTER FOURTEEN

A Tragic End

∞

In the seaside town of Boulogne, France, Gertrude rented a room in a small hotel and settled into a daily routine, taking a brisk walk each morning near the water, then hurrying along the cobblestone streets to 36 bis Rue Victor Hugo. Her work was at the Red Cross; the call of the suffragists (for and against) had been blotted out by the cries of war. Like many, she had volunteered to help and followed her friend Flora Russell to France.

She found her office dreary and choked with papers, and try as she might to cover over the drabness with wallcloth and chintz, or brighten it with jars of fresh lilac and narcissus, the job itself was too gloomy to allow much room for cheer. Each day was a painful struggle to trace soldiers who were wounded or lost in battle. From nine in the morning to nine at night, and sometimes later, she filed and indexed names and corresponded with the families of missing soldiers. Heart-rending letters from parents drove her to search for their loved ones. Often the task was impossible—their sons were missing or, worse, no longer alive—but she wrote to the families, gently, struggling to find any good news to report. And by Christmas 1914 she had taken charge of the office and reorganized the files.

It was only a way of marking time. She still ached for Dick, and no amount of work could numb the pain of being apart from him. He remained at his post in Ethiopia, and although her family encouraged her to return to Rounton, Gertrude rejected the notion of going home without him. "I shall not come to England for the present," she wrote to Domnul. "At any rate I can work here all day long—it makes a little plank across the gulf of wretchedness over which I have walked this long time. Sometimes even that comes near to breaking point."

If she wished to be anywhere else, it was in the East. The Turks were now in alliance with Germany (despite attempts by the British Government to neutralize them), and by December 1914, British troops in Egypt were prepared for a Turkish attack on the Suez Canal. In Mesopotamia, a fleet of forty-seven troop transports—the largest ever—sent from India, had already seized the vital city of Basrah from the Turks, and the British army was now on its way to try to take Baghdad as well. Only a few months before, Gertrude had felt so at home in Iraq; now there seemed to be no place for her out there. She wrote to Domnul, who was traveling through the Orient: "If only I were arriving in Mesopotamia at this moment! I do so long to hear of the occupation of Baghdad. You will see there will be little opposition. . . . I pine for details."

What details she did hear were the grisly fragments of the bloody tapestry of war. At her desk in the dreary office or over lunch at the cafés in town where some of the soldiers gathered, she listened to wrenching stories about the men at the front. They are "knee-deep in water in the trenches, the mud impassable," she reported. "They sink in it up to the knee, up to the thigh. When they lie down in the open to shoot they cannot fire because their elbows are buried in it to the wrist." Although the women who worked for the Red Cross were not allowed at the local hospital, Gertrude talked her way in and saw the horrors: adolescent soldiers, too innocent to grasp what the bombs had blown away, missing arms or legs or blinded by shrapnel. "A happier New Year," she wished her parents on January 1, 1915. She celebrated the evening at work at her desk, pausing only to eat some chocolates.

A few doors down from the office, in her small room at the Hôtel Meurice, she spent most nights overwrought, reading letters. A note from Dick arrived, filling her with ardor, and she answered feverishly:

"Dearest dearest," she wrote, "I give this year of mine to you and all the years that shall come after it. Will you take it, this meagre gift—the year and me and all my thought and love. . . . You fill my cup, this shallow cup that has grown so deep to hold your love and mine.

Dearest when you tell me you love me and want me still, my heart sings—and then weeps for longing to be with you. I have filled all the hollow places of the world with my desire for you; it floods out, measured to creep up the high mountains where you live. And when you walk in your garden I think it touches your feet. No, don't thank me. Take your own, hold it and keep it—fold me into your heart."

As poetic as her words were, his were filled with lust and wanting. But in his own crude way he tried to respond to her fears. "Is sex so much?" he asked, "and the senses and the contact and those bewildering things. They can be much—but not the best, they are only the landscape, the other thing is the sun we see it by—You once said you would still love me if I had a dozen wives—they would not matter—and that is true my dear that thing you knew by sunlight. . . . it's not a great thing sex—not really—it's always grossly overrated like chastity—which is only the faint beginning of a virtue and often a positive view. . . ."

"Ah Dick love me," she answered. "I live only for you."

∞　　∞　　∞

And then, like a starving waif suddenly handed a box filled with chocolates, she turned from despair to joy. Dick was coming back from Ethiopia. He would probably stop in France before going on to England to receive new orders, he wrote, but it was his wife whom he would see in Boulogne (ironically, Judith was working in the same city as a nurse). Never mind: there was no reason for concern; Judith would not leave her work, he reassured Gertrude, urging her to be with him in London.

Thrilled with the news, she left for England in mid-February so that they could have four intoxicating days together. Seeing him, touching him, she was enraptured, more certain than ever that he was everything she ever wanted: intelligent and understanding, gentle and caring, protective and strong. She took refuge in his arms. As they embraced, her smoldering dreams of the last year burst into flame. His lips pressed against hers, and she melted against his soldier's muscular body. He told her she was life itself, a fire that burned with passion. He needed her. He hungered for her. She listened in ecstasy, and more than anything, she wanted to give herself to him. Willingly, she began to yield, but as she did, some force, even stronger than all the desire burning inside her, rose up and held her back. In a panic, she recoiled. Then once more the yearning and the lust overwhelmed her, and they embraced and kissed. But again the force rose up and held her back. At the end of their tryst their love remained unconsummated.

In agony, a few days later she wrote to him:

> Someday I'll tell you, I'll try to explain it to you—the fear, the terror of it—oh you thought I was brave. Understand me; not the fear of consequences—I've never weighed them for one second. It's the fear of something I don't know: no man can really understand it; you must know all about it because I tell you. Every time it surged up in me and I wanted you to brush it aside—it's only a ghost, the shadow of a ghost. But I couldn't say to you, Exorcise it. I couldn't. That last word I can never say. You must say it and break this evil spell. Fear is a horrible thing—don't let me live under the shadow of it. It's a shadow—I know it's nothing. . . . Only you can free me from it—drive it away from me, I know now, but till the last moment I didn't really know—can you believe it? I was terribly afraid. Then at the last I knew it was a shadow. I know it now.

Tormented, she continued:

> I can't sleep—I can't sleep. It's 1 in the morning of Sunday. I've tried to sleep, every night it becomes less and less possible. You and you are between me and any rest, but out of your arms there is no rest. Life, you called me—fire. I flame and live and am consumed. Dick it's not possible to live like this. When it's all over you must take your own. You must venture—is it I who must breathe courage into you, my soldier? Before all the world claim me and take me and hold me for ever and ever. . . . Furtiveness I hate—in the end I should go under, and hate myself and die. But openly to come to you, that I can do and live, what should I lose? It's all nothing to me; I breathe and think and move in you. Can you do it, dare you? When this thing is over, your work well done, will you risk it for me? It's that or nothing. I can't live without you. . . .
>
> The people who love me would stand by me if I did it that way—I know them. But not the other way. Not to deceive and lie and cheat and at the last be found out, as I

should be. Yet I shall do that too, use all the artifices and run to meet the inevitable end. . . . If it's honour you think of, this is honour and the other dishonour. If it's faithfulness you think of, this is faithfulness—keep faith with love. . . . Because I held up my head and wouldn't walk by diverse ways perhaps in the end we can marry. I don't count on it, but it would be better, far better for me. . . .

Now listen—I won't write to you like this any more . . . I've finished. If you love me take me this way—if you only desire me for an hour, then have that hour and I will have it and meet the bill. I've told you the price. Whatever happens, whatever you decide, I will come to you and have that—I'm not afraid of that other crossing. . . . But don't miss the camp fire that burns in this letter—a clear flame, a bright flame fed by my life.

⌘   ⌘   ⌘

Horrified, Gertrude found herself facing the one person she did not want to see; Dick's wife appeared in her office in Boulogne. The two women had corresponded since the days in Turkey, and now they lunched together, talking casually about their work. Judith gave no hint that she knew of the relationship between her friend and her husband, but the meeting took a terrible toll on Gertrude. She begged Dick to discourage his wife from coming again. "I hated it," she wrote him; "don't make me have that to bear." She was torn with regret and desire and guilt. "Don't forget me—you won't leave me? It's not possible. It's torture, eternal torture, which loses its edge. Oh my dear it might be ecstasy."

Over and over she wrestled with what had happened in England during those four exquisite, excruciating days; questioning what she had done, trying to reconcile her feelings with her own behavior. If pregnancy had once been a fear, it now seemed a blessing. Gertrude, for years an atheist, now suddenly sounded devout: "And suppose the other thing had happened, the thing you feared—that I half feared—must have brought you back. If I had it now, the thing you feared, I would magnify the Lord and fear nothing. . . . Not only the final greatest gift to give you—a greater gift even than love—but for me, the divine pledge of fulfilment, created in rapture, the handing on of life in fire, to be cherished and worshipped and lived for, with the selfsame ardour that cherishes and worships the creator."

✺   ✺   ✺

Her letters reached him while he was on his way to war. When Turkey announced its alliance with Germany, the British reacted at once. A campaign was organized by Winston Churchill, First Lord of the Admiralty, to cut off Turkish forces on their way to Baghdad: thirty thousand Australian troops were sent to make a surprise landing at Gallipoli. The purpose was to open the Dardanelles for the British navy, capture Constantinople, and provide supplies for allied Russian troops while cutting off Turkey from German assistance. Dick Doughty-Wylie, already familiar with the Turks from his days as vice-consul in Anatolia, and decorated for his heroic actions in saving Armenians from Turkish slaughter, was chosen as one of the British officers to lead the attack.

In mid-March 1915, as Dick made his way to the Dardanelles, Gertrude was asked to supply the War Office with her unpublished maps of Syria. By the end of the month she was in London, called back to brief officials about the East; and at the behest of her friend Lord Robert Cecil, the Red Cross director, she was organizing the main Red Cross office in England. Once again the days were long and tiring, and as she walked from her gray townhouse at 95 Sloane Street to Norfolk House, her office across Piccadilly, she was haunted by memories of Dick.

A letter arrived from Doughty-Wylie just as his troops were about to embark for Gallipoli, and she knew he still cared deeply: "So many memories my dear queen, of you and your splendid love and your kisses and your courage and the wonderful letters you wrote me, from your heart to mine—the letters, some of which I have packed up, like drops of blood."

For Gertrude their love was a genesis. On April 21 she revealed to him: " . . . there is an eternal secret between you and me. No one has known, no one will ever know, the woman who loves you. Mind and body, a different creature from her who walks the common earth before the eyes of men—new born and new fashioned out of our joined love. Only you know her and have seen her . . . you gave her life but I made her, bone by bone; having begotten her you may love her without fear. And you will."

✺   ✺   ✺

Little information came from the front. War Office censors blocked out reports that might even have hinted at events, and letters that

reached England were so blackened with ink that, except for the saluta-
tion and the signature, they were hardly legible. But at a dinner party
with friends on the first day of May 1915, a casual conversation brought
Gertrude shocking news of Gallipoli. The landing had not gone well.
British forces had been unable to carry off the surprise attack; as they
landed on the crescent of open beach, they were met by Turkish troops,
who riddled them with machine-gun and rifle fire. In the bloodbath
that followed, Dick Doughty-Wylie had been shot in the head and
killed.

Gertrude was stunned. Quickly and quietly, she left the table and
rushed off to see her sister Elsa. Months ago, Elsa had reassured her
that, in spite of the difficulties, Gertrude had kept her integrity and
done the right thing. Now, in the comfort of her sister's home, Gertrude allowed herself to weep.

∞ ∞ ∞

After a while the crying stopped and a calm seemed to come over
her, but a few minutes later she turned her head away, losing control
again. She had coped with death before: at the age of three she had lost
her mother; at twenty-five she had lost her fiancé, Henry Cadogan, and
by the age of thirty she had lost both her favorite aunt, Mary Lascelles,
and her closest school friend, Mary Talbot. But now the loss of Dick
Doughty-Wylie was more than she could bear. She had lost the greatest
gift that life had given her. She could hardly keep from speaking of
Dick, and she shared her secret with Domnul, Lord Robert, her sisters
Elsa and Molly, and her chum, Elizabeth Robins. No one revealed a
word. Yet there was no one among her friends or family who could give
her solace, and for days she refused to see anyone except Domnul. "I
can't, I can't bear the anguish of it, except alone," she wrote to Lisa
Robins.

∞ ∞ ∞

For a few brief days, Gertrude retreated to Rounton. For her, the
familiar lair in the northeast was always a place of respite, its gardens a
source of repair. It was her England, a bulwark graced by brushwood in
leaf, pear trees in blossom. It was home, and as her grandfather's friend
John Ruskin had written, "the place of peace; the shelter not only from
injury, but from all terror, doubt and division." In her childhood,

Rounton had been the home of her grandparents, a comforting place for a child who was forced to wear black at the age of three.

Now, with Hugh and Florence to console her, Gertrude tried to regain her strength. She seemed a little better, Florence noted to Lisa Robins, but she was still "speaking hopelessly of the situation." Florence had little tolerance for such an attitude: "It's no good doing that. It's the business of the women of England to say 'Never say die'—and to stiffen up the whole country by saying 'yes, it's very bad—but will be better.'" But Gertrude was in far too much pain to mouth platitudes.

On a day when Lisa came to Rounton, Gertrude strode with her across the moors. She confided to her friend how much Dick had wanted her to go away with him; his greatest sorrow had been that she had refused to live with him, even while he was married to Judith. Gertrude stopped for a moment and paused. Her throat wrapped in a pink scarf, her arms crossed, her face tense, she looked up and described a recent dream: "I was falling into that pit of blackness, piercing a sword against my breast—and going down, down, me and my sword. . . ."

CHAPTER FIFTEEN

Escape to the East

∞

The London skies turned more somber than usual in the autumn of 1915, clouded with enemy aircraft and spattered with enemy bombs. The sound of the German planes, rumbling over Hampstead on one September day, drew Gertrude's attention as she watched the raid from Elsa's balcony. "We saw nothing, but the bursting shells," she wrote to Florence. "I gather they didn't do much harm."

A few words hastily scribbled, her note showed neither fear nor a sense of relief. Gertrude, who had routinely composed lengthy, picturesque letters, was no longer able to express much feeling at all. She was numbed by the terrible loss of Dick. As her sister Molly wrote in her own diary: "It has ended her life—there is no reason now for her to go on with anything she cared for. . . . It is difficult to see how she can build up anything out of the ruins left to her. Hers is not a happy nor a kindly nature, and sorrow instead of maturing her mellow has dried up all the springs of kindliness."

Friends could offer little comfort, and as content as she once had felt in solitude, she now ached from isolation. "It is intolerable," Gertrude had written to Florence, "not to like being alone as I used, but I can't keep myself away from my own thoughts, and they are still more intolerable." England had become a place of heartbreak, its cold damp air clinging to her.

By November 1915, as the war against the Turks extended on the Eastern Front from Gallipoli to Mesopotamia, Gertrude was more anxious than ever to be back in the East. The people, the climate, the sense of urgency about the region all made her eager for a summons, but until now, it was considered too dangerous for a woman, and the Government had refused to let her go. Toward the middle of the month, however, she strode into work at Norfolk House and, rushing across the office, seized the arm of her friend Janet Hogarth, and drew her aside. "I've heard from David," she told his sister excitedly; "he says anyone can trace the missing but only I can map Northern Arabia. I'm going next week."

David Hogarth had written to Gertrude from Cairo, where he was in charge of gathering information for the office of Military Intelligence. The small espionage bureau, established only a year earlier, was staffed with a handful of political officers, archaeologists and journalists. Like Gertrude, they had previously supplied the Foreign Office with relevant details from their everyday work in the field. Now, with the growing momentum of war and an increasing need for information about the Arabs, Hogarth urged Reginald Hall, the Director of Naval Intelligence, to draft Gertrude as a spy.

She had waited impatiently for this moment; after more than a year of marking time, filling her hours with bureaucratic busy work, she could at last return to the part of the world that welcomed her as a Person. What's more, she would go not as an observer, but as a participant, not as a bothersome traveler but as a knowledgeable practitioner, indispensible now to the same British officials who had tried so hard two years before to prevent her journey to Arabia. Her traveling expenses would be paid, and she would be given a billeting allowance. "I think I'm justified in accepting that, don't you?" she asked her father.

In the house on Sloane Street, her maid Marie packed a steamer trunk with tunics and peg-topped skirts, satin corsets, knickers, petticoats and silk stockings, adding capes and coats for the cool Cairo evenings and parasols to protect her from the hot Egyptian sun. A week later, clothing, books and toiletries in order, Gertrude said farewell to Florence and Hugh, not knowing how long she would be away nor how far she would travel beyond Egypt. That was enough.

Her spirits high, she boarded the *SS Arabia* on November 19, 1915, and set sail from Southampton. Storms raged all the way from Marseilles to Port Said; the rough seas pitched the boat day and night, tossing it dangerously, turning most of the passengers green with seasickness. It was a "horrible journey," Gertrude confessed, but she survived "triumphantly." Five days later, on the night of Thursday, November 25, 1915, the ship reached Port Said. The following afternoon Gertrude arrived in Cairo, invigorated by the sight of her mentor, David Hogarth. By his side was his subordinate, the fair-haired, blue-eyed young man named T. E. Lawrence.

∞ ∞ ∞

"Gerty!" the young man exclaimed.

"My dear boy!" Gertrude called in return. Lawrence had come—sloppily dressed, as always, his belt missing and his buttons unpolished—to meet her carriage and welcome her to Egypt. A ride on the dusty streets took them through a blend of East and West—a Levantine atmosphere thriving with Bedouin Arabs, Turkish traders, Jewish merchants, Sudanese servants, British officials and soldiers recalled from Gallipoli—until they reached the fashionable quarter of Ismailiya and the Hotel Continental, where Hogarth and Lawrence were billeted.

Gertrude surveyed the luxurious gardens and sumptuous surroundings, a whimsical combination of English gingerbread and Oriental elegance, and glanced at the guests sipping mint tea on the swag-covered verandahs. Egyptian bellboys in long nightshirts took her luggage, and she settled into her room, a well-appointed suite with modern fittings, private bath and covered balcony. After changing into a gown, she joined the two men and went down to her first dinner as a Staff Officer on the Military Intelligence team. There was much to catch up on, and as Gertrude sipped her Turkish coffee and puffed on a cigarette, she filled them in on news from home while Hogarth outlined the work to be done and Lawrence amused her with gossip.

When morning came, she marched to the telegraph desk to pen an urgent message home: send at once my new white skirt and purple chiffon evening gown, she wrote. That done, she was keen to start her day.

The local office of Military Intelligence, soon to be renamed the Arab Bureau, was installed in three rooms at the nearby Savoy. In peacetime, the hotel rivaled Shepheard's as a stylish meeting spot for women as well as men, but now, as headquarters for the War Office, it had become a bastion of uniformed British males—khaki-clothed officers in high suede boots, swatting the air with fly sticks. Gertrude marched through the Savoy, tall and erect, her head topped with a feathered hat, her confidence overbrimming, but her high spirit was met with a stony reception. "The military people here are much put about how she is to be treated and to how much she is to be admitted," Hogarth had written to his wife a few days before Gertrude arrived. "I have told them but *she'll* settle that and they needn't worry!"

He was right; Gertrude was impervious. Ignoring their suspicions, she stared them down and plunged into work, and after months of severe depression, her old enthusiasm reappeared. She was in her element, surrounded by males, toiling like a schoolgirl and excelling at her assignment. She was no longer a deflated balloon, left on the floor of a party, but a bubble floating higher and higher over the heads of the guests. On November 30, 1915, only a few days after her arrival, she wrote to Florence excitedly, "It's great fun." That same day Hogarth sent another letter to his wife: "Gertrude . . . is beginning to pervade the place."

∽   ∽   ∽

If there were sidelong glances from the military, there were welcoming smiles from others. Most of the members of the Intelligence staff— "Intrusives," as they were code-named, for their unorthodox ways— were old acquaintances who had come to Cairo in December 1914 to carry out new jobs: Lawrence, who had been digging at Carchemish, was now making maps and writing geographical reports; Leonard Woolley, another Oxford archaeologist who had worked at Carchemish, was now in charge of propaganda for the press. Several people were her friends from the embassy in Constantinople: Wyndham Deedes was an expert on Turkish affairs and had received her report after the trip to Hayil; George Lloyd, a family friend and financial expert, had provided her years before with her most loyal Armenian servant, Fattuh; the *Times* correspondent Philip Graves, an authority on the Turks, had often invited her to his Constantinople home to dine. Still others she had met on her earliest travels: the brilliant Aubrey Herbert, who spoke at least seven languages, had lunched with her in Japan in 1903 when she was on a round-the-world trip; the pragmatic Mark Sykes, now on a fact-finding mission for the War Office, was the fellow adventurer she had first met in Jerusalem in 1905; the erudite Ronald Storrs had been Oriental Secretary in Egypt, a position he described as "the eyes, ears, interpretation and Intelligence . . . of the British Agent, and . . . much more." In charge of them all was General Gilbert Clayton, a fatherly figure who believed in an Arab revolt. He had been working on the idea since November 1914, when he encouraged the ruler of Asir, near Yemen, to rebel against the Turks.

The office bustled with activity: men rushed about, bells rang and the air was charged with excitement.

∞   ∞   ∞

On the Eastern Front, the war had begun with the battle at Gallipoli. It had been a strategic attempt to stave off the Turks before they could make two serious strikes: one at Egypt and the Suez Canal; the other at Mesopotamia (Iraq) and the nearby oil refineries in Abadan on the Persian Gulf. The interests of Military Intelligence in Cairo had centered, at first, on Gallipoli: on the size and whereabouts of the Turkish army in the Dardanelles, where the regiments were, how large they were, who commanded them and what ammunition they held. But with the British defeat at Gallipoli, the bureau's focus had soon shifted to Mesopotamia, Arabia and the Gulf.

Success depended upon help from the Arabs. Years earlier, Gertrude had scoffed at the notion of Arab unity and denied the idea of Arab nationalism. But several factors had brought a change in Arab attitudes and, with it, an incipient Arab nationalist movement. The increasing weakness of the Ottoman Empire had caused the Sultan to reclaim his role as Caliph, the chief religious leader of the Muslims, threatening the religious leaders in Arabia. Concerned about competition from the Arabs, the Sultan had even exiled the Sharif Hussein, custodian of the holy places in Mecca and Medina and supervisor of the holy pilgrimage, to Constantinople. In addition, the desperate state of the Ottoman economy had resulted in higher taxation and deep inflation for the Arabs, while at the same time the thinly spread Ottoman army, engaged in too many costly wars, had relied on compulsory recruitment of Arabs. In Constantinople the Turkish reformers had forced a "Turkification" of the Ottoman world: Turkish rather than Arabic became the official language, angering the masses throughout the empire who spoke Arabic, the students and scholars who used Arabic as the language of education and the Muslims who considered Arabic the language of Islam. The reformers banned new political and ethnic organizations and shut down existing non-Turkish clubs, causing more resentment and pushing the Arab activists underground. Now that England was at war with the Turks, the Arab nationalists were a potential ally against the Ottomans.

In fact, the Arab tribes were torn between aligning themselves with the Turks (who, though they were unpopular occupiers, were also fellow Muslims) or the British (who represented a new rule but were, unfortunately, Christian infidels). There was even fear that the Arabs might call for a holy war against the British and the French. Nonetheless, if Military Intelligence could find the right Arabs—strong leaders, eager for independence and sympathetic to the British—they could pull off a rebellion against the Turks. The idea had been floating around for a while. In February 1914, a son of the Sharif Hussein of Mecca had arrived in Cairo to pay a call on the British Agent, Lord Kitchener, to test his support for an Arab revolt. Kitchener made no promises, but that same year Gertrude saw the importance of such a revolt when, in September 1914, after her trip to Hayil, she wrote in her official report, "I think we could make it pretty hot for the Turks in the Gulf."

The key to success was information.

For a while T. E. Lawrence had been assigned the task of collecting data on the Arab tribes. The Intelligence bureau had knowledge of the Arabs of Western Arabia and the Hejaz, where the Sharif Hussein was in control of six hundred thousand members of the Harb confederation; but they had few details on the tribes in Iraq, the Gulf, or the Nejd. Gertrude was a formidable expert, more knowledgeable about the personalities and politics of the Arabs in Northern and Central Arabia than anyone else (and the last European to have visited that region), not to mention—thanks to her six long desert treks—her familiarity with the tribes of Syria and Mesopotamia. As Mr. Lorimer, the British representative in Baghdad, said, he had "never known anyone more in the confidence of the nations" than Gertrude.

Now, seated at a desk in Hogarth's office, she quickly began to fill in the missing pieces in the files. Within a few weeks she was given an office of her own and took over the tribal work, while Lawrence was "mostly writing notes on railways, & troop movements, & the nature of the country everywhere, & the climate, & the number of horses or camels or sheep or fleas in it . . . and then drawing maps showing all these things."

With papers strewn everywhere, her ashtray overflowing, Gertrude worked till seven each night cataloguing the Arab clans. Her talent for detail proved invaluable: she recorded everything she knew about the tribes and the desert, recalling the campsites, the water wells, the railway lines, the topography and the terrain; she noted the tribes' numbers, their lineage and their sheikhs; she analyzed their personalities and assessed their political alliances. There were some who were feuding and others who were rivalrous friends; some who could be trusted and others who could not; some whose strength was waning and others who were on the rise. There were some, she wrote, like the weakened Ibn Rashid, whose territory ran close to the Mesopotamian borders, whose purse was filled by the Turks and whose headquarters, Hayil, had once been the center of operations for Ottoman influence in Arabia. And there were Ibn Saud and the Sharif Hussein of Mecca, who were now "the most powerful chiefs in Arabia," but whose authority over the desert was personal and fleeting, never permanent, and whose regard for each other was filled "with jealous anxiety."

Much of what she recorded she knew from personal experience, and what she did not know she learned by interviewing Arab nationalists who came to the office in search of British backing. "They come up and sit with me by the hour," she explained in an uncensored letter to Lord Robert Cecil, who was now Parliamentary Under Secretary for Foreign Affairs. With their help she corrected the names of places, people and tribes, and in the course of conversation she heard about "remote people and near people who were little but shadows before." Some of the nationalists were from Arabia and followers of the Sharif Hussein; some, like Aziz al Masri, lived in Egypt and were determinedly anti-Turk; others, such as the wily Sayid Talib of Basrah, the brazen Sharif Muhammad al Faroki, the sophisticated Nuri Said, and the military expert Jafar al Askari were Mesopotamians, officers of the Ottoman army who had created a secret Iraqi society against the Turks. For Gertrude, to talk with them was a taste of earlier travels, and she relished the discussions. "It is great fun," she wrote.

Her mornings entailed an hour session with an Arabic tutor, "a charming little man," who sat with her on the balcony as they read and practiced conversation, chatting about people and places they knew. The rest of her day she spent at the office, but only a week after she arrived in Cairo, she wrote disappointedly to Florence, "Mr. Hogarth leaves tomorrow, to my great sorrow. He has been a most friendly support." She favored quiet meetings with colleagues, and in the evenings, when she returned to her hotel, there were others to sit with at dinner, especially T. E. Lawrence. "Usually I dine here with Col. Wright, Mr. Lawrence and a party of people," she noted in her first letter home; "we all share the same table."

Although they came from opposite social strata—she, a scion of one of England's most prominent families; he, a bastard from the lower middle class—Gertrude and Lawrence were much alike. Oddities, and out of the mainstream, both were loners who felt more at ease in the empty desert than in the crowded drawing room. To them, the Bedouin were more accepting than the British. As Gertrude had written earlier: "You will find in the East . . . a wider tolerance born of greater diversity . . . the European may pass up and down the wildest places, encountering little curiosity and of criticism even less. The news he brings will be heard with interest, his opinions will be listened to with attention, but he will not be thought odd or mad, nor even mistaken, because his practices and the ways of his thought are at variance with those of the people among whom he finds himself." Her words described herself and Lawrence.

As protégés of Hogarth, Gertrude and Lawrence saw eye to eye on the East. Over their evening meal, they conspired about the Sharif Hussein and how to keep him in line; abhorred the French and talked about how to limit their role in Syria; worried about the government in India and how to convince it to support a desert revolt by the Arabs; and concurred over the feuds between the Foreign Office, the War Office, the India Government and their own Cairo bureau. Because of the censors, little of their conversations reached home.

∞   ∞   ∞

Despite the disastrous battle at Gallipoli, the war now going on in Mesopotamia and the constant threat of a Turkish attack on the Suez Canal, an eerie air of celebration surrounded Cairo; its inhabitants were like children at play, oblivious of the anxieties of the adult world. Prosperous civilians and smart-looking officers entertained themselves on the tennis courts, the polo grounds or the racetrack of the Sporting Club; Wednesday evenings meant dances at the Majestic Hotel, and every night there were lavish dinners at Shepheards or stylish parties at home. Cairo was exhilarating. Henry McMahon, the British Resident, and his "charming [and] agreeable" wife even extended Gertrude a standing invitation to dine with them whenever she liked.

When she visited and gave Sir Henry her unequivocating advice, they mostly talked about an Arab revolt against the Turks. Since June 1915, six months after he arrived in Cairo to replace Lord Kitchener, Sir Henry McMahon, with the help of the Arab Bureau, had been corresponding with the Sharif Hussein of Mecca. The Sharif was one of the three most powerful men in Arabia—the others being Ibn Rashid and Ibn Saud—his territory of the Hejaz extending across the western region of Arabia and including the holy cities of Mecca and Medina as well as the thriving port of Jeddah and the mountain resort of Taif. As a descendant of the Prophet Muhammad and guardian of Mecca, the Sharif Hussein was the most important religious figure of the three Arabian chiefs, and thus a welcome ally for the British. Letters and messages had been flying through the desert since Kitchener's time, and now McMahon was floating bubbles, negotiating the terms of an alliance in which, with the help of British funds and support, the Sharif

Hussein planned to strike against the Turks. In return for his help, the British made vague promises of an Arab kingdom after the war. As a show of good intentions, McMahon had already sent the Sharif a down payment of twenty thousand pounds.

"The negotiations with the Sharif have . . . been very skilfully conducted," Gertrude wrote knowingly to Lord Robert Cecil. Indeed, so skillful were they that the precise extent of British promises to the Sharif became the subject of bitter controversy for many years between Arab nationalists and British colonialists. But Gertrude was concerned about the Sharif Hussein. "From all the information that comes in he seems to have acquired a very remarkable position in Arabia, but his strength is moral, not military," she argued, and suggested that Hussein's rival Ibn Saud should also be drawn to the British side. At her insistence and upon the advice of others, the British put Ibn Saud on the payroll, at almost ten thousand pounds a month. By the end of the war he would defeat Ibn Rashid at Hayil, and by 1925 he would dethrone the Sharif Hussein and rule all of Arabia.

Nurtured by its British nannies in Cairo, an Arab uprising was in the air, coming closer to reality, but "meanwhile," she noted to Lord Robert, two troublesome factors stood in the way: the French, who controlled much of Syria; and India, whose Viceroy controlled British troops in Mesopotamia and the Gulf and who did not wish to see a war in Arabia.

McMahon's oblique letters suggested to the Sharif Hussein that he would have a kingdom extending from the parts of Arabia he already controlled to Mesopotamia and most of Greater Syria, including all of TransJordan and some of Palestine. But the British knew they did not have the authority to hand over these areas to the Sharif without the French having a say. Since the days of the Crusades, France had established and maintained strong political and commercial ties in Syria in the *vilayets* of Aleppo, Damascus and Beirut.

While Sir Henry McMahon was drawing a blurry picture of a future Arab kingdom, Mark Sykes was smoothing the way for a future pact between the British and the French. He had been sent by the Foreign Office in the summer of 1915 on a six-month trip to the region to assess the feelings toward a postwar Arab state. Gertrude and Lawrence tried to convince Sykes that the French should be given only a minimum of territory.

Just back from a tour of the Middle East and India, Sykes talked to Gertrude for hours, as they discussed the Arabs and their sentiments toward both the British and the French. Sykes agreed with Gertrude "that the Arabs can't govern themselves," she wrote to Lord Robert;

"no one is more aware of that than I." But she believed that the Arabs would be dependent upon the British and would willingly approach them for advice on running their new state after the war. Her major concern was the French. She believed that the French would ignore the Arabs' needs and thus provoke them, risking the possibility of a future Arab war against the West. She tried hard to convince Sykes that, on the heels of eventual victory, France should be given only a corner of northern Syria, along with the mostly Christian area of Lebanon. In spite of her efforts, however, by the time he returned to England in December 1915, Sykes was prepared to agree with a French official, François-Georges Picot. Picot demanded that Syria, from the Mediterranean to the Tigris, be given to France.

In the area of Mesopotamia—which included Basrah and Baghdad—however, Sykes agreed with Gertrude. There the Arab nationalists could help in defeating the Turks, but it was the British Government in India, not the administration in Egypt, that had political and military authority over Mesopotamia and Arabia.

∞   ∞   ∞

In November 1914, the India Expeditionary Force D had been sent to seize Basrah from Turkish troops, and, having succeeded, was now under the command of General Townshend, battling its way to Baghdad. Sykes's mission in Delhi had been to try to convince the Viceroy, Lord Hardinge, to support and finance an Arab revolt, which would lead to a future Arab kingdom, including Mesopotamia. But Hardinge considered the revolt a dangerous idea. Great Britain was the largest Muslim empire in the world. Its tens of millions of Indian Muslims were members of the Sunni sect; their holy leader, the Caliph, was the Sultan of Turkey. Hardinge worried that the Indian Muslims under his domain, who were not Arabs, would be unsympathetic to an Arab rebellion against the Sunni Muslim Turks, and that they would be angered by any turmoil near the Muslim holy sites. He refused to support an Arab movement.

But what upset him even more was that McMahon promised to give Mesopotamia to the Sharif Hussein. The port of Basrah was of vital interest to the British. It was a strategic point from which the British guarded the Persian oil fields and the installations at Abadan, the largest oil refineries in the world; in addition, Basrah served as a strategic link on the route to India. Furthermore, the city of Baghdad, where the British had been established since the 1600s, was an impor-

tant commercial center and involved all of their trade in the Gulf. To
the British officials in the service of the India Government, the Arabists
in Cairo were creating a "Frankenstein Monster."

The British Government of India wanted to annex Mesopotamia.
Furious with his Cairo colleagues, Viceroy Hardinge lashed out in a
letter to the Foreign Office: "I devoutly hope that this proposed Arab
State will fall to pieces, if it is ever created. Nobody could possibly
have devised a scheme more detrimental to British interests in the
Middle East than this. It simply means misgovernment, chaos and
corruption, since there never can be and never has been any consistency
or cohesion among the Arab tribes. . . . I cannot tell you how detrimental I think this interference and influence from Cairo have been."

By the end of 1915 the Arab Bureau was desperate. The British
administration in Egypt and the British Government in India eyed each
other as rivals: Cairo was in charge of Egypt and the Sudan; India was
in charge of overseeing the sheikhdoms and emirates of the Persian
Gulf. Both governments toyed with the question of who would control
the future Middle East. The India Government wanted to maintain its
authority in Arabia and to annex Iraq; the Egypt administration wanted
to create an Arab kingdom extending from Arabia to Iraq, over which
the British would have influence but far less control and, presumably, at
far less cost.

There was little communication between Cairo and Delhi, and the
telegrams that were sent were not much more than brusque formalities.
In a letter to her father, sent by diplomatic pouch, Gertrude wrote:
"There is a great deal of friction between India and Egypt over the
Arab question which entails a serious want of co-operation between the
Intelligence Departments of the two countries and the longer it goes on
the worse it gets."

In order to move ahead with their plans for an Arab uprising, Cairo
needed Hardinge's support. The Viceroy alone could provide the men,
the money and the arms. There was only one person who could possibly persuade Hardinge to change his mind. Gertrude had known Hardinge since her youthful trip to Bucharest when both he and Domnul
came to visit her uncle, Ambassador Frank Lascelles. Now, with
Domnul, a close friend of Hardinge's, in India working on a special
project for the government, she was encouraged by her chief, General
Clayton, to pay him a call.

"So I'm going," she wrote to her father. "I feel a little nervous
about being the person to carry it out . . . but the pull one has in
being so unofficial is that if one doesn't succeed no one is any the
worse."

∞ ∞ ∞

"I'm off finally at a moment's notice to catch a troop ship at Suez," she wrote on January 24, 1916, hardly betraying her anxiety; "I really do the oddest things." The *SS Euripides* was crowded with military men, two battalions of soldiers on their way to India. "The cat and I are the only two people not in uniform," she scrawled to Florence. The five-day cruise ended in Karachi; from there, she took the railway line to Delhi. She arrived, coated in dust on an icy cold morning; Domnul, still red-haired but plumper, was waiting on the platform.

Taking her in an official car, Domnul motored with her to her quarters, a luxurious tent with a sitting room, bedroom and bathroom, and stayed to talk while she breakfasted. A short while later the Viceroy appeared. Gertrude curtsied and launched her case. "He is very anxious that I should return to somewhere in the neighbourhood of my old hunting grounds," she wrote home excitedly, referring to Iraq.

After lunch at the Viceroy's residence, she presented him with a memorandum on what she felt she could do to improve relations between India and Egypt. For all his power as head of India, Hardinge was out of the loop. Actions were being taken and policies set in Cairo without his consultation. He was eager for better communications, and with his help she set to work, meeting with officials from India Intelligence headquartered in Simla, digging through Intelligence dossiers to add information to her tribal report, working with officials in India Foreign Affairs, using every opportunity to argue for support of an Arab revolt. She found them "curiously eager to talk—much more than I expected," and was asked by India Intelligence to serve as an editor for a publication they were compiling, a Gazetteer of Arabia. After three weeks she deemed her visit a success, writing proudly to her father: "I think I have pulled things straight a little as between Delhi and Cairo." In another note she added, "It is essential India and Egypt should keep in the closest touch since they are dealing with two sides of the same problem."

But her greatest interest was in Mesopotamia. In a note to Captain Hall, the Director of Naval Intelligence, she wrote: "I remember your putting your finger on the Bagdad corner of the map and saying that the ultimate success of the war depended on what we did there. You are one of the people who realised how serious are the questions we have to face."

Whatever happened, the British needed Iraq. Its huge grain supplies could feed the army, its proximity to oil could fuel the navy, and its location put it at the center of the land route to India. Mesopotamia, it was hoped, would be the place where the British could stave off the Turks by setting the Arabs against the Ottoman army. At the end of February 1916, Gertrude bade farewell to Domnul and Hardinge, and, having established a new line of communication between India and Egypt, with the Viceroy's blessing she set sail for Basrah.

From its position at the head of the Gulf, near the convergence of Iraq, Kuwait, Arabia and Persia, few places served as better listening posts, and few people were better equipped to listen than Gertrude. For the next few weeks, she was told by Hardinge, her mission was to gather information from the Arabs and to act as a liaison between British Intelligence in Cairo and India Intelligence in Delhi.

She would be the eyes, the ears, the lips and the hands of Great Britain, watching, listening, talking to and stroking the Arabs of Iraq. It would be her job to convince the Arab tribes to cooperate with the British. But she would be working without an official position.

CHAPTER SIXTEEN

A Remarkably Clever Woman

∞

The British troop transport steamed across the Indian Ocean, leaving behind the warm, muggy weather of Karachi, sailing north into the milder temperatures of the Persian Gulf. Past its ally of Kuwait it went, past the freshwater port where in 1899 the Sheikh had signed a protective treaty with the British; past Abadan, bowing to the refinery of the Anglo-Persian Oil Company, whose oil was used mostly for British warships; past Muhammerah, salaaming the friendly sheikhdom to the east. The steamer had entered the yellow waters of the Shatt al Arab, the narrow river uniting the Tigris and the Euphrates and linking the Gulf to Basrah, the vital Mesopotamian port.

From the rail of the ship Gertrude watched the shoreline as familiar groves of date-filled palm trees floated by, followed by Arab huts and mud-walled gardens graced with apricot trees. For thousands of years the river banks were home to people who had learned to harness the floods and enjoy the rice, barley, wheat, corn, dates and cotton yielded by the fruitful soil. "No doubt it was to the fertility of the country that earliest civilisation owed its existence," Gertrude wrote when she first explored these shores. Close to here Adam and Eve had dwelled in the Garden of Eden, the Ark of Noah had been constructed, the Tower of Babel built, Babylonia had thrived and the Sumerians had invented the written form of language. By the medieval era, a string of conquerors had dispatched their soldiers to this land of *The Thousand and One Arabian Nights*: first the early Muslims, then Abbasids, then Seljuks ruled, only to be quashed in 1258 by the maniacal Mongol Hulagu, grandson of Genghis Khan, who not only demolished Baghdad, murdered the intellectuals and destroyed the Islamic Caliph, but laid waste to the lands and ravaged the ancient system of irrigation. It was nearly three hundred years later, in 1534, that Suleiman the Magnificent brought Iraq into the Ottoman sphere.

For Gertrude the key word of Iraq was "romance. Wherever you look for it you will find it. The great twin rivers, gloriously named, the huge Babylonian plains, now desert which were once a garden of the world; the story stretching back into the dark recesses of time—they shout romance."

∞   ∞   ∞

On the morning of March 3, 1916, Gertrude stepped carefully onto the slip at Basrah, holding her long skirts with one hand, her hat with the other, dodging the black flies and the swarms of mosquitoes that buzzed around. Along the waterfront she caught sight of the odd Basrah houses made of yellow baked bricks, their latticed wooden balconies leaning out like busybodies over the mud streets mobbed with Arabs. She was glad to see it again, she scrawled in a note to her father soon after she arrived: "I feel as if I were in my own country once more, and welcome it, ugly though it is." Still, she was concerned, unsure about her assignment and uneasy about what kind of welcome she would receive. Would they find a job for her or would they send her away at once? "Now it remains to be seen," she wrote apprehensively.

In Delhi and Cairo, the Great War had seemed far removed, but in Basrah the reverberations of battle still shook the city. Seized from the enemy in November 1914, the Turkish *vilayet*, the governmental province of thirty-three thousand local Arabs, was now a British Occupied Territory, thick with thousands of British soldiers and ruled by military decree. Sir Percy Cox, the Chief Political Officer—"a very big person," Gertrude noted to her father—was on a visit to India Government headquarters in Bushire, but a warm greeting awaited her nonetheless. With few British wives in Basrah and almost no one to talk to, Lady Cox, whom Gertrude had met before, giddily showed her around their old Arab house and invited her to stay.

When morning came, Gertrude set off, decked out in her petticoats, stockings, dress and hat, through the palm gardens and across the irrigation canals, to present herself at General Headquarters. There, in the large brick building set along a canal, she introduced herself to Colonel Beach, in charge of Military Intelligence, and renewed her friendship with Campbell Thompson, last seen in Carchemish and now Beach's assistant in charge of decoding Turkish telegrams. They both were very welcoming, Gertrude reported to Florence, but the rest of the staff could hardly bother to hide their disgust.

Hardinge had sent her to Basrah with a fuzzy task. She had no specific job or title, nor was she even on the military payroll. To the rigid male world of India Expeditionary Force D, Miss Bell, as she would be known, was a flighty meddler, not to be allowed to interfere. She was lectured on military rules, told that her mail would be strictly censored and was limited on where she could go and what she could do; the woman who had entered the tents of scores of desert sheikhs was ordered not to visit any native homes without a chaperone. Gertrude stamped out her cigarette and listened impatiently.

She was to act as the informational link between Delhi and Cairo, contributing what she could on the Indian side for the Arab gazetteer, rousing support on the Egyptian side for an Arab revolt. But the Basrah military (attached to the Indian forces) had already shown their contempt for Cairo's ideas. "I should like to see it announced that Mesopotamia was to be annexed to India as a colony for India and Indians," Captain Arnold T. Wilson had written more than a year earlier, in November 1914, "that the Government of India would administer it, and gradually bring under cultivation its vast unpopulated desert plains, peopling them with martial races from the Punjab." The headstrong Wilson, Sir Percy Cox's second-in-command, was hardly ready to accept Miss Bell or any notions she carried with her from Cairo.

At least Colonel Beach cooperated. With his help Gertrude was given access to the Intelligence files for her research on the gazetteer. But with so many military personnel in Basrah, there was hardly space to set up a desk. Instead, for the first few days she was handed the tribal material, names and places that had become so much a part of her life, and was shoehorned alongside Mr. Thompson in Colonel Beach's bedroom—"a plan," she noted dryly, "which is not very convenient either for us or for him."

At teatime she joined the Political Officers—among them the handsome H. St. John Philby and the tall, dark-eyed A. T. Wilson—immersing them at once in a pool of gossip. She filled them with fresh news from Cairo, and dished up tidbits of the negotiations between Sir

Henry McMahon and the Sharif Hussein. "She had plenty to say for herself," St. John Philby remarked in his memoirs.

Later in the evening in her room at the Coxes', Gertrude sent off a reassuring note. "I think it's going to be exceedingly interesting," she wrote cheerfully to her father. "I'm now looking for a servant—oh, for Fattuh!" she moaned. "It's delicious weather but what Basrah is like! Frogs and mud are the sum of my general impressions; muddy stagnant creeks and crowds of Arabs—but I like it!"

For several days her routine remained the same, and then on March 8, Sir Percy Cox returned. She had met him before, in 1902 in India, and in 1909 at the home of their mutual friends the Ritchies, when Sir Percy had cautioned her strongly not to go to Arabia, not to attempt a visit to Ibn Rashid or Ibn Saud. Taking his advice, she had, instead, made the trip across the Syrian desert that led her to Ukhaidir. As disheartening as it had been to hear Cox then, it was only slightly more reassuring to see him now.

Dressed in army officer's uniform, but with the white tabs on his collar to mark him Political, Cox was fifty-one, four years older than Gertrude, tall, thin and distinguished-looking, with wavy silver hair, a firm jaw, large crooked nose and blue eyes that met hers directly. Known to be a cool, dispassionate soldier-statesman, he had been educated at Harrow and Sandhurst, had served in the region for nearly a decade as Agent for the Government of India and had won the respect of Arabs and British alike. He knew, of course, of Gertrude's reputation, but the reticent Cox showed her none of the fatherly encouragement she had received from Chirol, Hogarth or even Hardinge. He could barely hide his suspicions of her Cairo colleagues, and McMahon's promises to the Sharif Hussein seemed to him unwise, if not outrageous. Sending a woman to Basrah did little more to assure him. Yet a letter from the Viceroy Hardinge had advised him to take her seriously: "She is a remarkably clever woman with the brains of a man."

As Chief Political Officer, Sir Percy was to oversee the new administration in Mesopotamia. Good relations with the local tribes were of primary concern: the Arabs could not only ensure food and housing provisions for the British; they could help the army defeat the Turks. But the tribal sheikhs, many of whom owed their wealth to the Ottomans, were as likely to side with the Turks as with the Entente; if they did, the British could face disaster. Local tribes could block the British lines of communication, choke the oil pipelines, cut off food and water supplies and provide significant strength—tens of thousands of men and rifles—to the Ottoman army.

There had already been a series of frustrating rejections. When one important sheikh was approached by an American intermediary for the British, he told the man, "The Turks have offered me one hundred and twenty-five thousand dollars if we will join them." But, he went on, "if the British give me two hundred thousand dollars we will go with them and refuse the Turks." When the British officials heard his request, they turned it down, resenting the ransom. Shaking his head in disappointment, the Arab chief replied sadly, "I am sorry. I think the British are going to win, and I would like to be on the winning side."

When a meeting was requested with another chief, Ajaimi Sadun, who controlled four thousand Turkish rifles, the powerful Arab hemmed and hawed, fearing that his reputation would suffer if he abandoned the Turks for no cause; nevertheless, he allowed, it might be possible to find an excuse. He admitted he distrusted the Turks, but they had promised him all the Ottoman Crown lands in the Basrah *vilayet.* On the other hand, he said, if the British could assure him they would win, he would switch sides. But, then again, he added, the British Government was an unknown quantity of very uncertain stability. He was hesitant to decide. At last, he declared, he had made his decision: he would go with the Turks.

Such discord only added to the British generals' contempt for the local Arabs, many of whom raided army storehouses in Basrah, and did little to help the disdainful army win the tribes to their side. Cox believed the General Command was inept. For the past three months, IEF D had been struggling north toward Baghdad—without enough river transport, airplanes, doctors, medicine or food—into a quagmire of Ottoman territory, where, to make matters worse, as Gertrude noted later, the Arabs "backed the winner," thinking it would be the Turks, "and hung like jackals round our troops, looted our camps, murdered our wounded, stripped our dead." Cox had lost patience with the military leadership, particularly with the man in charge, General Lake. Thinking Gertrude might be a useful ally, Sir Percy was polite, promising to send on to her any Arabs he thought would be of interest.

∞ ∞ ∞

The day following her meeting with Cox, Gertrude lunched with the local command. General Lake, General Cowper, General Money and General Offley Shaw of the India Expeditionary Force stood stiffly, their khakis starched, their mustaches waxed to a point, as Gertrude entered the Officers' Mess, and, keeping her head high and her back straight, lifting her skirts ever so slightly off the floor, took her place at the table. As she had done at the time of her Oxford exams, she sat tall and prickly as a long-stemmed rose and faced the four iron men.

Across a sea of damask they raised their glasses, sipping the Rhine wine they had captured from local German cellars. From under his bushy brows, the gaunt-faced General Lake eyed her unruffled expression, and with exceeding politeness the officers fired away, asking her questions about the Arab Bureau. Like their colleagues in Delhi, they were opposed to a movement of Arab nationalism, opposed to an Arab revolt against the Turks, opposed to the Sharif of Mecca and opposed to giving up control of Mesopotamia. Most of all, they graciously omitted from their account, they were opposed to a woman messing in their business.

Nevertheless, they needed her help. Facing a Turkish force of equal size, the British troops had to march through unmapped territory—desert, swamps and palm groves—as they progressed toward Baghdad. They had to be sure the Arabs would not ambush them, and for that they required local guides, men who could be trusted so that the natives would not attack. And they needed maps to know where they were going.

Gertrude's green eyes pierced the room, and she began to speak in a deep and knowledgeable tone that shattered their words into splints. There was much she could do to help the generals, she assured them: she knew how important it was to establish ties with the Arabs; she had heard how frustrating it had been. No one was on a friendlier basis with the sheikhs and notables than Gertrude: not only did she know many of them by name; she knew their sons and their brothers, had sat in their tents and their salons, had drunk their coffee and shared their bread. With her help, the Arab chiefs might be persuaded to lend their support; with her help, the troops might have enough supplies for housing and food; and with her help, the maps could be drawn so that the army could find its way to Baghdad.

Their response arrived with the pudding. Later that afternoon, Gertrude wrote to her mother, "They moved me and my maps and books on to a splendid great verandah with a cool room behind it where I sit and work all day long." With great enthusiasm and a dash of naïveté she noted, "Everyone is being amazingly kind."

The war had put great distance between Gertrude and home. She longed to know how her brother Maurice, on sick leave from the European front, was faring, but mail from England took more than a month to reach Basrah, and with so many ships sunk by the enemy, letters often went down at sea. "One feels—and indeed is—awfully far away, and the echoes of war in France which must to you sound so deafening are nearly lost here under those of Mesopotamia," she wrote to her father.

There was little local news she could discuss in her letters because of the censors. She made small references to Kut al Amara, the peninsula town where, as a result of numerous command mistakes, several thousand British forces, struggling through swamps and muck as they inched their way from Basrah toward Baghdad, had been caught under siege. Forced to flee from a battle at Ctesiphon, only forty miles from their goal, they had retreated to Kut. There, in the muddy town on the Tigris, they were besieged, trapped without enough food, medicine or ammunition to fight their way out. For three months the soldiers— many wounded, others suffering from dysentery and malaria—had waited desperately for reinforcements. But British troops on their way to help were blockaded by a Turkish army composed of Arabs ten times their number. Again and again, boatloads of British soldiers were sent up the river to relieve the force; again and again, their bodies were paddled back by wooden barge. Still, the air was electric with suggestions that the Turks might be giving in.

In reply to questions from her mother, she said she had no idea how long she was going to stay or where she would go next or what she would be doing. It seemed, though, that she might be in Mesopotamia much longer than she had planned. The thought of the steamy summer two months ahead prompted a flood of requests: she needed hot weather clothes that would be easy to wash; petticoats, crêpe de Chine shirts and stockings; an evening gown in cream lace that touched the floor, narrow black velvet ribbon to wear around her neck, a pair of tussore knickerbockers and two pairs of thin stays. Finally, a pair of eyeglasses and a pair of spectacles, stronger than the ones she had now, since all the mapmaking was straining her eyes.

∞   ∞   ∞

Predictably, the spring rains came, flooding the city, causing the roads to excrete slime. On a morning drenched from cloud bursts, Gertrude walked from the Coxes' house to Headquarters, hurdling like an athlete over gulfs of mud, "tight rope dancing" on fallen palm trees, certain at any moment she might slip and sink into a pool of muck.

Word arrived that Colonel Beach wished to see her. He had some information, he said; it looked as if the British forces up north would soon be moving forward toward Baghdad, and if so, they would immediately encounter the local tribes. The colonel often called on Gertrude to meet with local Arabs and to help with the mapping and charting the tribes. More than fifty groups inhabited the land between the Tigris and the Euphrates, including the rice-growing Abu Muhammad; the nomadic Bani Lam, with their fine-bred herds of horses and camels; the troublesome Bani Rabiah of Kut; the two hundred thousand people, including the Sadun, who made up the loose confederation of the Muntafik; the two hundred and fifty thousand Anazeh, Bedouin who roamed the Syrian desert from Aleppo all the way to Central Arabia; and on the Euphrates, above Ramadi, the great shepherd tribe of the Dulaim. Tribal organization remained as it had been for a dozen generations, since nomad tribes had wandered north from Arabia; the power of the sheikhs was deeply rooted, tribal laws and customs held sway and tribal blood feuds provided the excuse for constant and bitter revenge.

This time Beach wanted Gertrude to send secret messages behind enemy lines: offer "a word of friendship" to Nuri Said, the Mesopotamian officer in the Ottoman army who had started a secret society against the Turks, he suggested, and to Fahad Bey, the Paramount Chief of the Anazeh, to encourage them to break free of the Turks. He was "eager to try the experiment." By the way, the colonel mentioned, he was having trouble getting through to a sheikh of the Dulaim tribe. "Why not send him a message through Fahad Bey?" Gertrude advised. "They will all be camping together at this time of year." Only two years earlier, on her way back from Hayil, she herself had stayed at Fahad Bey's camp near Karbala, and years before that she had sipped coffee in the tents of the Dulaim.

In the evenings she waded back through the mud to the Coxes', but aside from Sir Percy and his wife, there were few others who invited her to dine. Even at lunch in the mess she was shunned or scoffed and sneered at by the staff, most of whom still regarded her with suspicion. Only Henry Dobbs, a family acquaintance who had been made Political Officer, and his second-in-command, Reader Bullard, offered to take walks with her through the palm gardens. Thanks to them, as well, she met Dorothy and John Van Ess, an American missionary couple who would become two of her closest friends.

John Van Ess had traveled extensively into the marshlands, developing an expertise on the local villages and tribes. Almost from the moment the British conquered Basrah, he had been providing them with information and supplying them with Arab agents behind the Turkish lines. Despite his proselytizing profession and Gertrude's religious disbelief, the two had much in common, and it was not long before she started calling on him, seeking his help on the tribes. Later he composed a limerick about her:

G is for Gertrude, of the Arabs she's Queen,
And that's why they call her Um el Mumineen,
If she gets to Heaven (I'm sure I'll be there)
She'll even ask Allah, "What's your tribe, and where?"

∽   ∽   ∽

In spite of her fascination with the Arabs, however, Gertrude was less than keen about their women. She rarely entered the harems in the tents and spent almost no time with the wives in town. Nor did she care about Islam, any more than she cared about Christianity. Her lack of understanding irritated Dorothy Van Ess, who insisted that knowledge about harem life was essential to understanding the character and psychology of Arab men. Nor, she added, could one possibly ignore the profound influence of Islam on social and political conditions. Gertrude disagreed. Dorothy became exasperated. "I have sufficient regard for your intelligence," she chided, "to think that if you knew anything about either of these subjects, you would hold different opinions." Gertrude laughed. "Touché!" she replied.

The two women had actually become good friends. "I get rather tired of seeing nothing but men," Gertrude complained to her mother; "Lady Cox is absolutely no good to any mortal soul—she is so damned stupid. . . . She is as kind as ever she can be, but there's no possible subject on which you can converse with her. My great standby is Mrs. Van Ess." As for the Arab wives, they would remain only a mild curiosity. She might accept the fact that they wielded influence behind the scenes, but it was male political power, raw, intense, and directly affecting society, that she found so intriguing.

∽   ∽   ∽

"Letters are a great joy," Gertrude wrote wistfully to Hugh. Alone in her room in Basrah, she had little else to look forward to, and as quickly as the mail arrived, she composed her responses, maintaining a lifeline between herself and high-powered friends. Lord Cromer; Mr. Montagu, the Secretary of State for India; Mr. Asquith, the Prime Minister; all were recipients of her notes, in which she apprised them of activities in Mesopotamia. As for Captain Hall, the Director of Intelligence, she had sent him a long letter sketching out what people in

Delhi and Basrah were thinking about the future of Iraq—mainly that it should be run in some way in conjunction with Egypt, rather than by India. Afterward she wrote to her father: "You might find out some time, discreetly, whether he likes having letters from me. I write only when there are things I think it might be useful for him to know."

She was also corresponding with T. E. Lawrence in Cairo, where her colleagues were now celebrating some success. On March 9, 1916, the British Cabinet had voted to pay the Sharif Hussein a subsidy of one hundred and twenty-five thousand pounds per month in gold sovereigns, which they would continue for more than a year; in addition, plans were being made to send him five thousand rifles and a quarter of a million rounds of amunition in order to ensure his success against the Turks.

In Mesopotamia, too, activities were heating up; as Colonel Beach had mentioned, it looked as if the troops would soon be heading toward Baghdad. "There might be a good many things to be done, and it could be exceedingly interesting to see how the thing works out," Gertrude wrote to T. E. Lawrence. "My only regret is that you aren't here, but failing that please cable any advice or suggestions. . . . Do seize a moment of the night and send me a word of your news."

Still concerned about the lack of communication between India and Egypt, she continued: "I have always thought an exchange of people in the various Inter-Depts. would be an immense advantage . . . and I should think yet more favourably of the scheme if it included your coming out here.

"I've written enough," she scrawled. Then, ending her letter to Lawrence, she confided dejectedly: "To read it you might think I was a real person seriously considering affairs of the moment, but I don't feel like a real person at all—much more like some irresponsible flotsam carried here and there on the flood and floating aimlessly first round one eddy and then round another, until in the end I suppose I shall float back somewhere, and remembering all these months wonder what I was doing in them. And find no answer. I hate war; oh, and I'm so weary of it—of war, of life. Not of Basrah, especially; I would just as soon be here as anywhere—and as soon be anywhere as here, except as yet in England. Not there."

PART TWO

The Khatun

Chapter Seventeen

A Messy Situation

∞

British officials in London had been reorganizing the office of Military Intelligence in Cairo, officially renaming it the Arab Bureau and assigning as its head David Hogarth. With the bureau's work clearly focused on the coming Arab Revolt, Hogarth wanted Gertrude to leave Basrah and return to Cairo. To her superiors in Egypt she was a wellspring of information, and the following week Lawrence was dispatched to Iraq, hoping to find a replacement for Gertrude so that she could come back with him to Cairo.

Along with this overt task, Lawrence's mission was partly covert. Only a short while before, General Clayton had tried to help save the British force at Kut by offering to send Aziz al Masri, a former officer in the Ottoman army, to tempt away disgruntled Arabs from their Turkish troops. The scheme had been shrugged off by the generals in Basrah, who found it less than realistic. But now the situation was growing more desperate. Unbeknownst to Gertrude, a far more distasteful secret plan had been devised by General Townshend. The British commander, fighting an overwhelming Turkish force at Kut, had proposed to London that he offer a bribe to the Turkish army commander; with Whitehall's approval as much as one million pounds would be paid to free the British soldiers. The man who would carry the money was T. E. Lawrence.

At the beginning of March 1916 Lawrence had dashed off a note to his mother, aware, of course, that it would be read by the censor: "I am going away, for a month or 6 weeks, to consult with some people, and suggest certain things. Is this vague enough? I hope to meet Miss Bell shortly, since we are much on the same tack."

By the end of the month he was on a ship to Iraq and informed his mother that he could not write to her from Basrah. He would be "very busy ashore," he said, with things which he could not discuss. But, he added, "I want to bring Gertrude back with me, and our Arabian office will be complete." The rare use by him of a woman's first name was an indication of their unusual relationship.

It was late and raining heavily the night of April 5, 1916, when Lawrence walked into the office of Gertrude Bell and Campbell Thompson at Military Intelligence at Basrah. He had just maneuvered himself the three hundred yards from the boat dock, sliding "over the top of what seemed to be a bank of soft soap and toffee." Delighted to see their old chum, Gertrude and Thompson brought him directly to Headquarters to meet Sir Percy Cox. Lawrence handed the Chief Political Officer a letter from Sir Henry McMahon, explaining that he was "under orders from the War Office to give his services in regard to Arab matters."

Percy Cox had learned earlier of the scheme to bribe the Turks and had found the proposal appalling. He had no instructions for Lawrence, the dignified Cox declared. Furthermore, he wrote tartly in a memo to Colonel Beach, in no way did he want his name connected with such business: "You see, I am not a migrant—I am a permanent official in the Gulf and I may conceivably have to remain here for a time after hostilities are concluded. The project in view is pretty sure to become known sooner or later especially if it proves unsuccessful and I cannot afford as Political Officer of the Government of India to be identified with it."

Before Lawrence set off on the two-hundred-mile journey for Kut—fortified by tins of biscuits, beef, and jams and loaves of bread— he spent time with Gertrude, meeting people she admired, such as Reader Bullard; discussing at length the Arab Bureau and the future of the Middle East; and interviewing local Arabs he hoped would be interested in instigating a revolt. A Pan-Arab party had been formed in Basrah, but its leading member, Sayid Talib, an influential but ruthless Basrah nationalist, had been deported by Cox as a "state guest" to India; the others Lawrence met with showed no interest in the project and he referred to them as "jackals."

The week had been "greatly enlivened by the appearance of Mr. Lawrence," Gertrude wrote just before Lawrence left Basrah on April 10. "We have had great talks and made vast schemes for the government of the universe. He goes up river tomorrow, where the battle is raging these days. With what anxiety we watch for news it would be difficult to tell you."

His departure left her again without many allies. Her family friend, the linguist Aubrey Herbert, was coming to Basrah, but only for a day, heading north to join Lawrence in the bribery negotiations with the Turks. A year earlier, shortly before Doughty-Wylie had gone off to Gallipoli, Herbert, an Intelligence officer in Egypt, and Dick had dined together. Now, over dinner with Herbert in Basrah, she would have a chance to talk to him about Dick. "Oh how glad I shall be to see him!" she wrote. "One's extraordinarily lonely with no one of one's own. That's why even Mr. Lawrence was such a godsend. He speaks the same language at any rate." Lawrence may not have been of her class, but at least they saw eye to eye.

Looking out over the river from her new apartment, Gertrude felt cheered. The spring rains had subsided, the city was no longer coated with mud, and the flowers, which she missed, were now making their appearance. "Even Basrah has a burst of glory in April," she wrote enthusiastically to her father. "The palm gardens are deep in luxuriant grass and corn, the pomegranates are flowering, the mulberries almost ripe and in the garden of the house where I am staying the roses are more wonderful than I can describe. It's the only garden in Basrah, so I'm lucky."

She now wakened at five-thirty each morning, eager to exercise her favorite way, on horseback. Riding through the palm groves, then out to the edges of the desert, she passed "British troops, Indian troops of every kind, buffalo carts, mules, tongas, motors and motor lorries of the latest pattern, camels—reed huts and telephone wires." By eight-thirty, she had bathed and breakfasted and was in her office, and, except for the hot sun, she had no complaints. Her work on the gazetteer was almost complete, but in other areas there was much to be done; her days were spent debriefing Arabs coming into Headquarters, correcting maps, and circulating information between Cairo and Delhi, tasks that Hogarth had hoped someone else could do when Gertrude returned to Egypt.

In truth, she enjoyed the work in Basrah more than the work in Cairo. In Egypt she would be kept behind a desk and flooded with paper work. Here the material was all raw, fresh and firsthand. She was uniquely qualified for the job, able to read and speak fluent Arabic and alert to the politics of the place. No one else in the Intelligence Department could be relied on to do it satisfactorily, she informed Hogarth. She had already recommended Mr. Bullard for the job and had introduced him to Lawrence, who approved; but reluctant to give up the post, she shared her doubts with Hogarth: "As long as I am here I can get all the new stuff, but much of it walks in on two feet, in the shape of a sheikh down from Nasariyah or elsewhere, and when I am gone there will be no one to collect it."

The other likely choice to replace her was Campbell Thompson, but Gertrude found him inept. Bluntly, she reported to her chief, "If you will let me say so, he isn't any damned use—I think I have never come across anyone quite like this before, so amiable and so . . . futile." She was doing a great deal of work on new maps, work that Campbell Thompson might have done. However, she wrote, "he hates maps and can't look at them!"

Word had come in, she notified Hogarth, that there was a good deal of disaffection among the Arabs in the Turkish army, but frustrating as it was, until the situation at Kut was resolved, she was not allowed to travel north to investigate. Nevertheless, she had developed her own network of Arabs, who kept her informed. The chaperones she had been ordered to use had long been shucked, and she fluttered about like a young bird in spring from one native house to another. She would report back to Hogarth soon: "I am going out to Zubair tomorrow to see the Shaikhs and other notables."

❧   ❧   ❧

Driving through mud and water, Gertrude reached the hard sand that marked the start of the desert. Eight miles to the west was the oasis of Zubair—once, before the Euphrates had changed its course, the original city of Basrah, home of Sindbad the Sailor and burial place of Ali the Barmecide—now, "the funniest little desert place, something like Hayil," she described it. With the help of the local political officer, she found sleeping quarters in the post office and furnished the mud-floored room with the camp bed, chair and bath she had brought along.

The village had served for centuries as a marketplace for the Bedouin. Caravans coming up from Arabia poured into town, and purchasing agents of Ibn Rashid bargained in the shops for clothing, household utensils, rifles, corn, oil, coffee, tea and sugar, much of it to be delivered to the Turks. Tribal gossip buzzed through the air like worker bees in a rose garden.

The Sheikh of Zubair, who hosted visiting travelers at his coffee hearth, was the local authority on the politics of the desert. A wealthy man who counted his riches in date palm plantations, herds of camel and the tribute he taxed his tribe, he had made his peace with the British and now invited Gertrude several times to dine with him. She visited his palace, passing through the low-arched doorway leading to the courtyard, taking her place beside the sheikh on one of the long divans placed on the Persian rugs that covered the floors of the verandahs. Brown-hooded falcons lined the room, and the bearded sheikh, cloaked in a gold-embroidered robe, sat in elegant style. Over a Bedouin meal of whole roasted lamb, piles of rice, vegetables wrapped in cabbage leaves, chicken and hard-boiled eggs, he served the honored guest the eye of the lamb and fed her the latest news. She learned of the whereabouts of the Turkish troops and heard of the activities of a large group from Hayil who, turning their backs on Ibn Rashid, had brought their camels and tents close to the Mesopotamian border.

Even before Gertrude arrived in Basrah, the sheikh had been used as a medium through which to transfer information. Percy Cox had asked him to deliver a message to Ibn Rashid, "holding out a hand of friendship," as Gertrude described it in a letter to Lawrence, "warning him at the same time that he will in the future find it very uncomfortable to be on anything but good terms with us, since we shall control his market towns. This was sent before I came," she noted, "by means of a small Shammar caravan which dropped in at Zubair."

Now on this visit, she heard more about Ibn Rashid. "His intentions are . . . doubtful," she reported later, "but I don't think he is in a position to do much harm. But of one thing there is no doubt: we should be much more at ease if we were on terms with him." Gertrude wanted to send the young ruler a personal letter. As she explained to Hogarth, it was time to make peace between Ibn Rashid and Ibn Saud. The only problem was the dilemma of supplying arms. "We can't give arms to both of them, that would be manifestly absurd; nor can we give arms to one only, if we are friends with both; which brings us back to the point I always wish to reach, and leaves us with no alternative but to give arms to none."

∽ ∽ ∽

After a courtesy call on Sheikh Ibrahim's harem, where the un-veiled, tattooed women smoked *narghiles* and entertained her with coffee and conversation, Gertrude left the clean dry air of the desert to return to Headquarters and her mail. Two letters from her parents had arrived, but one of her father's was lost. "I fear his of March 23 went down in the *Sussex*," she wrote to Florence, "and also, I suspect, the clothes you sent me! Better luck next time."

A beastly, steamy heat permeated Basrah. Gertrude sat at her desk, enclosed in her room, the doors and windows tightly shuttered to ward off the sun, the blades of the electric fan spinning. It was three years since she had seen the daffodils coming up in springtime at Rounton. "Oh I wonder how my dear family is and wish for news," she wrote with an almost audible sigh. "One falls into a kind of coma when one is so far away and wakes up with a jump at intervals."

It was not the heat that bothered her, she assured them, but her clothes. Unlike her fellow officers, who could requisition a clean new uniform at any time, she had no one to make her new dresses. Her things were beginning to fall apart. "One wears almost nothing, fortunately, still it's all the more essential that that nothing should not be in holes." And she was still without friends, as neither Aubrey nor Lawrence had returned: "They go up river and disappear. I long for someone I know to come down so that I may hear what is happening for we get very little news."

∞   ∞   ∞

Word of the siege at Kut had already reached England, and in the mail from home her father had included an article from the *Economist*, blaming the Government of India for the military disaster. Gertrude may not have known that while the taking of Basrah was carried out upon orders from London, the premature thrust toward Baghdad had been General Townshend's initiative, agreed to only reluctantly by London. The *Economist* article triggered a furious response. Aware that Hugh would pass on her letter to influential friends at Whitehall, she took out pen and paper and, noting that the India Government was not alone in deserving blame for the military disaster, she answered angrily:

> Politically, too, we rushed into the business with our usual disregard for a comprehensive political scheme. We treated Mesop. as if it were an isolated unit, instead of which it is part of Arabia, its politics indissolubly connected with the great and far reaching Arab question, which presents, indeed, different facets as you regard it from different aspects, and is yet always one and the same indivisible block. The coordinating of Arabian politics and the creation of an Arabian policy should have been done at home—it could only have been done successfully

at home. There was no one to do it, no one who had ever thought of it, and it was left to our people in Egypt to thrash out, in the face of strenuous opposition from India and London, some sort of wide scheme, which will, I am persuaded, ultimately form the basis of our relations with the Arabs. And up to this moment, the battle against the ignorance and indifference of the people at home is waging—and is not yet won. The Milton sonnet is so often in my mind—there's no one to lead. Swollen with wind and the rank mists we draw—

Well that's enough of politics. But when people talk of our muddling through it throws me into a passion. Muddle through! why yes, so we do—wading through blood and tears that need never have been shed.

More than twenty-three thousand British relief soldiers had been killed by the time (two days before she composed her letter) that General Townshend met with the head of the Turkish forces and proposed that Lawrence and Herbert be allowed to speak with General Khalil. The offer was denounced with a flat refusal. Instead, the Turks insisted, the British soldiers must immediately abandon Kut and surrender. It was on April 29, 1916, that the radio operator at Kut sent his final message of goodbye: more than thirteen thousand British and Indian troops were taken prisoner and sent on a march to almost certain death. The fall of Kut was one of the worst defeats in British history.

Unaware of the surrender, Lawrence, Herbert and Colonel Beach left their trenches and, holding a white flag, edged their way a couple of hundred yards toward the Turkish side. An enemy soldier was sent to find out what they wanted, and led them, blindfolded, to General Khalil. Hearing that their countrymen had surrendered, the surprised threesome tried for an exchange of prisoners, but an agreement had already been made to trade the British sick and wounded for Turkish prisoners of war. Except for a pleasant Turkish dinner, the whole event was a fiasco. Newspapers around the world reported the humiliating story of the failed attempt at bribery, and by May 8, Lawrence and Beach were back in Basrah.

⚭   ⚭   ⚭

Outraged by what he had seen at Kut, Lawrence sent Cairo a scathing report. Iraq was a "blunderland," he announced, except for Sir

Percy Cox, who was "delightful," and Miss Bell, who he thought was first rate. But with Gertrude needed in Cairo, he had to find someone to take over her job as Basrah representative of the Arab Bureau. He approached Sir Percy Cox, but the Chief Political Officer handed the matter over to Colonel Beach.

Lawrence persisted, explaining to Cox that the Arab Bureau was a "Foreign Office affair" and that its representative must be "intimate with the work of the political side." For the present, he and Cox agreed, Miss Bell would continue to do the tribal and geographical work while they searched for a successor. But it would take at least two people to replace her. "I have a feeling that no one person will be able to supply us with all we want," Lawrence wrote. Only she had the female charm to extract what was needed: "I think Miss Bell, by her sex and energy and lack of self-consciousness, is peculiarly likely to per- suade Political Officers to send her what she asks for."

Nevertheless, competition for the job was growing. George Lloyd had been sent out from Cairo, and India had sent out their own choice. But the former spoke no Arabic, and the latter had never before been in the East. On May 14 Gertrude wrote to Hogarth, emphasizing the importance of being fluent in Arabic. "Even the information which comes to us from the Political Office," she said, required an under- standing of the language; "clan names, peoples' names, tribe names, spelt with so many variations that you are put to it to find out that two almost wholly different words are really the same. And the actual inter- course with the natives (of whom I now see a good deal) necessitates Arabic."

As difficult as it was, Gertrude was eager to stay in Iraq.

❧   ❧   ❧

A great deal of work needed to be done in Basrah. Ibn Rashid still had to be "roped in" and neutralized, and when several of his men came into the office to meet with her, Gertrude gave them a long letter for the Emir. She was now assigned all the liaison work between Basrah and Cairo and hoped that it would bring her in closer contact with Percy Cox. "I like him very much," she told her father; "he is a big man and it will be a great pleasure to work with him."

Her reports had also been appearing in the *Arab Bulletin*, the secret publication on Middle East personalities and politics initiated by the Arab Bureau in Cairo and circulated exclusively to the highest Intelli- gence officials. Gertrude's information, she told her father, came from natives as well as from the refugees now "tumbling in from Baghdad, fleeing from Turkish oppression." Many of them she knew; and if she didn't know them directly, she knew their friends. And since almost all of them had heard of her, she met them "on equal terms." It was great fun, she wrote. "It's also very valuable sometimes, the lead they give you into the recesses of Oriental opinions."

One analysis she wrote contained a cautious view of the future: "Men living in tents, or in reed huts almost as nomadic as the tent itself, men who have never known any control but the empty fiction of Turkish authority . . . men who have the tradition of a personal independence . . . ignorant of a world which lay outside their swamps and pasturages, and . . . indifferent to its interests and to the opportunities it offers, will not in a day fall into step with European ambitions, nor welcome European methods. Nor can they be hastened. Whether that which we have to teach them will add to the sum of their happiness, or whether the learning or inevitable lessons will bring them the proverbial attitude of wisdom, that schooling must, if it is to be valuable, be long and slow."

Not until the summertime, after the end of the siege at Kut, could Gertrude travel along the Euphrates, but with information to be gathered, she ignored as best she could the sun beating down on her back and the wind scorching her face, and sailed by steamer through the marshes with her friend General MacMunn. Past the man-made reed islands—villages rising and falling in the river floods—they rode to Nasariyah, where some of the tribesmen had been persuaded to serve as agents for the British. For several days in early June, she explored the town, working on her reports, filling in missing tribal data, visiting the homes of notables in the evenings and gathering Intelligence material on the Turks.

At a stop on the way back to Basrah, Gertrude met Captain Dickson, the Revenue officer at Suq al Shuyukh. To support the cost of their occupation, the British, like the Turks, taxed the local tribes, using the sheikhs to collect the money and giving them a percentage as a prize. Like all his colleagues, Dickson was challenged continually by the cleverness of the local Arabs. He liked to tell the story of one old sheikh from whom he tried to collect revenues. Since there were no records of how much money their predecessors, the Turks, had received, Dickson asked the first sheikh he encountered how many date palm trees he had been taxed on by the Ottoman administration. "By God, O Dickson, I know not," the sheikh answered.

"Rot," Dickson said, "of course you know quite well. Now how many trees did you pay on in 1914?"

"By your head, mine eyes, I know not," the sheikh responded. "Write fifteen hundred!" he commanded.

Dickson jotted down that number in his book and collected from the man the appropriate tax. Several days later an informer showed Dickson an old Turkish tax receipt stating that the sheikh owned five thousand trees. Dickson ordered the sheikh to appear at his office and asked him to explain.

"Five thousand, sayest thou, my dear?" asked the sheikh. "By God, it is very strange!" Then, with a generous sweep of his hand, he ordered Dickson, "Y'Allah! Write down six thousand, my friend. Let us not quarrel."

It was only several months later, however, after the sheikh had become a friend, that Dickson asked him how many date trees he really owned.

"God alone knoweth," the sheikh replied, "but there cannot be less than ninety thousand."

∞ ∞ ∞

Returning to Basrah from the Euphrates trip, Gertrude was struck again by the disdain of her colleagues and the humiliation of working without an official position. It was only because of Sir Percy Cox's kindness, she allowed, that she was able to continue her work. Her loyalty to Cox was growing stronger while her fealty to Hogarth, her friend and Cairo chief who refused to give her a title or pay her a salary, was weakening. Embarrassed and irritated by a number of things that had happened, on June 15, responding to a letter from Hogarth, she dropped her reserve and answered her old mentor angrily:

"I want to express some pretty strong feelings, if you don't mind. You say in this letter that you are putting something from one of my private letters into the Bulletin and I hear that you have done so on more than one occasion." Cox had telegraphed Hogarth not to publish this material, and she agreed. "You would not like it, would you, if you were to find bits of your private letters to me in the Basrah summaries. The position is exactly parallel."

But even worse, the work she was doing for Cairo was more a favor to Hogarth than an official assignment.

> I have no official status here with regard to Cairo; you have not given me one. I'm not your correspondent; if I

think there is something which you would be interested to have I must ask as a favour that it should be sent to you. [And, she reminded him,] I was not even sent here by you; I was sent by the Viceroy with the request that I might be allowed to see all secret papers and given every opportunity to study tribal history. But even if I were officially your correspondent, nothing that I sent you could be used officially except what had been passed by Col. Beach and Sir P.C. Private letters are private letters. They don't carry official weight. I now feel that you have made things very difficult for me. . . . I hope you will shortly define my duties more clearly. There are a number of things which I know would interest you that I don't get to you because there is no one whose business it is to send them.

There was some specific information that she wanted to send to Hogarth, but she needed Sir Percy's permission to do so. "He is immensely kind in such matters and raises no difficulties, but it would still be a great deal more convenient for both of us if I were not sending you such notes by special favour.

"I have also finished a number of Personalities on the Euphrates side and as soon as I have a typist I will get them ready for you. Again this is a matter dependent on Sir Percy's kindess—I have no *right* to a typist. Further I told Mr. Lawrence that I am in a difficulty about my board and lodging here." She was not receiving a salary and her land-lords were not charging her rent, "but they admit that if I were being billeted officially, that would be all right. I don't want a salary, as you know, but it seems monstrous that these good people should be keep-ing me out of the hospitality allowance they get from their firm." Cox had told her that if Cairo gave her an official position, they should also give her a salary. She didn't want much, she assured Hogarth, only "enough to defray my keep."

All of these matters, she continued, had been discussed with Law-rence. But "Mr. Lawrence left all these threads hanging and nearly two months have passed without any appreciable advance towards a solu-tion."

Two days later, still upset, she sent off a note to Domnul, now back in London after completing his work in India: "You don't know how difficult my job is here; but I continue to be very glad to be here." The more difficult it was, the more she felt she ought to stay.

Her mood changed dramatically a fortnight later, when she learned that her persistence and stoicism had finally paid off. Her status had been officially upgraded: Gertrude Bell was declared a full member of Sir Percy Cox's Political staff of the India Expeditionary Force D. With a fixed monthly salary of three hundred rupees and the title of Liaison Officer, Correspondent to Cairo, Major Miss Bell was now the only female Political Officer in the British forces.

CHAPTER EIGHTEEN

An Independent Woman

∞

It was Sir Percy's job to keep India informed of Arab sentiment in the Gulf, keep track of the intentions of Ibn Saud and Ibn Rashid and keep watch over the activities of German spies. He was to keep apprised of the Mesopotamian tribes from Basrah to Baghdad and in neighboring Persia, and to know the sheikhs and their mood. As a member of General Headquarters Intelligence, he wrote later, he was involved with "assisting in the examination of prisoners and spies, the sifting of information, and the provision of informers and interpreters."

No member of his staff was better qualified for this work than Gertrude. But she faced a Political Officers' clique as hostile as the Military Intelligence fraternity she had just left behind: Colonel Leachman was arrogant; Hubert Young ignored her; and A. T. Wilson, Cox's brilliant deputy who took particular pleasure in sending out piles of reports laced with references to the Old Testament or quotes from Bacon, Milton and Shakespeare, was suspicious of her friendships with influential men in Cairo, Delhi and London.

As she sat across from him at lunch in the Political Mess, only his snide allusions to St. John Philby or others at the table enabled her to deduce a few crumbs of the policy feast he was dishing up to Delhi and

London. Concerned about her plans for the future of Iraq, he made certain to exclude her from his decision-making process. He refused to give her access to information going out and refused to tell her the codes for his cables and secret telegrams coming in. Although he had won a Distinguished Service medal, the gallantry he was praised for played no part in his relations with Gertrude. Nevertheless, the temporary appointment of George Lloyd to Sir Percy Cox's staff made her feel less isolated. An occasional morning ride with him would give them a chance to talk things over.

As interesting as she found the work, the lack of friends left her lonely. "I feel rather detached from you," she lamented in a letter to her father. "I wish I could sit somewhere midway and have a talk with you once or twice a week." The "kind" and "generous" Sir Percy Cox, the Chief Political Officer, was still somewhat aloof, shy and reserved, and although she met with him several times a week, he was not the type whose advice she could seek or with whom she could ever gossip.

Daily events, large and small, sent her emotions reeling, roller-coasting from happiness to disappointment and back again. On Monday, June 5, 1916, the Sharif Hussein raised his standard and led his men in the Hejaz against Turkish forces. If the actual fighting at Mecca was only a prelude, Gertrude noted victoriously a few weeks later, it was still "one up to Egypt and my beloved chiefs there . . . the revolt of the Holy Places is an immense moral and political asset." When Hugh wrote to ask his daughter if she had been responsible for instigating the revolt, she confided, "No, I didn't stir up the Sharif! he stirred himself up. But, it was partly about all that business that I went to India."

The excitement she had felt in June was soon tempered by the open opposition to the Arab Revolt by the Viceroy of India, who called it a "displeasing surprise," and feared that the Muhammadans in India would see it as "Christian interference" with the Islamic religion.

More frustration came in July. After George Lloyd paid a visit to the front at Amara, where the British army was still fighting the Turks on the way to Baghdad, he returned from the scorching heat with harrowing accounts of confusion and incompetence, of soldiers suffering from a drastic lack of ice and a paucity of food. "Human skill in organization and human foresight have seldom had a less satisfactory advertisement than in this campaign," Gertrude charged in a letter to her parents. "Someday I'll tell you tales about it all—and you won't believe me. No one could who hasn't seen the things going on. I do not think the Indian Government can escape blame—I don't think it should." But she blamed the government in London for not carefully thinking out a policy: "We've paid for this negligence and want of forethought in blood and misery, in lives that can't be brought back."

Relieved to know that her own brother was safely in England and thankful he was not fighting in Mesopotamia, she acknowledged: "The real difficulty here is that we don't know exactly what we intend to do in this country. Can you persuade people to take your side when you are not sure in the end whether you'll be there to take theirs? No wonder they hesitate; and it would take a good deal of potent persuasion to make them think that your side and theirs are compatible." Neither the government in London nor the government in India had made firm plans for the future. Furthermore, to the dismay of many Arabs, the Sharif Hussein, who was counting on help from an uprising in Syria, had now drawn up a statement proclaiming himself King of all the Arabs.

To make matters worse, whatever persuasive powers she and Sir Percy had used to try to neutralize Ibn Rashid had been unsuccessful. "We didn't succeed in roping in Ibn Rashid," she reported unhappily. But, she continued, "it's not the immediate war problems here I think of most; it's the problems after the war, and I don't know what sort of hand we shall be able to take in solving them. However there's no harm in thinking about them and that's what I do. Write, too," she pleaded. "I've plenty of official openings for that."

Soon after, Percy Cox left once again for upriver, leaving her to his contrary deputy, A. T. Wilson. As the summer progressed, those who could, escaped Basrah's oppressive heat: by August, Mr. Dobbs, suffering from exhaustion, had gone to India, and George Lloyd had left for Cairo. "I have a good many acquaintances but no friends, except for Mr. Dobbs and Gen. MacMunn," Gertrude wrote home. She had found an ally in MacMunn, the Inspector General of Communications, "a nice creature, full of vitality and energy." They often went out on the river together in his launch. But, she added achingly, "I can't tell you what it's like to have nobody, nobody whom I have ever known before or who has ever known me before." Her only woman friend, Dorothy Van Ess, had also gone on holiday to India. Before she left, Gertrude asked her to bring back a few thin dresses. Mrs. Van Ess recalled seeing some frocks in a smart shop near the Taj Mahal Hotel. She cautioned, though, that they might be very expensive. "My dear," Gertrude said, "pay whatever you have to; I *must* have clothes!"

❧   ❧   ❧

The heat had become unbearable, as if the city were smothered under a heavy, wet wool blanket. All of Basrah had taken to their roofs to sleep. Outdoors, in the middle of the night with the temperature at well over 100 degrees, Gertrude awoke to find herself and her silk nightgown in a pool of sweat. "Everything you touch is hot, all the inanimate objects—your hair—if that's inanimate—the biscuit you eat, the clothes you put on." Malaria and typhoid were on the rampage, and clerks, typists and servants "go down before you can wink." Off and on through July and August Gertrude too was out with fever; in September she was stricken with jaundice.

For two weeks she lay limp as cloth, recuperating at an officers' rest house on the river. She had never been so ill before. But by September 20 she was strong enough to sit outdoors on the hospital verandah, noting that she had done nothing but eat and sleep and read novels. Her reading ranged from romantic fiction to philosophical fantasies, from Anthony Hope at one end to *The Crock of Gold* at the other, and she asked that her favorite London bookseller send her four to six books a month.

Two weeks later, still at the rest house, she gladly put on a woolen dress. The heat had disappeared: it was now only ninety degrees and she was shivering. With the cooler weather ahead, her thoughts, naturally, turned once again to clothes. She requested a violet felt winter hat, a black satin gown, some thick silk shirts, a purple knitted coat, a white serge motoring coat, and a satin embroidered Chinese coat to wear as an evening wrap. Joyfully, she informed her father that she was finally receiving her copies of *The Times*, but for some reason, Smith & Sons had neglected to include her weekly edition of the *Literary Supplement*. "Would you mind asking him what the deuce he means by it?" she bristled.

She had been out of the office exactly one month, and when she returned in early October, she learned that her official reports had evoked accolades in London. She noted proudly a few weeks afterward that she had received complimentary letters from various people, including Austin Chamberlain. Only a short while later, on December 16, 1916, upon his departure from Egypt, Sir Henry McMahon would shower her with praise: "I welcome the opportunity . . . of recording my high appreciation of the services of . . . Miss Gertrude Bell. . . . Her intimate knowledge of Arabia, ability and energy, have rendered her services of great value. The manner in which she has so long devoted herself to the work of the Arab Bureau, under the most trying conditions of country and climate, is deserving of special notice."

Her new duties now included acting as an intermediary between Sir Percy Cox and the Arabs, and it was this work which she found most satisfying: "I'm gradually becoming a sort of cushion between bewildered and mostly miscreant sheikhs and the ultimate authority," she explained. Drifting for a moment to memories of Doughty-Wylie, she added pensively, "Yes, it has been a godsend all this. I can't think what I should have done without it. And it stretches on into the future—but I don't think of the future; to live today and then sleep, that's enough."

She hoped that in the not too distant future, a letter she was composing to Fahad Bey would bring some rewards. The Paramount Chief of the Anazeh, who controlled the land along the western borders of the Euphrates, had resisted British attempts at friendship. Even when an envoy had been sent to plead the British case, the sheikh had stubbornly refused to see him; his sympathy lay, as it always had, with the Turks. The Ottomans had long ago earned his loyalty by making his father a "Kaimmakam," giving him the right to tax every caravan that crossed his land; Fahad Bey had inherited the title and the tribute that went with it. Nevertheless, since he had five thousand riflemen at his beck and call, Gertrude felt it worth her while to try to befriend him, and in the autumn of 1916 she sent a message to the tribal chief. It would be several months before she received a reply.

The intensity of the heat and the stress of war had taken their toll. Her hair was turning gray, and worse, when she washed it, it fell out in clumps. She had requested "two bottles of hair stuff" from Rudolfe on Sloane Street, but she feared her letter may have gone down with the SS *Arabia*: "Rudolfe might be asked if he got the letter, otherwise I shall be bald."

Bald or not, by mid-November she had gathered enough strength to travel, and packing some food and clothes and portable furnishings, she took the night train for Qurnah, dining in an empty train car on tinned tongue and tinned pears, lunching the next day with the local sheikh to draw out some needed information. The following week she made an archaeological venture on the Euphrates, west to Nasariyah, to visit the mounds of Ur of the Chaldees. The ruins of the ancient town from which Abraham had taken flight were being threatened by railway engineers and army generals, and she took it upon herself to protect the site from their ravages. But an urgent event hurried her back to Headquarters: Ibn Saud, the sheikh she had wanted to visit for so long, was on his way to Basrah.

⮾　⮾　⮾

The legendary Abdul Aziz Ibn Saud, husband of sixty-five wives, hero of swashbuckling exploits, including his escape from Kuwait, his seizure of Riyadh and his defeat of the Turks at Hasa in 1914, had earned the title of desert warrior and desert statesman. A commanding presence swathed in white robes and checkered *kafeeyah*, forty years old and massively built, six foot three inches tall, dark skinned, with black hair and black pointed beard, a straight nose and flaring nostrils, he arrived in Basrah on the night of November 26, 1916.

He came with Sir Percy Cox from Kuwait, where he had signed a treaty with the British and received investiture as Knight Commander of the India Empire. Three thousand rifles, four machine guns and a subsidy of five thousand pounds a month had been promised Ibn Saud in the hope of keeping him, the leader of the Wahhabi, the Bedouin Islamic fundamentalists, from attacking Britain's new ally, the Sharif Hussein, guardian of Mecca and leader of the revolt against the Turks. Hostility had grown between the two Emirs with every incremental increase in Hussein's power; now Ibn Saud resented furiously the Sharif's recent claim to being the King of the Arabs.

On the morning following Ibn Saud's arrival, surrounded by an audience of notables, the desert sovereign was presented with a jeweled sword in the name of the new British army commander, General Maude. There had once been hope that Ibn Saud would start the Arab rebellion, but the possibility had disappeared with the death of Captain Shakespear, a British agent killed in crossfire in the winter of 1915 while on a mission to see him; no treaty had been signed between the Emir and Britain. Sir Percy and the India Government officials believed that Ibn Saud represented the strongest weapon against the Turks. His victory over the Ottomans would have ensured him immediate control of all Arabia; furthermore, it would have kept Mesopotamia under the aegis of the India Government. But it was too late. The British Government in London and Cairo had backed the Sharif Hussein against the Turks. Now, at the very least, the treaty signed in Kuwait would keep Ibn Saud from attacking the Sharif. And if he fired his attentions on Ibn Rashid, so much the better.

A singular tour in Basrah had been organized in Ibn Saud's honor; he was given a show of British technology that was meant to dazzle. Within a few hours he stood before a parade of British forces, saw high explosives fired from an improvised trench and watched as antiaircraft shells burst in the air. He was taken on a brand-new railway and was driven through the desert in a motor car; at a hospital housed in a palace on loan from the Sheikh of Muhammarah, he was shown his own long, slim hand under an X-ray machine, and a short while later he witnessed an airplane zooming into the sky. Gertrude, wearing a silk-brimmed hat, smart jacket and skirt, with a camera case slung over her shoulder, stayed close to his side and, speaking in her classical Arabic, an accent strange to his ear, demanded: "Abdul Aziz, look at this," or "Abdul Aziz, what do you think of that?"

Amazing as the parade of British force might have been, it was not nearly as startling to him as Gertrude herself. He had never before met a European woman, and although he had been warned in advance, nothing had prepared him for the fact that this unveiled female was not only allowed in his sight but was accorded priorities and permitted to engage in all the procedures, whether they were discussions on Arabian politics or social functions in his honor. He looked down with heavily lidded eyes, dismayed at the Englishwoman who seemed to be everywhere.

She, in turn, found him "one of the most striking personalities" she had ever encountered, "full of wonder but never agape. He asked innumerable questions and made intelligent comments. . . . He's a big man," she observed, adding ironically, "I wish we could expound to him the science of peace, but we've got to get through this war first and hope that the better things will come after. Will they? It's an open question whether we don't do these people more harm than good and one feels still more despairing about it now that our civilisation has broken down so completely. But we can't leave them alone, they won't be left alone anyway, and whatever you may feel the world moves on— even in Arabia."

"Politician, ruler and raider, Ibn Sa'ud illustrates a historic type," Gertrude wrote in a communiqué for the Foreign Office and the *Arab Bulletin*. "Such men as he are the exception in any community, but they are thrown up persistently by the Arab race in its own sphere, and in that sphere they meet its needs. . . . The ultimate source of power, here as in the whole course of Arab history, is the personality of the commander. Through him, whether he be an Abbasid Khalif or an Amir of Nejd, the political entity holds, and with his disappearance it breaks." The echo of her words would ring throughout the region for the rest of the century, in men like Gamal Abdel Nasser, Yasser Arafat and Saddam Hussein.

Her detailed account of Ibn Saud and British relations with Arabia was finished the first week of December 1916 and sent off to the highest officials in England, Egypt and India. As important as her reporting was regarded, however, she felt restrained; a month before, T. E. Lawrence had left for his first adventure with the Sharif's army in Arabia. But as a woman, Gertrude was confined primarily to her desk. With a heavy sense of frustration, she wrote: "One can't do much more than sit and record if one is of my sex, devil take it; one can get the things recorded in the right way and that means, I hope, that unconsciously people will judge events as you think they ought to be judged. But it's small change for doing things, very small change I feel at times."

⚭   ⚭   ⚭

"Do you know," Gertrude mused, as she sat in her room ten days before Christmas 1916, writing her weekly letter to her father, "I was thinking yesterday what I would pick out as the happiest things I've done in all my life, and I came to the conclusion that I should choose the old Italian journeys with you, those long ago journeys which were so delicious. I've been very unhappy in the big things and very happy in the little things . . . only in that very big thing, complete love and confidence in my own family—I've had that always and can't lose it. And you are the pivot of it."

Her father had always been the source of her strength. From earliest childhood she had received his undiluted, never-ending love, and it was from him that she gained the self-esteem and self-assurance to reach as far as she could. "The abiding influence" in her life, her stepmother wrote later, "was her relation to her father. Her devotion to him, her whole-hearted admiration, the close and satisfying companionship between them, their deep mutual affection—these were to both the very foundation of existence."

Her father's affection served as a potent elixir, flushing away her disappointments, reinforcing her vigor. In return for his confidence in her, she trusted in him completely: he was the final authority; and even when he had caused her pain by refusing to accept her engagement to Henry Cadogan, she reluctantly agreed to his decision. From her youngest days, she and her father were friends; there were times when she played the role of Hugh Bell's child and times when she played his companion; and whatever role she played, he was always her guardian angel.

⚭   ⚭   ⚭

Twenty years later, she found another companion in the charming St. John Philby. They shared a common aversion to A. T. Wilson, whom Philby found "domineering," and enjoyed a common interest in charting the tribes and the genealogies of the sheikhs. But more than that, they became good friends. On December 21, 1916, Gertrude informed her family that she and St. John were going up the Tigris together. Philby had been asked by Cox to report on restless tribesmen up the river. Gertrude was reluctant to participate in the Christmas celebrations in Basrah, and thus felt relieved as they embarked together in Philby's launch. It was her fourth Christmas in foreign parts: "Arabia, Boulogne, Cairo and Qalat Salih. The last is where I expect to be on Xmas Day and I'm truly thankful to escape any attempt at feasts here." The celebration would only be a painful reminder of the husband and family she lacked.

On a warm and sunny day they steamed up the bending Tigris, sailing past villages of reed-built homes, pausing to look at the tomb where the Prophet Ezra was said to be buried, stopping finally at Qalat Salih, where their mutual friend Mr. Bullard had lent them his cottage. Gertrude and the handsome Philby talked for hours, and she described the stay enthusiastically: "We occupied his tiny house, sent for rations and prepared to lead a rough tin-fed life. But behold my boy developed a genius for cooking and we lived for 5 days on the fat of the land."

Explorations through the marshes took them to a part of the country that she had never seen before: village after village built of reeds, and fields of rice irrigated by the canals along the Tigris. After a week of meeting the marsh Arabs and dining with local sheikhs, Philby returned to Headquarters to welcome his wife, just arrived from India. Gertrude remained in the marshes a few extra days, gathering information about tribes and families that had baffled her in Basrah. She returned home alone, welcomed only by her mail from England.

The new year of 1917 brought with it rain and mud and the danger of walking to work, but Gertrude's life was made easier now by two servants and new living quarters—a two-room suite in the Political Office—allotted to her by Percy Cox. Her apartment contained a large sitting room and a dressing room screened off from the bed, "a blessing," she wrote, since she had been "miserably uncomfortable," lacking a place to work at night. Of course, there were still the small irritations: the tinned butter and tinned milk had grown so tasteless that she no longer even wanted them; the sheath of her pen had broken, requiring a new broad-nibbed fountain pen from England; her hair was still falling out; and a box of clothing sent from home by Thomas Cook & Sons had been waylaid in Bombay.

As soon as it was brought to her in Basrah, Gertrude hastily opened the carton. Eager to try on the black satin gown tucked inside, she sifted through the packing papers, but instead of running her hands over the rich, smooth fabric, all she could find was a small cardboard box and, in it, a black coat, a gold flower and some net. Nearly in tears, she wrote to Florence that the carton had been tampered with in India. "The gown has been abstracted. Isn't it infuriating?" she cried. Ten days later it was still bothering her: "Isn't it a tragedy about my black satin gown. Of course it's just the very gown most wanted . . . (I feel as if I were playing the leading role in the *Emperor's New Clothes*)." But even worse than the loss of her dress was the loss of her hair. "Presently I shall have to ask you to send me a nice wig. I haven't got enough hair left to pin a hat to," she moaned.

But these irksome matters were unimportant compared to the praise she had won for her work. "Happy to tell you that I hear my utterances receive a truly preposterous attention in London," she proudly informed her parents on January 13, 1917. One week later she received a commendation from the India Office in which it was noted: "They lectured her on the Indian Official Secrets Act and actually censored her letters. For a woman of her status the position must have been uncommonly galling; but she put up with it and I imagine that the improvement in the political attitude of Basrah to Cairo and H.M.G. [His Majesty's Government] is largely due to her work."

Her opinions were now more in tandem with the India officials in Basrah than with her colleagues in Cairo. In a message to Hogarth, while showing support for the Arab Bureau's policy, she indicated that she was a part of Sir Percy's team. "I think we'll still plump for the Sharif," she wrote. "His affairs seem to be taking a satisfactory turn and if they do, it will mean a good deal." But like Sir Percy Cox, she also supported Ibn Saud and wished he would join the Sharif in his revolt against the Turks. "He must be requested to do so, for now's the time." As for her nemesis, Ibn Rashid, whose ruthless family had once taken her prisoner in Hayil, reports were coming in that his brother-in-law, who served as his Vizier, was about to assassinate the truculent Emir.

Coincidentally, her work on Ibn Saud was to be published soon. "You'll see a piece of mine in the papers about Ibn Saud," she told her parents, adding somewhat cynically, "I gather the India Office are going to publish it. No, I don't suppose you will, for they usually publish these things in papers which no one reads."

By mid-February 1917 her writings on the tribes were also ready for publication, and she felt gratified as she read through the proofs. Of all her work it was, she told her father, the constant thread that gave her increasing satisfaction. *The Arab of Mesopotamia* would provide military and political officials with a complete and thorough background on the local tribes.

As the winter progressed, British troops under the successful command of General Maude finally took Kut and were edging closer to Baghdad. Gertrude's work in Basrah was nearly done, and on March 2, 1917, one year after her arrival, she wrote home that she had been asked to do an outline of modern Arabian history for Intelligence, "(the sort of thing I really enjoy doing), so I've turned to that. The amount I've written during the last year is appalling. . . . It comes to a great volume of material, of one kind and another. . . . But it's sometimes exasperating to be obliged to sit in an office when I long to be out in the desert, seeing the places I hear of, and finding out about them for myself."

Even worse was to be sitting idle in Basrah, yet, much to the disappointment of Lawrence and Hogarth, she had no desire to return to work in Cairo. Her feelings of loyalty toward Mesopotamia were growing, and equally important, her loyalty was becoming stronger to Percy Cox. As Hogarth wrote to his sister: "I hear from Gertrude Bell at fairly frequent intervals—She is still working hard and, as usual, feeling more and more under the influence of her chief. She varies in spirit apparently, which I expected. . . . Still, when you are as much behind the scenes as she is, things are not always so great as they are dished up to appear and I daresay I shall hear less jubilance from her. She has had several fever attacks evidently and would be the better for a time off in India or here . . . but she won't leave her present God."

The British now occupied Baghdad, and Gertrude waited impatiently to join Cox. On March 10, 1917, moments before the troops officially proclaimed the city taken, she wrote that she hoped to be called there very soon. The taking of Baghdad meant the end of the German dream of dominating the Middle East and the first big British success in the war. "We shall, I trust, make it a great centre of Arab civilisation, a prosperity; that will be my job partly, I hope, and I never lose sight of it." She reminisced about Baghdad and longed to hear exactly how it appeared. It was just three years since she had arrived there from Arabia, "3 lifetimes they seem as I look back on them."

Yet if anyone in her family harbored suspicions that she was homesick, she reassured them that, in spite of the drawbacks, "I would far rather be in the East among surroundings which are a perpetual interest to me, places and people which have no sharp edge of memory. . . . It has not been easy, in many ways. I think I have got over most of the difficulties, and the growing cordiality of my colleagues is a source of unmixed satisfaction."

Of all her colleagues, the friendliest at the moment was General

MacMunn. He returned from Baghdad with a purse of stories to tell her, and together, almost every evening, they sailed on the river or motored out to the desert. As they lounged on his yacht one evening, he turned to her and asked what part she intended to play in the future of Mesopotamia. "I think I shall have to keep an eye on it," she answered. Within a few days, she received word to come to Baghdad. Sir Percy Cox had already given her the title of Oriental Secretary, the key Intelligence post. Now she could keep her eye on the future.

CHAPTER NINETEEN

Baghdad

∞

Baghdad seemed as gossamer as the nighttime breeze, as alluring as the tales of *The Thousand and One Nights*. It was here, in the tenth century A.D., in the time of Harun al Rashid, that Scheherezade kept her murderous husband at bay, here that she spun her stories of beguiling women and lascivious men, here that she told of golden palaces and silver ponds, eunuchs and slaves, Ali Baba and Aladdin.

The citadel on the Tigris, built by the Abbassid Caliph Mansur eight centuries after the birth of Christ, one century after the death of the Prophet Muhammad, flourished for five hundred years. The heart of the Abbassid empire, it was the largest, most prosperous city in the world. More than a million people, of every imaginable race, color and creed, filled its narrow streets, worked in its shops, bathed in its bathhouses, gossiped in its coffeehouses. Sophisticated and cosmopolitan, the Baghdad of a thousand years ago boasted of bookstores and literary salons, banks and commercial houses, gardens and zoos. Its writers and poets produced some of the Arab world's greatest literature and translated into Arabic the works of Euclid, Plato and Aristotle. Its mathematicians, calculating in Arabic numbers, introduced the concept of zero; its scientists built an astronomical observatory and studied the round surface of the earth; its physicians earned their degrees in medical schools and served in public hospitals; its businessmen cashed checks at bank branches as far away as China. The cargo ships that sailed its river carried in gold from Africa, silver and spices from India, porcelains from China, pearls from the Gulf. Traders from East Africa arrived with ivory; desert caravans from Turkestan brought in slaves. In return, Baghdadi merchants exported to the world the finest cotton shirts, thick cotton towels, fanciful turbans of colored silk, healing oils and potions, excellent swords, fine leather goods and paper.

But history had swept it nearly all away. The tyrannical force of the Mongols, the feudal rule of the Persians, the corrupt occupation of the Turks and the plagues and floods of the nineteenth century had wiped out most of the city. When the British troops rode in, in March 1917, they found only two hundred thousand people—mostly Sunni Muslims and Jews—living in shabby buildings inside the crumbling city walls. Yet, as they do today, here and there grand Ottoman buildings of yellow brick, two or three stories high, stretched across acres of green grass; slender minarets and domed mosques glittered in the sunlight; statuesque palm groves fringed the city. Verdant gardens brought relief from the dry hot sun, and the perfume of jasmine, roses, oranges, lemons, peaches and pomegranates wafted through the early morning air.

It didn't take long for the British to spiffy up the place with horse races and polo matches, cribbage and dominoes, afternoon tea and lawn tennis. Gertrude arrived in April, pleased as punch to be part of the action. Not that it had been easy: General Maude, newly appointed Military Commander of Mesopotamia, had been determined to keep her away. He wanted no woman in Baghdad, least of all an official. But Sir Percy Cox came quickly to Gertrude's defense: she would be treated the same as the male members of his staff, he informed the general, and she could render services beyond the power of anyone else. As Cox struggled to organize a civil administration, replacing lax Ottoman rules with strict new laws, new institutions, new agencies, he needed Gertrude to act as his link to the people. Besides, she was not like other women.

∞   ∞   ∞

Exactly three years had passed since her last trip to Baghdad from Hayil. Exhausted from the trying journey to Arabia, dejected over her failures either to find important archaeology or to meet the warrior Ibn Saud, she had come out of the desert in 1914 bearing an enormous sense of defeat. Now she came to Baghdad as a victor, jubilant over her own success in Intelligence, exultant over her country's success in capturing the city. Masses of roses and cries of congratulations greeted her as anti-Turkish Arabs celebrated their liberation by the British.

Nevertheless, confusion followed. Against the advice of Cox, a flowery proclamation from London, read aloud, invited the Arabs of Mesopotamia to participate in the new government so that they could unite with the rest of the Arab peoples. But to the Mesopotamians, the proclamation raised more questions than it answered. What kind of government would be formed? How much independence would the Arabs have? What kind of connection would there be between themselves and the people of Syria and (what is today Saudi) Arabia? How would their future unfold? Would the Turks return? From the point of view of most of the Arabs, another foreign conqueror, heretic and Western, had come into their land, evicted their Muslim occupier and claimed the local people to have been liberated. Then, like all the others, it established itself as the ruling authority.

Anxiety abounded as people from all parts of Mesopotamia came to the city. A crush of visitors flocked to the British Residency, an Ottoman building that still stands along the Tigris. Old acquaintances and nervous petitioners swarmed the great courtyard outside. Indoors, clusters of black-robed women huddled on the floors, bearded sheikhs in flowing robes and braided headdresses waited on the sofas, white-haired elders and aspiring magnates paced the hallways, turbaned holy men and landowning sayids gathered in the inner courtyard.

Gertrude organized a space just outside Sir Percy's office where, as "official strainer" of Kokus (as Cox was now called by the locals), she interviewed the Arabs. Her job was to assuage the fears of all and assess the influence of each. Trustworthy civilians had to be found to serve the newly formed agencies. Notables and holy men, rich or influential, had to be befriended to win their loyalty. Tribal sheikhs, leaders of great numbers of people, had to be subsidized financially to gain their allegiance. Unknown tribesmen from the fertile Euphrates Valley, whose grain was needed to feed the civilian and army populations, had to be filtered out and appraised for their importance.

Her work, as she described it to her parents, was "the gathering and sorting of information," and though she was also given the role of Curator of Antiquities, her main title was Oriental Secretary. As the Intelligence expert and chief adviser on Arab affairs, she analyzed the power and politics of the local leaders, evaluated their links to the enemy Turks, judged their potential loyalty to the British. Within two weeks of her arrival she had already prepared maps, tribe lists and confidential reports on Baghdad's Personalities. "That's not bad going," she crowed. Not allowed to give more details of her highly sensitive work, she assured her family that she was content, happy at last to be eating fresh butter, yogurt and milk, pleased that the job was "a thousand times more interesting" than in Basrah. She was soon writing long reports on Turkey for the War Office, composing articles for them on Mesopotamia and Asia Minor, compiling Intelligence reviews, sending off essays for the secret *Arab Bulletin*, analyzing tribes, Shiite traditions and more.

Dressed in her frilly skirts and flowered hat, she paid a call on the elderly Naqib of Baghdad. The white-bearded Abdul Rahman al Gailani, chief religious figure of the Sunni community, and member of a family line reaching back to the Prophet, held a prominent role in the city, and indeed his power was nearly worldwide. It was a rare privilege for an unveiled woman even to be allowed in the Naqib's presence, yet she had been to his grand house on the Tigris several times in the past. Now, when she entered the columned, brick courtyard, and the robed and turbaned holy man received her with open arms, his welcome had even more significance. Her high position in the government confirmed her status as an "honorary man." The locals respectfully called her El Khatun, "the Lady" to some, the "lady of the Court who keeps an open eye and ear for the benefit of the State" to others. Yet in the eyes of the Arabs, her female gender all but disappeared when they heard her discourse knowledgeably on the complicated politics of the day. "A very shrewd woman," remembers one of the men she dealt with; "very, very, very, very, very, very shrewd."

She relished every moment. Days after her arrival, she marched off in search of a place to live, dismissing the house that had been assigned her as "a tiny stifling box of a place." In a busy part of town, across from the great arched building of the Lynch Company, the British export-import firm, she poked her head behind a blank wall and discovered three small summer houses set in a rose garden. The place needed work. But with help from the owner, her friend Musa Pachachi, a wealthy landowner from one of the city's most prominent families, she added a kitchen and a bath, hired a cook, a servant and a gardener. By May, she was settled in the first house of her own, living merrily under the blossoms, cooled by the breeze coming off the river just a block away.

Her life took on a pleasant routine. Awake before six, eager for exercise, she dressed in her breeches and bowler and rode her favorite pony along the river bank, sometimes toward the desert, sometimes to the gardens of Haji Naji. Six or seven kilometers outside the center, those vast gardens now comprise most of the diplomatic embassies and some of the commercial streets of Baghdad. The proprietor, Haji Naji, a slim, handsome Shiite, quickly became her friend, keeping her abreast of Shiite attitudes and offering her his counsel, along with fresh fruits and honey from his orchards. Their morning picnics soon became the talk of the city, and rumors flourished, as they do today, that their friendship had turned into romance.

For people who had never seen a woman accepted so unequivocally by men, it was difficult to believe that sex was not the reason. Indeed, she oozed femininity in her fancy dress. She percolated sociability in her outgoing ways. She even flirted with seductive charm. When one holy man paid her a call, he refused to look at her, an unveiled woman, in the face. It did not prevent him, however, from talking to her about his personal affairs. "And at the end of it," she wrote home delightedly, "I'll admit he tipped me a casual wink or two, just enough to know me again." But it was the power of her mind that won men over.

Six months earlier, Gertrude had sent Fahad Bey ibn Hadhdhal, the Paramount Chief of the Anazeh tribe, a letter beseeching his support for the Arab Revolt and English alliance. As the greatest nomad potentate on the western borders of Iraq, he controlled five thousand rifles and ruled the enormous desert that lay between Syria and the Euphrates River. With Germans, Turks and Syrians skulking across the sands, toting guns, trafficking in supplies, the British needed his help. If he could stop the enemy, they would pay him a generous allowance. But the Turks, still in command in the western desert, were willing to pay him too. The Turks, to whom his family owed some of its wealth, were a known commodity; the British were strangers. To side with the English meant he would be taking an enormous risk. Gertrude had labored carefully over the letter asking for his help.

Now, at the end of May 1917, the seventy-five-year-old sheikh was coming to Baghdad. It was three years since she had last seen him, slight and brown-skinned, seated in his tent, a falcon at his shoulder, a greyhound at his side. Their reunion was tenderly affectionate, "almost compromising," one of her colleagues teased. In a conference at the Residency with her and Cox, Fahad Bey revealed that it had been the "powerful effect" of Gertrude's arguments that won him over. With great detail, he described his transformation.

Upon receiving her eloquent plea, the Arab chief said, he summoned his men from the desert and read the letter aloud. Then, turning to his followers, he declared: "My brothers, you have heard what this woman has to say to us. She is only a woman, but she is a mighty and valiant one. Now we all know that Allah has made all women inferior to men. But if the women of the Anglez are like her, the men must be like lions in strength and valor. We had better make peace with them."

No words could have made her prouder. That women were seen as second to men was a painful given, whether in England or in Iraq. But there was no doubt in her mind that in the eyes of the Arabs, and in the eyes of Cox as well, she was more than the equal of any man.

∞ ∞ ∞

As successful as the alliance was with Fahad Bey, relations with colleagues in Cairo had hit a snag. In accord with the letters between Henry McMahon and the Sharif Hussein, the Arab Bureau had gone ahead with the agreement to back the Sharif's demands for an Arab kingdom if he led an Arab revolt against the Turks. Ronald Storrs, the Intelligence chief in Egypt, had journeyed to the Hejaz, the Sharif's headquarters in Arabia, carrying money, weapons and gold watches for the Sharif Hussein. Within days of their meeting, the Arab Revolt had been launched. Triumphantly, the Sharif's men had captured Mecca and forced the Turks to surrender at Jeddah.

Yet only recently, in April 1917, Sir Percy had learned of a pact signed by Mark Sykes and M. Georges Picot, to divide the Ottoman Middle East between Britain and France. Under the Sykes-Picot accord, actually signed a year before, the Turkish spoils were to be divvied up between the British and the French: a British zone of influence would be created in Mesopotamia, around the Euphrates and Tigris Rivers, to include Basrah, Baghdad and Khanaqin; a French zone of influence would be created in Syria, comprising the Syrian coast, including Beirut and the country betweeen Cilicia and the Upper Tigris. The pact also stated that France and Britain were "prepared to recognize and protect an independent Arab State or Confederation of Arab States . . . under the suzerainty of an Arab Chief," carrying out some of the promises made to the Sharif Hussein. In addition, it was decided that Palestine would be placed under international administration.

A year earlier, in 1916, when David Hogarth was informed of the Sykes-Picot pact, he had written at once to the Director of Intelligence, Captain Hall, urging that no one else be told: "The conclusion of this Agreement is of no immediate service to our Arab policy as pursued here, and will only not be a grave disadvantage if, for some time to come, it is kept strictly secret." The pact was concealed from Sir Percy Cox and Gertrude Bell for almost a year.

When Cox learned of the Sykes-Picot agreement, he was furious. Not only had he been deceived, but what would become of Mesopotamia? Cox had hoped that Iraq would be annexed under the India Government and that Ibn Saud would be appointed king. McMahon and the Arab Bureau had promised that position to the Sharif Hussein.

Now there was even talk that, under Sykes-Picot, Baghdad would have a local ruler, Basrah would belong to the British, and Mosul would go to the French. Cox demanded an explanation.

Arriving in Baghdad in June 1917 to present the Arab Bureau's side, Ronald Storrs was taken by river launch to Cox's house. As they stood, cocktails in hand, on the balcony overlooking the Tigris, Cox and Gertrude pumped him for information. At dinner, they questioned him more. What was the thinking in Cairo? they wanted to know, and what was happening in Arabia? Among other things, he reported to them on the Hejaz. He had returned several times, he said, and with T. E. Lawrence to assist him, had met the man who would set the desert ablaze. The man was Faisal, third son of the Sharif Hussein, slim and high-strung, a skillful leader, proven to be shrewd in strategy, strong in battle. As Storrs described the charismatic Faisal, Gertrude took note.

At the office the following morning, it was her turn to fill Storrs in. She described in detail the situation in Mesopotamia, ran down the list of tribes and chiefs, habits and traditions, rivalries and politics, checking off each with masterly ease. Then, like a schoolgirl skipping class, she led him on a fast-paced tour of the town, interviewing sheikhs and notables to hear their positions, taking the political temperature (as she often did) of the merchants in the bazaar. By the end of the visit, Gertrude had made her mark on the man who would soon be Governor of Jerusalem. Her knowledge of Iraq, her familiarity with the people, her understanding of the relationship between the Arabs of Syria, Arabia and Mesopotamia were unique, Storrs wrote in his diary. Her "first-class brain," her "universal" knowledge, her "level" judgment, outstanding. But for all her strength and drive, he wisely observed, she should be careful: "her frail body" needed rest if it was to endure the heat of summer.

For Gertrude, the visit had added a brilliant spark to her daily routine. Coupled with the recent arrival in Baghdad (thanks to her persuasive efforts with Sir Percy) of her good friend St. John Philby as able deputy to Cox, it sent her spinning. Her work in Mesopotamia now was exhilarating. There had never been anything quite like it before, she wrote to her father: "It's amazing. It's the making of a new world." Outlining a plan for Whitehall, she noted she wanted to take "a decisive hand" in the country's future. "I shall be able to do that, I shall indeed," she affirmed. "What does anything else matter when the job is such a big one?"

For the first time in years she began to think about what lay around the corner. Her work had reached a new level of excitement; her little house had begun to feel more like home. Friends like Philby and Bullard frequently came for dinner and good conversation, and over a well-cooked roast and the proper wines she enjoyed pronouncing her views on everything from the strengths and weaknesses of Turkish administration to the Labour Party's position in England, to the price of meat in Baghdad, to the eating habits of her newest gift, a gazelle. If the latest clothes that arrived fom England weren't quite what she had envisioned (one of them was "no more of an evening gown than it was a fur coat," she complained. "I shall just have not to dine out when it gets hot"), the friendliness of the local people, the warmth of the sunshine, the abundance of flowers and fresh fruits more than made up for her disappointments. "It's so wonderful here, I can't tell you how much I love it," she wrote her father.

Rather suprisingly, she refused his invitation to visit England on her vacation. With so much going on, she did not want to leave Iraq right now, she explained. Still, she reassured him, it was his love that gave her the strength to carry on. And in the strange way that she wrote to him, little girlishness combined with womanly passion, she told him their relationship was special: "unique. That's what it is, dearest beloved one. You know there's nothing in the world which I would not bring to you, big things and little, with complete assurance of your perfect sympathy and understanding and when necessary forgiveness. What you were to me at a time of sorrow so acute that I still wonder how one can endure such things and live, I shall never be able to say to you—but you know, and in the midst of all this new world which has grown up round me my regret is that I cannot share it more fully with you." As for the East, "It's a new life, a new possibility of carrying on existence. . . . I'm loving it, you know, loving my work and rejoicing in the confidence of my chief."

∞   ∞   ∞

Summer hit like a furnace blast; by July the daily temperature reached 120 degrees. Gertrude's parasol was useless; her fair skin baked in the sun, her cheeks stung from the swirling dust, her eyeballs ached in the fierce wind. Even at night the air hardly cooled. The only way she could sleep was to take her mattress to the roof and lie outdoors between wringing wet sheets; when they dried she woke and soaked them again in cold water. It wasn't long before a tropical illness landed her in the hospital, where she fastened the emerald pin her father had sent for her birthday onto her nightgown.

Sometime in August she was well enough to laugh at a story she heard about an Englishman who had visited a Turkish military hospital before the war. The hospital's official ledger listed patients as: "Admitted; Cured; Died; Ran Away." On the last page of the ledger was the total: "Admittances; 6. Cured; o. Died; 2. Ran Away; 4."

At the office, an ugly dispute with the army Commander-in-Chief had soured the air. As great a commanding soldier as he was, General Maude was imperious; arrogant toward Cox (his classmate at Sandhurst), intolerant of the Arabs. His interference in political affairs had brought the mild-mannered Cox to the point of thinking seriously about resigning. Sir Percy's presence, as mentor, father figure, and colleague, meant too much to Gertrude to let this situation go unheeded. She owed him more than her job; her life had become linked to his. In the way that people working together feel a sexual energy derived from thinking and acting intensely in tandem, she felt exhilaration. (She would never have put a sexual connotation on things related to Cox; more likely she would have called it admiration, but whatever its label, it held a strong pull.) With Cox's permission, she composed a scathing letter to her good friend Arthur Hirtzel, Permanent Under Secretary for the India Office, likening the army command to "denizens of a lunatic asylum."

The power of her friendships, and her words, were not to be taken lightly. Hirtzel forwarded her letter to Lord Curzon, Secretary of State for Foreign Affairs. It confirmed his worst suspicions, Curzon said, and promised to take up the matter with the War Cabinet (without, of course, mentioning Miss Bell). But before General Maude could be reprimanded, he was taken ill. Two days later, on November 16, 1917, the general died of cholera.

∞ ∞ ∞

While General Maude was being laid to rest, the Arab army under Faisal's command was on the move. Its main goal was to sabotage the Turkish railway line, the key communications link for the Turks, that ran from Medina in the Hejaz to Damascus in Syria. The irregular bands of Arab warriors were the perfect fighters for this campaign of guerrilla warfare, but it would take more than just the Sharifian army to make it a success. Tribes that were long-standing enemies had to be persuaded to fight side by side. With the understanding that Faisal would be their leader, the men of the Billi, the Juheina, the Harb, the Rwallah and the Beni Sakhr all agreed to join the Arab Revolt.

In the summer of 1916, when their revolt began, they took control of Jeddah, Rabigh, Yanbu al Bahr and Mecca. Six months later, in January 1917, with Lawrence serving as Faisal's political officer, the

Arab army, with help from the British navy, captured the seaport of al Wajh. Then, after marching eight hundred miles north from Mecca, the Arabs won a decisive victory at Aqaba. It was Gertrude's friends the Abu Tayi—the Howeitat tribe from northern Arabia—who led the attack, with Lawrence at their side, and the success made a hero of T. E. Lawrence. In September the Arab army had raided the Hejaz railway line at Mudawara; destroying a Turkish locomotive, they killed seventy Turkish soldiers, wounded thirty more and and took ninety Turkish prisoners. Later that autumn, after some serious mishaps in the Yarmuk Valley, they derailed a train carrying Jamal Pasha, the Governor of Syria and commander of a Turkish army corps. By the end of November 1917, assisted by two Iraqi officers, the skillful military expert Jafar al Askari and the politically savvy Nuri Said, the Arab army was clearing the way for Britain's General Allenby to march from Suez into Jerusalem and from there (with Lawrence and Faisal behind him) into Damascus. Armed with Lawrence's promise of future British backing, Faisal was on the path to become ruler of Syria.

David Hogarth would later credit Gertrude Bell for much of the success of the Arab Revolt by providing the "mass of information" about the "tribal elements ranging between the Hejaz Railway and the Nefud, particularly about the Howeitat group." It was this information, Hogarth emphasized, which "Lawrence, relying on her reports, made signal use of in the Arab campaigns of 1917 and 1918."

With help from the American writer Lowell Thomas, Lawrence was camel-riding the path to fame, but Gertrude deliberately turned her back on publicity. In October she was awarded the C.B.E., Commander of the British Empire, yet requests for interviews were tossed in the wastebasket and her parents chastised for talking to journalists. "Please please don't supply information about me," she scolded. "I've said this so often before that I thought you understood how much I hate the whole advertisement business." Self-promotion was abhorrent. Not that she had any self-doubts. One of the best Political Officers, Colonel Leachman, had even told her that her "unbounded conceit was the talk of Iraq."

When the Balfour Declaration was released to the public at the end of the year, Gertrude attacked it viciously. Sir Arthur Balfour, the British Foreign Secretary, had written a letter to Lord Rothschild, leader of the Jewish community in England, promising "a national home for the Jewish people" in Palestine. The Balfour Declaration vowed not to prejudice "the civil and religious rights" of the Arabs already living in Palestine.

"I hate Mr. Balfour's Zionist pronouncement," Gertrude wrote venomously to her parents. "It's my belief that it can't be carried out, the country is wholly unsuited to the ends the Jews have in view; it is a poor land, incapable of great development and with a solid two thirds of its population Mohammedan Arabs who look on Jews with contempt. To my mind it's a wholly artificial scheme divorced from all relation to facts and I wish it the ill success it deserves—and will get, I fancy." Part of her prediction came true: the trouble she forecast between Arabs and Jews was to continue for five generations, and not until almost the end of the twentieth century did the people of Palestine—Jews and Arabs—recognize each other's right to exist on the same land. But the "wholly artificial scheme" of a Jewish national homeland did, in fact, become a reality. Indeed, Israel became the only democratic state in the Middle East.

∽ ∽ ∽

As concerned as she was about Palestine, she felt besieged by problems closer to home. Shiite tribesmen in the Euphrates Valley had been helping the Turks, and Cox had given orders to stop their communications with the enemy. He had even visited the area himself. But the trouble continued, and in December 1917 Gertrude made plans to investigate. Few people knew the region as well as she did.

Piling her suitcases and camp furniture into an open Ford, she settled herself in the motor car and, with her servant at the wheel, drove off in the clear January sunshine, bumping along the familiar desert road southwest toward Karbala. She had been on that road before: once, years ago, euphoric, as she headed back to Baghdad with the plan of Ukhaidir, the great palace ruins she had discovered, in her pocket; once, downcast, as she returned from her imprisonment in Hayil in Arabia. She felt herself sliding back into that earlier atmosphere, savoring the innocence of those times, knowing full well that they had disappeared. She feared that even the good-natured Fattuh, her former servant and so much a part of those journeys, was a victim of the Turks.

For hours on end she looked out on little else but the past; the dirt road ran through endless vacant land, cutting through only two small market towns. Not until late afternoon, as the car wobbled through clouds of dust, did the dirt change to grass and the tufts of desert brush burst into palm and willow trees. Another whole day along the Euphrates, and she reached the holy city of Karbala. Like its sister city Najaf, it had once been a hotbed of fanaticism, a place where Shiites plotted *jihad*, holy war, against Christian nonbelievers. This was the founding region of Islam, where Ali, son-in-law of Muhammad, and

Hussein, grandson of the Prophet, were each treacherously slain and where their devout Shiite followers, many from Persia, still brought the corpses of their dead. (The schism between Muslims that resulted in Shiites and Sunnis came early on. The Shiites wanted the warrior Ali ibn Ali Talib, son-in-law of the Prophet, to succeed Muhammad as Caliph; the Sunnis accepted Abu Bakr, a close friend of Muhammad's, as his successor.)

Other travelers were coming here too: Persians serving as espionage agents for the Germans and the Turks; enemy caravans from Damascus and Aleppo, buying food and supplies. Karbala's merchants made a handsome profit on the goods, and its sheikhs collected a hefty tax on the loaded camels. What's more, the Syrian customers barraged the townsmen with anti-British propaganda. The locals were easy prey. The British had been depleting their resources, taking their flocks of sheep and cattle to feed the troops, demanding high taxes to cover the cost of administration; in addition, the British had set up blockades to try to stop the trafficking with the Turks. The Arabs of Karbala were in an uproar.

Gertrude moved cautiously through the narrow streets of the town, meeting with its notables, the first European woman to enter the dark, damp cell of its most renowned holy man. As strong as her arguments were, she needed every bit of her persuasive powers. Even then, it was too soon to know whether her words would have an effect.

At Najaf the situation was even worse. The city, a web of underground houses connected by tunnels, a malignant, fanatical place, drew her in with its mystery and beauty. There, she wrote, the holy men sat in an atmosphere reeking of antiquity, "so thick with the dust of ages that you can't see through it—nor can they."

Heavy trade in contraband and handsome payoffs from the Turks kept the population of forty thousand Arabs on friendly terms with the enemy. What's more, when tribes that were sympathetic to the British came to Najaf to purchase large amounts of grain, draining the food supplies, the locals expressed their resentment. As Gertrude phrased it after she met with the local sheikhs, "Things are not in a satisfactory state."

Stopping briefly at Babylon on the way back, she yearned even more for simpler times. She walked around the ruins, recalling the days when she had camped there with the German archaeologists. The war had turned the world upside down; now her former colleagues were the enemy. Her heart ached when she stood in the empty dusty room where Fattuh had put up her camp furniture and where she and the Germans had held eager conversations about her plans of Babylon and

Ukhaidir. "What a dreadful world of broken friendships we have created between us," she wrote.

By the time she returned to Baghdad and her office on the Tigris, her nerves were on edge. She was nearing fifty and experiencing symptoms that often strike women that age. But with no close female friend with whom to compare notes, she searched helplessly for a reason. Before the two-week trip to the Euphrates she had complained of listlessness and anomie, even temporary amnesia. She was constantly forgetting things, causing her to work more slowly and to continue later into the night. Tired and run down, she needed a companion, someone to look after her, to lend her a sympathetic ear. "What I really want is a wife," she wrote to her parents. "I quite understand why men out here marry anyone who turns up!" Never long on patience, she found her temper shorter than ever. When her new boots did not arrive on time from England, she denounced her bootmaker of fifteen years as "a rogue" and accused him of "abominable practices." When she sat down at the lunch table in the mess and a plate of bully beef was put before her, her body tensed. Fresh food was scarce, she knew, but it was the fourteenth day in a row she was being served the tasteless tinned meat. She looked at the plate of rations, threw down her knife and fork and burst into tears.

But these complaints were like paper cuts compared to the deeper wound that festered. Time had not yet healed the pain she still felt from the loss of Doughty-Wylie. "Oh Father, dearest," she wrote, "do you know that tonight (February 22) is just three years since D. and I parted. . . . I've lived again through the four days of three years ago almost minute by minute." Once again her father wanted her to come home for the summer; once again she was reluctant. "Dearest you know I love you but this sorrow at the back of everything deadens me in a way to all else, to whether I go home or whether I stay here in the East, or what happens. And yet . . . whether I'm with you or away from you, you're just as real a comfort to me always."

She had molded her house and garden around her like a protective womb. From her sitting room, with its comfortable, chintz-covered chairs, Persian rugs and pottery shards on the mantel, she wrote her letters to friends, pausing sometimes with pen in hand to peer out the window and watch her gazelle. Her Chaldean servant kept her house and clothes in order, her cook took charge of the food and her gardener followed her precise instructions, coaxing flowers from the same kinds of seeds as her favorite blossoms at Rounton. If only she had ordered bulbs of daffodil and narcissus! Still, she smiled, seeing irises and verbena flourish in their beds, violets flower bravely in their pots, roses almost always in bloom. As for the inevitable summer heat on the way, ceiling fans had been installed, along with new electric lights, and she felt a little bettter prepared. By the end of the year she would even add on another room.

To a friend she wrote that she had grown to love the East, its sights, its sounds, its people. She thought of it not as the land of her exile but as her second native country. If her family were not in Yorkshire she would have no desire to return.

Iraq was turning into her permanent home; England had become a dusty attic filled with ghostly memories.

Chapter Twenty

Disarray

∞

The situation with A. T. Wilson began rather differently from the way it ended two and a half years later. To start things off, when the insurrection came, in the spring of 1918, it was discovered that an Islamic committee of over a hundred Arabs, working under cover in Najaf, planned to incite the Euphrates tribes to rebel against the British. First, they murdered a Political Officer and plotted to kill three more men. At the time, Percy Cox was away, advising Whitehall on Mesopotamia (London was actually thinking of pulling out of Iraq), but the Acting Civil Commissioner, Arnold T. Wilson, handled the situation well. Some of the criminals were deported; the real culprits were hanged.

"I'm not sure you realize who he is," Gertrude informed her parents of Wilson, "a most remarkable creature, 34, brilliant abilities, a combined mental and physical power which is extremely rare." Known for his extraordinary memory and inexhaustible energy, Wilson alone exceeded Gertrude in his literary appreciation and endless working hours. Never without a classical book in his pocket, he quoted Bacon, Shakespeare, Milton, Virgil and Socrates in his dispatches home and mesmerized his dinner guests with Persian poetry or Indian dialects. "I'm devoted to him," Gertrude went on; "he is the best of colleagues and he ought to make a wonderful career. I don't think I've ever come across anyone of more extraordinary force."

Admittedly, in the early days in Basrah she and Wilson had been less than friendly. He had ignored her in the mess, excluded her from his work, even refused to tell her the codes used in his communications with London and India. And when he arrived in Baghdad to replace her good friend Philby (who had gone to Arabia to try to persuade Ibn Saud not to attack Britain's ally, the Sharif Hussein), he and Gertrude had eyed each other with suspicion. Wilson regarded her as a "born intriguer"; she viewed him with distrust. Yet now, in his role as Acting Civil Commissioner, he behaved with a cool conduct that earned her admiration.

∽ ∽ ∽

Gertrude had declined to go to England that summer of 1918, explaining that things were too critical for her to leave the country. If the Khatun left, the Arabs would feel she was deserting them. "I, in a small way, am one of the people who can help comfort them," she wrote to Hugh. As for herself, she was "unspeakably anxious" about the country's future, but "I do sometimes want you so much that I can scarcely bear it." Perhaps Hugh would come to Iraq.

For the sake of her health, she knew she would have to escape the heat of Baghdad. She would go to Persia instead, on the sort of holiday she enjoyed: a change of scenery, a bit of rest and a chunk of challenging work. Trouble was brewing next door to the east, in the country of the Shah. The Persian ruler was wavering in his neutrality, threatening to join Germany's side in the war. Moreover, Turks, Germans and Russians, running amok since the Bolshevik Revolution in November, were creating problems on the border with Iraq. The British were desperate to maintain a stable atmosphere. Yet added to their concerns over a peaceful frontier, the security of their oil fields at Abadan and the continued safety of their routes to India was the new Bolshevik state now looming over Persia. A weak British Ambassador in Teheran made the situation even worse.

The War Office had requested that clear borders be drawn, and for several weeks in the spring of 1918 Gertrude worked steadily, poring over maps of Mesopotamia and Persia, deciding vital boundary lines. Her office in Baghdad was cool and spacious, its tall shuttered windows facing the Tigris, its brick floors covered lightly with fine Persian rugs, its high whitewashed walls papered with maps. Persian vases stood on top of the black wood bookcase, and a white sofa, some white chairs, her writing desk, and a big map table on which she studied the desert outlines, made up the rest of the room. On the outdoor balcony that rimmed the building sat the *kavasses*, office servants in high felt hats, who fetched files or brought in tea. Next door to her, on the Residency's first floor, was Wilson's office, and she often went back and forth to speak with the tall, broad-shouldered Acting Civil Commissioner.

At the end of June she left for her vacation: a week in Teheran, more weeks camping in the mountains and the rest of the time riding through the countryside gathering information. She came back at the end of August, rested and refreshed, ready to compile an Intelligence book on Persia and looking forward once again to seeing Cox.

Upon her return, she was met with staggering news. The dark-eyed Wilson summoned her to his office and sat her down. Sir Percy Cox was leaving, he announced, assigned to Persia to oversee events. For Gertrude it came as a shocking blow. Not that she didn't think it was a good idea for the British Empire. Indeed it was. Persia was dangerous and the situation called for his shrewd mind, his dignified manner, his deft way with few words, his clever way of handling people. Many petitioners went into his office angry, but no one ever went out mad. Yet a wave of sadness overcame her when she thought of losing her mentor. As brilliant and indefatigable as A. T. Wilson was, he was also unsociable, obstinate and strong-willed; he had none of Sir Percy's gentle ways.

A few weeks later, just before leaving Iraq, the reticent Cox came to see her in her office. He had visited her parents while he was in England, and his attitude toward her now seemed more paternal. Was she being properly looked after by everyone? he asked anxiously. Was she happy? he wanted to know. In an unusual show of emotion, he bent down, embraced her warmly and said farewell. Then, collecting his wife, his parrot and his assistant Mr. Bullard, Cox was off in a convoy to Teheran, leaving behind A. T. Wilson as Acting Civil Commissioner and Gertrude Bell as Oriental Secretary. "Captain Wilson and I are excellent colleagues and the best of friends," she reported to her parents, "and I know I can do a good deal to help him by seeing people and being ready to sit and talk as much as they want." She was right; there would be plenty of people to talk to. But as for being on excellent terms with Wilson, that would be short-lived.

∞   ∞   ∞

Perhaps it was Cox's departure that made her sick, perhaps it was just the weather; but she spent much of that autumn in bed, swallowing quinine, fighting a bout of malaria. Nevertheless, she was cheered by some encouraging reports. General Allenby, with the Arab army under his command, had taken Damascus, and on October 1 the Sharif's son, Faisal, followed by several hundred mounted soldiers of the Arab army, rode into town. With the help of T. E. Lawrence, an independent Arab constitutional government was installed three days later in Syria and the tall, slim Faisal declared the ruler. It was a slap in the face for the French and the Sykes-Picot accord, but a recognition of promises made by the Arab Bureau, and Lawrence in particular, in return for the Sharif Hussein's revolt against the Turks.

Gertrude's spirits soared even higher when news arrived, on October 31, 1918, that the Allies had signed an armistice with Turkey. "War has ceased here," she wrote home in great relief. "It's almost more than one can believe."

Buoyed by the treaty, but still weary from the malaria, she welcomed an invitation from her good friend General George MacMunn. The Commander-in-Chief had become her favorite dinner companion, and now he offered to take her on a cruise. Relaxing on board his luxurious ship, she read novels, dined well and indulged in a bit of flirting with her friend. As they sailed down the Tigris word came that an agreement had been reached with Austria-Hungary, and, most comforting of all, a few days later, on November 11, 1918, they learned that the Armistice had been signed with Germany.

Nearly ten million people had been killed and another twenty million wounded; nations had been destroyed and empires disbanded in what was one of the most brutal wars of all time. Gertrude had seen the tortured faces of too many wounded soldiers and the battered corpses of countless dead. She had suffered herself from too little food and too much heat, from loneliness and isolation, from sickness and fatigue, and most of all from the death of her beloved Doughty-Wylie. But now she celebrated the end of the Great War. Peace was at hand. Or so it seemed.

The war to end all wars had left the Ottoman Empire in a state of disarray. The sick man of Europe, now in the throes of death, had abandoned his offspring, leaving them to the care of others. British and Arabs alike fingered their worry beads over the future of the East, rubbing them even harder after the announcement on November 8, 1918, of the Anglo-French Declaration. In Basrah and Baghdad, Aleppo and Amman, Jerusalem and Damascus, in public broadcasts, in newspapers and on billboards, England and France together proclaimed the "final liberation of the populations living under the Turkish yoke and the setting up of national governments chosen by the people themselves." Promises were made to help in creating new governments and to grant them recognition as soon as they became established. A new phrase, "the right of self-determination," declared by President Woodrow Wilson of the United States in his Fourteen Points, whirled through the streets like a Gypsy gone wild. But as much as the announcement of independence alleviated Arab concerns over the return of the Turks, it stirred up more fears about who would lead and how best to proceed. A year and a half earlier the Arabs had worried about how the British were going to rule them; now they worried about how they would rule themselves.

To Gertrude the declaration seemed surprisingly premature; in Baghdad alone, she remarked to her father, it "has thrown the whole town into a ferment. It doesn't happen often that people are told that their future as a State is in their hands and asked what they would like. They are all talking and mercifully they all come in to me with the greatest eagerness to discuss what they think. On two points they are practically all agreed, they want us to control their affairs and they want Sir Percy as High Commissioner. Beyond that all is divergence."

Beyond the divergence lurked suspicion. She continued: "Public opinion is very jumpy and the most unexpected things set the town afire with almost childish indignation. Every word we say they regard as pointing to things we have in our hearts which we won't fully explain. . . . I always speak quite frankly and they believe me. I think they know I have their interests more deeply at heart than anything else and they trust me in the same sort of way that they trust Sir Percy."

Gertrude's immediate task was to watch the local weathercock. The Secretary of State for India had asked her opinion on which way the political winds were blowing among the various constituencies: the educated Sunnis in town, the Shiite majority in the provinces, the large Jewish community in Baghdad, the Christians in Mosul. Did they want the British Crown or an Arab king? Most of the townspeople wanted an Arab emir, but they couldn't decide who it should be, she wrote home at the end of November. Some preferred a son of the Sharif Hussein, some favored the head of an important family in Mosul, some thought a member of the Egyptian royal family might be best, and still others wanted the Naqib, the Sunni holy man of Baghdad. The last, however, rejected the notion of either himself or one of the Sharif's sons and was firmly in favor of a British administration. As for the attitude of the Shiites, she would have to wait a while before they made their feelings known. Adding to the confusion, the Jewish community was so concerned about being ruled by Arabs that they petitioned for

British citizenship, while several thousand Turkish sympathizers, imprisoned during the war and now returned to Baghdad, were creating havoc as they began to engage in an anti-British campaign.

Gertrude spent time with everyone she could. In the mornings at the Residency, in her high-ceilinged office, groups of young men, some in *dishdashas*, long cotton shirts, most in Western suits and Turkish fezes, trooped in. The Khatun rang for coffee, and when Indian servants brought in refreshments, the men drank the rich dark brew and talked, while she smoked her cigarettes and made notes on their political views. Some days she motored outside Baghdad, visiting tribal sheikhs or seeing friends like her landlord, Musa Pachachi, who came from one of the most important trading families, or Haji Naji, who favored her with fruits from his orchards. She was gathering news, and at the same time fueling gossip that both men were her lovers. Afternoons, to smooth the way to other notables, she often called on their wives, and on Tuesdays she began to hold weekly teas. "And they come," she wrote proudly to Domnul, "even the veiled women. No one can do that here but me, you see."

A stream of women, mostly Muslims, many of them Jews, their children in tow, arrived at her walled retreat. They slipped off their face veils and long black *abbayas* and, dressed in Turkish silks or outfits made from the patterns of *Vogue*, entered a world they hardly knew. At the rear of her garden stood Gertrude, receiving her guests, her figure erect in a long silk dress, her head held high under a hat blooming with fruits. Without a doubt, Miss Bell was considered by all a formidable figure of British authority.

Chairs were placed around the garden, and her servants went from one guest to the next, pouring tea from the silver service, passing around biscuits, cakes and the cook's specialty, caramelized walnuts filled with thick buffalo cream. When the weather turned cold or rainy, the guests were entertained indoors, and a circle of thirty chairs—all that the room could hold—was arranged for tea parties in her sitting room. For two hours, over the clatter of china cups, female gossip and feelings about the future fluttered through the air. Gertrude listened, her ear trained to pick up any nuance of political change.

The meetings made an impact, as much on Gertrude as on the local ladies. The disdain she had once expressed to Mrs. Van Ess about Arab women disappeared. The conscious lack of interest in the harem had been discarded, replaced by knowledge and understanding. When a British education expert, Humphrey Bowman, arrived in Baghdad to set up a school system, he found her highly concerned about the future of the Arab girls.

She was sitting on the floor, a cigarette burning in the ashtray, her dress tucked under her knees, her head buried in the piles of maps and papers scattered about, when Bowman knocked on her door. She answered sharply, "Come in." With his arrival long overdue, he explained who he was and handed her a letter of introduction. Gertrude glanced at it quickly, threw it down with the rest and stared at the newcomer, piercing him like an X-ray machine. "I'm glad you've come," she said abruptly. "I can see we shall be friends." With that, she pointed him to a chair, stayed herself on the floor and proceeded to fill him in on the history and social conditions of Iraq.

Of all her concerns about the Arabs, Gertrude told him, her greatest worry was the Muslim girls. Unlike the young Jewish women, taught English, Arabic, Hebrew and French at the Alliance, the Muslims had had no education under the Turks. With few exceptions, they were illiterate. She had seen how helpless these women were, how vulnerable to the whims of the men.

"We must give the girls an opportunity for self-expression," she said with determination. "If you only knew the harems as I do, you would have pity upon the women. Nothing has been done for them— nothing." Here at last was an opportunity. She wanted schools for them and classes in domestic science, housecraft and hygiene. They would be willing and eager to learn, she assured him, and, of course, the teachers could only be women. With that, she dismissed him. Her interests were not forgotten; the educational system established by Bowman, still the best in the Arab world, served as a unifying force for the country and included the radical concept of education for the females.

The notion that women were undervalued was never far from her mind. When, a few days later, a letter arrived from Florence asking whether Gertrude was the author of a recently published major report on Mesopotamia, she took up her pen at once and answered sharply: "Why, yes, of course I wrote all *The Arab of Mesopotamia*. I've loved the reviews which speak of the practical men who were the anonymous authors, etc. It's fun being practical men, isn't it."

Her reports were highly thought of by those in power; coming out of her extensive travels and extraordinary friendships with the Arabs, they combined literary achievement with finely tuned political insights, historical perspective, a plethora of detail and a profound depth of cultural understanding. Her rare relationships had been underscored at a durbar, a convention of sheikhs and sayids, held in Baghdad in September 1918. Eighty tribal leaders, many from distant provinces and known neither to one another nor to the British authorities, were brought together in the public gardens by the British Commander-in-Chief. At the opening ceremonies the general shook the hand of each. Gertrude was sitting far down the platform, but as soon as the sheikhs caught sight of her they turned away from the dignified procession and walked across the stage to shake her hand.

Many of the notables came to her office and spoke of the positive change in relations, the amicability that had developed since the year before. "I thought that testimony to our friendly intimacy was worth everything," she noted.

It was about this time that she had a different encounter with one nomadic sheikh. He had come demanding compensation for a hundred head of cattle, which, he claimed, had disappeared since the British occupation. Gertrude promised that the government would pay him two pounds for each head. The deal was acceptable, the Arab replied gleefully. But the Khatun, who heard all the gossip, knew that the man had either transferred the cattle to a neighbor or traded them for wives. As he stood up and salaamed to leave, Gertrude inquired in Arabic, "And how many head of cattle hast thou now, o sheikh?"

"Five hundred," he answered.

"And how many before we came here?" she asked.

"Fifty."

"Ali of the River," she said solemnly, "thy flocks and herds have been well guarded by us except the matter of the one hundred. Take the bill of two hundred pounds; thou shalt be paid. But thou must pay the King of England for guarding four hundred and fifty head at the rate of ten pounds for each fifty head for three years."

The old sheikh paused for a minute, and replied: "O Just One, I pray thee not to press the bill. Mine I have forgotten."

As he walked out the door, Gertrude could hear him murmur, "She is Shaitan." She is Satan.

❦   ❦   ❦

On most afternoons she had work to do for the Foreign Office: a new state had been anounced, but the borders of the new country still had to be determined. At the request of Whitehall, she studied the maps of Persia, Turkey, Syria, Kuwait and Mesopotamia, examining every inch of the land she knew so well. Shaking her head at the blurred frontiers, she carefully drew in boundary lines, making sure to place the provinces of Mosul, Baghdad and Basrah within the territory of Iraq. As she told her parents: "It's an amusing game when you know the country intimately, as I do, thank goodness, almost all of it. Was ever anything more fortunate than that I should have crisscrossed it in very nearly every direction."

Exhilarated as she was over defining the borders, she was even more excited about constructing a brand-new state. There had never been an independent Iraq; no political entity, no administrative unit had ever existed. No borders like these had been drawn since ancient times (and even they had included only the region from Baghdad to Basrah); no Western banner had ever flown over it. Now she was not only deciding a country; she was devising its shape and determining its composition: who would lead it, how it would be governed, who would be included in its citizenry, what would be its laws and institutions. Imperialist and Orientalist both, she was creating an asset for England, constructing an entity for the Arabs. The power was intoxicating, and at the beginning of December 1918 she wrote home: "I feel at times like the Creator about the middle of the week. He must have wondered what it was going to be like, as I do."

An Arab king was being considered to head the new country, but Gertrude strongly opposed the idea of giving up British authority. With the excuse that it was too much trouble to establish a monarchy, she wished they would drop the idea of an Arab emir. "It tires me to think of setting up a brand-new court here," she wrote, "but at present they are that way inclined." Perhaps they would not be able to agree on an individual and Cox would be recalled. "Then we should have Sir Percy alone which would be splendid." Even more flattering, she noted, "I'm second choice for High Commissioner here, so I'm told!" But once again she felt the bothersome issue of gender: "What would all Permanent Officials say if we suggested it? It's really just as much a female job, however, as a male, because it's mainly concerned with the handling of people individually." She signed her letter to her family: "Your very affectionate High Comissioner. Gertrude."

All winter long, at lunches, at teas and at dinners in the Baghdad Political Mess, the British officers in the service of the India Government chewed over the question of authority, swallowing hard the Arab demands for independence and doubting whether stability could come from local rule. At the bequest of London, Wilson authorized a poll among the general public to find out what they favored. But the concept itself was naïve. Most people had no definite opinion and were in no position to form one. As Gertrude wryly noted later, "It was clearly impracticable to pursue the enquiry among the rank and file of the tribesmen, the shepherds, marsh dwellers, rice, barley, and date cultivators of the Euphrates and Tigris, whose experience of statecraft was confined to speculations as to the performances of their next-door neighbors." Accordingly, in the country districts and provincial towns it was the sheikhs and notables who were asked for their views.

The findings only added to the confusion. Although all believed that Mosul should be united with Baghdad and Basrah, the rest was as muddy as the ground in the rainy season: the Sunni nationalists wanted an Arab kingdom; the Shiites wanted an Islamic religious state; the Kurds in the north sought an independent Kurdish entity; the business community that had prospered under the Sultan wanted a return to the Turks. To the great disappointment of the Acting Civil Commissioner, the one thing made instantly clear was that no one wanted to be under the tutelage of India. But it was beyond consideration, in A. T. Wilson's view, and Gertrude's as well, to turn over control of the country to the local population. To give them total power would have been like handing over the reins to a riderless horse. Instead, Wilson proposed and Gertrude agreed that the new country be run with a British High Commissioner in charge, and with British officials serving as advisers to an array of Arab Ministers.

For Gertrude, this was the only sensible solution. Years before, in 1907, she had written, "The·Oriental is like a very old child." Her profound respect for family and strong sense of responsibility would never allow her to abandon her offspring; indeed, her child had to be not just created, but nurtured, educated and trained to look after itself. She may have lost the opportunity of marrying and bearing a baby, but she had conceived Iraq and borne it as her own. She would raise it in the best of British ways: controlled by a paternal British High Commissioner; nannied by British advisers; mothered by herself. And she expected Mesopotamia, like any good child, to return the favor in kind, with gratitude and loyalty, making safe the land route to India and giving back to its parent, Britain, its wealth of agriculture, archaeology and oil.

∞ ∞ ∞

But a clique of Arabs, driven by nationalism, demanded more. In January 1919, Gertrude remarked that "a small vociferous group . . . thinks they could get on quite well alone and certainly have much more fun individually without us. They would have immense fun for a bit, but it would be a very short bit." It would end, she said, in "anarchy and bloodshed." She was to be proved right.

In London, officials with little understanding of the Arabs were debating policy, deciding the fate of the Middle East. Government voices were rising in anger over the cost of staying in Mesopotamia. Yet the idea of pulling out and leaving the place to the Arabs sent shivers of fear through those on the ground. A knowledgeable person was urgently needed to advise Whitehall, and in late January, Wilson asked Gertrude to return to London for a few months' leave, to "give a guiding hand." He wanted her to report the experiences and information they had gained in Iraq while keeping him closely informed of activities in England. By now she looked forward to going back, to rest, to see friends, even to taste real mutton. "That's not poetic is it, but you should see—and try to eat—the meat we live on. I can't think what part of the animal it grows on." And the thought of buying new clothes and seeing her father delighted her as she prepared for the journey home.

Chapter Twenty-one

Paris and the Arab Question

∞

On instructions from the British Government, General Allenby had appointed Faisal, the son of the Sharif Hussein, as the new ruler of Syria (including the interior cities of Damascus, Homs, Hama and Aleppo, but excluding Beirut and the rest of coastal Lebanon). According to the terms of the Sykes-Picot pact, however, as Allenby explained to Faisal, Syria would be within the sphere of influence of France. The Sharifian prince would rule with Arab governors and an Arab administration, but his rule would be under French supervision. His government would have an Arab flag, but it would also have French advisers; its finances and its policies would be driven directly by France.

Faisal had been given a different scenario. The commander of the Arab Revolt had been promised by T. E. Lawrence, his trusted British liaison, military and political adviser and friend, that the only outside influence in Syria would belong to the delicate hand of the British. But with little choice, a reluctant Faisal agreed to do what Allenby asked. Disgusted (and embarrassed by his own deceits), Lawrence requested home leave and left Damascus immediately. An anxious Faisal, disappointed and worried over the role of the French, stayed on to rule.

❧   ❧   ❧

In Iraq, reports from neighboring countries were scarce, and the news from Reuters, at the beginning of 1919, that Faisal had been proclaimed the Arab ruler of Syria, came as a surprise. The idea of an Arab king heightened the fears of Christians and Jews that they would be exploited by the Muslims; it raised doubts among those whose wealth had depended upon the Turks, upon the British or upon the French; and it fired the ambitions of those who strove for Arab rule. Fueling the mixed emotions were the reports that Faisal was representing his father as King of the Arabs at the international peace talks, begun in Paris.

❧   ❧   ❧

Before leaving Baghdad, Gertrude summed up the political information she had garnered and composed a major memorandum. In *Self-Determination in Mesopotamia*, her weighty report, dispatched by Wilson to the India Office, she noted that prior to the release of the Anglo-French Declaration of Arab liberation, most Iraqis had accepted the idea "that the country would remain under direct British control." The publication of this declaration, however, "opened up other possibilities which were regarded almost universally with anxiety, but gave opportunity for political intrigue to the less stable and more fanatical elements."

On one side of the Iraqi tug-of-war stood the groups whose self-interests lay with the British. At the other end were the nationalists who wanted British forces withdrawn (or overthrown) so that the Arabs could rule themselves.

Sooner or later, Gertrude noted, a nationalist party would have sprung to life. But as a result of the Anglo-French Declaration, it had happened sooner. Its early appearance, however, pushed "the stable elements" that opposed Arab nationalism (fearing it as extremist) to take cover under the British flag.

Of those who identified with the British, one man, in particular, stood out. The Naqib of Baghdad, religious leader of the Sunnis, influential as far away as India and China, had been a wise and reliable friend for years, and although the holy man refused to make any public statements on the subject of politics, he confided his feelings to Gertrude. Firmly opposed to an Arab emir, he believed the country was not yet ripe for any form of Arab rule. He emphasized the need of

British troops to maintain the peace and hoped that a British administration would slowly incorporate Arabs into its government. Only over time, he believed, could the rivalrous factions—townsmen versus tribesmen, Sunnis versus Shiites, pro-British versus pan-Arabists— come together, and only over time could the Iraqis learn to rule themselves.

On the polite orders of the British military, the well-to-do Naqib had lent his large residence on the river to the occupying officials. He was now ensconced in his smaller house opposite the great Gailani mosque, where the tomb of his revered ancestor, the Islamic theologian Abdul Qadir al Gailani, was encased in silver. Gertrude had requested a meeting with the Naqib, and on February 6, 1919, she paid him a call.

She climbed the familiar courtyard staircase to the balconied first floor, entered his whitewashed study and made her way toward one of the hard white sofas that lined the perimeter of the room. Through the windows she could see the courtyard garden planted with orange trees, and under one corner window inside the room, where the devout man liked to sit, a book had been left on a small, white cloth-covered table. The Naqib's grown son entertained her for a while, and then the holy man appeared; she stood to greet him. Old and white-bearded, his body bent by rheumatism, his figure cloaked in a long black robe layered over white, his head covered with a white turban wrapped around a red Turkish fez, he moved slowly toward her and, giving orders not to be disturbed, welcomed her warmly and settled himself on a hard settee.

She had known the Naqib since her earliest trips to Baghdad, and she had called on him almost at once when she arrived to work for Cox in April 1917. Now they talked about her departure for England and about the future of Iraq: they discussed the French, whose culture he loved but whose government he despised, and contrasted them with the British, whose government he admired and whose policies he considered firm and fair; to her delight she heard him say that he hoped they would stay and rule in Iraq.

"Khatun," he spoke in Arabic, "your nation is great, wealthy and powerful; where is our power? . . . You are the governors and I am the governed. And when I am asked what is my opinion as to the continuance of British rule, I reply that I am the subject of the victor. You, Khatun, have an understanding of statecraft. I do not hesitate to say to you that I loved the Turkish government when it was as I once knew it. If I could return to the rule of the Sultans of Turkey as they were in former times, I should make no other choice. But I loathe and hate, curse and consign to the devil the present Turkish Government.

The Turk is dead; he has vanished, and I am content to become your subject."

Yet even he had reservations about a permanent British presence. The war was over, he said, wiping his hands with the words; it was time for the British to end their military rule; it was time for them to install a civil government. He knew she was going to Whitehall as an adviser, and he begged her to request that Kokus, Percy Cox, be returned to Baghdad. "There are a hundred and a thousand men in England who could fill the post of Ambassador in Persia," he stated, "but there is none but Sir Percy Cox who is suitable for Iraq. He is known, he is loved and he is trusted by the people of Iraq. He is a man of sober years." And commenting on A. T. Wilson, who had acted at London's instructions, the Naqib continued, "I bear witness that if Sir Percy Cox had been in Baghdad we would have been spared the folly of asking the people to express their wishes as to the future."

The old man told her exactly what she should say when she appeared at Whitehall: "We wish to be governed by Sir Percy Cox." But, he advised, "do not say, even though it be true, that you yourself have become a Baghdadi and that your mind is wholly occupied with the welfare of Iraq, for that will cause your words less weight in London and we shall have the less profit from you."

He went on to discuss the notion of self-determination, a thoughtless idea, he believed, which he blamed on the American President. "Does Sheikh Wilson know the East and its peoples?" he asked rhetorically. "Does he know our way of life and our habits of mind? You English have governed for three hundred years in Asia and your rule is an example for all men to follow. Pursue your own way. Do not submit to guidance from Sheikh Wilson. Knowledge and experience are your guides."

Gertrude drew the discussion back to recent events in Baghdad. "Most of those who have spoken against you are men without name or honor," the Naqib said. "But I tell you to beware of the Shi'ahs. I have no animosity against the Shi'ah sect," he hastened to assure her. She nodded and gave him no hint of her own underlying doubts. "They love and respect me," he continued, "and I am regarded by them as their Sheikh. But turn your eyes on the pages of history and you will see that the salient characteristic of the Shi'ahs is their *khiffah* [volatility]. Did they not themselves murder Musa ibn Ali whom they now worship as a God? Idolatry and mutability are combined in them. Place no reliance upon them."

The conversation had reached the point where Gertrude felt she could tread on tender soil. Like the Sharif Hussein, the Naqib was a

Sunni and a descendant of the Prophet Muhammad. Cautiously, she asked the holy man his opinion of the Sharif. The Naqib answered that they were distant relatives. "I come of the same stock and I share the same religious opinions," he said. Nonetheless, he confessed, "I would never consent to the appointment of himself or of his son as Emir." The Sharifians were strangers to Iraq, he explained; they came from the Hejaz, in Central Arabia, an environment totally foreign to Iraq. "The Hejaz is one and the Iraq is one, there is no connection between them but that of the Faith. Our politics, our trade, our agriculture are all different from those of the Hejaz."

The holy man repeated that, as much as he hated the present secular, nationalist Turkish Government, he "would rather a thousand times have the Turks back in Iraq than see the Sharif or his sons installed here."

What about the Naqib himself as ruler? Gertrude asked. Her hand was resting on the wooden arm of his sofa, and he tapped it reproachfully with his finger. Leaning forward, he said with a laugh, "How can you put such a question as that to me? It would be contrary to the deepest principles of my creed to become the political head of the State." Besides, he added, "I am an old man. These five or six years which remain to me I wish to spend in reflection and in study." Then, raising his voice, he emphasized: "Not if it were to save Iraq from complete destruction would I alter what I have now spoken." She accepted his no for an answer. Despite all her experience in the Arab world, she did not consider the possibility that he was waiting for her to insist.

They talked for ninety minutes before Gertrude begged his permission to leave. The Naqib expressed his personal affections and reminded her of their long friendship. She valued it greatly, she answered, and thanked him for his confidence. He hoped that she would regard him as her father, he said touchingly, and prayed that she would return soon from England. With that, he bade her go in peace.

∞   ∞   ∞

Whitehall promised to "take no action if they can avoid it until Miss Bell arrives," so she left Baghdad, heading not yet for England, but for France. There, at the Paris Peace Conference, the leaders of Europe were meeting to divide the spoils of the First World War and carve up the remains of three empires: Austro-Hungary, Russia and Turkey. At A. T. Wilson's request, Gertrude would make sure that when the talk turned to Mesopotamia, British interests would be well represented. But that would prove more complex than the Acting Civil Commissioner had believed: Lawrence and Faisal, who had fought side by side in the desert battle against the Turks, were now fighting side by side in the political battle against the Allies. They were already in Paris, and Gertrude's opinions would soon swerve away from Wilson and swing toward them.

⧂ ⧂ ⧂

The journey to Europe went via Egypt. Gertrude sailed on the *Ormonde*, and on the morning her boat docked at Port Said, she dressed with great anticipation. She slipped on her calf-length dress, topped her hair with a flowered hat and waited excitedly for David Hogarth. Her friend and former mentor, traveling from Cairo to see her, found her "more affectionate than ever," looking "a little older," he wrote to his wife, "but still wonderfully alive and well turned out." They spent two hours together, clarifying some questions he had, discussing her mandate to Whitehall.

Gertrude reached Paris on the seventh of March 1919. The French capital was electric, glittering with power and charged with the current of international conspiracy. Each nation had come with its own agenda: the Italians to dismember the Austro-Hungarian Empire; the French to disarm the Germans, regain Alsace and Lorraine and the Saar region and gain their share of the Ottoman Empire (including control of Syria); the British to win the German colonies in Africa and the South Pacific, keep control of Mesopotamia, have protectorates in Persia and Egypt and see the end of German naval power; the Americans to establish their dream of a League of Nations. And, in addition, each one wanted control over oil. The highest officials of every country had arrived, blocking the streets with their hired cars, booking up tables at Fouquet's and the Pré Catalan, chattering at the Paris Opéra and enlivening the hotel lobbies with the buzz of global schemes. "It was a gathering of the nations such as the world had never seen or dreamed of before," wrote Domnul Chirol, who had come from London in January at the opening of the winter conference on behalf of the British Government to lobby the French press.

The inner circle of white-haired leaders was meeting every day at the Élsyée Place on the rue de Foubourg St. Honoré. Armed with heavy leather pouches and giving off a whiff of violet hair wash, the Council of Ten, accompanied by military aides, interpreters and advisers, paraded along parquet floors through thick double doors to the plushly carpeted study of the French Foreign Minister. In M. Picot's splended paneled chamber, where the smell of typewriter ribbons and polished furniture mixed with the scent of secrecy, chandeliers blazed and draperies of red damask were drawn tight so that not a sound nor a signal escaped from the privileged room. A long baize table, covered with blotting papers, tracing tissue and maps, was lined with facing rows of great gilt armchairs, behind which two more rows of little gold seats were reserved for secretaries and advisers.

At the head of the vast stretch of green-covered table, with his back to a glowing fire of huge logs, sat the French Prime Minister, Georges Clemenceau, dressed like all the others in a black wool suit, starched white collar and crisp white cuffs. With his gray-gloved hands resting on the arms of his seat, he rose to address the group, and with his head thrown back and his shoulders hunched, he spoke. Out of his droopily mustachioed mouth he hurled his words, slowly and deliberately at first, then faster, like the rat-a-tat of a machine gun. When a resolution had already been drafted, he stated it, refused to hear any discussion, and with his phrases still reeling toward his confrères, he announced, "*Adopté*," and sat down, the half-closed eyes under his bushy eyebrows surveying the room.

On either side of the Tiger sat the magnetic British Prime Minister, David Lloyd George, in town with his mistress, Frances Stevenson; and the enigmatic American President, Woodrow Wilson, whose idealistic thoughts were purely on his new concepts of the League of Nations and the mandate system. "The peoples of the world are awake and the peoples of the world are in the saddle," Wilson would declare, hoping to spur the former territories of the Germans and the Turks to self-determination.

Down the line from Clemenceau were leaders of Italy, Belgium, Greece, Romania, China, Japan, Australia—the only missing country being Russia. The proceedings were as formal as the gardens below the tall windows on the far side of the room, and the ministers' discussions as delicate as the snowflakes that fell outside. The conversation centered on Europe; the East was only a sideshow.

In fact, the delegates sneered at the notion of self-government for either Mesopotamia or Syria, and an often-repeated conversation was overheard among four very high officials:

1st Minister: "I fear that the country may be badly governed."

2nd Minister: "The country *will* be badly governed."

3rd Minister: "The country *ought* to be badly governed."

In the end, neither Syria nor Mesopotamia would be given immediate autonomy; instead, like other regions of the Turkish Empire, they would be placed under the mandate of Britain or France, which hoped to use Wilson's concept to keep control of the region.

But before that fateful day, and while the discourse continued at the Élysée Palace, a few blocks away in their suites of the Hôtel Crillon the American delegation conferred, and at the Hôtel Majestic and the neighboring Astoria the British contingent held its private meetings. Under the potted palms in the lobbies, and in every corner of the private rooms, the flow of words was tinged with the quest for oil. Petroleum had become the substance of vital interest; without it the British, French and Americans never could have won the war. "The Allies floated to victory on a wave of oil," proclaimed the British Secretary of State, Lord Curzon. It was evident that it had become a strategic necessity; national security now depended upon oil, and the leading figures of Britain were called to the conference for consultation. "Every day," Chirol observed, "there was a constant coming and going of experts specially summoned from England, of legislators and jurists, of bankers and economists, of captains of industry and commerce, of all the best brains in fact which the country could muster." On issues of the East, the potential source of that precious petroleum, Arthur Balfour, Arthur Hirtzel and Edwin Montagu huddled intently, while the exotic figure of Faisal, robed in flowing silks, moved like a graceful symbol through the corridors; at his elbow always was the small, odd figure of a khaki-suited, *kafeeyah*-clad T. E. Lawrence.

In the aftermath of the war, the Sharif Hussein, who, with his son Faisal had helped the British defeat the Turks, expected to be duly rewarded. His expressed desire was to create an Arab kingdom that included Arabia, Syria, Lebanon, Palestine and Iraq. He wanted the throne of the Hejaz, his Arabian turf, for himself, and he wanted two of his sons formally installed to the north: Faisal (already there) in Damascus; Abdullah, his eldest son, in Baghdad. If the French wanted to keep Lebanon, with its mostly Christian population, he might agree. But the French were not willing to give up any of Syria nor were the British delegates ready to hand over Iraq.

Faisal and Lawrence had come from London, where, on January 3, 1919, Faisal signed an agreement with the Zionist leader Chaim Weizmann on the principle of a Jewish homeland in Palestine. Afterward they set off for Paris, where the three met again. With the help of Colonel Richard Meinertzhagen, General Allenby's Chief of Intelligence and a member of the British team, Faisal composed a letter to Felix Frankfurter, head of the American Zionist delegation:

> We feel that the Arabs and Jews are cousins in race . . .
> [and] have suffered similar oppression at the hands of
> powers stronger than themselves. . . . We Arabs, espe-
> cially the educated among us, look with the deepest sym-

pathy on the Zionist movement. . . . We will wish the
Jews a hearty welcome here. . . . People less informed
and less responsible than our leaders and yours, ignoring
the need for co-operation of the Arabs and Zionists, have
been trying to exploit the local difficulties that must
necessarily arise in Palestine in the early stage of our
movements.

The letter, signed by Faisal, became a fragment of a history torn
apart by bitterness and tragedy.

It would take nearly thirty years of violent uprisings and a brutal
war between the Zionists and the Arabs before the Jewish state would
come into existence, in 1948, and almost a half-century more before the
Jews of Israel and the Arabs of Palestine recognized each other's right
to a homeland. But this early letter is testament to the fact that the
Hussein clan, alone among the Arab leaders, was well intentioned
toward the Jews. Later, Faisal's brother Abdullah, the first ruler of
TransJordan, and his successor and grandson, King Hussein of Jordan,
would make that clear in their readiness to accept a Jewish state.

But it was a far greater ambition that brought the desert prince
Faisal to Paris. Together with Lawrence he set out to convince the
French that, with his government already installed in Damascus, they
should anoint him King of Syria. The Paris Peace talks had com-
menced on January 23, 1919, and within two weeks the colorful pair of
Lawrence and Faisal was called to appear before the Council of Four.
Lawrence, dressed in white robes and gold-braided headdress, had no
official position; an eccentric at once flashy and shy, he held his only
acknowledged role as Faisal's translator. As an advocate for the Arab
leader, he was a questionable character; to many in the British Foreign
Service, he was not to be trusted. He had even been shunted off to the
Continentale, a lesser hotel.

It was to the gold-robed Faisal that Clemenceau, Wilson, Lloyd
George and the Italian Premier, Vittorio Emanuele Orlando, leaned
forward and listened closely. Without notes, without hesitation, in a
resonant voice and mesmerizing cadence, the Arab commander spoke.
No one of Western origin, not even Lawrence, matched the Emir's
mystique. When Faisal opened his mouth, said an American lawyer at
the talks, "his voice seemed to breathe the perfume of frankincense and
to suggest the presence of richly coloured divans, green turbans and the
glitter of gold and jewels." He delivered his speech in Arabic, with
Lawrence loosely translating, but the Turkish-educated Faisal stunned
his audience by answering questions in colloquial French. Faisal's presence had the force of an electromagnetic field, drawing in Lloyd

George, who declared firmly that the British would not let down their Arab allies, repelling Clemenceau, who angrily reminded his English colleague of the Sykes-Picot Agreement. The fate of that pact seemed oddly marked: only a few days earlier, on February 2, in the midst of an epidemic in Paris, Mark Sykes had died of the flu.

For several weeks the Eastern question was on the table. Faisal and Lawrence did all they could, beguiling, cajoling, even rattling sabers as Faisal threatened to rouse the Arabs of Syria and the Hejaz in a *jihad* against the French. But that not only angered the French; it infuriated the British, who were caught in a compromising position. They had made promises to both Faisal's father, the Sharif Hussein, and the French, vowing that each would have control over Syria. Britain had no wish now to support either one in another costly war. The problem had reached an impasse: Faisal, the self-declared King, was insistent on keeping the throne; the French, who long ago had claimed their stake, were not about to give up Syria.

When Gertrude arrived at the Majestic on Easter Sunday 1919 to promote the Arab cause, she was introduced at once to the intriguing figure of Faisal. Few knew his background: his parents were cousins; his father, the guardian of Mecca; his mother, an Arab peasant from the same town. Born in the desert, he had been taken to Constantinople when his father was put under Ottoman watch. He grew up sickly. As a young man he picked at his food, smoked a great deal and developed a love of classical Arabic poetry, but along the way he also learned to shoot well and to ride horses and camels with the skill of the Bedouin he was. Tall, thin, darkly dramatic, a noble born of fine stock, he had the virile look of a desert Arab, the polished manners of a cosmopolitan Turkish pasha, the charm and charisma of a leader. Talking with Gertrude, he knew how to flatter her femininity, excite her with his own political ambitions.

They spoke for only a few minutes before Faisal went off for a meeting. Left with his doctor and his private secretary, Rustam Haidar (French-speaking like Faisal, educated at the Sorbonne), Gertrude told them what she had heard. Conditions in Syria were not good, her informers had said. Daily living had become more difficult. Faisal must make an agreement with the French, she advised. The Americans could not help, and the British did not want to interfere. Later, the two men repeated the conversation to Lawrence. "Miss Bell has a poor mind," he retorted. "You should not attach any importance to what she says." But Lawrence's romantic attitude would fail Faisal in the end. Gertrude's approach was far more pragmatic.

Exhilarated by Faisal and Lawrence (she had not heard his nasty remark) and by her own important role in representing Mesopotamia,

Gertrude was swept up at once in the frenzy. The air was tainted with anxieties and conspiracies over the Arabs: muddled misunderstandings, complicated by the conflicting promises of the Sykes-Picot Agreement (which gave Syria to the French), the McMahon-Hussein letters (which promised an Arab kingdom to the Sharif Hussein), and the Balfour Declaration (which promised a homeland in Palestine to the Jews). All these were further splattered with the need for oil; the purported petroleum wealth of Mesopotamia was causing much excitement. It left the loquacious Gertrude nearly speechless.

A few nights later, alone in her room, she sat at the desk and wrote to her father: "I've dropped into a world so amazing that up to now I've done nothing but gape at it without being able to put a word onto paper. I'm not going even now to tell you what it's like partly because I can't—but it is clearing up a little. Our Eastern affairs are complex beyond all words and until I came there was no one to put the Meso-potamian side of the question at first hand." She had talked that day with Lord Milner, had plans to lunch with the questionable Mr. Bal-four and utimately hoped to catch Mr. Lloyd George. "If I can manage to do so I believe I can enlist his sympathies."

Her immediate task, she continued, was to speak to the French delegation. "The Mesopotamian settlement is so closely linked with the Syrian that we can't consider one without the other," she explained, "and in the case of Syria it's the French attitude that counts." There was so much to do, she needed help. A. T. Wilson was coming from Baghdad, and she suggested summoning Hogarth. As soon as they arrived she proposed to include them with herself and Mr. Lawrence to form a solid Near Eastern bloc. In the meantime she would tell her story to plenty of people in Paris, among them her friends Domñul Chirol and Sir Robert Cecil. And, despite his asides, T. E. Lawrence was at the top of her list as an ally.

If most British officials were repelled by Lawrence and his kinship with an Arab emir, Gertrude found him appealing. If most thought him difficult, she thought him dynamic; if most found him obstreper-ous, she found him enchanting. True, before the talks she had told a friend she thought Lawrence an "inverted megalomaniac," but Law-rence alone could understand her passion for the East. After they dined with Domnul at the Paris home of *The Times*'s editor, Wickham Steed, she wrote admiringly to Hugh, praising T.E.L.'s explanation of the situation with Faisal and the Syrians on the one hand and the French on the other: "He did it quite admirably. His charm, simplicity and sincerity made a deep personal impression and convinced his listeners."

Sometimes separately, sometimes together, Gertrude and Lawrence raced around town, from the Majestic to the Crillon to the Élysée

Palace, rushing from one conference to another. After one frigid morning in the office of Arthur Hirtzel, where she huddled close to the hot water pipes and reading reports, Gertrude hurried to keep a lunch date with Lawrence. Standing in the hall together, they spied Lord Milner, a close adviser to Lloyd George. "You go and ask him to lunch with us," Lawrence urged her. Boldly, she went up to the minister and invited him to join them. Milner said yes. It was a delightful lunch, unofficial and open, she reported, but realizing that he had said too much, Milner made them promise they would not quote him. "We assured him that people who lunched with us always were indiscreet," Gertrude wrote. "It's Mr. Lawrence, I think, who induces a sort of cards-on-the-table atmosphere."

Lawrence laid his own cards on the table when he confided in Gertrude about the book he planned to write. He hoped it would clear up the myths promulgated by Lowell Thomas. He sought her advice on how to treat the tales: whether to embellish them with the stories that had surrounded him as the legendary Lawrence of Arabia, or to go with the lesser truth and be diminished by the facts. Ever the one for truth, Gertrude assured him his book was a splendid idea and encouraged him to proceed with his work on *Seven Pillars of Wisdom*.

Gertrude was spending most of her time with Lawrence. When her father arrived for a weekend stay, she took him to lunch with her "beloved boy," and they discussed the situation in Syria. Hugh, friendly with some of the Americans, introduced his daughter to President Wilson's delegation and, during several days of lunches and dinners, she expounded on the Arabs, trying to teach the Americans something about the subject and persuade them to take over the mandate from the French. Temporarily, at least, the results seemed good: on March 25, the Americans announced they would send a commission to the region to study the situation. Upon hearing the news, the abstinent Faisal toasted them with champagne. "The Arabs would rather die than accept the French mandate," he told an American delegate. (The American King-Crane Commission took three years to issue its report, keeping the United States out of the political hotbed until it was too late to have an impact on events.)

Just after her father left, Gertrude dined with Harold Nicolson. She had known Nicolson and his bride since 1914, when they were newlyweds in Constantinople. Now he was part of the British delegation, and his wife, Vita Sackville-West, had reluctantly agreed to join him briefly. Their marriage was beginning down its rough road. Vita, in the midst of a romance with Violet Markham, had refused to leave her lover; in three years more, she would begin her affair with Virginia Woolf. "Mrs. Vita was over for a day," Gertrude scrawled. "She is a most attractive creature and would be more so if she didn't whiten her nose so very white."

Aside from such fluffy gossip, however, her talk stayed mainly in the realm of the East. Frantically working the hallways, lobbies, restaurants and conference rooms, grabbing the arm of anyone she could, she lectured him on the Arabs. She knew more about the desert and its people than anyone else, including Lawrence, said Domnul. When A. T. Wilson arrived on March 20, he immediately recognized how difficult her work was. Dismayed to discover how little was known about the region, he later wrote:

"Experts on Western Arabia, both military and civil, were there in force, but not one, except Miss Bell, had any first-hand knowledge of Iraq or Nejd or, indeed, of Persia. The very existence of a Shiah majority in Iraq was denied as a figment of my imagination by one 'expert' with an international reputation, and Miss Bell and I found it impossible to convince either the Military or the Foreign Office Delegations that Kurds in the Mosul *vilayet* were numerous and likely to be troublesome, that Ibn Saud was a power seriously to be reckoned with or that our problem could not be disposed of on the same lines as those advanced for Syria by the enthusiasm of the Arab Bureau." Indeed, while Wilson was still in Paris, word arrived that the Assistant Political Officer posted in northern Mesopotamia had been ambushed and killed by the Kurds. The incident was dismissed, but it foreshadowed much trouble with the northern tribes.

Wilson's accolades for Gertrude were but a momentary applause. As firmly as he believed that the only solution for Mesopotamia was a British High Commissioner, she was beginning to lean toward an Arab head of state. Numerous hours with Lawrence and Faisal had planted the seed that a Sharifian ruler was not only good for Syria; it was the best answer for Iraq.

Squalls of anger arose between the colonialist A. T. Wilson, fighting for the British to hold on to power, and Lawrence, whom he blamed for Britain's problems with the French. Wilson sighed with relief when he learned that, at the end of the negotiations, Lawrence planned to return to England and retire. After the conference had ended, the oil agreements were made, the League of Nations was established, the remains of Eastern Europe were divided up and a covenant adopted that called for mandates over formerly Turkish territories, the delegates departed; but the Arab issue hovered like a giant question mark in the air. Little had actually been ensured; instead of putting Syria and Mesopotamia firmly into French and British hands, the negotiators, deeming the issue too difficult to settle, deferred, in true diplomatic style, for two years, to another time and another place.

∞   ∞   ∞

Gertrude had left for Belgium to meet her father, where he had gone for a well-deserved rest. After a month she was finally back in London, catching up on new books, having fittings for new clothes. The styles had changed dramatically, as she had already discovered; the long dress lengths that she cherished were replaced by skirts just below the knee; the long evening gowns were now cut low in the back. She ordered one new dress fringed with ostrich feathers, the latest rage, and, instead of the old stiff fabrics, she tried on knitted silks and wool jerseys, worn with sheer stockings and the new pump-style shoes. At the milliner's she chose a brimmed hat piled with plumes and one of the tricornes that had just come into vogue.

She shopped, she read, she dined with friends. It was four years since she had seen them, and one of her Oxford colleagues—David Hogarth's sister, Janet—described her afterward: "She had aged a bit, her bright hair had silvered, and she looked like finely tempered steel."

At the beginning of June 1919, Gertrude retreated to Rounton. On long walks with her father or when riding through the rolling fields, swimming, gardening or just talking with friends, she could work off the tensions of the long war and the current frazzle of Eastern politics. With time to reflect on what she had learned, she sat at the desk in her childhood room and wrote lengthily to Wilson, summing up:

"This letter has been all business but I am going to end with a little sentiment . . . all these things have happened since I last sat in this beautiful room of mine, lined with books and looking out on an exquisite country-side. I cannot recapture the former world which this room and its books stood for, nor can I ever quite lay to rest the anguish which lies between that world and this, but I can, and I do, accept with wonder and gratitude what the new world has given me, and in that you play a large part—you yourself, and the Service of which you have made me feel I am one."

Toward the end of September, with her new wardrobe stashed in her trunks and her maid Marie in tow, she launched once again for the East. Sailing on the *Nevasa*, she dressed on a warm morning in comfortable muslin and searched for a place away from the other passengers. Finding a quiet spot, she stretched out on the wooden deck chair, took out her writing kit and penned a note to her father. "I'm glad to be plunged into Arab politics again and almost to think I'm a person," she wrote. "It's very curious to be part of the official East. I always used to wonder what it must be like to be coming on a ship of this kind and not to be an outsider. I find it quite amusing, not having had too much of it."

She planned to return to Baghdad via Cairo, Jerusalem, Damascus and Aleppo. It was important to examine the local problems for herself, to see and hear what the Arabs felt about the French, about the British, about the Turks, about the Zionists, about Arab nationalism. At the end of her trip to Egypt and Syria, she would write an official report. She had no idea of the trouble to come.

Chapter Twenty-two

The Arab Mood

∞

As Gertrude arrived in Cairo, the thick warm breeze held the fragrant scent of bougainvillea and the fragile hope of rebirth in the Arab world. Local Egyptians, clad in thin *djallabahs*, shuffled along the sandy streets on either side of the Nile, ignoring flies that swarmed around them as they stopped to buy sugarcane from street vendors; women, balancing stacks of baskets on their heads, brushed past scrawny donkeys and sad-eyed oxen dragging overloaded carts. *Feluccas*, ancient-style Egyptian boats, sailed silently along the river, while the rumble of modern trams and motor buses competed with the singsong sound of the street hawkers and the wails of the muezzin calling the faithful to prayer.

In the wealthy sections of town, in Giza, Zamalek, or Garden City where the British Embassy stood, upper-class Muslims, Coptic Christians and Jews lived alongside Europeans in splendid villas or elegant apartments overlooking the Nile. The men engaged in brisk business, trading cotton, commodities and stocks on the Cairo bourse, while their women shopped for fine fabrics at Cicural's, the Jewish-owned department store, ordered their foodstuffs from Vazelakis, the oldest and best Greek grocer, and bargained over gold and jewels with established Armenian dealers.

On top of Cairo's rich Oriental tradition lay a crust of British colonalism, an anomaly of English manners and mores. English-speaking doctors, lawyers, bankers and merchants read the gossipy *Egyptian Gazette* to learn that Mr. Macan Murkar, the jeweler from Ceylon, was showing a splendid selection of set and unset gems at Shepheard's Hotel; that Mr. and Mrs. England of Los Angeles were arranging a shooting expedition to British East Africa in order to secure some trophies for the L.A. Museum; that the Duke and Duchess of Alba had just arrived in town; and that the Crown Prince of Siam and his family had checked into the Luxor Winter Palace Hotel.

Cosmopolitan Cairenes relaxed together at the spa in Halouan, indulging in treatments of electric lights or needle baths; or they golfed at the Gezira Sporting Club, where the ladies were requested not to wear long skirts because they destroyed the surface of the greens. The putting greens, like the fairways, were composed of sand, painstakingly raked, brushed and watered into a smooth surface.

On sun-filled afternoons the smart set drove out to Mena House. Sitting on the terrace of the hotel, once the Khedive's hunting lodge, then a guest house for special visitors to the opening of the Suez Canal in 1869, they took their tea enjoying the view of the Pyramids. It was after the season in 1919 when Gertrude arrived, but had it been winter or spring, she would have joined the well-dressed women in long trailing gowns and tiaras, the men in white tie and tails, for an evening at the Cairo Opera House. There, world-famous singers performed *Tosca* or *La Traviata* and British actors such as Sybil Thorndike performed the latest West End theatrical rage. Or she would have dined and danced at Shepheard's, rubbing elbows on the ballroom floor with at least one visiting European monarch.

Yet despite the civility, a lingering stench of violence greeted Gertrude in September 1919. Rebellion had been in the air and clouds still trembled over the Nile. As a British protectorate, Egypt had been forced by Britain to provide men, supplies and four million pounds in money to fight the Turks; at the end of the war, when the Anglo-French Declaration of Arab liberation was announced, the Egyptians demanded their self-determination. But British officials in London refused to hear of it, and the Egyptians took up arms. At first the crowds turned angrily on the property of British subjects, then on the property of Egyptian Anglophiles. In the end, they not only destroyed homes and shops; they attacked British soldiers on trains, pulled them off, beat them and left their corpses behind. The overpowering British army quelled the uprising, but the insurrection gave an ugly taste of things to come. The bitter facts of nationalism and resistance, as told to Gertrude by General Gilbert Clayton, the Interior Minister, would make a significant impact on her views.

Sitting in the garden of the British Residence, a splendid Neoclassical building on the Nile, Gertrude smoked one cigarette after another while Clayton spoke. Despite the actions of the British Government in London, he confessed, he believed the Egyptians were mainly in the right. It was true that certain security positions would have to be kept by the British, but others could be turned over at once to the Arabs. If not, the situation would turn to disaster. "We must maintain control of the Suez Canal, the Nile water, the army and the police," he explained; as for the administration itself, "leave the Egyptian Ministers without British advisers, but give the High Commissioner a British adviser in each department." No doubt, he acknowledged, "the Egyptians will make mistakes and tie the departments into serious knots," but they were entitled to a fair trial. If the British refused to take these bold measures, they would end up with an "Oriental Ireland."

Gertrude asked his opinion on Iraq. He advised her to take the right steps from the start. "Begin as you intend to go on," he suggested. Look at the mess we have here, he said, and avoid it at all costs. But she shook her head in protest. Not only were the Iraqi Arabs at odds with each other; they had little experience running a government. How could they take charge of an embryonic country, an entity just being formed? Unlike Egypt, a modern state since the early nineteenth century, Mesopotamia had no solid framework, no infrastructure to build on. Indeed, the British were trying to create a country out of three entirely separate Ottoman *vilayets*—Basrah, Baghdad and Mosul—trying to unify a population of Sunnis, Shiites, Jews, Christians and Kurds, all with different interests. But Clayton insisted that even with poor material to work with, he would create independent Arab ministries, guided by advisers to the British High Commissioner. The ministers could form a council led by an Arab president who eventually might become the head of state. Gertrude listened carefully to his ideas. Whatever seeds of Arab self-rule had been planted in her mind by Lawrence and Faisal were beginning to take root under Clayton.

There were several Iraqi nationalists he wanted her to meet. One was Sayid Talib Pasha. A former politician from an influential family in Basrah, he had led the movement for Arab nationalism even before the war and now was seen as its spokesman. Smooth and smart, he had developed a large constituency. But Talib's methods were infamous. Robin Hood to some, blackmailer and murderer to others, he gave generously to the poor but with money taken from others; it was even rumored that he kept a dungeon in his house to hold his enemies. Gertrude viewed him with deep suspicion, but she took Clayton's advice and went to see him. Charming, urbane and ambitious, Talib told her he wanted to go back to Basrah, to return home and cultivate his estate. "To the best of my recollection," she later observed dryly, "he has none." Rather, she believed, the "cunning" fellow was plotting his way to become the Emir of Iraq.

Others on Clayton's list included Yasin Pasha, an extremist, but highly intelligent; Jafar Pasha al Askari and his brother-in-law Nuri Pasha Said, both impressive Iraqis who had fought alongside Faisal during the Arab Revolt and were now in power with him in Syria. She made a note to interview them when she reached Damascus.

The other matter on her agenda was the Arab Bureau in Cairo. Sharing information with the French and the Italians had weakened the British agency during the war, and now it was nearly destroyed. The network needed to be restored. She had been given the assignment of coordinating exchanges of information between the British posts in Egypt and Iraq. "Interchange of intelligence is a matter I have much at heart," she remarked.

∞ ∞ ∞

From Egypt she moved on to Palestine. Of the dozens of Arabs she spoke with, one, a "remarkable Muslim woman," railed against wearing the veil. The attractive twenty-five-year-old Nasirah Haddad, widowed once and then married to a lawyer, did charity work for the poor. But, she complained, being veiled interfered with her work at every turn; she hoped it would end with the next generation. "She is the only woman in Jerusalem who holds views so advanced," Gertrude observed.

The issue on everyone's minds, however, was Zionism. The Balfour Declaration and its promise of a Jewish homeland had terrified the Arabs, who saw themselves being displaced. But in the narrow alleys of the Old City, Eastern European Jews, who had fled pogroms in Poland and Russia, were already proving the need for a permanent home of their own. Gertrude spent hours discussing the situation with Ronald Storrs, now Governor of Jerusalem. To stop the newly arrived Jews from being absorbed into Palestine, Storrs informed her, the Arabs had created an anti-Zionist organization. Led by a Muslim president in Jerusalem and a Christian president in Jaffa, it was in constant touch with the British Chief Administrator. But the Arabs viewed the British as responsible for the Zionists, and with anti-Zionism as its only basis for existence, the group was becoming anti-British as well. The organization was destined to become a vociferous, violent force in the region, targeting both British and Jews.

Of the others she met, Kamil al Husseini, the Mufti of Jerusalem, stood out. The leading religious and political personality in the city, he had been appointed by the British and was strongly anti-French. An Arab nationalist, like many Palestinian Arabs he saw himself as a Syrian and aligned himself with Faisal, now ruling in Damascus.

With the situation in Palestine hopelessly divided, Gertrude summed up her observations in a letter to her family: "There is practically no question but Zionism in Jerusalem. All the Muslims are against it and furious with us for backing it and all the Jews are for it and equally furious with us for not backing it enough. Our attitude, meantime, is to halt between the two and wonder what to do for the best. Like the people in authority I feel a great deal of sympathy with both sides and I believe that if both would be responsible they would each of them have not very much to fear. But they won't be reasonable and we are sowing the seeds of secular disturbance as far I can see."

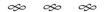

On the evening of October 7, 1919, Gertrude arrived in Damascus, annoyed to discover that the consulate had not been notified she was coming; "bad staff work," she jotted in her diary. She settled into a room at the Damascus Palace, the same hotel that had been her headquarters before she set off for Hayil five years earlier, and the following day she walked around the city. In only three years Syria had gone from Turkish to Arab administration, and in the course of much trouble and turmoil, Damascus had changed a good deal. Near the great Umayyad Mosque, the covered bazaar had been stripped of its roof, bringing sunlight to its shops. Jafar Pasha, the Arab Governor under Faisal, had made other improvements, too, creating thoroughfares, opening up crowded streets. Overall, she observed, the people were not as friendly, the town filthier than she had ever seen it, but there was little doubt that the Arabs were capable of governing themselves.

Sadly, the war had impoverished many. Nevertheless, on a visit to her old friend Sheikh Muhammad Bassam, she smiled a little when she learned that, despite her own attempts to stop the smuggling of goods from Mesopotamia into Syria, he had grown immensely rich. The man who had helped her make arrangements for her trip to Arabia in 1914 had run supplies successfully during the war, reselling them at hugely inflated prices.

The Arab Government had been in place for a year, but the French still refused to recognize Faisal as the legitimate, independent ruler of Syria. He was away in England, lobbying for support; he had appointed his closest aides as administrators and had left his younger brother, Zaid, temporarily in charge. Gertrude went to pay him a call. Entering his house, she found it filled with khaki-clad Arab officers and a throng of black Abyssinian eunuch slaves, imported from Mecca, ready to serve the ruler. The nineteen year-old Zaid seemed to be a "nice boy" and "very friendly," she noted, and when they conferred about Iraq, he told her that "the return of Sir Percy to Mesopotamia would be welcomed by all."

Faisal's government was composed of a group of self-reliant nationalists, nearly all of Mesopotamian origin, who had once served in the Turkish army and then switched to Faisal's side. It was this strong clique of Iraqis, now living in Damascus, that she wanted to meet the most. Yasin Pasha al Hashimi, Jafar Pasha al Askari and Nuri Said would one day, she suspected rightly, be the core of an Arab Government in Iraq. Yasin, a small, thick-set man in his thirties, headed Al Ahd al Iraqi, an intensely nationalist group whose fervent goal was Arab independence in Mesopotamia. It wanted the country free from all foreign control and, under the rule of the Sharifian family, sought an Iraqi alliance with Syria. She was pleased to hear him acknowledge, however, that for several years, at least, the Iraqis would not be able to function without British advice; Sir Percy Cox, he thought, should be appointed High Commissioner to an Arab king. But he was certain that Faisal's brother Abdullah, who had been proposed as King of Iraq, would become even more popular than Cox.

At Faisal's house she also met Jafar Pasha. A fat, jolly man, he was nonetheless a judicious authority and outstanding soldier who had won military honors from both the British and the Turks. Jafar, who was of Kurdish origin and came from Mosul, was fluent in seven languages— English, French, German, Arabic, Turkish, Kurdish, Persian—and tested her in all. (She did well in the first five, had never learned Kurdish, and had forgotten most of her Persian.) Knowing of her affection for the Arabs, he asked her to help him return to Iraq. She promised to try. "He is an honest man who would be useful to us," she noted correctly, "and said to be by far the most capable administrator in the Arab Government."

Nuri Said had been Faisal's chief of staff in the Arab army and held a similar role in Faisal's court. Born in Baghdad to a father who was an attorney, he was reserved and more of an introvert than Jafar but, like him, highly Westernized. The two men made a good team. They had met in military school and formed a strong bond, made even stronger by a pact to marry each other's sister. If Jafar had the common touch, Nuri was politically more shrewd. Gertrude wrote with fore-sight, "Probably the best of them, a man of considerable intelligence." Continually loyal to the British, Nuri would serve as Prime Minister under fourteen different Arab Governments in Iraq.

In a letter to her parents Gertrude described what she had seen in the city. Wherever she went, the desire for self-determination, "the Spirit of 1919," had overtaken all. "If the French won't recognize it, there will be risings and massacres and Heaven knows what."

By October 12, her stay in Damascus complete, Gertrude went on to Aleppo, where she found her old aide-de-camp, the loyal Fattuh, living with his wife in a tiny, rented house. He was still suffering from the war. "The Turks dropped on him," she wrote in her diary, "because he was my servant." He had lost weight, his once round face was now haggard and he had aged a great deal. His years of service to the woman who had become a leading intelligence agent for the British had cost him dearly. Nonetheless, he was delighted to see her and, after warm embraces, told her what had happened. Drafted twice into the Turkish army, he had managed to buy his way out; but later he had been imprisoned and then impoverished by the Turks. Stripped of his two homes, his garden, his horses and even his carriages, he was drained of everything, forced to earn a meager living by carting wood.

He still had some of her camp kit from their desert travels, and pulling out her old plates and cups, he prepared a picnic for her motor trip to Iraq. Her old equipment brought to mind much happier days. "Oh Fattuh," she said, "before the war our hearts were so light when we traveled; now they are so heavy that a camel could not carry us."

Smiling, he answered good-naturedly, "My lady, no, a camel couldn't carry you."

"My poor Fattuh," she grieved and gave him some money, promis-ing to help him rent a garden from the Muslim authorities. They hugged again, and she left for Baghdad, unaware that in her absence A. T. Wilson had used his authority and abolished the Arab Bureau office in Baghdad. And in an ominous letter to a colleague in London he had written: "I shall be interested to know what Miss Bell is going to do when she comes here. She will take some handling."

CHAPTER TWENTY-THREE

A Change of Thinking

∞

A wave of happiness surged through Gertrude as the motor car approached her walled house and lurched to a stop. Eight months had gone by since she left for the Paris Peace Conference, and she hurried to see her garden—a riot of zinnias, marigolds and chrysanthemums. Her villa, with its narrow columns in front, had been improved with the addition of new rooms; and her servants, happy to have her back, came running out to greet her. Word spread like wildfire that the Khatun had returned, and within hours of her arrival a stream of notables flowed through her doorway. She was home, happy to be there, amidst the familiar sights of the Tigris and the date palm groves, the familiar sounds of Victoria carriages clopping along the Baghdad streets, the familiar smells of fresh baked bread and sweetened turnips floating through the Mesopotamian air.

Now, besides seeing people, what she wanted to do most was to write her Syrian report.

At the office, visitors filled her days, taking up too much of her time, she complained. She had already been to see the Naqib, the holy man, informing him of what she had learned in Paris and London and on her trip through the East, and she had paid a condolence call on the family of one of her Arab friends, Abdul Rahman Jamil. Although he had been dead for a month, the women of the family were still in deepest mourning, his wife and sisters dressed in somber black, their hair shorn, their cheeks covered with streaming tears. "I'm very sorry he's dead," she wrote to Florence, adding tartly: "But I'm glad he won't have the opportunity of doing it again, so that I shall not have to pay a another visit of condolence. It was awful." No one, she remarked, "unless they determine to do so, can cry solidly for a month." She seemed to forget how long she mourned for Doughty-Wylie.

◆ ◆ ◆

The influx of five hundred and fifty British wives, children and relatives, given permission to arrive after the war, had dramatically changed the lives of the British officials. "Brides come out in swarms to be married here," she wrote. Two weddings took place just after she came back. A social whirlwind was sweeping the town, and she was carried along, in her new clothes, to a round of receptions and teas given by British, Muslim and Jewish women. A public library was being built, a law school opened, a female ward built in the civic hospital and a school opened for Muslim girls. But all too soon her colleagues' wives became a moaning brigade complaining about the heat and the dust, the sloppy mud, the awful food, the horrible Arabs. "These idle women" were getting on her nerves, demanding that she pay them social calls, yet when she asked them to attend ceremonies for the Arabs, they refused to come. "They can think what they like about me but I won't bother about them any more," she wrote angrily to Florence.

She was more at home among the Arab men than among the British women. When, in early November, her colleague Sir Edgar Bonham Carter hosted an at-home for Arab notables, Gertrude was one of only five British officials invited to attend. She arrived, dressed in a high-necked, long-sleeved gown and frilly hat, and looked around the room: fifty Arab men were seated in typical fashion, chairs arranged in a circle. As soon as they saw her they rose, and she walked around the room, going from one to the next, shaking hands, knowing them all by name, saying something significant to each. How was his wife? she asked. How was the health of his eldest son? What was the state of his crops? What did he think about the political situation?

Not only did she enjoy the company of the Arab men (and used their friendship in her work), but her special status appealed to her snobbishness. Toward the end of November, she was invited to visit one of the most learned Muslims in Baghdad. The notable did not like the British, yet he always treated her as a friend. "He doesn't consort with Europeans at all," she wrote home, but "he had a select little party to meet me. I must say I feel a sense of personal triumph when I sit in that house as an intimate."

Her own house was more comfortable than ever: with some good bargaining in the bazaar, she had acquired a charming black cupboard and a chest; her maid Marie, who had just arrived by ship, was sewing curtains and busily fixing up the rooms; her new cook was preparing vegetables from the garden. She wished only that the new furniture and crockery she had ordered from Maples in England would arrive so that she could increase the size of her parties. With her staff in place, she hosted dinners for friends like Frank Balfour, the new Governor of Baghdad, Bonham Carter, the Justice Minister, and General MacMunn, the Commander-in-Chief. Whoever the guests, she dominated the conversation. Her voice deep from the smoke of tobacco, her eyes sparkling, her enthusiasm boundless, she magnetized the men. Her conversation leapt from French to English to Arabic; it bounced from politics to gossip, from the attitudes at Whitehall to how best to administer the Arabs; from how to do the newest dances, to the number of stitches to the inch in the finest Persian carpets, to the proper way to dine in the tent of a sheikh, to the excavations at Babylon, to the horse given her by General MacMunn, to the pair of salukis—tall, slender, silken-haired dogs—that had just arrived from Fahad Bey. "On any subject that arose," said the enchanted Sir George MacMunn, "she was sure to be interesting and entertaining."

∞   ∞   ∞

But before it all, she worked on her report. Reviewing for the Foreign Office what she had seen and heard, she detailed everything on her trip, from Zionism to nationalism, emphasizing the Arab Government that stretched from Damascus to Aleppo and the importance of the Arab nationalist cliques. At last, after toiling in her office late into the night, every night for three weeks, she finished. Ending with a lengthy analysis of Syria, she dated her report November 15, 1919, and signed it *GLB*.

Her ideas had turned almost one hundred and eighty degrees from where they had been before her trip. She had gone from believing the

Arabs could never rule themselves to seeing them govern themselves in Syria. She had gone from denying the notion that there is an Arab nation comprised of one Arab people to seeing the fervor of Arab nationalism in Palestine and in Syria. She had gone from assuming that Britain must stay in total control to recognizing the need for it to cede considerable authority. With General Clayton's help in Cairo, she had seen the light: compromise would prolong British importance, not reduce it. The more the British helped the Arabs achieve self-rule, she now proposed, the longer the British could retain their economic and political influence. The paper marked a seminal change in her thinking.

It was useless to speculate on who was to blame for the current situation in Syria—the British installation of an Arab government while the French claimed control—or why it had happened, she wrote: "A more profitable line of thought lies in the direction of considering how the twelve-month existence—even if it fails to exist longer—of an independent Arab State [in Syria] has affected and will affect Mesopotamia. It is true that the Arab administration [in Syria] has left much to be desired, and equally true that it has been artificially financed by our subsidy to the Sharif; but it has presented, nevertheless, the outward appearance of a national Government; public business has been kept going, tramways have run, streets have been lighted, people have bought and sold, and a normal world has been maintained." If Faisal's government failed in Syria, she said, the Arabs would blame the British for their lack of support as much as they would blame the French for their aggression. "If it crumbles . . . its failure will be attributed, not to inherent defect, but to British indifference and French ambition."

Referring to the Anglo-French Declaration of November 1918, which promised self-determination to the Arabs, she wrote, "We have stated that it is our intention to assist and establish in Syria and in Mesopotamia indigenous governments and administrations. I believe that events of the last year have left us no choice in Mesopotamia." Yet, she acknowledged, the choice was not an easy one. "Local conditions, the vast potential wealth of the country, the tribal character of its rural population, the lack of material from which to draw official personnel will make the problem harder to solve than elsewhere." But, she could envision no other response. "I venture to think that the answer to such objections is that any alternative line of action would create problems the solution of which we are learning to be harder still."

Then came her inescapable conclusion: "An Arab State in Mesopotamia . . . within a short period of years is a possibility, and . . .

the recognition or creation of a logical scheme of government on these lines, in supercession of those on which we are now working on Mesopotamia, would be practical and popular."

∞   ∞   ∞

The report threw Wilson into a rage. And it hardly pleased most of her other colleagues in Baghdad. Britain's commercial interest in Mesopotamia was long and deep, emmeshed in a marketplace that imported nearly half its goods—including coal and iron, textiles and manufactured goods—from British supplies, and provided Britain with some thirty-five percent of its exports, including dates, figs, olive oil and grain. In addition, Britain's navy and its newly emerging air force needed to find substantial sources of oil. Unlike the United States, which was already producing 376 million barrels a year, England had no oil of its own; to retain her independence, she had to develop her own fields.

The same month that Gertrude called for self-rule in Mesopotamia, the General Staff in Baghdad issued a memorandum stating Mesopotamia's critical importance to the British Empire: "The future power of the world is oil," they wrote. "The oil fields of southern Persia, now under British control, are the most inexhaustible 'proved' fields in the world. The Mosul province and the banks of the mid-Euphrates promise to afford oil in great quantities, although the extent of the fields is not yet proved. . . . With a railway and pipeline in the Mediterranean, which is forecast within the next ten years, the position of England as a naval power in the Mediterranean could be doubly assured, and our dependence on the Suez canal, which is a vulnerable point in our line of communication with the East, would be considerably lessened."

A. T. Wilson was well aware of the value of oil; he would not take the risk of losing Mesopotamia. When Gertrude's report reached his desk, he seethed with anger. Writing a cover letter to Whitehall that said, politely, "I have the honour to enclose herewith an interesting and valuable note by Miss G. L. Bell CBE, entitled 'Syria in 1919,'" Wilson went on to include a few of his own observations to London:

"The fundamental assumption throughout this note and, I should add, throughout recent correspondence which has reached me from London, is that an Arab State in Mesopotamia and elsewhere within a short period of years is a possibility, and that the recognition and creation of a logical scheme of Government along these lines . . .

would be practicable and popular; in other words the assumption is that the Anglo-French Declaration of November 18th, 1918, represents a practical line of policy to pursue in the near future. My observations in this country and elsewhere have forced me to the conclusion that this assumption is erroneous."

The dispute was irreparable; the bridge that Gertrude and Wilson had built between them was shattered.

CHAPTER TWENTY-FOUR

Desert Storms

∞

Shunned by most of the British staff, who were vehemently opposed to her Syrian report, Gertrude could at least take solace in the Arabs who flocked to her office seeking advice. Umm al Muminin, they called her, the Mother of the Faithful. "The last person who bore that name was Ayishah, the wife of the Prophet," she wrote proudly to Hugh. But by December 1919, all sorts of problems were cropping up. Small personal matters, like her need for household supplies: sheets, blankets, pillowcases and towels, and damask cloths for her new dining room table. And oh, the high cost of living since the end of the war! Meat was very expensive, eggs less, but as a civilian no longer receiving army rations, she had suddenly come face to face with the price of food. She was paying her cook a hundred and eight pounds a year, her butler eighty-four pounds, and he was due for a raise. Even Harrods had sent her a bill for four pounds, but she'd paid it "somehow!" she swore.

She felt saddened too over the sudden death of her generous land-lord, Musa Pachachi. He was one of Baghdad's most prominent fami-lies and along with the Naqib, had been her earliest Baghdad friend. "It wasn't only unvarying affectionate kindness I got from him," she explained to her father, "but a very frank and valuable appreciation of politics. He was fearless and outspoken, had no axe to grind and I could go to him for information and advice as I could go to no one else. I do grieve for him—Baghdad isn't the same place without him."

His wise political counsel might have saved her heartache over the difficult issues arising in the north. But he was gone, and the tribes along the Euphrates were becoming of some concern. There were signs that a major uprising was about to begin. An Arab force had seized Dair al Zor, a Euphrates town four hundred miles north of Baghdad, where the border with Syria was still undefined. The local tribes were caught up in the Syrian nationalist movement. A question had arisen over who would administer the territory: a British Political Officer from Mesopotamia or a representative of the Arab Government in Syria. When it was rumored that an Arab force was moving down to attack the area, the British Political Officer in Dair rushed to the scene to make a recconaissance. Finding no trace of any unusual movement, the Political Officer tried to return to his post, but on the way back he was ambushed and fired at by tribesmen. Only with difficulty did he reach Dair.

Still not suspecting serious trouble, but just to be safe, he alerted Baghdad and arrested the Mayor of Dair (who he thought had been conniving with the agitators). Early the following morning, a force of tribesmen marched in from the south, joined the townsmen and ransacked Dair: they raided the hospital, the church, the mosques and the Political Office, where they broke open the safe and stole the contents. They blew up the oil dump, wounding ninety people, released all the prisoners in the jail and attacked the British army barracks. When the Political Officer tried to make peace in the town, the sheikhs attacked him in a fury. Just as they were about to kill him, two British airplanes flew overhead, spraying the town with machine-gun fire. "The sheikhs changed their note at once," Gertrude reported. Minutes after the airplanes left, the notables signed an armistice with the British. But it was only a temporary truce.

That afternoon, Ramadhan al Shallash, a leader of Mesopotamian origin and a member of al Ahd al Iraqi, the nationalist group, arrived from Damascus. He promised the British officers safe passage, but then, changing his mind, kept them hostage. He quickly established himself in authority, called in the local sheikhs from the region around the Euphrates, gave them generous payments and incited them to rebel against the British. He even encouraged them to carry the war to India. Fortunately, a few of the sheikhs, including Fahad Bey, the Paramount Chief of the Anazeh, remained loyal to the British.

For two weeks the situation in Dair remained extremely tense. In Baghdad the mood was hardly better. Gertrude and Wilson were sliding farther apart. He ignored her in the mess and belittled her in front of colleagues. In a letter to a friend, Wilson wrote, "I am having some trouble with Miss Bell. On political questions, she is rather fanatic." At about the same time, on December 20, Gertrude wrote home: "Rather a trying week, for A. T. has been overworked—a chronic state—and in a condition when he ought not to be working, which results in making him savagely cross and all our lives rather a burden in consequence."

Things seemed to improve, briefly. Faisal's government in Syria protested strongly against the mutinous Arab takeover in Dair, and the British authorities were released on December 25. That same evening, Wilson was giving a Christmas party for all the Political Officers and their wives. Prepared to shiver from the cold, Gertrude dressed in her evening gown and set off for the dinner. But the sight of her colleagues only irked her. "To judge from appearances most of them have two wives," she bridled, "and I wish I could get their names and faces by heart." When the music started and the guests got up to dance, she said her good nights and left. "I dance no longer," she explained.

∞   ∞   ∞

Instead, she caught a special train the next morning to celebrate the New Year in Babylon. Away for a week, she sailed by motor launch down the Euphrates to Shamiyeh, where the sheikhs were seething with anger over the taxes the British were forcing them to pay. Then it was on to the holy city of Najaf, where she listened carefully for unsaid words of *jihad*. With the tribes rebellious in the north, she had to assess how far the trouble was spreading, how great the threat of holy war.

The visit gave her a new perspective. Having seen the sheikhs and other notables, her ideas had crystallized. She sent a note to her father when she returned to Baghdad: "I have written to Edwin Montagu [Secretary of State for India] an immense letter about the sort of government we ought to set up here and even sent him the rough draft of a constitution. . . . I've done my best both to find out what should be done and to lay it before him. The rest is, as we say, *alla Allah*, on God. I sometimes feel that it's the only thing I really care for, to see this country go right."

Gertrude's private correspondence with Montagu and others infuriated A. T. Wilson. Not only was she advising Whitehall to form an Arab government, blatantly contradicting him; she was writing to friends in high places, undermining his authority. Unsaid, but far worse, she was indisputably a woman. A woman! An interfering, emasculating woman. Officially, Wilson was her chief, and the rigid officer of the India Service seethed at her gall. He sent off a letter to Cox, suggesting she be fired.

∽   ∽   ∽

The return mail carried sad news. Her favorite uncle, Frank Lascelles, her host in Bucharest and Persia, who had introduced her to Domnul Chirol, Lord Hardinge, Henry Cadogan and so many others, and who had opened her eyes to the East, was dead. "I do grieve so much," she wrote to Florence in January 1920. "When I remember how much I owed him, how many delightful experiences and how much sympathy, my heart aches with the thought that I didn't give him enough in return."

She grieved, too, over the situation surrounding Mesopotamia. To the north, the Turks, frustrated that no peace treaty had yet been signed with Britain and France, were embracing Bolshevik propaganda; and the Kurds were co-operating with anyone ready to massacre Christian heretics. To the west, the Arab Government in Syria, bound to fail without financial aid, was angry and unwilling to accept the help of the French; while Egypt, whose nationalist yearnings had been ignored by officials in London since the end of the war, had been torn apart, she wrote, "turned into a second Ireland, largely by our own stupidity." And Mesopotamia was up for grabs:

"This country, which way will it go with all these agents of unrest to tempt it?" she asked. "I pray the people at home may be rightly guided and realize that the only chance here is to recognize political ambitions from the first, not to try to squeeze the Arabs into our mould and have our hands forced in a year—who knows? perhaps less, the world is moving so fast with the result that the chaos to north and east overwhelms Mesopotamia also. I wish I carried more weight. I've written to Edwin and this week I'm writing to Sir A. Hirtzel. But the truth is I'm in a minority of one in the Mesopotamian political service—or nearly—and yet I'm so sure I'm right that I would go to the stake for it. They must see; they must know at home. They can't be so blind as not to read such gigantic writing on the wall as the world at large is setting before their eyes."

But as firmly convinced as she was that an Arab government had to be created in Iraq, Wilson and his team of officers were adamantly opposed. Shunned in the Political Mess, where the men snidely referred to her walled house as Chastity Chase, she sought refuge inside her home. Standing at the window, stroking her dogs, she looked out at her garden and watched the mulberry trees drop their leaves.

∞   ∞   ∞

The trouble up north continued. Faisal's government, like the British, did not want to divide the tribes around Dair by drawing boundary lines. But the renegade Arab, Ramadhan al Shallash, who had seized control and held the British officers hostage at Dair, acted in defiance of Faisal and pushed his authority harder. He declared that the British had to withdraw their occupying forces fifty miles below their existing lines in Anah, and, he announced, he was sending his forces farther north, on the attack toward Mosul. He collected taxes inside British territory, sent threatening letters to the Political Officers, excoriated the sheikhs under British control, encouraged the tribes to rob and raid, and spurred on his men to hijack and plunder the Baghdad gold merchants as they transported their goods across the desert from Syria. The British threatened reprisals and machine-gunned the insurgents.

The tensions continued into February 1920, growing only more hostile and dangerous when Ramadhan al Shallash was replaced by Maulud al Khalaf, another, even more prominent, member of the nationalist al Ahd al Iraqi. Then the entire situation grew murkier. It was difficult to understand whether Faisal's government in Damascus had succumbed to nationalist pressure and was waging war on the British in Iraq, or whether the trouble was coming from some anti-Faisal, extremist nationalist group.

To make matters worse, officials in Cairo, despite Gertrude's pleas, were still not sending up-to-date information about either Egypt or Syria. "We get no news from Egypt," she complained to Domnul in London, "though they must know more about Syria than we do. We don't know whether Faisal has returned nor whether he has come to terms with the French." But Arab tribesmen, whom she knew from earlier days, were beginning to trickle down from Aleppo. In exchange for official favors, her informants were providing her with news about Syria and Turkey.

"I've got a very complete system of intelligence with the Agail of Baghdad," she wrote to Domnul in early February, "and I don't think many people of interest arrive without their letting me know." As for circumstances in Mesopotamia, she told him, "if, when we set up civil government, we do it on really liberal lines, and *not be afraid*, we shall have the country with us." The key was to protect the rural, tribal population from the Baghdadis, who knew and cared nothing about the tribes. The Arab officials, she explained, would almost invariably be townsmen—Baghdadis and Syrians—because there was no other educated class. "And the tribes (mostly Shi'ahs remember), hate them."

Animosity and suspicion defined the relationship between the educated townsmen, who were mainly Sunnis, and the nomadic tribesmen, who were mostly Shiites. And more and more it defined the relationship between Gertrude and Wilson. On February 9, 1920, she received a letter from Sir Percy Cox in Persia, dated three months earlier, and hastened to open it. She read:

"Dear Khatun, It is good to know that you are back; how I wish we could forgather and have a confab. What a lot you must know of the doings of the mighty! . . . Your welcome letter of August 7th took three months to reach here."

She noticed a note scrawled on Cox's letter, the handwriting, Wilson's: "Miss Bell—what an extraordinary long time this has taken to come." Wilson was reading her mail!

Even worse, unbeknownst to Gertrude, he had been writing about her to Cox, first in December, then in January, complaining bitterly of her letters to government bigwigs. To Gertrude, her letters home seemed perfectly natural. But Wilson regarded her correspondence with deep suspicion. He wanted her sent home. The situation had become so tense and she had become so distraught that, responding to Sir Percy's letter, she even suggested it herself.

Sayid Talib arrived in Baghdad at Wilson's invitation. It was true that, as an Iraqi native and the son of the Naqib of Basrah, a direct descendant of the Prophet Muhammad, he was seen by many Arabs and even some British as the most logical candidate to rule the country, but he was feared and hated by many others. Gertrude had met him in Cairo in 1919 and was suspicious of him then, when he expressed a desire to come back to Iraq. He was still the one nationalist she really despised. Nevertheless, she wanted to gain his confidence; better to know what he was thinking than have him sneaking around her back. She attended a big Arab party for him (she was the only woman) and hosted a dinner in his honor.

Invited to dine at her table were British and Arabs, among them Sir Edgar Bonham Carter, Major Humphrey Brown, the Mayor of Baghdad and a son of the Naqib. As the candles flickered and wine glasses were held up in toasts, the conversation crackled with energy. The mustachioed Talib, well traveled and polished from years of living abroad, was as dignified and charming as he could be, but was known to be a man who killed those in his way. As Gertrude led the discussion, they talked about Syria, the tribes in the north, the problems in Egypt (where he had lived in exile for the past five years) and the current conditions in Baghdad. And then, coquettishly, she turned to her right and asked her guest of honor, "Tell me, Pasha, how many men have you done to death?" Politely Sayid Talib answered, "Nay, Khatun, it's difficult after all these years to give the exact number."

He was, she wrote, "the cleverest and perhaps the greatest rogue unhung . . . probably the best known man in Mesopotamia—a *succes de crime*—Talib is as sharp as a needle, nothing escapes him, and if he came to Baghdad to see how the land lay, why he has seen." He had been given a cooler reception than in the past. Later she would freeze him out entirely.

For now, he was a mere intrusion; she had more pressing matters on her mind. Shiite holy men in Karbala and Najaf in the south had banded together with notables from Dair and Mosul in the north to incite rebellion against the British. In early March 1920, they sent their representatives to an Arab Congress in Damascus.

The religious leaders' influence was undeniable; their hold over their followers, tenacious. The British wanted to be in touch with them, but communication had been impossible. The Shiite holy men had been overtly hostile; attempts by the Political Officers had met with blank rejection. Even Gertrude had been cut off, because, she explained, she refused to wear a veil: "Their tenets forbid them to look upon an unveiled woman and my tenets don't permit me to veil—I think I'm right there, for it would be a tacit admission of inferiority which would put our intercourse from the first out of focus." Nor did it do her any good to try to make friends through the women: "They would veil before me as if I were a man. So you see," she remarked on the confusing problem of gender, "I appear to be too female for one sex and too male for the other."

Yet it was essential to make contact. If the Shiite religious leaders could be persuaded to stop inciting holy war against the Christian infidels, or, at least, if they could be convinced to start a dialogue with the British, then progress could begin toward a peaceful solution. After months of ingratiating herself, in March she was invited by a leading Shiite family for a visit to Kadhimain. The third holiest city in Iraq was just eight miles from Baghdad, yet "bitterly pan-Islamic" and bitterly anti-British. Accompanied by a Shiite from Baghdad, Gertrude walked along the town's narrow, crooked streets, the only European among the black-shrouded women, stopping in front of a small mysterious archway, hesitating and following for fifty yards through a pitch-dark, vaulted passage, until she reached the courtyard of the house of the holy man, Sayid Hassan.

The place was at least a hundred years old, its upper floor enclosed by wooden latticework, its rooms all opening onto the inner court, surrounded by a pool of silence; no hint of the outside world could be felt. The holy man's son appeared, a sinister-looking figure in black robes, black beard and black turban, and bade her welcome. The old divine himself, Sayid Hassan, a formidable figure with a long white beard that reached to his chest and a huge dark turban on his head, awaited her inside.

Gertrude folded her skirt and squatted cross-legged on the carpet. No other woman had ever been invited to drink coffee with such a holy man or listen to him discourse. She wanted to make a good impression. As was his way, the old man began to speak. But never one to merely sit and listen, Gertrude joined in, and they spoke of many different things: of his family, the Sadrs, considered the most learned family in the entire Shiite world; of their branches in Persia, Syria and Mesopotamia; of books and book collections in Cairo, London, Paris and Rome. He showed her his library catalogues from every city, talking "with such vigour," she noted, "that his turban kept slipping forward on to his eyebrows and he had to push it back impatiently on to the top of his head." They spoke for nearly two hours, until, finally, she brought up the subject of Syria. She told him everything she knew, including the latest telegram she had just received, saying Faisal was about to be crowned king in Damascus.

"Over the whole of Syria to the sea?" the holy man asked.

"No," she replied; "the French stay in Beirut."

"Then it's no good," he said, wiping his hands, and they discussed the matter from every angle. From Syria they jumped to Bolshevism and she observed that it was "the child of poverty and hunger." The *mujtahid* agreed, "but," he added, "all the world's poor and hungry since this war." Gertrude added that the Bolsheviks wanted to sweep away everything that had been built before, but the problem was they had no knowledge themselves of the art of building. Again he agreed.

The conversation seemed to have come to an end. She made signs of leaving, but the holy man stopped her. "It is well known that you are the most learned woman of your time," he said, "and if any proof were needed it would be found in the fact that you wish to frequent the society of the learned. That's why you're here today." She thanked him profusely, and amidst "a shower of invitations to come again," she rose to go. She had established a line of communication with the influential Shiite leader. Her visit had been a success.

∞ ∞ ∞

On her return to Baghdad, she learned that the Arab Congress convening in Damascus had indeed proclaimed Faisal King of Syria. Following that, with the approval of Faisal, the Mesopotamian representatives to the meeting had pronounced his brother Abdullah King of Iraq. The reports on Abdullah's character were unclear, however. David Hogarth, who had never met him firsthand, had described his contradictory personality in a telegram the year before:

Abdullah was "indolent, pleasure loving," the "least scrupulous of the brothers," and "more vicious than the others," Hogarth wrote. He did not have "a dominant personality" nor "much will to power," and was "not born to rule." Nevertheless, said Hogarth, "he seems the ablest," and was "regarded by Arab Intellectuals as the one cultivated member of the Family." Hogarth believed that Abdullah was "intelligent enough to grasp real facts and conform to them" and "would make a presentable titular ruler. . . . Failing him," the British official warned, "I see no possible outstanding Arab for Mesopotamia."

The announcement about Faisal and Abdullah put Gertrude on the alert. "Well, we are in for it," she wrote Florence in March 1920, "and I think we shall need every scrap of personal influence and every hour of friendly intercourse we've ever had here in order to keep this country from falling into chaos."

CHAPTER TWENTY-FIVE

A Taste of England

∞

The news of Abdullah's appointment as Emir of Iraq had turned the usual havoc into frenzy. Gertrude spent a frantic week feverishly writing reports, meeting with jittery locals, hosting dinners for excited guests. Now, at home, she glanced at her watch and felt an anxious pang. With an impatient call to her servants to quickly gather her things, she left in haste, late for the train to Basrah. Her driver steered the motor car as swiftly as he could through the twisting streets, muddy from weeks of rain, but as they approached the station platform, her heart sank: the train was about to leave. There was nothing to do but make a dash for it; leaping onto the train, she found her compartment and settled herself in place. She heaved a sigh. After months of letters and preparation, her father was coming to Mesopotamia and she was on her way to meet him.

The journey on the newly opened railway line took thirty hours from Baghdad to Basrah, a winding adventure along a rugged roadbed. Nevertheless, she ignored the shaking train, brushed aside the annoying sand seeping into the carriage and arrived in Basrah in her smartest frock, with little time to spare. But the only thing she saw was a telegram: Hugh Bell had been delayed in Karachi and would not arrive for several days. "Paf!" she cried. At least she had brought along some work to finish, and perhaps she could recuperate from her recent cold;

"so there's a soul of goodness in things evil," she wrote to Florence. The wait would also give her some time for serious talks with local sheikhs on the shape of the future government.

Her American friends, the missionaries Dorothy and John Van Ess, welcomed her to their house, and she spent most of the day in their study, curled up on the settee, her feet tucked under her, Arab style, smoking one cigarette after another, arguing with John Van Ess about the kind of government Iraq should have. He agreed with A. T. Wilson that the Arabs could not govern themselves. The American churchman, who had spent years on intimate terms with the tribes, did not believe that Iraq was ready for independence. Like Wilson, he wanted a British High Commissioner to rule, and a Cabinet of Arab Ministers to be trained by British advisers. Gertrude agreed that the British advisers were necessary, but she was convinced that there should be an Arab head of state with Arab Ministers to help him rule. For her it was the only answer.

"But, Gertrude!" Van Ess implored, appealing to her respect for the past. "You are flying in the face of four millenniums of history if you try to draw a line around Iraq and call it a political entity! Assyria always looked to the west and east and north, and Babylonia to the south. They have never been an independent unit. You've got to take time to get them integrated; it must be done gradually. They have no conception of nationhood yet."

They discussed the tribes, their loyalties, and whether there was any Arab leader their chiefs might accept. Van Ess supported Sayid Talib. Far more popular than anyone else and with religious credentials as a descendant of Muhammad, Talib was also hardworking and a natural leader, Van Ess reminded her. But Gertrude bristled at the notion. She favored either Faisal, who was still in Syria, or Abdullah, his older brother. "Abdullah is a gentleman who likes a copy of the *Figaro* every morning at breakfast time," she wrote home later. "I haven't any doubt we should get on with him famously." The American insisted that the tribes would never accept a Sharifian ruler, because, he argued, they were outsiders, foreign to the land of Iraq and to its people.

"Oh, they will come around," Gertrude answered confidently.

∾   ∾   ∾

While Gertrude and John Van Ess discussed the fate of Iraq, the country was also the topic at Whitehall. A strong contingent felt that

Mesopotamia had already cost Britain too much money and too many lives (there were 17,000 British and 44,000 Indian troops in Iraq, and combined with the 23,000 troops in Palestine it was costing England 35.5 million pounds a year to keep the garrisons in place), but few could deny Mesopotamia's importance as a future source of oil. In addition to powering the navy and the newly developed air force, petroleum had become the fuel of choice for industrial nations; it was now driving the engines of factories and farm machinery, ensuring smooth runs for ships, railroads, airplanes, automobiles, tanks and trucks. The dependence on oil made England dependent on a friendly Mesopotamia.

In Parliament, Mr. William Ormsby-Gore defended the British position in Iraq. He promised to take fourteen thousand cultivable acres ravaged and destroyed by the war and restore them to their former productivity as one the world's great granaries. "The development of Mesopotamia is one of the things which must be looked to to reduce prices and increase the produce of the world," the colonial affairs expert argued.

Mr. Asquith opposed him. He urged that Britain confine its Iraqi obligations to Basrah. With its port and its proximity to Abadan, it was the most vital of the three former *vilayets*.

But Prime Minister Lloyd George disagreed. He wanted to keep all three of the former Ottoman areas:

> We might abandon the country altogether. But I cannot understand withdrawing from the more important and more promising part of Mesopotamia. Mosul is a country with great possibilities. It has rich oil deposits. . . . It contains some of the richest natural resources of any country in the world. . . . It maintains a population now of a little over two million. . . . What would happen if we withdrew? . . . After the enormous expenditure which we have incurred in freeing this country from the withering despotism of the Turk, to hand it back to anarchy and confusion, and to take no responsibility for its development would be an act of folly and quite indefensible.

In the end, a British commission was formed to seek a mandate from the League of Nations.

∽ ∽ ∽

The echoes of Parliamentary debate still rang in the air as Gertrude welcomed her father to Basrah. Hugh Bell arrived on March 29, 1920, tall, lean, white-haired and white-bearded, his cheeks pink, his blue eyes as lively as his daughter's. His daughter was overjoyed to see him, in his seventies and still fit. They spent a morning in Zubair with the sheikh and an afternoon at a tea with forty notables, hosted by Gertrude. Her father's charm and dignity impressed them all. "It's more amusing than words can say showing him round," she exclaimed. "I feel as if it must be a dream."

From Basrah they headed by train to Nasiriyah, then to Hillah, where she showed him an agrarian renewal project, and to Najaf, the holy city. She took him to Kadhimain, where they had tea with the mayor; she led him across the desert to meet the sheikhs; she brought him as far north as the oil fields in Mosul. In the course of his stay, she showed him her Iraq, and she showed Iraq her father. She was proud of her country and even prouder of her parent: Hugh was an admirable reminder of her noble roots; a strong affirmation of herself (especially in the hostile atmosphere). In Baghdad she pinned on her straw hat, replete with peaches and cherries, and took him to lunches, teas and dinners; she introduced him to everyone she knew, Arabs, Jews and British, from the landowner Haji Naji to the holy man the Naqib, from the Jewish brothers Sasun and Sha'ul Effendi Eskail to her good friends the Tods (he was the agent for Lynch's), from her colleague Mr. Bullard to her nemesis A. T. Wilson. And if Wilson whispered to Hugh that perhaps his daughter needed a rest and a return to England, Gertrude pretended not to hear him.

For one sweet month she ignored the knives in the air and doted only on her father, a sweet taste of England in his well-tailored tweeds and polished Oxfords, seated before the fireplace in the floral covered armchair, reading *The Times*. She indulged in the pleasure of having him in her home. While her servant Zaiya poured them tea and her Persian cook brought in freshly baked cake, they talked for hours on end, discussing A.T.'s stubbornness toward the Arabs and his envy of her friendships; Parliament and its debate over Mesopotamia; the tribes, the nationalists and the possibility of a mandate. She had always relied on her father's judgment; watching him size up the problems confirmed her trust in him.

"He happens to have arrived at a very crucial time," she wrote to Florence. "I think we're on the edge of a pretty considerable Arab nationalist demonstration with which I'm a good deal in sympathy." But the demonstration, she acknowledged, could force a British decision to withdraw from Mesopotamia. And that might lead to disaster: "If we leave this country to go to the dogs it will mean we shall have to reconsider our whole position in Asia. If Mesopotamia goes, Persia goes inevitably, and then India. And the place which we leave empty will be occupied by seven devils a good deal worse than any which existed before we came." She saw that the fall of Mesopotamia would lead to the end of India, and the end of India inevitably meant the end of the British Empire.

For the moment, at least, everything seemed saved. At the San Remo Conference on April 25, 1920, Prime Minister Lloyd George and Premier Georges Clemenceau finally came to an agreement on the division of the Arabic lands formerly under Ottoman rule. Arabia would remain as it was, an independent peninsula, though it would be guided by the British. Syria, including Lebanon, would be mandated to France; Mesopotamia (and Palestine) would be mandated to Britain; in both cases, until such time as they "could stand on their own." In exchange for the area of Mosul in northern Iraq, which France agreed to give to Britain, the two European nations would share in the exploration and production of oil in Iraq. It was not the issue of oil, however, but the matter of mandate that was on everybody's mind.

The news reached Baghdad on May 1, 1920 and was published a few days later; as Percy Cox wrote afterwards. "It set all the tongues wagging." Wilson issued a communiqué stating that the aim was "the creation of a healthy body politic," with Britain serving as "a wise and far-seeing guardian." Steps had been and would be taken, he announced, to "prepare the way for creation of an independent Arab State of Iraq."

Every morning and late into the night secret meetings took place. And in the bazaars and the coffee houses the Arabs argued over the meaning of "mandate." The nationalists opposed it as a superior body with the power to command; the holy men opposed it as an organized secular government threatening their very existence. To some it came as a relief; to many it betrayed the promise for self-determination given eighteen months earlier in the Anglo-French Declaration.

The twist of events had defeated Wilson's efforts to prevent an Arab government from being formed. Now, in a desperate attempt to appeal to the moderates, he telegraphed the Foreign Office, asking permission to publish proposals for a constitution, although he did not believe a constitution should be immediately adopted. But London refused his request; his plea to be replaced at once by Percy Cox was also turned down. Neither the constitutional proposals nor the announcement of Cox's return could be made until a peace treaty with Turkey had been signed, Whitehall said.

⌘ ⌘ ⌘

When Britain received the mandate for Mesopotamia from the League of Nations, and France received the mandate for Syria, the French gave up their claim to Mosul, as promised in the Sykes-Picot pact. But in exchange for territory, the French demanded a share of Mosul's future oil. With the Armenian entrepreneur Calouste Gulbenkian, known worldwide as Mr. Five Percent, as a partner, the British and French signed an agreement calling for "the permanent provision of industrial and commercial purposes of petroleum products." The demand for oil was growing at such a heated rate that the agreement acknowledged "the supply is admitted to be increasingly inadequate." England and France would share a common policy of development, construction of pipelines, facilitation of land acquisition for depots, refineries, loading wharves and whatever else was required.

Their rival was the United States. With almost two thirds of the world's production of oil, the American Government feared that its own resources would soon be depleted. The United States Congress (which refused to ratify President Wilson's League of Nations or to accept some of the Ottoman areas as American mandates, voting instead for isolation over engagement) was enraged at its allies' ambitious quest. "England is taking possession of the oil fields of the world," thundered Henry Cabot Lodge, the patrician senator from Massachusetts.

The debate would continue for years, but Britain's position was clear: she desperately needed oil for her vital interests and military power. The control of Iraqi oil fields would allow the British people to sleep well at night; the security blanket of coal could now be replaced with a smooth coating of oil.

⌘ ⌘ ⌘

Gertrude's spirits had lifted since her father's visit. "I wonder how anyone can complain about anything when they have a Father like you," she wrote adoringly. "One takes for granted where you are concerned that no matter how unfamiliar or complex things may be that you're seeing and hearing you'll grasp the whole lie of them at once, and it's only when I come to think of it that I realize what it is to have your quickness of intelligence. Anyhow, I feel certain that you know the general structure here as well as we know it ourselves and I'm enchanted that you should, not only because it makes my job so much more interesting knowing that you understand it, but also because it's

Gertrude Bell flanked by Winston Churchill *(left)* and T. E. Lawrence *(right)*
at the Pyramids during the Cairo Conference in 1921.
Churchill slid like jelly off the camel before the photo was taken.
(University of Newcastle)

Gertrude Bell and
T. E. Lawrence in Cairo, 1921.
"You little imp!" she chastised
Lawrence at the Cairo Conference.
(University of Newcastle)

The Cairo Conference, 1921. Gertrude Bell was the only woman among the forty
delegates called by Winston Churchill to the conference. *Front row center:*
Winston Churchill *(with legs crossed); to his left,* Sir Percy Cox. *Second row: second from left,*
Gertrude Bell in her flowered hat and furs; *second from right,* Arnold Wilson; *fourth from*
right, T. E. Lawrence. *On the floor:* baby Somali lions brought for the Cairo zoo.
(University of Newcastle)

Sharif Hussein, descendant of
the prophet Muhammad,
guardian of Mecca,
father of King Faisal of Iraq.

Faisal *(right)*, deposed by the French
from his throne in Damascus, walking
in Cairo with his chief aide,
Nuri Said, 1921.

Sayid Talib of Basrah,
"rogue" and rival to Faisal.
(Kerim. Baghdad)

King Faisal
shortly after
his coronation
in Baghdad, 1921.
(University of Newcastle)

The coronation of King Faisal, Baghdad, August 23, 1921.
Front row left to right: Sir Percy Cox *(in military whites),*
Kinahan Cornwallis *(with helmet),* Faisal *(in front of throne),* General Aylmer.
(Kerim. Baghdad)

Dinner party in a Baghdad garden,
1921. Lady Cox *(with mosquito netting
around her hat)* at head of the table.
Gertrude Bell to her left,
King Faisal to her right.
(Kerim. Baghdad)

Gertrude, aged fifty-three.
(University of Newcastle)

Gertrude in 1921, at a picnic with Faisal *(foreground, right)*
near Ctesiphon, Iraq, site of a seventh-century Arab victory.
(University of Newcastle)

The Naqib of Baghdad, holy leader
of the Sunni community, 1921.
Gertrude was the only unveiled
woman allowed to visit with him.
(Kerim. Baghdad)

Gertrude and her father, Hugh Bell,
in front of the biplane she flew in from
Baghdad to Ziza, 1922.
(University of Newcastle)

Gertrude Bell *(left)* at a farewell party for Sir Percy Cox.
Lady Cox, covered with mosquito netting, chats with a guest while
Sir Percy holds her flowers. Baghdad, 1923.
(University of Newcastle)

A 1923 garden party in Baghdad with sofas and rugs laid out on the lawn.
Foreground: Gertrude and King Faisal.
(Kerim. Baghdad)

Detail of above photograph.
Under her parasol Gertrude confers with King Faisal.
(Kerim. Baghdad)

A thoughtful and lonely
King Faisal, Baghdad, 1923.
(University of Newcastle)

Gertrude Bell and some of her colleagues in Baghdad, 1924.
Seated, second and third from left: Kinahan "Ken" Cornwallis, Sasun Effendi Eskail.
(University of Newcastle)

good for us all that you should be able to put in a word for us at home."

She not only needed her father's advocacy for Mesopotamia; she needed his moral support for herself. A. T. Wilson was making her life miserable. After another clash at their offices in the Residency, he denounced her to her face. "You are the most objectionable and intolerant person I've ever met," he snarled. A few days later she lamented that office lunches were becoming unbearable: "A.T. presides, and is often cross as a bear so that the only thing is to leave him alone and not talk to him. He doesn't like that either, but what can one do?"

The Political Officers, loyal to their chief, had lined up solidly against her, and Wilson had cut her off from the daily routine. To make matters worse, Frank Balfour, one of her few reliable friends, had become engaged to be married. "I'm very glad about it. I like her," Gertrude remarked, adding snidely, "and should like her better doubtless if I could catch a glimpse of her face through the paint." Then there was the stream of letters to Hugh from Florence: "Letters continue to arrive from Mother which I duly return. I hope she will soon begin writing to me instead of to you." But determined to do what she believed in, she held her head high and carried on with her work.

CHAPTER TWENTY-SIX

The Clash

∞

The Pleasant Sunday Afternoons of Miss Gertrude Bell, or the "P.S.A.'s," as the British officers called them, began in the middle of May 1920. After breakfast and a morning ride, Gertrude returned home to decorate her garden. Stringing old Baghdad lanterns around the trees, she arranged a circle of chairs and waited eagerly for her male guests to arrive. Along with Balfour, Bonham Carter and a few other officials, thirty of the city's Arab political intelligentsia, most of them supporters of Faisal and the Sharifian family, strolled in. Over cold drinks, fruit and cake, they discussed the political issues of the day: Zionism and the Balfour Declaration, the Anglo-French Declaration, Mosul and the Turkish question, the mandate. Most important of all, they expressed their own hopes and fears. If trouble was in the air, Gertrude believed, it was better to hear it firsthand. "A capital plan," Balfour called it. Knowing that Wilson might object to her meetings, she had asked him in advance whether he approved. "I like to have a foot in both camps," he replied.

No Arab guest could have been more welcome than the one who arrived the following week: on Sunday, May 23, her former servant Fattuh appeared on her doorstep. He had served as driver for a man from his home town of Aleppo, and, after a harrowing ride through the desert, dodging robbers who still prowled the sands, had made his way at once to Gertrude's house. She welcomed him with hugs, and almost immediately he inquired of her father. "Is His Excellency the Progenitor still with you?" he asked.

"How did you know he has been here?" she responded, surprised.

"Oh," said Fattuh, "one of the Bedouin in the desert told me that the Khatun was well and her Father was with her."

"So," Gertrude wrote to Hugh, "I suppose it's the talk of Arabia." She missed her father badly, thinking of him as she passed the railway station, remembering their train rides up and down the country, how they had shared a thermos of tea and discussed the wealth of antiquities, the dearth of local leadership, the daily problems with Wilson. Her adversary had been made a Knight Commander of the Indian Empire, an honor slightly higher than her own. The hurt came through even as she wrote: "I'm very glad. He well deserves it. I confess I wish that in giving him a knighthood they could also endow him with the manners knights are traditionally credited with!"

∞ ∞ ∞

The loyal Fattuh could not have come at a better time. Outdoors the temperature was still a tolerable 100 degrees at the end of May, but in the mosques the heat was rising. Eighteen months had gone by since the Anglo-French Declaration, the mandate already had been declared, yet there was still no sign of an Arab government. Now Ramadan, the month-long holy period of daylight fasting, was under way, and the *mujtabids*, the highest Shiite authorities, were using their pulpits to stir a *jihad*. In the past the Sunnis had looked askance at such preachings of holy war, worried that they would lead to an Islamic state. But for the first time in anyone's memory, Sunni townsmen and Shiite tribesmen put aside their bitter prejudices and joined together against a common enemy: the British. "The underlying thought," Gertrude explained, "is out with the infidel." When one young hothead made wild speeches, Frank Balfour, Governor of Baghdad, had him arrested. Gertrude thought he was probably right, but, she acknowledged, "it is always a delicate line of decision." As was so often the case, his arrest only fed the fire.

The following evening, May 30, 1920, a mob of townsmen gathered at the large mosque on New Street. Worried about a riot, Balfour sent two armored cars to patrol the streets. When an Arab instigator threw a rock at one of the uniformed drivers, the driver drew his revolver. Gertrude heard the gun shots from her bed. In the morning, the Arab who came daily to inform her of all the meetings told her the driver had fired over the heads of the crowd, but one blind Muslim had been run over; the rest of the throng had scattered quickly. That day Balfour called in the leaders: the mosques were not to be used for political speeches, he ordered. But the damage had been done. The nationalist urge, egged on by extremist propaganda from Syria, and coupled with the British Government's refusal to present proposals for a constitution, brought on a rash of violent demonstrations. A general strike was declared, and as Gertrude walked to work through the bazaar, she found the shops shuttered and business ground to a halt.

On June 3, 1920, Wilson spoke with the new army commander, General Sir Aylmer Haldane (he had replaced General MacMunn who had been sent to India) and warned him that trouble was expected in the lower Euphrates "within a few weeks." To Wilson the coming disturbance only underscored his belief that the Anglo-French Declaration was ill advised and that the Arabs were incapable of governing themselves.

Fiery rumors were spreading like a flame on kerosene, burning nationalist ambition as far away as the mosques in Karbala and the mud huts in Basrah. Reports that the Arabs under Abdullah were on their way from Syria encouraged the nationalist hopes of the northern tribes. But the same tales incensed the Shiites in the south, who resented the presumption that they were to be governed by a stranger and a monarch, sparking a series of raids across the Euphrates.

Fattuh brought Gertrude the gossip from the coffee houses, where he heard bitter complaints about her colleague Colonel Leachman. The Political Officer had been sent to Dulaim, known for its dangerous raids, to keep a watch on any instigators. Leachman had been well known as an adventurer and traveler but his tactics were rough; his snarling attitude had made him an enemy of the tribes. Word was out that they despised him. Ignoring Wilson's rude manner, Gertrude passed on the information to him.

On June 4, the Shammar, the most powerful of the three northern Sunni tribes that roamed the desert between the Euphrates and the Tigris, attacked Tel Afar, a city forty miles to the west of Mosul. The Shammar sheikhs, led by Jamil Maidfai, announced falsely that Abdullah was on the march to Baghdad to proclaim himself King. Using that as justification for rebellion, they urged the local Arabs to show their alliance with the Arab nationalists and kill any Englishmen they could find. Six men were murdered: two clerks, two drivers, the Levy Officer, Captain Stuart, who had won an award for distinguished service during the war, and the Assistant Political Officer, Captain Barlow. Wilson responded at once.

He ordered the areas to be machine-gunned, the insurgents imprisoned and their leaders deported. The residents of the town were all
turned out of their houses, and every house was destroyed. Nor would
the British allow the town to be rebuilt. It was a punishment Wilson
would use again and again.

The same day that the news came in about the murders, Gertrude
was having lunch with General Haldane. To the irritation of the civil
administrators, the general was about to take his high command on
holiday in Persia and would not be back until October. After chatting
about common acquaintances in London, Gertrude got up to leave. If
news reached him that the tribes had taken Baghdad, would he return
before October? she asked.

The general shrugged his shoulders. "Oh, I don't feel any responsibility for what happens while I'm away," he replied.

The shock over Haldane's indifference served as a momentary
bond between Gertrude and Wilson. They both viewed him with disgust. But just as quickly, it underlined their disagreements: while Wilson wanted to see the British military presence strengthened, Gertrude
wanted to see an Arab government installed. She wished the Arabs
would settle for the cultivated Abdullah as Emir. That would solve
everyone's dilemma, including the British who opposed self-rule. Then,
the Iraqi leaders advising Faisal in Damascus—including Jafar al Askari
and Nuri Said—should quickly be brought back to Iraq to set up the
government; they were "capable men with considerable experience," she
noted. "If we meet them on equal terms there won't be any difficulty in
getting them to act with wisdom."

In Baghdad a clique of nationalists approached Wilson, who arranged a meeting on June 7, inviting not just them but all the leading
notables—Muslims, Jews and Christians—to attend. Standing tall, his
dark eyes penetrating the crowd, Wilson expressed regret at the delay in
establishing a civil government. It was beyond the control of the British,
he told them, using the excuse that although the mandate had been
declared at the beginning of May, the terms of the mandate had not yet
been defined. Nevertheless, he warned, if the delegates incited the people to riot, it would only lead to dangerous and uncontrollable results,
which could end with all their hopes destroyed. The delegates responded by demanding the immediate formation of a committee to
draw up proposals for an Arab government as promised in 1918. Wilson
answered that as soon as the terms of the mandate had been formu-
lated, steps should be taken to summon a Constitutional Assembly.
They would be consulted on the future form of Government, he promised. With that, he left.

Fattuh reported that from the talk he heard in the coffee houses the meeting had been a success. "A.T.'s speech took the wind out of the sails" of the extremists, Gertrude wrote with relief, and the general talk "was that the town had made a fool of itself." Indeed, when Wilson flew in an air force plane the next day to Hillah and Najaf, he found that no one was even interested in joining the rebellion. "Meantime," Gertrude observed, "our opponents are now quarrelling busily among themselves." The alliance between the Shiites and the Sunnis was broken.

In a note to General Haldane, she wrote that "the bottom seems to have dropped out of the agitation." From the coffee house talk, the daily visits of her informers and "heart to heart interviews," she had heard that "most of the leaders seem only too anxious to let bygones be bygones." Calm seemed to prevail. The end of Ramadan, near at hand, would put a stop, she hoped, to the heated meetings taking place in the mosques. General Haldane ignored Wilson's earlier advice and listened instead to Miss Bell; he ordered his army to take no further military action.

∽   ∽   ∽

In the hope of encouraging the moderate Arabs, Gertrude slipped some secret documents about a constitutional government to an influential Arab nationalist. Meeting with Wilson in his office the following day, she casually mentioned what she had done. A.T. flew into a rage. Your indiscretions are intolerable, he berated her. You shall never see another paper in the office. Miss Bell apologized. "You've done more harm than anyone here," Wilson went on. "If I hadn't been going away myself I should have asked for your dismissal months ago—you and your Emir!" he snapped, choking with rage.

Wilson's behavior infuriated her. "I know really what's at the bottom of it," she wrote to her father, referring to her Syrian report. "I've been right and he has been wrong; I need not say I've been at much pains not to point it out, but it's all on paper."

It was time for Wilson to leave, she told Hugh. He had never supported the official policy of Arab self-government laid down in the 1918 Anglo-French Declaration; "he has in fact always ignored it. The people know that he isn't in sympathy with it and don't trust him.

"Meantime," she admitted, "it may be I who goes. But I shall not send in my resignation. I shall only go if I am ordered. Thank heaven Sir Percy will be here next week, on his way to England, so I can consult him if necessary."

Ramadan ended in the middle of June 1920, but the tribes still bellowed with defiance. When Gertrude rode out one morning to visit her Shiite friend Haji Naji, she found him in a state of agitation. The extremists had roughed him up and threatened him with more if he did not join the insurrection. Haji Naji had refused and had protected his house with watchmen, but he was worried. He begged her to come and visit more often. She would come "constantly," she promised.

In several towns placards covered the bazaar, urging the people to rise up against the British. In the holy city of Karbala, where thousands of pilgrims had gathered for the Id al Fitr, the feast to celebrate the end of Ramadan, Islamic agitators whipped the people into a frenzy while a group of sheikhs and notables plotted a revolt for an Islamic state. In Kadhimain the son of the holy man Gertrude had visited was now firing up the town. Near Najaf a small tribe, known for stealing from Persian pilgrims, was robbing everyone on the road. In the north two large tribes attacked each other in a major raid; and along the southern Euphrates near Diwaniyah, the tribes, bombed from the air for refusing to pay their taxes, were now in open rebellion and had cut the railroad line in three places. Wilson responded by bombing villages, burning houses, machine-gunning insurgents, deporting instigators and imprisoning activists.

Wilson's tactics were too harsh, Gertrude believed. In fact, they functioned like a pressure cooker: the more he bore down on the insurgents, the more their fury increased. But Gertrude was in the minority. At the office she was shunned for being too soft on the Arabs; Wilson spoke to her brusquely and refused to eat with her in the mess.

Within a few weeks the rebellion was in full bloom. Trouble had spread to Rumaithah, where Major Daly, the Political Officer in the southern Euphrates region, had arrested two leading local personalities and sent them down to Basrah by train. Knowing where they were, the Euphrates tribes attacked the train, rescued the prisoners and cut the railway lines. When two hundred troops were sent in to help the stranded soldiers, the Arabs captured at least one relief train and grabbed the guns on board. With only a limited number of railroad cars in Mesopotamia, the British resorted to airplanes, flying low and dropping food supplies for the troops. But the Arabs used the captured guns to shoot at the planes. "As far as I can make out," Gertrude wrote, "the matter was pretty badly handled at the beginning, partly no doubt, because the whole of G.H.Q. was up in the Persian hills and refused to realise the importance of the rising."

But if she blamed the army for doing little about the uprising, Wilson and his staff blamed Gertrude. Her earlier assurance to General Haldane, that there would be no more trouble, now cost her dearly with her colleagues. Wilson claimed their loyalty and admiration, and like him, they treated Gertrude with contempt. The Political Officers were solidly against her sympathy for Arab independence. In their view, Wilson's tough policy was exactly right; Gertrude was mush in the hands of the Arabs. The Mesopotamians' cry for independence only irritated their British colonialist ears. It was not accidental that *The Times* called Wilson "a sun-dried bureaucrat set on Indianizing Mesopotamia."

Chapter Twenty-seven

An Unpleasant Victory

∞

Percy Cox arrived in Baghdad toward the end of June, and for a brief moment, at least, Gertrude could breathe more easily. He was a rock she could cling to in a sea of turmoil. She saw him almost at once, breakfasting with his wife in the mess, and "felt as if a a load of care had been lifted." The following afternoon, Cox came to her house after tea. She quickly informed him of what had been going on: the inflammatory preachings in the mosques, the extremists among the nationalists, the anger seething within the tribes and the antics of General Haldane (who had been upbraided by a sharp telegram from the War Secretary, Winston Churchill). She gave him what she believed was "the correct view of the whole Arab situation," she wrote her father: that they had been forced to wait too long for an Arab government and an Arab ruler, and that the matter had been badly handled "for the last eight months." But one subject she left untouched. She did not tell Cox about the ugly scene with Wilson. She regarded it as "sheer lunacy."

In a meeting with Wilson, however, Cox asked how he and Miss Bell were now getting on. Wilson complained bitterly that she was still writing private letters to Asquith and others. It seemed to be driving him to a state of paranoia, Gertrude had noted. Nevertheless, she and A.T. had now arrived at a *modus vivendi*: Wilson sent her the usual papers, they ate together in the mess and he bent over backward to be polite, while Gertrude did the same. Afraid of setting off another fit of rage, she avoided A.T.'s office and offered him the minimal courtesy when he came to see her. "As he wants a good many things he has to come pretty often," she sniffed. "And I laugh in my inside, for it's my trick, isn't it. In fact, I think it's my rubber." She was living in misery, but she had won the game: Cox told her he was coming back in the autumn as High Commissioner.

During his two-day stay in Baghdad, Sir Percy approved a statement drafted by Wilson calling for a Constitutional Assembly. The announcement declared that Mesopotamia was to be made an independent state under the guarantee of the League of Nations and subject to the mandate of Great Britain; Sir Percy Cox was to return to establish a provisional Arab government.

Cox set off for England the following day, leaving his parrot in Gertrude's care, but carrying home half her major report for Parliament on the length and breadth of the British civil administration in Mesopotamia. With the government in London so upset over the cost of staying in Iraq, it was important to publish something, she explained, to show them the enormous amount of work that had been done. "Please will you do as much propaganda as you can," she wrote to her father, hoping he would lobby Parliament on her behalf. And then she begged, "Don't forget to go on loving me."

∞   ∞   ∞

For several months Gertrude had been urging Wilson to allow Jafar Pasha Askari, one of Faisal's inner circle, to come to Baghdad and discuss the situation in Syria. Wilson had flatly said no. But now even he knew that steps had to be taken to placate the Arabs. Receiving official permission from Whitehall to call for the Constitutional Assembly, he invited Jafar Pasha to Baghdad. Yet Wilson refused to discuss the matter with Gertrude.

"I am rather in the dark about all this because A.T. never tells me anything," she wrote home. "I fancy his chief idea is that I should be kept in my place, though what this is exactly no one can say." The best policy was to avoid any discussions until Cox returned. She refused to let Wilson interfere with her work; instead, she sent him a memo suggesting a joint committee of Sunnis and Shiites from Baghdad be sent to the holy cities to try to quash the rebellious tribes. A.T. ignored her; she suspected he threw her memo in the wastebasket.

With the convening of the Constitutional Assembly, Sayid Talib also arrived in town. At one time a supporter of the Turkish group that rebelled against the Sultanate, he later turned his back on them, raising suspicion among some Mesopotamians. Known for his underhanded tactics, he was, nonetheless, an able politician, regarded by some of the Iraqi nationalists exiled in Syria as their spokesman. Now, he told Gertrude when he called on her, his interests and those of the British were the same. He aimed to cobble together a moderate party, for which he wanted British support. But Gertrude, more wary than the locals, refused to back him, saying, somewhat disingenuously; "We cannot bind the Arab government, once we've established it, to select any particular person as its head."

∞   ∞   ∞

The gathering of nationalist leaders in Baghdad did little to quiet the rest of the country. Reports came in that the tribes along the middle Euphrates were on a rampage, destroying the farms of Sunni townsmen in their wake. The Political Officer at Kufah was being held prisoner, and near Hillah four hundred English soldiers were attacked on a march; almost half were taken prisoner. The story of the incident flew through the country, and rumors of British weakness encouraged thousands of others to rise up in arms. The rebellion had raced out of control.

Panic spread among the Baghdadis: their vast country estates were being ravaged by the tribes; moreover, the threat of an Islamic state stared them in the face. The old hatred between the Sunnis and the Shiites had intensified. The townsmen were now terrified of the uprising, which, as Gertrude pointed out, they themselves had started with the Shiites in May during Ramadan. Two distinguished Sunni notables from Baghdad visited the Khatun in her office, seeking advice. She welcomed the turbaned magnates, offered them coffee and asked how she could be of help.

"Everyone in Baghdad praises you. What they say is—'*if only their men were like their women!*'" they began, their flattery tipping her that they wanted something. They had come, she discovered, to find out whether anything could be done to pacify the tribes.

Gertrude suggested they form a joint committee of Sunnis and Shiites and pay a call on the leaders in the holy cities of Karbala and Najaf. It was the same proposal she had made to Wilson ten days earlier, but she framed it in such a way that the Sunni notables thought it was theirs; despite their resentment at having to join forces with the local Shiites, they accepted her idea.

But when she talked to Wilson about it, he bristled. He would hear none of it from her. He would consider the proposal only if it was presented to him through the proper channels, by Captain Clayton (brother of her friend in Egypt), now a member of his (male) staff. Gertrude consented, but since Clayton had only recently arrived and was not yet acquainted with any of the local Arabs, she insisted on being allowed to sit in. Wilson bowed to her logic. When the session took place, she noticed, both Wilson and the notables took credit for the idea. But Gertrude knew better. As she had done so often, she silently swallowed her pride. "It's my scheme from end to end," she confided to her father.

∞   ∞   ∞

In Syria, after nearly two years of Faisal's pleas to the French, and of France's refusal to recognize the Arab Government, events were coming to a head. On July 14, 1920, with an expanded French army advancing from Beirut to Damascus, General Henri Gouraud sent Faisal an ultimatum, demanding acceptance of the French mandate and French control over the Arab army, the economy and the railroads. Faisal ordered his troops to disband, and although some refused and fought a desperate battle, the end was in sight.

On July 20, 1920, the Emir Faisal and his brother Zaid quietly left Damascus. The Arab Government had lasted twenty-one months. Gertrude believed that Faisal, angry and feeling betrayed by the British, who had not kept their promises to the Sharifians, would soon gather his army and try to return. Whatever happened, the emotions would spread across the desert. If the French were forced out of Syria, the British might have to leave Iraq. "Well," she informed her father, "if the British evacuate Mesopotamia I shall stay peacefully here and see what happens. It will be very nice . . . like old times!"

Like old times for Gertrude. But not for Hugh. The fortune that the Bell family had taken for granted was suddenly beginning to disappear. Within a decade the wealth from iron would turn to dust. The Bells' business had suffered terribly from the strikes and the Depression that hit England after the war. Hugh and his partner were now trying to borrow money to refinance their company. A letter had arrived from him asking Gertrude for power of attorney to sign her name on bank loans.

"I'll go a dash with you," she responded cheerfully, echoing King Lear. "Then when we're both in the workhouse we'll write our life and times." She understood that by signing the papers she would ultimately owe the bank seventy-two hundred pounds, which she hoped she would earn as the Dorman Long stock increased its dividends. Meantime, she would watch her expenses carefully, she promised. Her salary was not enough to live on, and entertaining at home was a necessary part of her job, but she could reduce her extra allowance from England to thirty pounds a month.

Whatever happened, she had no intention of leaving Baghdad. At the worst, she suggested, the British would withdraw from Mesopotamia, land values would drop and she would finally be able to buy her house. There was a silver lining after all, she told herself.

Yet she felt a pang of remorse for not being with Hugh at this troubling time. "Darling Father," she continued, "I do hope you enjoy my letters as much as I enjoy writing them! If they seem to you rather mad, I can only offer as excuse that I'm living in a perfectly mad world. Added to which the heat makes one a little light-headed. One just accepts what happens, from day to day, without any amazement."

In spite of such confidence, Gertrude was stunned when, on August 6, 1920, a telegram arrived from Edwin Montagu. It was not, as she might have hoped, a message of congratulations on her fifty-second birthday, but an official reprimand, a response to a complaint from Wilson. "Private and Personal," Montagu wrote:

> I hope you will understand from me that in the present critical state of affairs of Mesopotamia when the future of the country hangs in the balance we should all pull together. If you have views which you wish us to consider, I should be glad if you would either ask the Civil Commissioner to communicate them or apply for leave and come home and represent them. You may always be sure of consideration of your views but Political Officers should be very careful of their private correspondence with those not at present in control of affairs. Apart from all questions of usual practice and convention it may increase rather than diminish difficulties a result which I know you would deplore.

Gertrude immediately drafted a reply:

> I am also wholly in agreement with policy which has been pursued since April. You are sufficiently aware of my general attitude towards the Arab question to know that I regret it was not embarked on earlier. To express this view in public would now however be valueless and even harm-

ful. With regard to correspondence except for private letters to my Father I cannot recall letters on political subjects to unofficial persons which have not been previously
submitted to Colonel Wilson. Your remarks are however
a useful warning.

⚭   ⚭   ⚭

She sent her response, along with Montagu's telegram, to A.T.,
asking if he had anything to add. In an interoffice note, he scrawled:

> Miss Bell. When Sir Percy Cox passed through he
> asked—a propos of events earlier in the year—whether
> my relations with you were happier. I said that I could
> not say they were—that your divergence of opinion was
> marked and a matter of public knowledge and indeed of
> comment. (Sayid Talib mentioned this to me rather
> pointedly today.) I said the position would be untenable
> but for the fact that I was hoping before long to be
> relieved. You have always maintained your right as an
> individual to write what you like—to whom you like—
> you have, I gratefully admit, shown me letters e.g. to
> Asquith, but I do not like their being written and the fact
> that I am cognisant of them must not be held to include
> approval. Otherwise I have no comment to make.

The following day Wilson requested a meeting. She glowered at his
rough demeanor, her reedlike figure in sharp contrast to his iron hulk.
"It had been quite inevitable that people should have known that our
opinions diverged because I had always said so—to you first and fore-
most," she told him. "But in that respect I hadn't differed in any degree
from the declarations of H.M.G." The particular instance he had mentioned from Sayid Talib, that scurrilous rogue, was "manifestly absurd,"
she snapped. If she was being "made a peg on which to hang opposition," it would be much better if he would send her on leave to India
until Sir Percy returned. Indeed, a holiday in India might allow her
some rest.

But Wilson refused to grant her leave. He himself was going home
soon, he answered, and besides, he conceded, knowing that she was the
key to good relations with the Arabs, he thought she might be of use to
his successor. She listened and smiled to herself.

They discussed the matter of her correspondence with friends. His note had left her "in amazement," she said. She reminded him that they had talked about the letter she wrote to Mr. Asquith last week; it was "scarcely fair" for Wilson to complain now. After all, he had said nothing, not even that he preferred it not be sent. But it wasn't only the letter to Asquith that made Wilson anxious, she discovered. Had she written to Domnul Chirol and to the India Office? he now wanted to know.

Domnul was one of her closest friends, she reminded him; her letters to him were personal. And when she wrote to Sir Arthur Hirtzel, she had done so, "almost invariably," with Wilson's knowledge and sometimes with his hearty approval; she had even written once in Wilson's defense, she made him recall, and he had been grateful to her for the letter. Furthermore, she injected, "Edwin's warning specially mentioned non-official persons."

Wilson answered that he "objected to any private communications with the India Office."

That was "quite preposterous," Gertrude growled; nevertheless, she would certainly comply with his wishes.

Thanking her for her "frankness," Wilson shook her hand. They parted as amicably as two firebrands could: Gertrude, pleased that he soon would be leaving; Wilson, pleased that she soon would be out of his life.

It was true, she confessed to her father, that she was not entirely in the right. She admitted that Wilson's "insolent rudeness" sometimes threw her into a rage. And that might have shown itself to the Arabs. But she did not intentionally want them to present a divided front; that could do the British nothing but harm. They needed a show of strength, especially since their troubles in Mesopotamia were hardly at an end.

The news that began the week of August 16 made her heart sink. Gertrude's most trusted Agaili informer came to the office to tell her that Colonel Leachman, the Political Officer in Dulaim, had gotten into a bitter feud with Sheikh Dhari of the Shammar tribe. The Agaili had heard a few days ago that Leachman had viciously berated the sheikh for not maintaining peace along the road to Mosul. Afterward, he ordered some of the Shammar to repair a drain in the path. Sheikh Dhari, known to be vindictive, nevertheless ordered his men to cooperate. But as the Political Officer turned around to leave, he was ambushed; one of the tribesmen, the son of the sheikh, shot Leachman in the back. "He always used extremely unmeasured language to the Arabs and Shaikh Dhari had many grudges against him," Gertrude explained in a letter home. "He was a wild soldier of fortune but a very gallant officer and his name was known all over Arabia." Now, she moaned, "Lord knows what's going to happen here."

In Baghdad, where a curfew had been installed, an uneasy calm had descended. But in the rest of the country the three-month uprising was still raging. Thousands of tribesmen were out looting; the entire political staff at Shahraban had been savagely murdered. The flames roared around Gertrude, fueled not only by the infernal rebellion but by Wilson's fiery rage. When another message arrived from Montagu, upbraiding her for her correspondence with London, she responded sharply: "To allay anxiety I now confine myself to writing to my Father and shopkeepers."

Wilson's temper, the nasty cables from home, the brutality of the tribes and the hot, miserable weather left her depressed. On August 23 she wrote despondently to Florence: "We have made an immense failure here. The system must have been far more at fault than anyone suspected. It will have to be fundamentally changed. I suppose we have underestimated the fact that this country is really an inchoate mass of tribes which can't as yet be reduced to any system. The Turks didn't govern and we have tried to govern—and failed."

She felt numb, "half dead," from the turmoil. "I feel as if I were living from day to day without trying to make any plans for the future." Yet a glimmer of hope remained. "At the bottom of my heart I think it possible that the situation may clear as unexpectedly as it has developed, though it's equally possible that it mayn't. Oh dear! I wish the world were a little more normal. Or do you think war and revolution may now be reckoned as normal?"

Through it all, she worked on the second half of her comprehensive report on the civil administration. Nearly completed now, it was, she told her father, the most difficult task she had ever undertaken. "One can't write history while it's all in the making and hasn't arrived at any conclusion." Nevertheless, she added, "to my stupefaction A.T. thinks it a masterpiece."

⁓ ⁓ ⁓

Sayid Talib brought her a pleasant surprise. A skillful politican, he had helped the British immensely by quieting the insurrection in Baghdad. Now he was working hard to organize a moderate political party and sought British support. Lobbying anyone he could, he crudely told her friend Mr. Tod, a businessman: "What's needed in this administration is experience. I've got it. A doctor before he learns his trade will kill at least two hundred people. I've killed my two hundred—no one knows it better than yourself." Added Gertrude, in a note to her father, "And Mr. Tod couldn't honestly say he hadn't."

On Sunday morning, August 30, Gertrude was eating her breakfast of eggs and fresh figs when Talib appeared at her house. After florid inquiries as to her health and her family, he sauntered into the conversation. He regarded her as a sister and not as a member of the government, he said. Will you give me some advice? he asked coyly. She listened intently. He explained that he did not know whether to take financial support for his political party from the British Government. What did the Khatun think he should do? She pointed out that like his father, her father was a wealthy man, and like Sayid Talib, she too was doing valuable work for the government and justifiably taking a salary. "Rather than being indebted to any Tom, Dick or Harry, who would have a claim on you later," she told him, he would be better off taking money "for services rendered."

"I must say I liked and respected him," she wrote somewhat naïvely to Hugh, "for having come to consult me about it. We're often wondering what his real game is; though he has so far played perfectly straight—I'm sure he must wonder the same thing about us, though we've been equally straight. As long as he comes to me and talks openly it's much easier to keep the balance level, but I'm not at all sure he would do it to anyone else. And so I stay, just on the chance of being useful."

Talib was also being useful. His presence in Baghdad had calmed the angry townsmen; whether out of fear or respect was momentarily unimportant. Nevertheless, Gertrude still viewed him warily. If he hadn't received financing from the British, she noted wryly, "he would get what he wanted by a system of blackmail, an act at which he's adept." Nevertheless, she told Hugh, "he's bound to play a big part in the future and till that time comes we've got to try and keep him out of mischief." Later, her own mischief would keep him from playing what some believed was his well-earned part.

❧　❧　❧

Except for some minor incidents, by late fall of 1920 the insurrection that began in May against the British had quieted down. It had cost Britain fifty million pounds and hundreds of British lives. More than ten thousand Arabs had been killed. Wilson's tone had changed with the announcement of the mandate, but, as Gertrude noted, for the Arabs the change had come too late. They had already raised a storm of protest, and it was their own violent actions, the sheikhs believed, that had caused the turnaround. In fact, Gertrude acknowledged, "No one, not even H.M.G., would have thought of giving the Arabs such a free hand as we shall now give them—as a result of the rebellion!" A provisional government would soon be installed.

By the end of September Wilson was set to depart. The night before he left, he walked into her office to say goodbye. The two stood in her whitewashed room, he, tall and strapping, his dark hair slapped flat across his forehead; she, slim and almost delicate, her gray hair in a topknot and curls. She had won the game, Gertrude knew, but as teammates they had both been failures. She was "feeling more deeply discouraged than she could well say," she told him. She "regretted acutely that they had not made a better job of their relations."

He had come to apologize, Wilson said.

She held up her hand to stop him. It was as much her fault as his, Gertrude admitted. She hoped he wouldn't carry away any "ill-feelings."

He felt the same way, Wilson cordially replied. Then he left, still holding on to the dream of expanding the India Government's power, believing, he later wrote, that "the eastward trend" of Britain's responsibilities was "destined to increase." Wilson went on to represent British oil interests as an official of the Anglo-Persian Oil Company. Later, he would become a Member of Parliament and a supporter of Adolf Hitler.

For the moment Gertrude felt only relief. "What he really thinks about it all Heaven alone knows," she wrote to Hugh. "I have no reason to be satisfied with my part in the story and I suspect there's nothing to choose between us, or if there is a choice I'm the more blame worthy because I need not have stayed when I found my views to be wholly divergent from his. Nor would I have stayed if I had known how deeply he resented my attitude." But now that difficult part of her life had come to a close.

CHAPTER TWENTY-EIGHT

Cox Returns

∞

Rarely did Gertrude ready herself with such elation. Wearing a new silk dress, she pinned up her graying hair in a topknot, frothed the curls around her forehead, slipped on her favorite hat, smoothed her stockings, patted her pearls in place, grabbed her parasol and, tucking away some handkerchiefs for her chest cough, headed gaily for the train station.

It was only four-thirty P.M., on Monday, October 11, 1920, but a large crowd had already gathered at Baghdad West, where she was ushered into the reception room and asked to wait. Within a short time some two dozen local dignitaries and the leading British officials joined her in the lounge. At precisely five-thirty, the British soldiers fired a seventeen-gun salute, but the wind carried off the sound in the opposite direction, and without other warning, the distinguished group was suddenly told to hurry along and take their places in the railed-off space near the platform. To the right stood Gertrude with the Judicial Officer, Sir Edgar Bonham Carter; the heads of the civil departments; the consuls and the religious leaders. To the left stood the Commander-in-Chief with his staff; Sayid Talib and the other deputies of the Constitutional Assembly; the Mayor; and the eldest son of the Naqib. The rest of the throng—British officers and their wives, Arab notables and others—were kept outside the enclosure.

A buzz of excitement fizzed the air, and Gertrude watched in triumph as the train pulled slowly into the station. After months of Wilson's torturous rule, they were celebrating the return of Sir Percy Cox. But before anyone could let out whoops of cheer, the ceremonial duties had to be performed. With proper formality, the Commander-in-Chief, clad in khaki, walked forward to greet the new High Commissioner. Sir Percy, tall, smart, crisp in his snow-white uniform and gold-braid trim, emerged from the train, shook hands with General Haldane and stood at attention while the band played "God Save the King."

"I thought as he stood there in his white and gold lace, with his air of fine and simple dignity that there had never been an arrival more momentous—never anyone on whom more conflicting emotions were centred, hopes and doubts and fears, but above all confidence in his personal integrity and wisdom," Gertrude recalled later. With all eyes focused upon him, Cox strode into the enclosure, and as he did, Sir Edgar presented Miss Bell. Nearly giddy and flushed with joy, she curtsied deeply; it was all she could do to keep from crying.

Out of the train stepped her longtime friend Mr. Philby, serving as Cox's deputy; Captain Cheesman, Cox's personal secretary; and Lady Cox. Like everyone else, Gertrude stared in amazement at the wife of the High Commissioner. After a ten-hour journey through showers of dust, she looked, Gertrude said, "as if she had emerged from the finest bandbox—'a miracle,'" the group told Lady Cox as they all exchanged warm greetings.

After each of the dignitaries in the enclosure was presented to Cox, a welcoming address was read by Jamil Zahawi, a famous Baghdad orator. Sir Percy responded in Arabic, saying that he had come "by order of His Majesty's Government to enter into counsel with the people of the Iraq for the purpose of setting up an Arab Government under the supervision of Great Britain."

This was the first time the name "Iraq" was used officially by the British, a deliberate decision by Sir Percy to recognize the Arabic identity of the future state. Iraq would belong to the Arabic people and be ruled by the Arabic people. His words aroused a swell of pride and a chorus of cheers from the people gathered around.

Charged by Lord Curzon to obtain "a stable spot in the Middle East" and redeem the country "from misrule and anarchy," Cox planned to fulfill his mission at once. As the crowd interrupted his speech with murmurs of praise and words of agreement, he asked that "the people cooperate with him in the establishment of settled conditions" so that he could proceed immediately with his task.

Then, it was off to Sir Percy's house. Lady Cox (who had brought some things for Gertrude, among them her fur coats, an afternoon gown for the winter, a billycock riding hat, a pair of black riding boots and more flower bulbs from Kent and Brydon), now the official hostess, supervised the servants as they brought in tea, but she soon dashed out to see the new home being built for the High Commissioner.

It was then that Gertrude, Philby and Cox sat down to talk, and the moment Sir Percy spoke, Gertrude felt the pain of the past few months wash away. He intended to form a provisional Arab Government at once, without waiting for a complete halt to the rebellion, which was still going on in more than a third of the country. He planned to set up an Arab Council, call on a local notable to serve as Prime Minister and have him head a provisional Cabinet made up of Arab Ministers (whom the British would choose). Cox himself would appoint a British Adviser to each of the Arab Ministers; and he wanted the cabinet to take on the job of preparing and holding the first general election. Gertrude, Philby and Cox all agreed how difficult it would be to find the right person to serve as Prime Minister, but Sir Percy thought that the Basrah politician Sayid Talib, with his substantial constituency, could do the job.

Hearing the name made Gertrude anxious. "You had better see people here and form your opinion," she said, trying to hide her distaste for the nominee. "But whatever you do," she promised Cox, "we will do our utmost to further. The main thing is to decide on something and get it done." She knew she would not have to worry. Sir Percy never jumped to decisions but moved with caution and care. A seasoned statesman, the model of a British diplomat, he was a man who projected strength in his very presence and offered wisdom in whatever he said. And if he had his eccentricities, like his passion for birds or keeping a pet bear in his home, they made him all the more an Englishman. Cox belonged to that special world inhabited by her father and few other men; she held him in the highest esteem.

Respected by the Arabs (as he still is today) and sympathetic to their plight, Cox was the antithesis of the imperious Wilson, who had belittled her and the Iraqis for desiring independence. Only a few days after Wilson's departure she felt as if she had awakened from a nightmare. "I didn't realise till he had left how horribly oppressive it had been," she admitted in a letter home. "One thing is certain. I'll never again work for A.T. If he comes back here, I step out, that instant. I can't work with any man as unscrupulous as he. I'm not the first; Mr. Dobbs had the same doubts." So too did the able Mr. Philby, who had clashed with the arrogant Wilson years before in Basrah and refused to work for him under any circumstances. But as for Cox, she revered him: "It is quite impossible to tell you the relief and comfort it is to serve under somebody in whose judgment one has complete confidence," she wrote in girlish wonder; "he brings a single-eyed desire to act in the interests of the people of the country."

To her delight, at the dinner given by the Commander-in-Chief that evening, Sir Percy was seated beside her. Her excitement nearly heated up the drafty room—not enough, however, to keep from making her bronchitis worse. Nevertheless, early the following morning she made her way cheerfully to the Residency. Sir Percy summoned her almost at once. "We talked over some telegrams," she reported to her father, "I trying to conceal the fact that it was a wholly novel experience to be taken into confidence on matters of importance!"

Returning down the hall, she found her own office deluged with visitors and letters, but it took her aback when she learned they had all come to express their anger: the notables invited to the welcoming ceremonies had been herded together, kept outside the privileged area, left to stand humiliatingly in the open dust. They hadn't even had the opportunity to shake Sir Percy's hand, they complained. One old sheikh cried furiously, "We came in love and obedience, and when we tried to get near His Excellency we were pushed away." Kokus was enormously admired by the Arabs, but she knew this sort of rebuff could lead to a dangerous reaction. It was clear that something had to be done to heal the wounds.

"I decided at once to invest myself with the duties of Oriental Secretary," Gertrude explained to Hugh. The title had been hers under Wilson, but all of its power had been stripped. Now, using the position to full advantage, she called in her colleague Philby, and together they drafted a letter to one hundred Baghdad notables, inviting them to meet the next day with Sir Percy Cox. Then, in view of the fact that in at least half the country, the insurrection, although it had quieted down, had not ceased, they planned for the High Commissioner to take a trip to Mosul to explain his ideas. Lastly, as she explained later to Cox, it would be good for him to confer with the Euphrates sheikhs and Fahad Bey of the Anazeh. The High Commissioner Cox agreed enthusiastically to all her proposals. "I shan't go on running the affairs of Mesopotamia," she acknowledged to Hugh, "but for the moment there wasn't anyone else to do it and as there wasn't a second to lose I just upped and did it."

The following day she and Cox talked confidentially about possible Arab Ministers. The biggest question of all was: Who should be asked to take on the job of Prime Minister and form the Arab Cabinet? To her vast relief, Cox had already learned of the animosity toward Sayid Talib. Many people were now suggesting the Naqib as Prime Minister. As the religious authority, he was held in the highest esteem, and though he was elderly and ill, he would make a fine transitional leader.

When Sir Percy asked if she would like to be his Oriental Secretary or take some other job, she answered yes to her old post without a moment's hestitation. It was, undoubtedly, the perfect place for her; as liaison between the High Commissioner and the Arab Government she could promote the interests of both and, not incidentally, poke her nose in everyone's affairs. She had struggled hard under Wilson just to stay in place; now, those on the staff who felt loyal to Wilson had been dismissed, and she was in the lead brigade advancing toward an Arab state. Her spirits were stronger than they had been in years, but the bronchitis was getting the better of her; her body racked from the chest cough.

As weak as she was and confined to bed, she was besieged by a stream of Baghdadis. On the pretext of inquiring after her health, the Mayor, the son of the Naqib and a string of Euphrates sheikhs, led by the eighty-year-old Fahad Bey (who had recently married two new wives), appeared at her doorstep, made their way to her dining room and, plopping down on the new Persian sofa, poured out their hopes and fears. At the end of each day she wrote up her notes, turning their rumors and gossip into valuable reports.

While she was still at home, a message arrived from Cox that he had called a "Council of State"; since Gertrude could not come to the office, he informed her, the council would come to her. Sir Percy, Philby, Bullard, Bonham Carter and two others arrived to discuss a scheme for the provisional Arab Cabinet. At the end of the meeting Sir Percy said he would now approach the Naqib to head it up as Prime Minister. Far and away the best-qualified candidate, the holy man was moved by considerations that were above suspicion; his influence among the Sunni community was unequaled; his religious and social position commanded universal respect. Gertrude was all in favor, but she was sure the Naqib would turn it down. For two days she heard no news. Then, on Saturday, after she had received the portly Jafar Pasha, the first of the Iraqis to return from Faisal's Syrian Government, Sir Percy rushed in, breathless with excitement. Gertrude waited anxiously. "Well," said Cox at last, "he has accepted."

"No one but Sir Percy could have done it," she wrote admiringly; "it's nothing short of a miracle."

∞ ∞ ∞

The following week was fraught with delicious tension. The Naqib's acceptance was well worth celebrating, but the provisional Arab Cabinet still had to be formed. On Monday Gertrude invited two of her colleagues to dine with her and Jafar Pasha. It was hoped that the extroverted Jafar, an able military commander, would accept the offer to become Minister of Defense. His success during the Arab Revolt and afterward as a Military Governor in Syria, she believed, would ensure a strong Arab army, able to control the insurgent tribes. Over dinner at her house, they discussed the bitter disappointment of Faisal and his coterie of Mesopotamian officers, their sense of betrayal when they found themselves without British support in Damascus. To repair his feelings, she confided her conviction that one of the sons of the Sharif Hussein should be chosen by the Mesopotamians as Emir. Unlike the experience in Syria, she vowed, in Iraq the British Government would not oppose the choice, nor would it rescind its support.

But Jafar worried about the extreme nationalists. Troublesome in Damascus, they were still unreasonable to deal with in Iraq and demanded total withdrawal by the British. Yet he was aware that Mesopotamia did not have the infrastructure nor its people the experience to assume complete independence. He explained his position vis-à-vis the nationalists: "I say to them: you want complete independence? So do I. Do we not each and all dream of a beautiful maiden, her age fourteen, her hair touching her waist? She does not exist! So complete independence under existing condition is impossible." He turned to Gertrude: "But because I believe in your honesty of purpose, I am ready to work with you for the salvation of my country—and when I go to my brothers to persuade them to help they turn aside and say: 'You're English.'"

Gertrude empathized. She had often been accused by her colleagues of being too sympathetic toward the Arabs: "It's your turn," she answered. "For the last year when I spoke to my brothers they turned from me and said: 'You're an Arab.'" But, she reassured him, "complete independence is what we ultimately wish to give." The canny general was quick to reply: "Sitti [My lady]" he said, "complete independence is never given; it is always taken."

❧   ❧   ❧

Things were progressing well, yet every day seemed to bring a small crisis. One of the worst came when the pro-British Sasun Effendi Eskail ("the ablest man here," she had called him), a well-known Jewish businessman, who, it was assumed, would become Minister of Finance, turned down the post. When Gertrude heard the news she left the cup of tea on her desk and rushed to tell Philby, but he was out. Spying the light on in Sir Percy's office, she reported at once to him. The High Commissioner was obviously upset. Make Sasun change his mind, he demanded.

Leaving the Residency, she went off, "feeling as if I carried the future of Iraq in my hands," and arrived at Sasun's house in the nick of time. Philby and Captain Clayton were already there, but they had made no headway convincing their host to take the job. It seemed that Sasun Effendi wanted nothing to do with a cabinet that included Sayid Talib. Yet the British had little choice but to include him. Talib was too powerful with the people to be left out of the government. Nevertheless, if Sasun refused to join the Cabinet, Gertrude believed, it would be damned from the beginning, doomed to failure.

Quickly taking the reins of the conversation, she tried to persuade Sasun that the British were not pushing Talib on anyone, but the man must be given a chance. Give him enough rope, she argued; if he failed, he would hang himself. After an hour, Sasun still would not give in. But he did agree to think it over. That night she hardly slept, tossing and turning, going over the arguments she had used. Could she have done a better job? How else could she have convinced him? At ten o'clock the next morning the tall, slim Sasun appeared at her office. To her great relief, he announced that he had decided to accept the post.

❧   ❧   ❧

Her work entailed constant meetings with Iraqis; editing local newspapers for propaganda in Arabic and English; compiling fortnightly Intelligence reports on the Arabs' activities for the Foreign Office; maintaining a network of agents throughout the country; reading secret reports that arrived from around the world; and at least three times a week hosting teas and dinners at home for British and Arab notables. In short, her house became the center of Baghdadi power. On one Saturday night, when the guests included leading

Iraqis—Sasun Effendi, Jafar Pasha and Abdul Majid Shawi—and three of her most important British colleagues—Philby, Captain Clayton and Major Murray—the talk turned to the insurgents. Jafar pleaded eloquently for an end to the tribal rebellion: "The peasant must return to his plow, the shepherd to his flock. The blood of our people must cease to flow and the land must once more be rich with crops. Shall our tribes be wasted in battle and our towns die of starvation?" he asked.

"Long Life to the Arab Government," Gertrude wrote to her father the next day. "Give them responsibility and make them settle their own affairs and they'll do it every time a thousand times better than we can. Moreover, once they've got responsibility they'll realise the needs and the difficulties of government and they'll eliminate hot air in favour of good sense. Because they've got to run the show, and they can't run it on hot air."

∽   ∽   ∽

"The Council of State of the first Arab government in Mesopotamia since the [thirteenth-century] Abbasids" met on Tuesday, November 2, 1920. Along with Sasun Effendi as Minister of Finance, Jafar Pasha as Minister of Defense, and six other ministers, the Council included the inevitable Sayid Talib as Minister of the Interior. For the most part, the members did little besides trying to figure out the relationship between the Arab Ministers and their British Advisers. Nevertheless, there were problems. The Shiites, almost to a man, stood entirely against the Arab Government; it looked to them like a British scheme, and worse, although there were a million and a half of them and fewer than a million Sunnis, few Shiites were in the Council. The Sunnis made every effort to keep them out of power, arguing that they had never taken part in any administration under the Turks and had not the slightest knowledge of public affairs. The only way to stall more rebellions was to hold an election as soon as possible for a national assembly. Gertrude was certain the assembly delegates would ask for a son of the Sharif Hussein—either Faisal or Abdullah—as Emir. "I regard that as the only solution," she affirmed.

A few nights later, at another of her dinners, her partner, a wise politician, turned to her and said: "You British wish to build the Government of Iraq in the usual solid English fashion. You want to begin with the foundations and then follow with the walls, the roof and then the decorations. That is not my idea of the way to build now for Iraq."

Gertrude was taken aback. "What do you mean?" she asked.

"Begin with a roof," he answered, "supported by a few pillars. The roof will encourage us to continue. Otherwise the slowness of building may discourage us. Give us a king. He will be our roof and we will work downwards." She took careful note of his words.

❦   ❦   ❦

November's cold weather coaxed her chrysanthemums to bloom, and although Marie had not yet had time to make new coats for the dogs, nor to sew a new winter gown for Gertrude, it mattered little; for the month that followed, the Khatun's thoughts were focused mainly on the machinations of Sayid Talib. The most feared yet most able and influential representative on the Council, he took up everyone's attention. One day he demanded to become Emir, the next day he threatened to resign. Jafar Pasha, she learned, had joined the Council just to make sure that Talib did not abscond with power.

Yet Gertrude's own opinion of Talib wavered. In early December she called him "a rogue" and wrote to her father: "If they select him as Emir all I can say is they've got what they deserve. But they won't," she added, as if to reassure herself. The following week Sayid Talib paid her a call. "I must confess that he made a favourable impression on me," she said. "He told me frankly that he wished to be Emir of Iraq. We discussed his position at length and I thought he showed wisdom and good sense."

The Cabinet member whose wisdom she admired throughout was Sasun Effendi. "He is out and away the best we've got and I am proud and pleased that he should have made friends with me. One can talk to him as man to man and exchange genuine opinions." Like other, though not all, Baghdadi Jews, he appreciated the treatment by the British and had prospered under the reign of the Turks during much of the Ottoman period. The ancient Jewish community, largest in the Middle East, had thrived since Babylonian times; its educational system reached the highest standards, its medical care was good, and its people flourished among the Arabs. To many, the cry for a Jewish homeland in Palestine struck a discordant note; it meant only trouble from the Arab world. That Sasun was anti-Zionist was not unappealing to Gertrude.

She was enraged that British money was spent on maintaining troops in Palestine. She wanted it for Iraq, and wrote home bitterly: "If they withdrew the two Divisions from Palestine we could keep them here for a couple of years where they're so urgently needed. But no," she went on vindictively; "there's the Jewish interest to reckon with. The Jews," she added spitefully, "can buy silence on the subject of expenditure."

∞   ∞   ∞

For several weeks while the Cabinet kept a close eye on the activities of Sayid Talib, it engaged in hot debate over whether or not to include the provincial Shiites in the Council. The Ministers looked to Gertrude for advice; even the Arab Government considered her the leading authority on the tribes. She knew that the big landowners on the Council, including the Naqib, would try to keep them out. Nevertheless, she thought it not only fair, but essential for the survival of the Arab Government, that the Shiite tribes be included in the Council. They did, after all, represent a majority of the population. If they were not included, there could be another major rebellion.

But if she bowed to their demand for representation, she did not fall blindly in the face of their claims. Indeed, she observed, they had to be controlled by a strong Arab army. "Mesopotamia is not a civilised state," she explained to her father; "it is largely composed of wild tribes who do not wish to shoulder the burden and expense of citizenship. In setting up an Arab state we are acting in the interests of the urban and village population which expects and rightly expects that it will ultimately leaven the mass." But until that time, an Arab force would be needed to control the tribes and maintain order.

∞   ∞   ∞

Every Arab, it seemed, whether townsman or tribesman, was finding his way to her door. "The number of heart to heart talks which take place in my office would surprise you!" she wrote glowingly to Hugh. "The Arabs who are our friends . . . constantly come to me, not only for advice on immediate conduct, but in order to ask about the future: 'But what do you think, Khatun?'" Her response to them was far different from what it had been less than two years before, when she had urged caution. "I feel quite certain in my own mind that there is only one workable solution," she explained to her father; "a son of the Sharif and for choice Faisal." Yet among Iraqis there was not much sympathy for the Sharif. They scoffed at his assertion that he spoke for all the Arabs. They were Mesopotamian; he was from Mecca. They felt that he represented Britain; they wanted someone who represented them.

Nevertheless, now that the French had thrown Faisal out of Damascus, he was, she announced, "very very much the first choice." His military experience in the Arab Revolt against the Turks, his administration of Syria, his diplomatic skills, his depth of character and his charisma would make him the perfect leader. Others might stand in the way, but she would do everything she could to ensure that none other than Faisal became the first King of Iraq.

CHAPTER TWENTY-NINE

The Cairo Conference

∞

"Upon my soul I'm glad I don't know what this year is going to bring. I don't think I ever woke on a first of January with such feelings of apprehension," Gertrude declared at the start of 1921.

The new year began with a torrent of rain, but it wasn't only the weather and the political situation that made her apprehensive. Except for her closest colleagues, she had very few friends. (The only woman she was close to was Aurelia Tod, the Italian wife of Lynch's representative in Baghdad.) She cared little for socializing, and her contempt had left her without much of a personal life. Even the entertaining she did was part of her work, and guests who failed to conform to her style were simply banished from her mind. In the middle of a dinner to which she had invited one of her favorite Political Officers, Major Dickson, and his young bride, Violet, she turned to another male guest and, switching from Arabic to English, announced, "It is *such* a pity that promising young Englishmen go and marry such fools of women."

"As Harold had been one of her 'promising young Englishmen,'" Mrs. Dickson commented later, "I felt most uncomfortable." To the bride, the evening was long and miserable, her hostess "rather aloof and unprepossessing." But when Gertrude wrote home, she declared the dinner a "real success."

Coats of numbness had hardened her. Resilient before, she was impervious now, her passions buried in the war, in the tombs of her lovers and friends and family members, her sensitivity crushed by the vicious behavior of A. T. Wilson. She protected herself as she had learned to do as a child: pushing away the pain, consuming herself in her work. It had left her bitter and lonely. On Christmas Day 1920, alone in her sitting room, she scrawled to Hugh: "As you know I'm rather friendless. I don't care enough about people to take trouble about them and naturally enough they don't trouble about me—why should they? Also all their amusements bore me to tears and I don't join in them; the result is that except for the people I'm working with I see no one."

She had been to the Coxes' to help prepare for a dinner that night, and to the Tods' for a Christmas tea with twenty children—English, Circassians, Jews, Christians and Arabs—all playing together "as if they had been born and bred in the same nurseries." But joyful gatherings like the ones celebrated at Rounton were long gone; she noted that this was her eighth Christmas away from her family.

Sir Percy Cox was the steady factor in her life, the "Rock of Gibraltar," gentle but firm, courteous but determined. She worked closely with him at the office, lunched with him every day and relaxed with him sometimes on weekends, boating, picnicking or shooting. A man of few words, he rarely spoke but listened carefully to those with something to say. Her influence over him was increasing. In fact, it was becoming so great that Philby later observed, "Gertrude Bell exercised an excessive and almost mesmeric effect on his judgment and decisions."

The closer she was to Cox, the more jealous her colleagues became; with few exceptions, the Political Officers used every opportunity to mock her. On a day when she was having coffee with visiting sheikhs and the conversation lagged, she asked one of the Arabs how things were going in the desert. "The wind is blowing," the sheikh replied. After he left she quickly repeated his words to the High Commissioner. But the dangerous agitation she predicted turned out to be nothing more than an actual weather report, and for a long time afterward her message was used against her. "The wind is blowing" became a regular, in-house British officers' joke.

❧ ❧ ❧

Reports of her brilliant opus, *Review of the Civil Administration of Mesopotamia*, prepared by Miss Gertrude L. Bell, C.B.E., arrived mid-

January in the newspapers from home. A literary achievement as well as a factual compilation, the official, 147-page publication had been presented as a White Paper to both Houses of Parliament. Loaded with anthropological, sociological, historical and political facts, it encompassed every important personage and explained every significant event that had taken place in Mesopotamia over the course of the six years since India Expeditionary Force D had entered Basrah, in November 1914, up to the current steps to establish an Arab Government. Beginning with a description of the lax and corrupt Ottoman rule, it went on, in highly detailed and descriptive prose, to account for the British occupation during and after the war; the problems with turbulent and pro-Turkish tribes; the difficulties in winning the loyalty of the sheikhs; the disaster at Kut; the occupation of Basrah, Baghdad, Mosul and the holy cities of Najaf and Karbala, with their inflammatory religious leaders; the Anglo-French Declaration and the problems the British encountered up until the time of the mandate; the organization of the Civil Administration, including the establishment of schools and a unified educational system, the building of hospitals and medical care, the creation of a judicial system, the formation of a police corps, a commercial department and tax agencies; the pacification of the tribes during the 1920 uprising; the relations with the Arabs and the Kurds; and the nationalist movement.

It had taken Gertrude the better part of a year to write, and it won accolades in England. Nevertheless, she was more than a little annoyed at the sexist tone of the praise. Intellectually, she may have viewed herself as a man and even prided herself on being accepted by men as an equal, but being a woman, a capable woman herself, was never in dispute.

She wrote home angrily: "I've just got Mother's letter of December 15 saying there's a fandango about my report. The general line taken by the press seems to be that it's most remarkable that a dog should be able to stand up on its hind legs—i.e. a female write a white paper. I hope they'll drop that source of wonder and pay attention to the report itself, if it will help them to understand what Mesopotamia is like." She wanted it clearly understood that the request for the report had come directly to her from the India Office and not, as suggested on the cover page, from A. T. Wilson. Moreover, she wrote, "I insisted, very much against his will, on doing it my own way, which though it might not be a good way was at least better than his. At any rate it's done, for good or bad, and I'm thankful I'm not in England to be exasperated by reporters."

But other events in England soon aggravated her even more: the debate over Mesopotamia had taken a bad turn. Severe unemployment from the post war Depression had brought on a taxpayers' revolt; the public was fed up with the expense of supporting Britain's newly mandated areas in the Middle East. Winston Spencer Churchill, now Colonial Secretary, had suggested that, to protect the oil interests in Persia and the route from Egypt to India, the base at Basrah should be maintained. But due to the high cost of keeping troops in the region, he proposed that the British pull out of the rest of Iraq. Gertrude and Cox found the notion absurd.

"As far as statecraft I really think you might search our history from end to end without finding poorer masters of it than Lloyd George and Winston Churchill," she scoffed to her father. She had already suffered enough from Churchill's poor decisions: his resolve to send in troops at Gallipoli had killed Doughty-Wylie. Now she foresaw, at his whim, the destruction of Mesopotamia.

In the face of such a threat, Cox had composed a letter to Whitehall explaining the risks of abandoning Iraq and the impossibility of keeping only Basrah. At Gertrude's urging, and in the hope of quickly establishing a solid Arab government, he suggested choosing Faisal as Emir. On the morning of Sunday, January 10, Cox called Gertrude to his house. She found him sitting in the dining room, where he handed her a telegram he had just received from Churchill. Mortified by what she read, she went home and whisked off a note to Hugh:

"EXTREMELY CONFIDENTIAL. We have reached, I fear, the end of the chapter. . . . H.M.G. had placed the decision as to their policy in Mesopotamia in the hands of the Secretary of State for War and he therefore informed the High Commissioner and the Commander in Chief that he could not burden the British public with the expenditure necessary to carry out the programme suggested—i.e. Sir Percy's recent proposal that we should bring about the selection of Faisal as Emir of Iraq, that being, in his view, the one hope of establishing speedily a stable Arab Govt and reducing the British army occupation."

It was impossible, she insisted, to establish a native government without British support. And she still chafed at Wilson, calling him the source of the problems. From the day in May when he had first spoken contemptuously of an Arab Government, she explained, the nationalists had intensifed their anti-British campaign. It was true that the idea of a *jihad* appealed to the masses, and the prospect of looting and not having to pay taxes inspired the tribes, but, she emphasized, "A.T. stands convicted of one of the greatest errors of policy which we have committed in Asia—an error so great that it lies on the toss of a halfpenny whether we can retrieve it."

A few weeks later everything changed.

Pressed by the fury in England over the cost of Mesopotamia

alone—twenty million pounds sterling for the year of 1920—combined
with the confusion in Baghdad over who should become Emir—a son
of the Sharif Hussein or Sayid Talib or even a Turkish prince—and the
dilemma over what to do with Palestine and TransJordan, Churchill
summoned a small group of Orientalists to Egypt. The British Empire's best minds on the Middle East would determine the fate of
Mesopotamia, TransJordan and Palestine. From England, Churchill
called in Air Marshal Hugh Trenchard of the RAF; Kinahan Cornwallis, an Intelligence expert attached to the Finance Ministry in Egypt;
and the newest member of his team, the fair-haired, formerly retired
Arab expert Colonel T. E. Lawrence. From Palestine Churchill sent for
High Commissioner Sir Herbert Samuel and Mr. Wyndham Deedes;
from Aden, General Scott; from Somalia, Sir Geoffrey Archer, who
brought along two baby lions destined for the Cairo zoo; from Persia,
A. T. Wilson, now representing the Anglo-Persian Oil Company; from
Arabia, General Ironside and Colonel Trevor. And from Mesopotamia
he summoned Sir Percy Cox and the only woman among the forty
official delegates, Miss Gertrude Bell.

By the middle of February Gertrude was preparing for the urgent
conference in Cairo.

To represent the Iraqis, two members of the Council were picked to
join the delegation: Jafar Pasha and Sasun Effendi; Sayid Talib, to his
great disappointment, was kept at home. The night before they left,
however, they all dined with Talib. Gertrude reported: "Amid potations
of whisky he whispered in my ear in increasingly maudlin tones that he
had always regarded me as his sister, always followed my advice and
now saw in me his sole support and stay. And I, feeling profoundly
that his ambitions never will and never should be fulfilled, could do
nothing but murmur colourless expressions of friendship." The following morning, February 24, 1921, the group was off, sailing down the
Tigris, and after dinner that night, Gertrude sat down with Percy Cox,
Major Eadie and Jafar Pasha for the most popular form of Baghdad
evening entertainment, a game of bridge.

At Basrah, where they switched from the boat to a ship, Gertrude
rushed off to see the Van Esses. A warm welcome, lunch with her
friends, and the conversation turned to the rebellion still weighing
heavily on their minds. For seven years John Van Ess had lived as a
missionary among the Euphrates tribes that had started the 1920 uprising; he was certain, he said, that the roots of the revolt were not in a
struggle for nationalism but in a war of religion, an ongoing battle
between Shiites and Sunnis. He had supported Wilson's harshest measures and, even less to Gertrude's liking, was a fan of Sayid Talib.

Nevertheless, she appreciated hearing his analyses. "There's no one better to talk to than Mr. Van Ess," she wrote to Florence.

∞ ∞ ∞

As the Mesopotamian delegation sailed to Egypt on the *Hardinge*, Winston Churchill walked briskly past the crowds at Victoria Station, and slipping into his private compartment on the boat train, he lighted a cigar and set to work. "I'm going to save you millions," the Colonial Secretary had promised the press. Only a few days before he had noted to Parliament that the great success of the Allies in World War I, the break-up of the Ottoman Empire and the consequent possession by the British of Palestine and Mesopotamia had pushed England into a situation of enormous responsibility. It had come at a high price, he told them: twenty-five million pounds just to fight the rebellions and ward off anarchy and chaos in the Mandates. Now he would do something to cut the cost. He would establish an Arab Government in Mesopotamia and ease the burden on the British public.

∞ ∞ ∞

Gertrude stood in her striped silk dress and silver fox boa, looking out from beneath her flowered hat, and in the hall of the familiar Cairo train station she spotted her old chum Lawrence, come to meet them. With the huge success of Lowell Thomas's lectures and the publication of Thomas's book, *Lawrence of Arabia*, T.E.L. had become world famous; for the first time since they met, he was more well known than Gertrude. "Dear Boy," she cried out, extending her gloved hand to the shy and awkward fellow. "Gertie," he greeted her and looked around. "Everyone Middle East is here," he said.

A horse-drawn carriage took them to the palm-fringed Corniche, the road overlooking the Nile, and on the way they could hear Islamic students from al Ahzar University chanting anti-British slogans. Inside the Semiramis Hotel, a sense of expectation fluttered through the lobby. For days the staff had bustled about, feverishly polishing brass, watering potted palm trees and flowering plants, readying rooms, scurrying across the marble floors delivering telegrams, carrying hatboxes, toiletry cases and steamer trunks, ushering in a glittering array of distinguished guests.

Gertrude led Lawrence to her room. During the 1920 uprising in

Mesopotamia and the debate over the cost of the mandate, Lawrence had written letters to the British press, sometimes praising, more often condemning the work of the civil administration in Baghdad. "I'm largely in agreement," Gertrude had written back to him at first. But as the weeks wore on, his criticism grew more hostile. "The people of England have been led in Mesopotamia into a trap from which it will be hard to escape with dignity and honour," he wrote unfairly in *The Sunday Times*. "Things have been far worse than we have been told, our administration more bloody and inefficient than the public knows." Gertrude responded angrily, rightly describing his ideas as "tosh" and "pure nonsense." Now the pair enjoyed "a private laugh over two of her letters, one," Lawrence explained, "describing me as an angel, and the other accusing me of being possessed by the devil."

They discussed the costs of Mesopotamia and the need to withdraw some troops, and they agreed that, with an Arab Government installed, Great Britain could begin to decrease the size and expenditures of its administration. Most important of all, in the confines of the Semiramis Hotel they conspired over Faisal as the future ruler of Iraq. Lawrence had already smoothed the way with Churchill in London, and Gertrude had done the same with Cox in Baghdad; now they would work together to make sure the man they wanted was anointed Emir. An hour later they emerged from her room, and while Lawrence drifted off, Gertrude went with Sir Percy to pay a courtesy call on the Churchills. The following day, Saturday, March 12, 1921, cloaked in a shroud of secrecy, with not a single word to the press, the Cairo Conference officially opened.

"I'll tell you about our Conference," Gertrude wrote to Florence two weeks later. "It has been wonderful. We covered more work in a fortnight than has ever before been got through in a year. Mr. Churchill was admirable, most ready to meet everyone halfway and masterly alike in guiding a big political meeting and in conducting small political committees into which we broke up."

∞   ∞   ∞

On the first day of the sessions, as the Political Committee convened at the table, Gertrude puffing on her cigarette, Churchill puffing on his cigar, Percy Cox described the events in Baghdad over the past five months: a Provisional Government had been established, and the Naqib invited to form a Cabinet. Now without delay, he said, an announcement had to be made that a new authority would soon replace the provisional Council of State. The delegates concurred that the new authority must be an individual ruler. But who? The Naqib of Baghdad was mentioned, and the names of Sayid Talib, the Sheikh of Muhammarah, even a relative of the Turkish Sultan were tossed around; almost without argument, they were dropped. With the McMahon-Hussein promises of an Arab kingdom for the Sharifian family still hanging over them like a cloud of conscience, the best choice, the group agreed, was a son of the Sharif.

But why, Churchill demanded to know, would Faisal, the younger son, be better than his older brother, Abdullah?

Cox explained that it was important to establish an Arab army to control any incipient rebellions; Faisal's experience in leading the desert revolt, and his involvement with the Allied army under Allenby, made him better qualified than Abdullah. The fact that Faisal was no longer in Damascus made him available. That he had been let down by the British did not need to be said.

The conversation moved around the table. "The first ruler should be an active and inspiring personality," Lawrence observed. It was important to have a charismatic figure to "counteract the claims of rival candidates and pull together the scattered elements of a backward and half-civilized country." Abdullah, he added, "was lazy and by no means dominating."

Churchill pointed out that choosing Faisal to lead Iraq would give the British some leverage over the rest of the Sharifian family. If Faisal knew that his own behavior (that is, his cooperating with the British) affected not only his father's subsidy and the protection of the holy places from attacks by Ibn Saud, but also influenced the position of his brother Abdullah in TransJordan, he would be much easier to deal with. And his father and brother, in turn, would also behave in acceptable ways.

Gertrude acknowledged that if Faisal were chosen, they might encounter opposition from Sayid Talib. He was, after all, one of the most powerful men in Iraq. But, she assured the group, it would be negligible compared to the acclamation Faisal would receive.

By the end of the day, as Gertrude had hoped, they voted in favor of Faisal. Churchill cabled home: "Prospects Mesopotamia promising." The Sharif's son Faisal, he wrote, offered "hope of best and cheapest solution."

Gertrude had changed her opinion completely about Winston Churchill. And no wonder: the meetings had gone almost exactly according to her plan. It was she who had set her sights on Faisal as King of the new Arab state; it was she who had fought to include the *vilayets* of Basrah, Baghdad and Mosul, and to embrace Shiites, Sunnis and Kurds; it was she who had decided the borders and drawn the lines in the sand around Iraq. All that she had envisioned was beginning to take shape.

∽ ∽ ∽

At the following session Gertrude and Lawrence laid out plans for bringing Faisal to Iraq. As a Sunni ruler in a country with a Shiite majority, Faisal would have to base his legitimacy on his Sharifian roots; he was, most important, a descendant of the Prophet Muhammad. Thus, they explained to Churchill, although the Emir was currently in London, he would need to travel to Mecca, the birthplace of Muhammad, the holiest site in Islam and the symbol of Faisal's religious importance. There it would be announced that Faisal had been invited by the Iraqi people, and as he journeyed from Mecca, north toward Baghdad, Gertrude felt sure that, with help from British and Arab sympathizers, support for him would snowball.

The Iraqi delegates, Jafar Pasha al Askari and Sasun Effendi Eskail, were called into the room and asked what they thought. As Gertrude knew they would (she had already spent hours with them discussing this very same subject), the two men wholeheartedly agreed with the decision.

∽ ∽ ∽

At further conference sessions, debates ensued over Mosul, the Kurds and the costly size of the British military presence. When they turned to the turbulent area in the north of Iraq, Churchill proposed autonomy; a Kurdish region would serve as a buffer zone between the Arabs and the Turks. He feared that an Iraqi ruler might "ignore Kurdish sentiment and oppress the Kurdish minority." Gertrude disagreed. The north was too important to Iraq, she insisted: Mosul not only had oil; it had long been the breadbasket of Mesopotamia, its fertile soil providing grain for the entire country. Moreover, its population provided a substantial number of badly needed Sunnis to counterbalance the Shiite majority. As for the Kurds (who were also Sunnis), she believed that within six months they would be eager to join the Arab Government. But Lawrence objected: the Kurds should not be placed under an Arab Government, he warned. The issue was left in abeyance; for the immediate future, Kurdistan would be kept separate, overseen by the High Commissioner.

In the midst of the week-long debate, Lawrence, who had been on his best behavior, began to revert to his old ways. When, becoming obstreperous, he made an impudent remark, no one knew what to say. Finally, Gertrude shot him a look with her piercing eyes. She brooked no insolence. "You little IMP!" she jeered. His ears and face turned red, and Lawrence, rarely if ever taken aback, retreated in silence.

A discussion arose on the annual allowances paid to influential Arab chiefs to keep them loyal to Britain. The subsidy for Fahad Bey, whose desert provided landing strips for airplanes and roadways for the motor cars traveling between Palestine and Iraq, was kept at thirty-six thousand pounds. The Sharif Hussein of the Hejaz was to receive one hundred thousand pounds, and although Cox pushed for more for Ibn Saud, who had received sixty thousand pounds, he was to be given the same amount as Hussein. But, it was agreed, Ibn Saud would receive his raise only if he promised to stop his warring campaign against Hussein, make peace with the Shammar tribe on the southern border of Iraq and avoid the threat of war with the Emirate of Kuwait.

The troubling size of the British military presence was high on Churchill's list. Churchill (who still retained the title of Air Minister) believed that through the use of airplanes instead of land troops, Iraq could be controlled at less expense and in a more efficient manner. Furthermore, the same air bases used in Iraq could provide a strategic link to India. Since the British army would be replaced by both the Royal Air Force and an Arab army, and since they would have armoured cars and an effective Intelligence system, British interests would still be secure. As for the Kurds: the members of the conference were all sure that air power and a few squadrons overhead would be enough to contain the rebellious tribes.

The last item on the Mesopotamian agenda, once again, was Faisal and the timing of his entry into Iraq; it was agreed that he should be invited to Baghdad before the Iraqi elections for a ruler took place. Churchill wired home: "Both Cox and Miss Bell agree that if procedure is followed, appearance of Faisal in Mesopotamia will lend to his general adoption." But it would be tricky business to make the Iraqis believe that Faisal was their personal candidate and not the proxy of the British.

Decisions still had to be made on the remaining mandates of Palestine and TransJordan and on the rest of the Sharifian family. Hussein, who had already declared himself a king and was considered "tyrannical," "autocratic" and greedy by the British, and his son Ali were left to rule in the Hejaz (although they would be driven out within four years by Ibn Saud); Abdullah was awarded TransJordan, the Arab area that stretched from the east bank of the Jordan river to the western border of Iraq (and where his grandson King Hussein rules today); and although Churchill supported the Balfour Declaration, the fate of Palestine was left ambiguous.

∞ ∞ ∞

Taking a break from the wearying sessions, the peripatetic Churchill could not resist a trip to the Pyramids. Gertrude, invited to join him, climbed onto a waiting camel at Giza, but Churchill was a mass of sliding gelatin as he struggled onto the wooden saddle resting atop the hump. The animal rose from its knees, and as the bulbous Churchill reached for the thin cord, the camel lurched. Churchill fell to the ground. "How easily the mighty are fallen!" his wife, Clementine, chided. But when a horde of Egyptian riders rushed forward to offer their horses, the stubborn Churchill brushed them away. "I started on a camel and I shall finish on a camel," he growled. A little later, with the Sphinx behind them, the group sat poised on their camels, Gertrude flanked by Churchill and Lawrence, as they posed for one the few photographs taken at the conference.

In the evenings, she and the others dashed from one social event to the next. Her father had come out to Egypt to see her, and with Hugh as her escort, Gertrude went off to a tea at Shepheard's arranged by a visiting sheikh and to a banquet at Gezira Palace given by King Fuad. They waltzed at a ball at High Commissioner Allenby's residence and dined at the Semiramis Hotel, where their host was Herbert Samuel, the High Commissioner of Palestine, and on the last evening, they celebrated at a banquet at Abdin Palace. The Sultan's home was an enchanted city with acres of luxurious gardens, private living quarters complete with sunken tubs in gilded bathrooms, and a *samalek*, where the royal ladies received their guests. In the palace's great Byzantine hall, the forty delegates, now called jokingly by Churchill "the forty thieves," clinked their glasses and dined in splendor, enjoying their great success.

The Cairo Conference ended on March 25, 1921. A triumphant Churchill would soon tell Parliament that he had achieved what he had set out to do in Mesopotamia: the British garrisons would be reduced from thirty-three battalions to twenty-three battalions; expenditures would be dropped by five million pounds the first year and by twelve million pounds the next; communications lines would be installed and strategic air routes created to connect and strengthen the entire Empire.

Always a loner, Lawrence had written to his brother only a few days before the end of the conference: "It has been one of the longest fortnights I ever lived. . . . We lived in a marble and bronze hotel, very expensive and luxurious—horrible place: makes me Bolshevik."

But Gertrude had had a marvelous time. Now, sitting on deck in the open air on the boat back to Iraq, she scrawled a letter to her friend Frank Balfour. She had been so pleased to see her father, she told him, and felt sad that she would not see him again for another year. Nevertheless, she wrote: "When we get our Amir he will need a great deal of help and guidance and it's more than I could bear not to be there to give whatever hand I can. Oh Frank, it's going to be interesting!" Almost everything she had wished for now had a chance of coming true. The country would consist of all three *vilayets*—Baghdad, Basrah and Mosul; the Sunnis, Shiites, Jews, Christians and Kurds would be united under a Sharifian king; and Iraq, rich, prosperous and led by Faisal, would prove a loyal protégé of Britain. If Gertrude could bring it all off, it would be more than interesting; it would be a model for the entire Middle East.

CHAPTER THIRTY

Resistance

∞

Gertrude's challenge now was to put Faisal on the throne. Without allowing it to appear in any way that he was a British proxy, she had to convince the Iraqis that Faisal was their best and only choice. The plan was that the Sharif Hussein would announce his son's candidacy for the position as ruler of Iraq; after that, Faisal would leave Mecca and travel by train from Basrah to Baghdad, delivering speeches, building a groundswell along the way. By the time he reached his destination, it was hoped he would have gained enough supporters to make it seem that the people themselves had chosen him as their leader; to those who wanted the British to rule, it would be made clear that Faisal had British approval. Iraqi elections were to be held, and with the British expressing their endorsement, Faisal would be crowned King.

Thirteen centuries earlier the same scenario had been played out by Faisal's ancestor Hussein, grandson of the Prophet Muhammad. But as Gertrude was keenly aware, the results had been nothing short of disaster. Called from Mecca by the Iraqi people to become their Caliph, Hussein arrived at Karbala in A.D. 680, ready to assume the role of the highest religious leader. But in an unexpected turn of events, Hussein was savagely betrayed; instead of being welcomed by supporters, he was met by a rivalrous army. Only a handful of followers stayed with him, and almost all of them were killed; on the tenth of Muharram, Hussein himself was slain. Lighting torches, beating their breasts in somber processions, Shiite Muslims still mourn Hussein during that holy month. "*Absit omen*" (May it not be an omen), Gertrude murmured to herself.

Even before she and Cox returned to Baghdad, the air was being poisoned; during their absence the scurrilous Sayid Talib had been hard at work campaigning for the aged Naqib. The wily Minister of the Interior hoped that the frail old man would be chosen Emir; after he died, Talib himself would likely be named his successor. With the slogan "Iraq for the Iraqis," he stressed the Naqib's (and his own) Mesopotamian roots, as opposed to Faisal's distant origins in the Hejaz. Making an extensive tour around the Euphrates, Talib assured the public he was a British favorite, and, while making threats of intimidation against the opposition, gave away thousands of British pounds to potential friends.

Indeed, one of the most powerful sheikhs in the region, Ali Suleiman of the Dulaim, supported the Naqib. But Gertrude believed that Talib had been less than successful. "He cut very little ice," she wrote after her return on April 12. She suspected that because the recalcitrant tribes of the middle Euphrates mistakenly thought Talib was bolstered by the British, they would refuse to give him their support. On the other hand, she went on. "The last thing they think we should like would be a son of the Sharif." After all, she recalled, the tribes had asked for a Sharifian the year before and were "jumped on" for their efforts.

Suspicious that the British Government was backing Faisal, Talib hosted a dinner party for Percival Landon, a visiting English journalist with the *Daily Telegraph*. The thirteen guests at Talib's that night included the Tods, the French and Persian Consuls, and two important Arabs. The Khatun was not invited.

The morning after Talib's dinner, Gertrude was greeted with news of the event by some of the guests. Plied with liquor, Talib had proclaimed himself "wholly satisfied" with Sir Percy Cox and the attitude of the British Government, but, he had said, "there were British officials in H.E.'s entourage [an obvious reference to Gertrude] who were known to be partisans and who were exercising undue influence." Pointing out the power of his Arab guests (and, more important, his own power) to the English correspondent, Talib had threatened, "If any attempt is made to influence the elections, here is the Emir al Rabi'ah with thirty thousand rifles . . . and the Sheikh of Chabaish with all his men." Then, reminding them all of the religious leader's wide influence, he warned, "The Naqib will appeal to Islam, to India, Egypt, Constantinople and Paris."

Talib's remarks made Gertrude livid, and she immediately wrote up a report for Percy Cox. "It was an incitement to rebellion as bad as anything which was said by the men who roused the country last year, and not far from a declaration of *jihad*," she fumed. Talib was "capable of anything," she warned. His reputation for evil had not diminished. His power came from ruthless medieval methods: blackmail, extortion and cold murder. Known to have given orders to eliminate a Turkish official before the onset of the war, he had now summoned to Baghdad the very man who had carried out the killing. She feared that, at the very least, Talib, using the power of the Naqib's name, would organize a tribal rebellion, a *jihad*, against the British; worse, she felt certain he would attempt to assassinate Faisal. The man was too dangerous; something had to be done at once.

Later that same afternoon, the innocent Lady Cox held her regular Saturday tea. Although Sir Percy announced that he was too busy to come and went off to the races, a number of guests, including Gertrude and Major Bovill (who had been keeping a close surveillance on Talib for Cox), attended. At four-thirty Sayid Talib arrived, stayed half an hour to chat, and said goodbye. Gertrude escorted him to the front door of the Residency and, after seeing him to his car, walked back inside. With his chauffeur at the wheel, Talib drove off, but as soon as his car reached a nearby bridge, it was blocked by a broken-down truck. Talib's automobile was forced to stop, and at the order of Major Bovill, who suddenly appeared—and who himself was under orders from Percy Cox—the putative candidate was arrested and removed to an armored car. Talib had driven directly into an ambush. "The wiliest man in Arabia had walked into the simplest of traps," Philby said. Two days afterward Talib was deported to Ceylon.

Cox had taken a big risk. By deporting Talib, he could have roused sympathy for the politician and turned him into a martyr. But instead, as Cox believed would happen, the public felt eased by Talib's removal and reacted acquiescently to the show of British power. "Not a voice has been raised against Sir Percy's coup, on the contrary the whole country is immensely relieved at Talib's disappearance," Gertrude wrote.

A major barrier to Faisal's election had been removed and Gertrude breathed a sigh. "Lord! how glad I am that I gave in a careful report of that speech," she rejoiced to her father. "Didn't I tell you there was no one like Sir Percy in the handling of a delicate political problem! I feel a load off my mind." Once again she blamed her former enemy: "It's the final unravelling of the harm that A. T. Wilson did, for no one knows what he promised Talib when he brought him up."

But the problems surrounding Talib were not over yet. Each of the Arab Ministers had been assigned a British Adviser. Talib's Adviser, Philby, felt deeply distressed over the seizure of his charge. Strongly opposed to a monarchy, and fearing that Talib had been removed to make way for Faisal, Philby immediately went into Cox's office and offered his resignation. But the High Commissioner assured him that the British had no intention of imposing Faisal as King. Moreover, he added, he needed Philby to run the Interior Ministry.

Gertrude and Philby had long been close. They had worked well together since their days in Basrah, had developed a personal friendship and even spent one Christmas together along the Tigris. They shared a common loathing of Wilson and a common vision of an Arab Iraq. But now, knowing of her support for Faisal, Philby blamed Gertrude for Talib's downfall and grimaced whenever they passed in the halls. His chilliness was painful, and finally she insisted they talk. She told him that she had done only what was "obviously incumbent" upon her. He did not dare quarrel with Cox, and she refused to let him quarrel with her. They were back on speaking terms, she reported a few days later, but whether or not her colleague would stay in Iraq if Faisal was chosen Emir, she did not know.

Two weeks later, on May 21, she attended a dinner at the Coxes'. Thanks to Sir Percy's passion, the house was a zoologist's dream, a menagerie of birds, dogs and a fully grown bear (that would one day turn wild). Ignoring them all, Gertrude marched proudly into the drawing room, her fifty-two-year-old figure strikingly thin, her head high, her posture erect, her dress a cream lace gown stylishly flounced. With one exception, she wrote her parents, the evening was "very friendly and pleasant." Mrs. Philby, however, was "markedly stand-offish." Gertrude could not imagine why. "It's conceivable, after all, that she just doesn't like me." As for Mr. Philby, she wasn't seeing him very much, but when she did, he was "quite pleasant."

Not pleasant enough. With Talib gone, Philby was running the Ministry of Interior and was thereby in charge of all internal organs. When Gertrude proposed, with Sir Percy's approval, to start a nationalist newspaper as a tool to promote the Sharifians, Philby said, flatly, no. "He has a strong prejudice against Faisal," she complained to her father.

Philby's attitude continued to upset her: "It seems most unnecessary that your official policy should be in any way hindered by one of your own officials. He never comes to see me so I suppose he looks on me as the arch enemy—or not far from it. And I can't give him a friendly word of warning. But he is spinning a bad cotton for he is earning a name as an opponent. I'm very sorry, but I've done my best to make a bridge and if he won't walk over it I can't help him."

His frostiness only added to her frustration. Faisal's arrival was long overdue. Several secret messages had been sent by Cox to the Sharif Hussein asking him to announce that Faisal was coming to Iraq. But for nearly two months there had been no answer. Then, on June 12, 1921, to the great relief of Cox and Gertrude, the telegrams arrived: Faisal was on his way. For all the excitement, however, Gertrude worried over what would happen once he appeared:

"At the back of my mind there's the firm conviction that no people likes permanently to be governed by another," she wisely observed. "Now we're trying to foster nationalism, but I'm always ready to admit that nationalism which is not at the same time anti-foreign is likely to be a plant of weak growth. Faisal walking hand in hand with us will not be so romantic a figure as Faisal heading a *jihad* might be! He won't head a *jihad*; that's not his line. Can we get enough of the breath of life into him, without that, to enable him to put real inspiration into the Arab State. . . . All depends on his personality and Sir Percy's discretion in keeping in the background."

At least she knew she could rely on her chief: "He is a master hand at the game of politics," she said deferentially; "it's an education to watch him playing it."

∞   ∞   ∞

The announcement in the *Baghdad Times* (the government's English-language newspaper) of Faisal's imminent arrival prompted the Mayor and a number of younger, pro-Sharifian politicians to call at her office. They asked her suggestions on what to do next. "We had to settle on a temporary flag," she reported to her father, "and then there was the difficult question as to where Faisal should be lodged." Through Gertrude's persistence, rooms were readied in the Serai, the former Turkish Government offices which had been under repair, and on her advice a town meeting of five hundred people was called. Sixty men (including Haji Naji, Gertrude's "personal spy") were chosen to form a delegation to go down to Basrah to welcome the future Emir. To mollify Philby, Cox appointed him as Faisal's official escort.

In the midst of it all, Gertrude opened her mail and found an invitation from the Philbys to attend a ball. "It's a perfect mania here," she groused. "They dance at the Club four times a week. It's accursed, I think. Men who are as hard worked as our officials can't sit up till one or two in the morning and be in their office at seven or eight. It's the wives that do it, confound them—they take no interest in what's going on, know no Arabic and see no Arabs. They create an exclusive (it's also a very second-rate) English society quite cut off from the life of the town. I now begin to understand why the British Government has come to grief in India, where our women do just the same thing."

The night of the ball at the posh Alwiya Club, where British officers could swim, play tennis or shoot pool, Philby politely danced with Lady Cox. Then, dancing with Gertrude, he let her know that the plan for Faisal was no longer a secret. "The Cairo cat is out of the bag," he declared. By the end of the evening, as they twirled around the floor, he was drunk and argumentative.

The following week, dressed once again in a long gown, Gertrude left her house at nine P.M., stopping first at the train station to say farewell to Mme. Talib, who was joining her husband in Ceylon. Then she was off again to another ball, this one given by Lady Cox. She reached the Sports Club to find the guests outdoors, gliding on carpets spread on the grass, but she declined to dance. Instead, she supped with Sir Percy and came home at midnight with Mr. Tod. "The gay Lady Cox," she noted snidely, "danced till 4 A.M." Only a few weeks before, with Gertrude's help, Lady Cox had given a garden party for four hundred guests. Carpets were laid on the lawn, couches and chairs brought outdoors and lights strung up in the trees. But after Gertrude had done most of the work, the High Commissioner's wife took her breath away. Wasn't it "a pity we hadn't had all the trees washed," said Lady Cox; they were "so dusty!"

∞ ∞ ∞

On June 23, Gertrude received word that, with Philby there to welcome him, Faisal had arrived in Basrah. The plan was for Faisal to travel directly to the Shiite holy cities of Karbala and Najaf, underscoring his religious importance as a descendant of the Prophet, and then continue north to Baghdad. In preparation for his arrival, people in town started flying the Sharifian flag, and as Gertrude walked through the bazaar on her way to work, she saw the banner waving from the shops. "The intention is good but the flag heraldically bad," she noted to Hugh, her critical eye offended.

Early on Wednesday morning, June 29, 1921, Gertrude motored through town with Colonel Joyce, Military Adviser to the Iraqi Government. Past throngs of people waving Arab flags, past scores of buildings decorated with flags, flowers and triumphal arches, the car rode along the big street to the Baghdad train station. An immense crowd had gathered, impatient for Faisal's arrival. She and the colonel made their way to the special seats reserved for dignitaries, but after they had waited an hour, there came instead a disappointing message: the train was delayed and would not arrive before noon. Midday was much too hot for a reception. Word was sent back asking Faisal to stay on board and delay his arrival to six P.M. Home they all went, to return again in the late afternoon.

Faisal stood at the carriage door, slim and splendid in his flowing robes and gold-braided headdress, saluting the honor guard. Sir Percy Cox and General Haldane greeted him ceremoniously, and the crowd broke into applause. "He went down the line of the guard of honour, inspecting it," Gertrude reported. "Sir Percy began to present the Arab Magnates, representatives of the Naqib, etc. I hid behind Mr. Cornwallis, but Faisal saw me and stepped across to shake hands with me. He looked excited and anxious—you're not a king on approbation without any tension of the spirit—but it only gave his natural dignity a more human charm."

She chatted eagerly with the tall, distinguished Kinahan Cornwallis, "a tower of strength and wisdom." Indeed, he towered over the crowd, an eagle, with his large beak of a nose and penetrating blue eyes. Highly intelligent and dependably wise, he had been Director of the Arab Bureau in Cairo, and then Faisal's adviser in Damascus; he had worked closely with the Emir for five years, earning his great respect. In fact, Faisal had refused to come to Baghdad without him.

Yet as the eminent Cornwallis stepped off the train, Gertrude noticed that he looked glum. The reception in Basrah, he quickly told her, had not gone terribly well. The crowds that came out to see the candidate had been restrained and had given no cheers; indeed, as the train progressed toward Baghdad, the response had ranged from quietly curious to outright hostile. The Political Officers in each of the towns along the route had listened to Philby, who, undermining Percy Cox, discouraged their participation or any show of support; and Philby himself, who had been sent to welcome Faisal, had been less than kind to him. The British officials, Philby informed the Emir, had been instructed that the elections were to be "absolutely free." If Faisal thought he could win the people's votes "on the grounds that he was the nominee of Great Britain," Philby warned him, his "chances of success were slender." The people wanted a republic, Philby insisted, and he himself supported Ibn Saud as its leader. In addition to these disheartening words, Faisal heard rumors along the way that Philby was against him, the Khatun was in favor of him and that Sir Percy Cox was neutral. Bewildered, Faisal wanted to know whether the High Commissioner was on his side. And if so, why were Cox's own officials against him?

Instead of finding a welcome embrace, Faisal had found a wall of resistance. In Basrah the leaders wanted autonomy to govern their own enclave. Along the lower Euphrates, the tribes were readying a petition for a republic. In Karbala and Najaf the Shiite holy men were opposed to a Sharifian. Around the country pro-Turkish factions believed the Turks would return. And in Baghdad the Naqib and his followers were reluctant to give their support. Shades of Hussein and Muharram: the great reception that Gertrude had hoped for had not occurred. The snowball had melted in the sand.

CHAPTER THIRTY-ONE

Faisal

∞

It was not yet seven A.M. but the waves of heat that shimmer over Baghdad in July were already beginning to appear. The temperature was racing to its daily high of 120 degrees as Gertrude, on her way to work the morning after Faisal's arrival, stopped at the Serai. The long brick building sat on the riverfront, not far from her house, a sprawling display of strength and grace. She handed her calling card to the aide-de-camp, expecting that Faisal would invite her later that day or the next. Would the Khatun please wait? the man inquired. The Emir would like to see her. A servant led her into a large salon, and a short while later Faisal, thin and angular even in his flowing robes, walked across the room to greet her. It was two years since they had spoken at length at the Paris Peace Conference, but he had not forgotten. His eyes warm and welcoming, he reached out, took both her hands in his and said gratefully, "I couldn't have believed that you could have given me so much help as you have given me."

After leading her to a sofa, he sat beside her and as he smoked one cigarette after another, divulged his fears. Gertrude did what she could to comfort the anxious candidate, assuring him that Percy Cox was "absolutely with him." You must speak your mind to Sir Percy, she advised. Furthermore, make certain you see the Naqib and do what you can to win him to your side.

The Naqib and his followers had watched with disappointment when Faisal and his men took the throne in Damascus, only to lose it to the French. Now the Baghdadi elders were concerned that the coterie around him was too weak to take control in Iraq. Gertrude was aware that the elitist notables did not like the idea of ordinary young men coming into power. When Faisal arrived in Baghdad, the Naqib remained at home, too sick, it was claimed, to greet the train.

Knowing that Faisal resisted the idea of appeasing his enemy, Gertrude counseled him nonetheless to do what he could to gain the Naqib's support. "I shall make you responsible," Faisal replied, but he took her advice. Playing the game by the Naqib's rules, he called on the old man at home and wished him a speedy recovery; the visit broke the ice.

That evening, at an outdoor banquet she had arranged, Gertrude looked around with delight at the electric lights and the decorations, and listened with pleasure when the orator called Faisal the King of Iraq. But the behavior of some of Faisal's guests left her appalled. "I shall have to set about getting a proper ceremonial for Faisal's court," she remarked; "none of them have the least idea of what to do next." Several times during the evening, the guests walked off to talk among themselves, leaving Faisal standing alone.

When dinner was served, and course after course slowly brought to the table, the would-be king ate sparingly, impatient and obviously eager to jump from his chair. "There is a great deal to be said for an Arab dinner party," Gertrude observed. "All the viands are before you, you eat what you want and when you're done you get up and go back to your coffee and cigarettes." To make matters worse, the after dinner speeches went on for far too long. Tired and bored, Faisal stood up, went over to Gertrude and, with the weariness of a long-time politician, moaned confidentially, "I used to do all I could to avoid speeches in Syria and I'm afraid they are going to be much worse here."

∞　∞　∞

In spite of a few bouquets that were tossed, the path Faisal walked was thorny. He had never before set foot in Iraq; he knew little of the people he would rule, of the land over which he would reign, of the history he would inherit. He had no knowledge of the Iraqi tribes, no friendships with their sheikhs, no familiarity with the terrain—the marshes in the south, the mountains in the north, the grain fields, the river life—and no sense of connection with its ancient past. He even spoke a different dialect of Arabic, a mixture of Hejaz, Egyptian, Syrian and Turkish. Yet Gertrude knew he had the intelligence to learn quickly and the charisma to lead effectively.

He sent for her frequently to ask her advice. In the privacy of his quarters, in a large cool, underground room with a vaulted ceiling, the two conferred, and after servants brought in glasses of iced lemonade, Gertrude suggested what he should do: what to say to Sir Percy, how to handle the Baghdadi businessmen, how to form his Cabinet, how to approach the Kurds. And day after day, dressed in her prettiest clothes and using her most feminine ways, she spread out her maps and taught the charming Faisal the tribal geography of Iraq.

Opposition to Faisal was strong. Some tribes wanted a republic; others, such as the Anazeh, led by Fahad Bey, wanted British rule; and still others, such as the Dulaim, favored the Naqib. As Gertrude struggled to convince the contrary factions, the tension took its toll. "I'm beginning to feel as if I couldn't stand it much longer!" she cried. She was "straining every nerve," trying to sell her candidate, "talking, persuading, writing," even arguing in her sleep.

Walking to work each day, she picked her way through throngs of curious sheikhs and notables, sitting for hours under the Residency's courtyard awnings, waiting to meet the candidate. At least, she noted, Faisal's great charm was a help. "He has been roping in adherents," she reported. That, combined with her assurances to the people who favored the British that Faisal had Sir Percy's approval, was beginning to sweeten the brew, convincing the magnates that the Sharifian was the best if not the only choice for Emir.

One of the most important dignitaries to fall in line was the venerable Naqib. On Thursday, July 7, the holy man gave a dinner at home. One hundred people were seated at tables in the open space of the courtyard, while the most distinguished were led to places on the roof, carpeted and lighted for the occasion. Tottering forward to the head of the stairs to meet his honored guest, the Naqib kissed the white-robed Faisal on both cheeks and, walking with him hand in hand, brought him together with the influential leaders of the town. "We are making history," Gertrude proclaimed. The following week more dinners were held, first by the Coxes for Faisal and then by Faisal for the sheikhs of the Tigris and the Euphrates. "Dinners!" she groaned. "In this weather they are a real trial." The nights were hardly any cooler than the days, and sweat poured off the guests' brows as they ate their way through heaping platters of eggplant, stuffed grape leaves, roast lamb, rice, fresh fruit, listening all the while to endless speeches.

But if Gertrude was able to persuade the Naqib and his followers to lend their support to Faisal, she had less success with her colleague Philby. Sent away for a ten-day rest by Cox, Philby on his return was called to the High Commissioner's office. Could he accommodate his views? Cox wanted to know. Philby refused; he could not go along with the official agenda for an Arab emir. Cox was furious and informed his aide he had no choice but to relieve him of his duties. It hurt Gertrude to see Philby destroy himself. "It's a real tragedy, he's dismissed," she wrote disappointedly, "but he has himself to thank." Cox had given him "a long rope" and every chance to use it. "Sir Percy, who never hesitates in what he thinks to be his duty, has cut the knot in the only possible way. I am, nevertheless, very sorry."

Wanting Philby to know how bad she felt, she paid a call on him at home. "Jack, I'm so sorry to hear this news," she said. But instead of extending their hands in friendship, he and his wife practically slapped her face. "No you're not," Mrs. Philby snapped and burst into tears. Accusing Gertrude of having been the cause of her husband's dismissal, the woman turned and ran out of the room. Philby glowered: "You've won this time," he snarled, "but we shall still meet at Philippi." She would not be at the battle scene, Gertrude retorted, adding curtly that it was not she "but His Majesty's Government that had won and always would." Reminding Philby of their long friendship, she told him she had done everything in her power to persuade him not to run counter to orders. "How he could embrace the cause of that rogue Talib passes all belief," she wrote.

At lunch at the Coxes' the following week, Gertrude found herself face to face with the Philbys once again. But by now their mood had changed. "The Philby business is clearing up," she wrote home. "It has been horrid for me, for in their angry amazement at having to suffer for what was entirely his own fault they have accused me of being the cause of his dismissal—at least Mrs. Philby has. But I think she has thought the better of it." Philby told her he was quitting politics, but Gertrude acknowledged sadly, "He's not a man we can afford to lose."

∞   ∞   ∞

The large Jewish community also had to be won over to the Sharifian side. Reluctant to accept an Arab ruler (they had once petitioned that they be granted British citizenship if an Arab government was installed), Gertrude worked to convince them that Faisal had British support. Her spirits rose when they agreed to host a large reception for him. On Monday morning, July 18, Jewish, Christian and Arab notables gathered in the courtyard of the Grand Rabbi's official house, where an awning covered the open square, and flags and streamers in Arab colors—green, red and black—hung from the second-story gallery. Children crammed the balcony and women peered out from the upper windows to watch the scene in the courtyard. Row upon row of chairs were filled with turbaned Jewish rabbis, prominent Christians, all the Arab Government Ministers, the leading Muslims and Shiite holy men.

The official party came in, took their seats and the crowd burst into applause. Gertrude was given the honored place to the right of Faisal. "You know the absurd fuss they make about me, bless them," she wrote. The program began, and for two hours, in the sweltering heat, cool drinks and refreshments were passed while the audience listened to speeches and songs. The Rabbi, she thought, looked "straight out of a picture by Gentile Bellini"; the well-prepared oratory was "interesting" because of the underlying tensions—"the anxiety of the Jews lest an Arab government should mean chaos, and their gradual reassurance, by reason of Faisal's obviously enlightened attitude."

The heavy Torah, encased in gold cylinders, was removed from the Ark and carried first to the Grand Rabbi, who kissed it, and then to Faisal, who repeated the gesture. Next, the future Emir was presented with a gold copy of the Ten Commandments and a beautifully bound copy of the Talmud. Gertrude leaned over to Faisal and whispered that she hoped he would make a speech. He hadn't meant to say much, he whispered back, but thought he must. "You know I don't speak like they do," he added. "I just say what is in my thoughts."

At the end of the ceremonies Faisal stood up. "There is no meaning in the words Jews, Muslims and Christians in the terminology of patriotism," he told the crowd; "there is simply a country called Iraq, and all are Iraqis. I ask my countrymen the Iraqis to be only Iraqis because we all belong to one stock, the stock of our ancestor Shem [Semites]; we all belong to that noble race, and there is no distinction between Muslim, Christian and Jew."

"He spoke really beautifully; it was straight and good and eloquent," Gertrude noted approvingly. "He made an immense impression. The Jews were delighted at his insistence on their being of one race with the Arabs, and all our friends . . . were equally delighted with his allusion to British support."

❧ ❧ ❧

As Gertrude celebrated in Baghdad, her father was suffering defeat. His attempts to boost the value of his business had failed, and now, after an exceedingly long coal miners' strike, he was heavily in debt to the banks. At the end of July she received a despairing note and wrote hurriedly to comfort him: "Darling Father. I'm sending you a letter by aeroplane in the hope that it will reach you in seven or eight days—just to feel as if you were so near instead of so far. Your letter of June 28th was rather despondent about the fortunes of the family, and indeed it's very hard that you should have fallen on such difficult times, but you will see it will work out all right, *inshallah*, just as I'm seeing our difficult task here work out in success. Anyway, dearest, don't bother too much about it—what happens, happens and we adapt ourselves to it. The only thing that matters is that you should be well and happy."

Sadly, the glory days of the Bell family were beginning to decline.

❧ ❧ ❧

A variety of groups was needed to form a consensus for Faisal. The Sunni townsmen, the Jews, the Christians and the Armenian orthodox were all important in Baghdad, the Kurds in Mosul and Kirkuk; but in the provinces it was the predominantly Shiite tribes that made up most of the population. Each tribal nation had to be approached and won over. Yet the very idea of a centralized state was anathema to them. Their major concern was the tribe. Their laws were the vengeful laws of the tribe, their leader the chosen head of the tribe, their immediate interest, grazing land for the herds of the tribe. They had no wish for borders, no respect for bureaucracy and no apparent need to be ruled by a king. Only a dynamic personality could convince them otherwise. Gertrude called on her friend Fahad Bey to organize an assemblage of two of the largest tribes, the Anazeh, who favored British authority, and the Dulaim, who preferred the Naqib.

At four o'clock in the morning of July 30, having already breakfasted and dressed, Gertrude quickly pinned on her hat, gathered her parasol and camera and, climbing into the large black Ford, gave crisp orders to the driver to speed toward the Euphrates: Faisal and his entourage had already left. Halfway to the river, her car caught up with his motorcade. As the driver pulled alongside Faisal's automobile, Gertrude shouted to him, asking permission to go ahead. She wanted to be in front so that when they arrived at the town of Fallujah, she could take their photograph. Faisal nodded, granting her request.

Crowds of howling horsemen lined the road for several miles. Fallujah itself was ablaze with flags, packed with people. She drove past the village and the shrieking mobs, continuing on toward the river. Scores of tribal horsemen encircled the motorcade, bellowing cheers, wheeling around the cars, kicking up clouds of dust. More tribesmen crammed their route as the cars wobbled along to the ferry, where they were greeted by the son of Fahad Bey.

A big black tent had been installed for Faisal to hold a *majlis*, a court to hear petitions, and after the Dulaim tribesmen came before him, a meal of chicken and rice was served. Then, while the cars were driven over a flying bridge, Gertrude and Faisal crossed the river by boat. Fahad Bey was waiting on the other side. "It was a great moment," Gertrude exulted. The Paramount Chief of the Anazeh had been "bitterly opposed to an Arab government" and was wary of giving his allegiance to the son of the Sharif Hussein; a man who had no desire to lose Britain's financial support, he had bowed to the Khatun's urging and was there to greet them.

As the motorcade drove away from the river and toward the desert, the fighting men of the Anazeh loomed in the sands in front: a phalanx of warriors on camels and horses, their flag held high, their rifles slung across their hips. The cars stopped, and Faisal saluted the forces, Gertrude doing the same. The Chief of the Dulaim, Ali Suleiman, came out to meet them and led them to another huge ceremonial tent, its walls covered with great boughs of fresh greens. Outside the two-hundred-foot-long black tent stood the Dulaim—hundreds of riders on horses and camels—and a single black-skinned man on a tall white horse, holding the standard of the tribe. Inside the tent were crammed four or five hundred more tribesmen. Faisal, in white robes and long black cloak, his flowing white headdress heavily braided with silver, was led to the front, where a dais had been installed. With Fahad Bey on his right and Gertrude on his left, he took his seat.

"I never saw him look so splendid," Gertrude exclaimed. "Then he began to speak, leaning forward over the small table in front of him, sitting with his hand raised and bringing it down on the table to emphasize his sentences. . . . He spoke in the great tongue of the desert, sonorous, magnificent—[there is] no language like it. He spoke as a tribal chief to his feudatories."

"Brothers!" Faisal's voice rang out in Arabic, "my word is yours and I deal with you as brother towards his brother, and as a friend towards his friend and not as a ruler towards his subjects. I am not a foreigner to you. You may accept my word in all confidence. I came to you knowing you to be Arabs and Bedouin, and for four years I have not found myself in a place like this or in such company." Iraq, he told them confidently, as though he had already been elected, was to rise to their endeavors with himself as their head. He slammed his hand on the table. "O Arabs, are you at peace with another?" he asked.

"Yes, yes," they shouted; "we are at peace. The truth, by God, the truth."

"From this day—what is the date?" he asked, "and what is the hour?" They told him, and he continued: "From this day and this hour of the morning any tribesman who lifts his hand against a tribesman is responsible to me—I will judge between you, calling your sheikhs in council. I have my rights over you as your lord."

"Yes, yes," they acknowledged, repeating the phrase. "The truth, by God, the truth." A gray-bearded man interrupted. "And our rights?" he called out.

"And you have your rights as subjects which it is my business to guard."

"Yes, yes!" the crowd shouted. "We agree. The truth, by God, the truth."

When he was finished, Fahad Bey, the Paramount Chief of the Anazeh, and Ali Suleiman, the Chief of the Dulaim, stood up. "We swear allegiance to you because you are acceptable to the British Government," they declared.

The words struck Faisal by surprise. Turning to Gertrude, he smiled and stated firmly, "No one can doubt what my relations are to the British, but we must settle our affairs ourselves." He looked at Gertrude again, and she held out both her hands, clasping them together as a symbol of the union of the Arab and British Governments.

"It was a tremendous moment," she recounted, "those two really big men who have played their part in the history of their time, and Faisal between them the finest living representative of his race—and the link ourselves." It was indeed a tremendous victory for Faisal and for Gertrude.

⊗⊗   ⊗⊗   ⊗⊗

After what now seemed a very short time—only five weeks of preparation—the coronation would take place. At the Cairo Conference it had been decided that Faisal's election would be held by the Constitutional Assembly; but fearing it would take at least three months to convene, and that the Kurdish provinces might vote against him, at Cox's will the Arab Cabinet of Ministers swiftly passed a unanimous resolution declaring Faisal to be King. Nonetheless, to show that this was a "free and fair election," a general referendum had been sent to the public. The question was asked: "Do you want Faisal to reign over you?" The answer was nearly certain.

The installation of Faisal was an event of momentous importance. Gertrude wanted him to understand not only the immensity of the occasion but its historical significance, its profundity of meaning. She had already spread before him maps of Iraq to give him lessons about the tribes. Now, like an eager teacher with her favorite pupil, she yearned to show the future King the greatness of his past. Much of her life had been spent among the ancient ruins of Mesopotamia, and she invited Faisal to join her for a visit to Ctesiphon. The grand palace, built in the sixth century A.D. by the Persian Sassanids for their leader Khosroes, was seized by the Arabs one hundred years later, its stones used to build the city of Baghdad.

On Tuesday, the second of August, Gertrude organized an early morning ride. Faisal, two of his aides de camp and Mr. Cornwallis joined her in their motor cars, and they set off before five A.M., stopping to breakfast along the way. Carpets were spread by the servants, china laid out for a picnic of eggs, tongues, sardines and melons, and they settled down, she in a silk dress and straw hat, Faisal in his army uniform. An hour's drive more, and they spotted the great arch of Ctesiphon; for nearly fifteen hundred years it had marked the site. Leading Faisal around the ruins, speaking to him in Arabic (as she almost always did), Gertrude expounded on the structure and how it was built, the rounded yellow brick vault still standing and, beside it, the massive brick arch. Vividly, she reconstructed the palace and showed him the figure of Khosroes sitting on the throne. She took Faisal to where the high windows that once existed faced the south and, pointing out the Tigris, told him the legendary story of the Arab conquest: legions of Muslim soldiers marching from Mecca to Iraq. "It was the tale of his own people," she wrote home. "You can imagine what it was like reciting it to him. I don't know which of us was the more thrilled." We shall make Iraq as great as its past, she promised the future King.

Almost deliriously, she continued in her letter: "Faisal has promised me a regiment of the Arab Army—'the Khatun's Own.' I shall presently ask you to have their colours embroidered. Nuri proposed that I should have an Army Corps! Oh Father, isn't it wonderful. I sometimes think I must be in a dream."

Nuri Said, Jafar Pasha's brother-in-law, had arrived a few months before. Although Jafar Pasha was likable, Gertrude had written, "he lacks force. He is naturally easy going, colossally fat, with a beaming smile. He responds at once to friendliness and sympathy, and at once gives you his confidence. The wonder is that a man of his mental and physical characteristics should be so ardent in his political convictions. But he doesn't carry over the footlights." Nuri Said was different. Noticeably slender and lithe, with keen gray eyes, he was quieter than Jafar, more percipient, a man of deep understanding and insight. She recognized instantly that he was "a strong and supple force."

The only disturbance now was Ibn Saud, who threatened Faisal's claim over the nomadic Iraqi tribes. He had sent a message to Fahad Bey, demanding the loyalty of the Anazeh, but the note had only angered the Paramount Chief. In the well-known way of the Middle East, "the enemy of my enemy is my friend," Ibn Saud had relied on tactics that forged an unexpected bond between Fahad Bey and Faisal.

At dinner a few nights later, Faisal turned to Gertrude: "I take witness in God, if we don't stop Ibn Saud, in three months' time there will be another battle at Ctesiphon like that which you described to me." Gertrude felt confident that Ibn Saud could be staunched. "We shall stop him," she said determinedly; "his claims are absolutely inadmissible." For the time being she could claim success; but the feud between the families would soon intensify. Indeed, it still surfaces in the tense relationship between the Hashemite Kingdom of Jordan, where upon occasion King Hussein has referred to himself as "Sharif," and the monarchy of Saudi Arabia, which has sometimes treated him with disdain.

By August 14, the referendum had been completed. Although some would argue that the negative votes were simply ignored and not counted, Gertrude felt vindicated. Faisal had won almost unanimously. As soon as the numbers were in, she dashed off a note to the Van Esses. "Faisal will romp on our shoulders!" she rejoiced.

The following week, after a round of calls with the towering Mr. Cornwallis, Gertrude left the office in the early evening to take some exercise. Riding along the river bank, she passed the new house being readied for the future King and spotted his car out front. She stopped and handed the reins of her pony to one of Faisal's slaves. The Emir was on the roof, she discovered, escaping the heat with some of his aides-de-camp. In the glow of the sunset, she looked out from the top of the house and could see the curves of the rocks just below, the groves of palm trees surrounding the town, the pink desert just beyond them. Faisal welcomed her warmly and she sat with the men and talked.

"Enti," Faisal said. "Enti Iraqiyah, enti Badawiyah." He paid her the greatest compliment. The Englishwoman who doted on flowery hats and fancy dresses, who gardened every morning and took tea every afternoon, who wore the honorary letters of C.B.E. and would inherit the title of Lady, who bore her heritage with regal carriage and had risked her life for the Empire, wanted more than anything to be accepted by this Arab Emir. Her own people had cast her aside; her personal life had shriveled into spinsterhood; her professional life had proved a lonely path. Most of the British men refused to see her as an equal, and the British wives returned her contempt in kind. But the Arabs had made her one of their own. "You're an Iraqi," Faisal had just told her lovingly. "You're a Bedouin."

The next evening Gertrude agreed to meet with Lady Cox and others to take a river launch to their favorite spot, near Faisal's new house. But when she arrived at the Residency, she found poor Lady Cox in a twitter. Sir Percy's mania for animals had gone too far. He was making a collection of Mesopotamian birds and his latest catch was an eagle. It wasn't the bird that upset Lady Cox; it was the food that it ate. The huge fowl existed on live bats and liked to eat them in the morning. Since the bats could be caught only in the dark, they were kept overnight in the kitchen icebox. When Lady Cox opened the icebox door, she found the faces staring at her.

Calming her down, Gertrude and the others set off with her on the river. As their boat landed, Gertrude noticed several people across the way: Jafar Pasha, looking fatter than ever in his Arab clothes; some aides-de-camp; and Faisal, regal and handsome, trailing his robes in the sand. With no room on the launch to change out of her swimsuit, Gertrude reported, she went to a "familiar dressing room in the willows above the sand." Walking back to the boat, her hair wet, her feet bare, she was "hailed to Faisal's dinner." She sat with the Arab men and talked until it was time to go back to her English dinner.

She added a fillip of gossip. "This is a secret," she scrawled; "there's a breeze on. The Colonial Office has sent us a most red-tapy cable saying that Faisal in his coronation speech must announce that the ultimate authority in the land is the High Commissioner. Faisal refuses and he is quite right. We are going—as you know—to drop the Mandate and enter into treaty relations with Mesopotamia."

∞   ∞   ∞

Nothing was as dreamlike as the day that thirty-six-year-old Faisal was crowned King. It was eleven years since Gertrude had attended a coronation, and from a seat in Westminster Abbey had watched in awe as the crown was placed on the head of George V. It was only a few months later, in the spring of 1913, that Gertrude had lost herself to the lusty Dick Doughty-Wylie. How many lifetimes ago that decade seemed. How different her life might have been if she had never gone to tea in the garden of his consular house in Anatolia, if she had never shared with him her secret ambitions to penetrate the East. But she had relished every moment, even quivering at the sight of his words on the written page. The pain of his death would never heal completely; it would remain a dull throbbing in her heart. If other men came into her life, they would never blind her with such a lightning charge. Yet as she sat now, in the front row of a coronation that she had orchestrated, another romance was slowly beginning to blossom. And even before that, like a schoolgirl with a crush, she was losing her heart to the King.

On Tuesday, August 23, 1921, at six A.M., when the air was not yet scorched by the burning sun, a crowd of fifteen hundred dignitaries— British and Arabs, Jews and Christians, townsmen and tribesmen, holy men and politicians—gathered in the courtyard of the riverfront Serai. Faisal stood in the distance, a somber commander in his khaki uniform and spiked helmet. Behind him stood High Commissioner Sir Percy Cox, tall and lean in his white diplomatic uniform bedecked with ribbons and stars; General Sir Aylmer Haldane dressed in his officer's whites; Faisal's Adviser, the towering Kinahan Cornwallis; and a phalanx of aides-de-camp. The procession marched down the steps of the splendid Ottoman building, parading along a path of Persian carpets spread on the ground, past the Dorset honor guard, and on to the dais in the center of the courtyard. The crowd rose as the honored group arrived, and once the royal entourage had reached their places, all the others took their seats. "Faisal looked very dignified but much strung up," Gertrude observed sympathetically. She was his mentor, he, her protégé. "It was an agitating moment. He looked along the front row and caught my eye and I gave him a tiny salute."

Sir Percy's proclamation, read in Arabic, announced that Faisal had been elected King by ninety-six percent of the people of Mesopotamia. "Long live the King!" the orator cried. Gertrude rose again with the crowd, and now, playing the role of subject, she grandly saluted her new master. The new national flag was hoisted beside him, and, with no anthem yet composed, the band played "God Save the King," followed by a twenty-one-gun salute. "It was an amazing thing to see all Iraq, from North to South, gathered together," she extolled. "It is the first time it has happened in history."

CHAPTER THIRTY-TWO

The King

∞

An extraordinary few weeks followed in the wake of Faisal's corona-tion. Like corks bobbing in on a sea of champagne, delegations organized by Gertrude pervaded the town. Only moments after the crowning ceremony, she returned to the Residency to find the cor-ridors swarming with turbaned men, some of whom she had never met before, others who had never been to Baghdad. From the Qadir Agha of Shush, huge and fat in his baggy striped trousers, to the ten-year-old Archbishop of the Nestorians, wearing a huge gold cross around his neck, to the religious leader of the devil worshippers, they thronged her chamber, eager to devour information about the new King. "Fun isn't it?" she asked her father, basking in the glow of her own success.

On Saturday of that first week, Faisal summoned Gertrude to a private tea. She spent "a happy hour" that day at the now-completed palace, a modest, two-story house close to the edge of the Tigris, where she and the King discussed a range of matters, from Ibn Saud's worri-some raids to the west and south of Iraq, to the new national flag of the country, to the personal flag of the King. "We arranged provision-ally this," she wrote to Hugh, drawing a sketch on her note; "the Hejaz flag with a gold crown on the red triangle. . . . Do for heaven's sake tell me whether the Hejaz flag is heraldically right. . . . Also whether you have a better suggestion for Faisal's standard."

They had become the closest of friends, the dark-skinned, black-bearded Arab Emir and the pink-cheeked, blue-eyed British lady, and while the charming King enfolded her in his flowing robes, the imperial Englishwoman protected them both with her parasol. Calling her constantly to the palace, he complimented her on her gowns and confided in her his deepest fears. He consulted with her on the settlement of tribal feuds (between the Anazeh and the Shammar), took her advice in choosing the members of his inner council, and depended on her to arrange the palace household. They picnicked, played tennis, attended the races, swam and took tea. And while a few flirtatious giggles passed between them, they spent most of their time working together to build a state.

"The week has been entirely occupied with subterranean agitation over the forming of the new Cabinet," Gertrude reported to Hugh at the beginning of September 1921. "These first appointments are of extreme importance to Faisal because he will be judged by them. If he puts in figureheads, just because they are known to be safe men and loyal to us, all the ardent people," she acknowledged, "will say the new Cabinet is a farce and Faisal not a King but a puppet of the English. On the other hand," she recognized, "it should be staunch and steady."

The choice of Cabinet members caused chaos in the ranks. British bickered with British, Arabs argued with British, and Arab nationalists, Shiite extremists and pro-Turkish politicians vied with one another for positions in the government. After her longtime friend the Naqib accepted the job of Prime Minister, and Jafar Pasha, Nuri Said and Sasun Effendi took their respective posts, the King conferred with Gertrude on the Minister of the Interior, "vacant," she noted, "since Talib was bundled out." They debated over Naji Suwaidi, well meaning enough for her and Mr. Cornwallis, but too unsteady for Percy Cox, and settled on Taufiq Khalidi, clever and well educated, but too pro-Turkish to have the complete confidence of Faisal. One of the leading pro-Turkish sheikhs was urging an uprising in the name of Islam.

With a beady eye on the proceedings of the Arab Government, she took charge of appointing the right man to be Treasurer to Faisal's household and, without mentioning it to anyone but Cox, added a new portfolio, Ministry of Health, supplying a Christian physician from Mosul at its helm. "I must tell you in confidence that he is my appointment," she revealed to Hugh; "everyone is delighted, but they don't know it was I who did it."

Her plans for Iraq were nothing less than grand. At tea with the King, in the reception room of the palace, she showed him first some photographs she had taken of him at a picnic, and then pulled out a map of Syria from *The Times*. Placing it in front of the monarch, she pointed out how the French had cut up the country into provinces.

"By God, it's forbidden," the King said scowling, swearing over the maps.

"There is only one hope for Syria," Gertrude responded, knowing full well that Faisal still dreamed of ruling Damascus; "that we should sit quiet here and do our own job." She turned to Jafar Pasha and Nuri Said, who had just arrived, and explained. "When we have made Mesopotamia a model state, there is not an Arab of Syria and Palestine who wouldn't want to be part of it. Before I die," she vowed, "I look to see Faisal ruling from the Persian frontier to the Mediterranean."

To some, her endeavors appeared the efforts of a generous friend; to others, the hateful symbol of British imperialism or, worse, those of a female puppeteer pulling the strings behind the throne. But whatever their feelings, British and Arabs alike were calling her "the uncrowned queen of Iraq." Faisal's coronation was her own crowning achievement. Catching the attention of journalists, her name spread like a sandstorm around the world, from Arabia to Europe to America. Yet when, in July, an American newspaper published an article trumpeting her power, Gertrude winced, calling the publicity "unspeakable."

"MESOPOTAMIA'S UNCROWNED QUEEN," shouted the headline of the *New York Herald*:

> Miss Gertrude Bell, Called Blessed by the Natives and All Wise by Downing Stret, Gives Invaluable Aid in Problems Arising from Mandate—English Ironmaster's Daughter, Famed for Explorations and Later for First Line Service in War, Carries White Man's Burden without Loss of Feminine Charms.
>
> As "El Sitt," "The Woman," every Arab in the peninsula knows her. When you speak of "Gertrude" every Englishman from Cairo to Teheran knows whom you mean. And if he knows that middle eastern land too, that cradle of the race, he calls a fervent blessing on the name.
>
> For in the Colonial Office in London, and in Baghdad, where Sir Percy Cox is trying to impose that newest fangled of Occidental governmental devices, the mandate, upon the oldest of all lands, she is the uncrowned Queen of Mesopotamia. She is Miss Gertrude Bell.
>
> Bedouin sheiks and Bedouin beggars bless her—and call her wise. Learned university gentlemen who delve in the glories that were Sideon [sic] and the pomps that

were Tyre admire her—and call her wise. People who design and sell the loveliest and the smartest of frocks in Hanover Square and the Rue de la Paix gladly give her of their best and call her wise. But when the tangled skeins of middle eastern affairs become inextricable at the nerve centre of the British Empire in Downing Street, they call in "Gertrude" and know that she is all-wise.

∞   ∞   ∞

"Impertinent balderdash," Gertrude retorted. "It's not true that I've determined the fortunes of Iraq but it is true that with an Arab Government I've come into my own. It's a delicate position to be so much in their confidence."

She had become the subject of an Arabic children's rhyme:

> "*Miss Bell*
> *Rikbat trambell*"

they chanted as they skipped down the street;

> "*Miss Bell*
> *Rode in a motor car*"

Their parents made their own verse:

> "*Miss Bell dhirtat fi al dira*
> *W'al hakim dhiay'a tadbira,*"

commenting on her political power;

> "*Miss Bell farted in the district*
> *And the high official lost his bearings.*"

"One of the reasons you stand out so," Nuri Said told Gertrude as he rode beside her on horseback, watching her return the salutes of villagers, "is because you're a woman. There's only one Khatun," he explained. "It is like when Sidi Faisal was in London and always wore

Arab dress, there was no one like him. So for a hundred years they'll talk of the Khatun riding by."

"I think they very likely will," Gertrude remarked.

The telephone rang in her office later that September day, the voice on the other end asking her to dine with the King. Two Arab Ministers were already invited to her own house, but she called them quickly to cancel. "I think it's best to treat Faisal's invitation as commands," she observed.

Dressed for the evening in her cloak and gown, Gertrude motored to the east bank of the Tigris and drove through the sandy entrance of the small brick palace. Curtsying, as always, before the King, she joined his three Arab guests. After dinner Faisal asked her to sit with him outdoors. On the balcony overlooking the river, the two friends smoked their cigarettes and spoke about the future. Thanks to a talk earlier in the day with Nuri Said, Gertrude now understood the sadness in Faisal's face.

The object of scorn as a child, Faisal had suffered the unhappy fate of being a middle child. Squeezed between his brothers Abdullah and Ali, he had been derided, not only by them, but by his mother. After she died, Faisal became close to Zaid, the child of his father's second marriage, creating even more of a gulf between him and Abdullah and Ali.

Faisal's personality, calculating and profound, stood in sharp contrast to Abdullah's candid, straightforward character. When Abdullah wanted something, he made it clear. But Faisal kept his intentions hidden and bore a *gravitas* that made him seem older than his years. It would be said later that when Abdullah died at the age of seventy, he looked fifty, but when Faisal died at the age of fifty, he looked seventy.

Now, as King of Iraq, Faisal was the target of of Abdullah and Ali's envy. Feeling alienated and alone, and worried about troublesome signs in the country, he could hardly ignore the shadowy fact that it was also the middle of Muharram. Every night processions of black clothed Shiite figures marched through the streets, pounding drums, swinging chains, beating their backs in mourning for Faisal's ancestor, the Prophet Muhammad's grandson Hussein.

The King unlocked his heart to Gertrude. Like a wounded bird, he appealed to her nurturing soul. She had urged him to bring his wife and children from the Hejaz to Iraq, but he was nervous, he said, "so uncertain of the future." He had not yet won the loyalty of the people, he confessed; large portions of the country seemed to be wavering back toward the Turks and their reformist leader, Kemal Atatürk. Lighting another cigarette, he went on. He was eager to sign a treaty with Britain granting protection to Iraq, but he had no idea what terms the British would insist on or whether he could accept them. On the other hand, pressure was growing from extremist nationalists to break the status of mandate. "The truth is," Gertrude had told her father a few days earlier, "there is very little real patriotism in this country and won't be until people see that the Arab Govt, *with us behind it*, isn't going to come to grief. Meantime there is a considerable population of asses who conceive that they'll either manage the show or overturn it. They can do neither."

But for now, she reassured the King, there was no reason to be anxious. We might be thankful for Your Majesty's winning personality, and why, she added coyly, doesn't Your Majesty use it more?

Yes, he replied eagerly, he wanted to be more in touch—should he not have little dinner parties? he suggested. But whom should he ask?

She would draw him up skeleton lists of dinner parties, English and Arab, she promised. He mustn't mind if they were boring, she warned. "The notables here mostly are boring, but the more you know them the better you like them."

"*Wallahi!*" he burst out enthusiastically; "you're the mistress of the house—ask whom you think best."

"It looks as though I shall run the Court till it gets on its feet," she remarked the following morning as she arranged for a series of dinners. She sent off invitations to be printed, instructed the staff on how to fill in the lines and showed them how to address the envelopes.

On October 2, a dozen guests, half of them Arab, half of them British, arrived at the palace for Faisal's first official dinner. Under Gertrude's watchful eye, servants poured champagne into the proper glasses, and the aides-de-camp moved people around so that everyone had a chance to talk to the King. She declared the evening a great success and Faisal a charming host, but it had taken enormous preparation and more than a bit of coaching to pull it off.

As comfortably as she fit into the shoes of mistress of the Arab palace, Gertrude herself was struck by the oddness of it all. It was as though she had been transformed from a girl in a Yorkshire garden to a princess in the East. She compared her background to Faisal's and to that of her landowning friend Faiq Bey: "I sometimes think how curious it all is, whether it's Faiq Bey or King Faisal. People whose upbringing and assocations and traditions are all so entirely different, yet when one is with them one doesn't notice the difference, nor do they. Think of Faisal, brought up at Mecca in a palace full of eunuchs, educated at Constantinople, Commander-in-Chief, King, exile, then King again; or Faiq, tending his palms and vines, and jogging into Baghdad to seek out the best market for his dates—and both of them run out to greet me with outstretched hands and then sit down to tell me in their several fashions what they make of life, as if I were a sister. And I feel like a sister, that's the oddest part."

❦   ❦   ❦

Sister, daughter or lover, associate or friend, it was to men that she swore her allegiance. She "was always the slave of some momentary power," T. E. Lawrence later wrote with hubris; "at one time Hogarth, at another Wilson, at another me, at last Sir Percy Cox." It was men who appreciated her political skills, respected her keen intellect and admired her commanding personality, and she, in turn, appreciated, respected and admired them. And if her sharp tongue and impatience intimidated some of her colleagues, so be it. But with rare exceptions, she had little regard for their wives, and they felt the same about her. The women's superficial interests, she believed, were equalled only by their deep suspicion of anything strange. Her one good friend, Aurelia Tod, who was Italian, had moved away, and the only other person she felt close to was Haji Naji. The kindly Shiite who sent her baskets of fruits and flowers was "an odd substitute for a female friend, but the best I can find," she confessed. "That's partly why I talk so much in my letters!"

At a fancy dinner with Arab magnates, given at the British Military School, Gertrude chatted with her friends Haji Naji, Nuri Said and Jafar Pasha, but out of the corner of her eye she inspected the women up and down. Lady Cox was a "model of discretion," she observed, but Mrs. Slater's brilliant green-and-gold gown, cut sleeveless and "outrageously low," sent Gertrude rushing off to curse privately in Sir Percy's ear. "I do wish that our women would show some suitability in their attire," she sniffed. The venerable Arabs' conception of female dress "is that it should leave no female visible," she wrote home. "I hope that Sir Percy will send out a sumptuary order . . . but not in my report—I don't want to antagonize the whole feminine world, with which I stand badly enough already, damn women!"

Like a chef in a Middle East kitchen, she stirred up a pungent stew, pouring in a mélange of spicy intrigues and, every so often, taking a spoonful of tantalizing power. In her own home, Arab politicians, British officials, and visiting writers like John Dos Passos of the *New York Tribune*, came regularly to dine. She still had her Tuesday teas for the Arab women, and with great sympathy for some, she still paid calls on the harems. After visiting the home of Daud Bey, "a worthless vicious man who spends all his money on dancing girls," she came away in a fury. A popular figure among the British officers (due to his skill at polo), Daud was a far less popular man in his own home. Although by Muhammadan law the women in his family had a right to a share of his property, he refused to give either his mother or his nine beautiful sisters any money to spend. After hearing the women's story, Gertrude summoned Daud. He cringed and bristled as she told him what she thought of him, but to her satisfaction, he eventually caved in. "Muslim women who never go out of the house and see no one are absolutely helpless in the face of their menfolk," she chafed, "and there's such a feeling against interfering in a man's domestic affairs that no one does anything to help. I am in the strong position of being a woman so that I can go and see the women and take their part. But how I do hate Islam!"

Not all her visits to Arab women were gloomy. She enjoyed showing them how to dress in the European style, and once in a while she took it upon herself to teach a child, such as the daughter of Musa Chalabi, to read English, or to train some youngsters to sing. Gathering them together in a quivering chorus, she pounded out the melody on an old piano. "Open those mouths! Exaggerate the sounds! Louder! Louder!" she ordered. And standing like shaking leaves, the Arab children sang out "God Save The King."

∞ ∞ ∞

Gunshots in the north soon shattered the autumn air. Promises had been made to the Kurds that a republic would be established after the war, but with no formal treaty yet signed between Britain and Turkey, Kurdish activists were inciting their tribes to rebel. The Sunni Kurds made up one fifth of the Iraqi population, and if the new state of Iraq was to succeed, Gertrude believed it had to include the oil-rich region of Mosul and the grain-growing areas of Tikrit and Kirkuk. Nor could an independent Kurdistan survive; economically, the Kurds could not afford to exist alone and the British could not afford to defend them. "We haven't a penny to spend in furthering Kurdish independence," she insisted, "for if we encourage them we shall only have to abandon them in the hour of need, which would be the worst thing possible."

In October 1921, after Faisal made a tour of the Mosul area, he came back to Baghdad convinced that he had won the loyalty of the Kurds. "On both sides a feeling of personal confidence has been established," Gertrude wrote to her father. "That's exactly what one wants to see, the establishment of mutual confidence between the King and his subjects."

But an international conference was soon to be held in Lausanne to settle the issue of Mosul, and once again the natives started skirmishing. Pro-Turkish Kurds were trying to reclaim the territory for Turkey before the meeting took place. As an ethnic (non-Arab) group, the Kurds felt more allied to Persia and Turkey, with their large Kurdish populations, than to Iraq and its Arabs. Yet as Sunni Muslims, they were essential to Faisal's kingdom, helping to balance the scale with the Shiites.

Smelling trouble, on November 3 Gertrude took the train north. "Kirkuk," she said, "has refused rudely to swear allegiance to Faisal." Half its population was Kurdish and the other half Turkish and, the latter wanted to restore their ties to Turkey. But, she noted, "since Kirkuk is in the middle of Iraq, [it] can't be countenanced." She would brook no nonsense, and urging Sir Percy to send a message to the instigators, she advised: "We must regretfully inform them that if they come they'll have the warmest welcome they ever met with. The guns they've heard; the Levies are ready and behind them aeroplanes enough to obscure the light of the sun."

Adding to the instability in Iraq was the dispute over the southern border. After years of menacing raids, Ibn Saud had finally struck and captured Hayil, the home of Ibn Rashid. Angry Shammar tribesmen stuffed their camel bags with revenge as they fled north, seeking refuge with the Anazeh. Border raids blazed the sand as Ibn Saud threatened not only Faisal in Iraq, but his brother Abdullah in TransJordan and his father, Sharif Hussein, in Mecca. "The underlying bitterness between him and the Sharifian family baffles description," Gertrude observed.

Sir Percy Cox wanted a conference to clarify which tribes and lands belonged to Ibn Saud in Arabia and which to Faisal in Iraq. The frontier still needed to be clearly defined, and Gertrude spent time poring over a map, plotting the water wells claimed by the Shammar and those claimed by the Anazeh, drawing the boundary lines with Arabia. Seated beside her in the office were an Arab from Hayil and her favorite chieftain, Fahad Bey: "The latter's belief in my knowledge of the desert makes me blush," she chirped. "When he was asked by Mr. Cornwallis to define his tribal boundaries all he said was: 'You ask the Khatun. She knows.' "

She stood at the pinnacle of her power. Yet as she peered out at the lofty vista, she could feel the earth beneath her beginning to slide. "I think I have been of some use here but I suspect I've come very near the end of it," she confided to Hugh. "I often wonder whether I am right to stay here." For the moment, however, she faced an enormous amount of work. A treaty of alliance between Britain and Iraq remained to be signed, but the issue of the mandate smeared the paper.

The British tied the treaty to the mandate they had received from the League of Nations; the Arabs saw the treaty as a means of breaking the humiliating mandate. Winston Churchill, then the Colonial Secretary, intended to hold on to British influence as long as possible, and the treaty was a subterfuge for keeping control. The pact would give the British almost complete authority over the financial and foreign affairs of the infant Iraqi state. But to the Arabs, the treaty represented a way of breaking loose, of gaining their honor, of restoring their pride, of establishing their independence. As King, Faisal intended to make Iraq an equal of England. If and when a treaty was signed, he wanted it to supersede the mandate.

Encouraged to seek independence by the United States, which had never recognized the mandate and wanted, in part, to reap its own financial rewards from the Arabs, the Iraqis would put up a strong fight against the mandate. "Oil is the trouble of course—detestable stuff," Gertrude complained.

The path was hardly smooth, she wrote to a friend: "You know well enough that to travel along any oriental road at present is a breathless adventure. The worst stumbling blocks are however of our making—broken promises, impossible and therefore unratified treaties, mandates. It's the last which touches us most here.

"From the very beginning," she explained, "the King told us with complete frankness that he would fight the mandate to the death. His reason is obvious. He wants to prove to the world of Islam which is bitterly anti-British that in accepting the British help he has not sacrificed the independence of an Arab state—that he has gained that which he has already told the world he could gain through free and equal alliance with us."

A thorn in everyone's side, the mandate nettled the feelings of Iraqis and British alike, causing the entire relationship to come into question. As confidante of the King and close adviser to Cox, the Khatun was entrusted with the secrets of both. But when her love for Iraq clashed with her pride in the Empire, she remained on the side of her motherland, England. Despite her objections to the mandate, she recognized the need for British officials to toe the line. "We had no alternative," she acknowledged. "We have told the King that under our instructions we must point out to him that he has only two courses. One is to reject the treaty with its underlying mandate, in which case we go; the other is to accept it and with it our help."

Whatever rumblings shook the ground between Iraq and Britain, for now the bond between Gertrude and Faisal remained strong. "I can't tell you how delightful our relations are," she wrote glowingly, "an affectionate confidence which I don't think could well be shaken. He usually addresses me with 'Oh my sister' which makes me feel like someone in the *Arabian Nights*. He is of course an exceptional beguiler—everyone falls under the charm—and his extremely subtle and quick intelligence is backed by a real nobility of purpose of which I'm always conscious."

Chatting one afternoon with the King, Gertrude let drop that she planned to go home the next summer. "You're not to talk of going *home*," Faisal replied severely; "your home is here. You may say you are going to see your father." Despite his sharp tone, his words pleased her; her fear of not being needed seemed premature. And adding color to her blush was the budding of a new romance.

Chapter Thirty-three

Ken

∞

A man of Olympian height, with an outsized nose and piercing blue eyes, Kinahan Cornwallis had the strong looks and keen mind that Gertrude found attractive. Like her, he had been at Oxford, making his mark in athletics as well as in academics, and like her, he had been attached to the Arab Bureau, serving first as liaison to the Sharif Hussein and his son Faisal, and then as chief of the Cairo Intelligence office. He spoke in a slow, gruff voice, exhibited a quiet manner and evidenced a leadership that inspired trust. He was "forged from one of those incredible metals with a melting point of thousands of degrees," Lawrence described him; "he could remain for months hotter than other men's white-heat, and yet look cold and hard." For Gertrude, he was "a tower of strength and wisdom," who bore the triumph of the Arabs over the Turks, of practicality over pipe dreams, of wisdom over whim. If she was the romantic breeze, he was the steady rock.

Personal Adviser to the King and Chief Adviser in the Ministry of the Interior, Kinahan Cornwallis was the only other British official besides Gertrude in whom Faisal had great confidence. The two had been placed side by side, supporting stakes behind the sapling King.

"He seems to me so wise and unacademic in his appreciation of the Arab point of view," Gertrude wrote in describing Cornwallis to

Hugh. "I hope it's not because he and I see eye to eye that I rate his discernment so highly!" Thousands of miles from his wife and children, he had separated himself from his family, not just by geographic distance but by environment and emotion. As it had for Gertrude, Iraq had become the central place, the central point in his life. Peering together through the same camera lens, she and Cornwallis focused on a similar picture.

On an afternoon when she invited him to tea, Gertrude sought his advice. Should she stay on in Iraq? she asked him anxiously. Sir Percy would be retiring in a year; after that, what role did he think she would play? And would she have a role at all? she wondered. Cornwallis replied in a steady voice, his calm demeanor a rock for her to lean on. They were the only two people in the foreign service of Iraq who had no ulterior objective, he said. Nothing but real necessity ought to call her away. Cheered by his confidence, she put aside her fears and finished her tea.

✆ ✆ ✆

A gloomy letter from England about her father's declining fortune, and a bout of appendicitis suffered in Baghdad by Faisal, gave a damp start to the year of 1922, but the knowledge that her job was secure, at least until Sir Percy retired in 1923, and that she had the intimate confidence of Faisal and a growing friendship with Cornwallis, kept her spirits buoyed. By early spring her garden bloomed with daffodils, marigolds and wallflowers, her cook was serving up platters of ripened truffles and her wardrobe was replenished with new dresses and cloaks from home. And in February a parcel from England landed on her desk, and when she quickly tore it open, a diamond tiara rolled out. "I nearly laughed aloud," she wrote to Florence, "it was such an unexpected object in the middle of the office files. But it's too kind of you to let me have it. I'd forgotten how fine it was. I fear in wearing it I may be taken for the crowned Queen of Mesopotamia."

To Hugh she wrote euphorically: "I want to tell you, just you, who know and understand everything, that I'm acutely conscious of how much life has given me. I've gone back now to the wild feeling of joy in existence—I'm happy in feeling that I've got the love and confidence of a whole nation, a very wonderful and absorbing thing—almost too absorbing perhaps. You must forgive me if it seems to preoccupy me too much—it doesn't really divide me from you, for one of the greatest pleasures is to tell you all about it, in the certainty that you will sympathise. I don't for a moment suppose that I can make much difference to our ultimate relations with the Arabs and with Asia, but for the time I'm one of the factors in the game." She did not mention Cornwallis, but his affection underscored her joy.

Thinking back to the lost opportunities for marriage and children, she added pensively, "I remember your saying to me once that the older one grows the more one lives in other people's lives. Well, I've got plenty of lives to live in, haven't I? And perhaps, after all, it has been best this way. At any rate, as it had to be this way, I don't now regret it."

∽   ∽   ∽

Neither the Cabinet's dismissal by Faisal, who had lost his patience with all the Ministers, nor a suspicious meeting in Karbala of the sheikhs and holy men, could shake her spirits. Her father was coming out to Jerusalem, and on the morning of April 29, 1922, Gertrude drove to the Baghdad airstrip. Skirting the rules against female passengers— "I'm an officer and I'm sexless,"—she climbed aboard one of the two British air force mail planes flying to TransJordan. From there she had hoped to travel with Hugh to Damascus, but the situation had become too dangerous. Even the flight to Amman was risky, she explained. "It's clear that any journey of mine in Syria would be classed in their Criminal Investigation reports under the heading of Movements of Suspects. . . . Anyway I expect Father and I will be happy even if he has to come and hold my hand while I'm sitting in gaol!" Ironically, it was near Amman that the Turkish authorities had tried to stop her in 1914 on her way to Arabia, the very trip that had led to her imprisonment in Hayil and to her Intelligence work in Iraq.

After three weeks of travel through TransJordan, Palestine and Lebanon, Gertrude took leave of her father and headed home. On the six-hour flight to Baghdad, while the plane, battered by a north wind, sped at one hundred miles an hour, Gertrude stared out the window, following tire tracks in the sand, keeping count of the landing sites so that she would know where they were. "I fear I've become the confirmed aviator," she announced after the plane touched down.

Faisal welcomed her back with an invitation to tea. Telling him what he wanted to hear, she reported how poorly the French were doing in Syria: their officials spoke no Arabic, had no personal relationships with the Arabs, and patrolled the streets with soldiers, "in deadly fear of an uprising." She was convinced that Iraq was "the only Arab province set in the right path."

The King asked her advice on an ultimatum he had received from

Churchill. The Arab Government must accept the fact that in order to have the treaty of independence, they would have to accept the mandate, Churchill said, even though it guaranteed British control. If Iraq refused to accept those conditions, the Colonial Secretary announced, the British would pull out by Christmas. There seemed little choice but to go along with Churchill's demands.

A short while later the King admitted that he owed his throne to the British and needed their protection; if they withdrew from Iraq, his Arab opponents would overthrow him. What's more, the country would be eaten alive, the carcass torn apart by townsmen, tribesmen, Shiites, Sunnis, Kurds and Turks all fighting for a piece of the territory.

Almost as soon as Faisal declared his consent, he changed his mind. Under pressure from the nationalists, he announced his willingness to sign the treaty, but only if it had equal status with, and was not subordinate to, the mandate. Iraq should be seen as an equal partner with Britain, he insisted, and he called for total abrogation of the mandate. But Churchill gave a brusque reply: Britain could conclude a treaty only with a mandate; that was the status given Iraq by the League of Nations under international law.

When a group of extremists held a demonstration against the British, Faisal refused to stop them, even showing support for the most radical of the nationalists. The Khatun had learned that, among his advisers, some had been trying to persuade him to declare himself an independent Islamic king; if he did, they assured him, the whole country would fall in line. Now he was succumbing to their advice. "The country will rally round him," Gertrude had written Hugh, "but not because of a sudden and miraculous change of heart. What is needed is several years of stability and decent government, not a miracle but a reward earned by steady work."

For more than a year she had struggled to make Faisal king, and now he was not merely destroying her work; he was destroying the special bond between England and Iraq. It was only with British support that Faisal could stay on the throne, and it was only through Faisal that the British could maintain their influence. Turning to Mr. Cornwallis, "her great standby," as she called him, she discovered that, like her, he too was "feeling bitterly disillusioned."

Distraught over Faisal's bias toward the extremists, she decided to tell him exactly how she felt. When an invitation came for tea on June 4, 1922, she put on her dress and hat and steeled herself for a confrontation. Waves of heat rose off the ground as she made her way to the palace, and on the streets, sweat poured off the brows of men and animals. In the whitewashed reception room of the King's house, the electric ceiling fans whirred with agitation. Faisal appeared, dramatic with his dark eyes and white robes, and when he welcomed her, she curtsied, but as she lowered her body, her eyes glowered angrily. Beneath the gracious formalities, she knew that Faisal knew how enraged she was. "I am playing my last card," she told him flatly. Did he believe in her personal sincerity and devotion to him? she asked.

He could not doubt it, he answered, because he knew what she had done for him during the past year.

In that case, Gertrude announced, she could speak with perfect freedom. "I am extremely unhappy," she said. "I had formed a beautiful and gracious snow image to which I had given allegiance and I saw it melting before my eyes. Before every noble outline has been obliterated, I prefer to go; in spite of my love for the Arab nation and my sense of responsibility for its future, I do not think I could bear to see the evaporation of the dream which has guided me day by day."

She had believed the King to be moved only by the highest principles, she asserted, but she saw him now as victim of every malcontent and every form of malicious rumor. He listened to men who, during the war, had betrayed the Arabs who served the British, giving their names to the Turks, and tomorrow, when the British left and the Turks returned, these same men would turn around and betray the Arabs who served under Faisal. The King responded by taking her hand and kissing it.

When they had taken their tea, the King explained his position. It was his task to reassure the extremists, he said; better to rein them in than to let them run wild. But, he reminded her, the British had consistently refused to recognize them. That made his task far more difficult.

She replied calmly that there was no reason why a *modus vivendi* could not be found; if only the King would lend his support to the mandate, they could live together in harmony. He would, Faisal finally said; he promised to try.

Pleased by what had transpired, Gertrude rose to leave, and taking Faisal's hand, she tried respectfully to kiss it. But the King demurred. Instead, with great affection, he embraced her.

"I'm still *sous le coup* of this interview," she wrote when she arrived at her house. "Faisal is one of the most lovable of human beings but he is amazingly lacking in strength of character. With the highest ideals, he will trip any moment over the meanest obstacle—he has hitched his wagon to the stars, but with such a long rope that it gets entangled in every thicket. You can't do anything with him except by immense personal sympathy—it isn't difficult to give it to him, but one must remember that he veers with every breath. I've left him tonight convinced that my one desire is to serve him; tomorrow he will be full of doubts. But at the bottom of his mind, with many deviations from the course, he trusts us and believes that one or two of us—Mr. Cornwallis and I and Captain Clayton for instance—would go to the stake for him and that's the strongest hold we have with him."

Two days later Faisal had veered back toward the extremists. "Oh the King, the King," she wailed. "If only he would be more firm. He is missing the opportunity of a lifetime—but what can one do?"

∞ ∞ ∞

A fortnight later, when another invitation arrived from the King, Gertrude grabbed the new parasol sent by her sister Elsa and, making her way to the palace, mulled over what she would say. Her worries were needless: it turned out to be "the most interesting talk" they had ever had.

Faisal's reluctance to accept the mandate stemmed from his sense of betrayal in Syria. The British had made great promises to him during the war: Damascus, the seat of early Muslim empires, of the Omayyads and the Mameluks, would be his to rule. Visions of Greater Syria danced before his eyes, a land that once stretched from the Taurus Mountains in Turkey to the Euphrates in Iraq, from Alexandria to Arabia, and included Jerusalem and TransJordan. But the British had let him down.

As Faisal described the whole background of his current feelings, Gertrude hung on his every word. With sadness in his eyes, he discussed the events of the Paris Peace Conference and his gradual understanding that even though England had made him promises, it would abandon him to France. He spoke of his determination to establish an Arab Government in Syria and how he was finally forced out by nationalist extremists on his own side as well as by the French.

"In my opinion," Gertrude responded, "there were scarcely words strong enough to express my sense of our responsibility for the Syrian disaster."

"You must remember," Faisal cautioned, his sorrowful eyes reflecting his disappointment, "that I stood, and I stand, entirely alone. I have never had the support of my father or my brother Abdullah. They were both bitterly jealous of the position which the successful issue of the Arab campaign had given me in Syria. When I was summoned to Europe after the Armistice, I was so conscious of their feelings towards me that I begged my father to send my brother Abdullah to Paris instead of myself. He refused but it was not because I had the confidence of my family. I have never had it."

He reminded her of the Arab conference in March 1920, when he was proclaimed King of Syria. "Do you realize why I encouraged the handful of Iraqis in Syria to nominate my brother Abdullah, King of the Iraq?" he asked. "I knew that the whole business was laughable, but I gave it my countenance in order to appease my own brother. He is as you know older than I am—I wanted to give him a status in the Arab world in order to disarm his hostility. He and my father never cared to accuse me of working solely in my own personal interest. What did it matter to me whether I or another was King of Syria? My task was to obliterate family dissensions and therefore I encouraged the nomination of my brother Abdullah to the Iraq. I knew that it was absurd."

But it was time to move on, he acknowledged. "I must form a new Arab ideal. Where shall I begin?"

"You must begin with Iraq," Gertrude answered.

She could not but feel sympathy for the man. Later she noted, "We betrayed him and he has not only forgiven the betrayal but has continued to trust us. It is a great deal more than we deserve."

Before Gertrude left the palace that afternoon, Faisal confided that he would never forget the gracious image she had drawn of snow; he did not want it to melt. If the British government gave him a treaty to which he could honorably (and that was the key) set his name, he would go ahead along the lines she suggested.

At the party in her garden that night, Gertrude moved happily among her guests, glittering as the lanterns she had strung through the trees. The draft of the treaty had arrived from London, and as servants passed coffee and ices, her Arab and English guests savored the terms. But the following day, when the document was presented before the Cabinet, the Ministers refused to approve it; it was all that she and Cornwallis could do to persuade them to continue the debate.

∞　∞　∞

The summer air was thick as a hornet's nest with controversy, the very word *mandate* stinging the Iraqi public. Once again the Shiite holy men called for an uprising against the British, and two Euphrates sheikhs who favored the mandate were murdered. In Baghdad large groups of notables visited the Naqib, warning him of shocking disasters if the treaty were accepted.

While the Cabinet Ministers argued heatedly over what to do, the

King came out clearly against the mandate. Even the British offer to help Iraq obtain a seat at the League of Nations once the treaty was signed did nothing to placate the Arabs' anger. Rumors spread that a large demonstration was being organized, and the foul smell of insur-rection grew stronger. The debate raged on and the King kept stalling, raising objections, until, after another week of hearing one exception after another, Cox disgustedly declared that no further alterations to the treaty would be allowed.

Through it all Gertrude consulted with Ken Cornwallis. The King had become their excuse for a flirtation, and they not only talked about the King, they swam together and picnicked on Sunday afternoons, laughed together over weekday lunches, confided over dinners and teas, shared stories, compared notes on Faisal's temperament, and agreed that, as much as the King embraced Ken, it was Gertrude's hand that he preferred.

But even Faisal's charm had its limits. Gertrude was livid at his double-dealing. Assuring her again and again privately that he was in favor of the treaty, he then did everything publicly to under-mine it. When she ran into Nuri Said, she told him how she felt. The attitude of the King was entirely indefensible, she scolded; she did not see how she could continue to confide in him. Early the next morning, on July 6, a message arrived inviting her to the palace for tea. She begged to be excused. But two hours later, after Ken Cornwallis phoned and urged her to go, Gertrude marched reluctantly into the palace.

The warm welcome from Faisal did little to calm the Khatun. She was in no mood to be disarmed. She had come against her better judgment, she announced, and for fifteen minutes they talked acrimoni-ously. She did not believe a word he said, she told him. But if she left him at that, she knew, she would never come back. "We had better find a *modus vivendi*," she finally said.

The King nodded in agreement.

Gertrude presented the evidence that showed his duplicity: al-though he had said he was for the treaty, he had deliberately worked to defeat its passage. Faisal admitted he "had worked and would continue to work against the acceptance of the principle of the mandate." The heated discussion went on. At last, after two hours, she rose to go. The King stood too, and taking her in his arms, he embraced her warmly. But it was a standoff: "We parted on rather unsatisfactory terms of close sentimental union and political divergence!"

Her only hope was that the British could persuade the King to go along with the treaty on the premise that, soon afterward, H.M.G.

would abrogate the mandate. Surely, Churchill could give this assurance privately to Faisal. "The mandate is tosh," she wrote home. "If we can't do that, hell will be let loose in Iraq, Faisal will lose his second throne, and where do you think he will find a third? At the moment," she confided, "I feel spiritually exhausted."

CHAPTER THIRTY-FOUR

Farewell to Cox

∞

For several more months in 1922 Iraq floundered in a sea of crises: Cabinet Ministers resigned almost as soon as their names were announced, and Faisal seemed to float along, oblivious of the danger of a teetering government, treading against the Naqib, swimming against the advice of the pro-British Nuri Said and nearly drowning in the clutch of the extremists. As fond as she was of the King, Gertrude felt that he might destroy both himself and the British with his fatal flaw. "The King is rather a beloved himself," she wrote. "Weak as water, he is full of the finest instincts. He reacts at once to everything that is noble and generous; he is naturally fine and discriminating; but he has the fatal defects of the Oriental—lack of moral courage and lack of intellectual poise; the latter, I suppose, a necessary corollary of ignorance . . . his indecision and cowardice may after all defeat us."

In spite of the dizzying pace of protests by the extremists and more waffling by Faisal, first to the side of the nationalists, then to the side of the British, the month of July ended on a satisfying note. Dining *en famille* with Faisal on her fifty-fourth birthday, Gertrude won the King's support for a law she had written to protect the country's archaeological excavations. Even better, Faisal agreed—with Cox's approval—to make her provisional Director of Antiquities.

Two weeks later, on Sunday the thirtieth, after receiving Arab guests at home, Gertrude set off for the weekly swimming party with Ken Cornwallis and their British colleagues Captain Clayton and the Nigel Davidsons (he, the new Judicial Adviser). This time, they were joined by Faisal. "The King was immensely pleased with himself," Gertrude noted. He had just bought a bathing costume, but she added with a scoff, "he's not much of a swimmer."

With fig trees for her dressing room, she stepped out of her jersey swimsuit to change into dry clothes, and munching a ripe green fig, she toweled her hair. Over a bonfire of palm fronds, the King's servants had roasted ten huge fish, surrounding them with an array of Syrian dishes. As the guests lay like the ancient Greeks on cushions plumped up on carpets that covered the grass, they ate by moonlight and chatted under the tamarisk trees. Faisal talked to Gertrude about his family, still living in Mecca, confiding his worries over whom his daughters would marry and how his son would be educated.

"It didn't seem at all fantastic in that setting of crescent moon and quiet river," she mused later, "but when I come to think of it, it is curious to be settling the family affairs of a descendant of the Prophet who is also King of Iraq." But her concern over losing influence still lingered. "I hope he'll go on being as devoted to me as he is now," she wrote nervously, "for it does make things easier to deal with. Mr. Cornwallis also—it's we two who ultimately guide him, and with him the destinies of the Arab world, if I'm not mistaken."

∞   ∞   ∞

On the first anniversary of Faisal's accession to the throne, in August 1922, the country remained deeply divided over the treaty. Gertrude believed the majority of the people still wanted the King to sign it. If Faisal rejected the pact, Gertrude felt they would push him to abdicate the throne. But she was equally convinced that even if he did accept the treaty, ultimately the British would be forced to evacuate. Either way, the British were doomed. The Cabinet had resigned in protest against the King's support for the Shiite extremists. Ten days later Gertrude remarked, "The Humpty Dumpty Cabinet is not up again yet, nor are the King's horses and the King's men going the right way to do it." The unending conflict permeated her thoughts.

On August 23, the day of the anniversary celebration, Gertrude set off, wearing her lace dress and parasol; meeting up with the uniformed Percy Cox, she motored with him in a procession to the palace. Several hundred people had already crammed into the royal courtyard, and as the two British officials plunged through the mob, a voice shouted something they could not quite hear. The crowd applauded, and although neither Sir Percy nor Gertrude could understand what was said, the air seemed to ripple with anger. Inside the palace, their audience with Faisal went smoothly; yet to add to their suspicion, the King was noticeably nervous. Later in the day, after querying her informers, Gertrude learned the mob had been part of a popular protest; the demonstration had been sanctioned by the King. "Down with the mandate!" was the cry that had been shouted in the courtyard. It was a slap in the face of the British Empire. Cox dashed off an angry letter, but a public confrontation was avoided; once again, appendicitis felled the King.

Faisal lay in bed, feverish and in pain, waiting for the doctors to perform an emergency operation. With the physician's permission, Percy Cox and Kinahan Cornwallis marched past the servants who guarded the door and entered the room where a crowd of slaves, armed and suspicious, hovered as they talked. The political position had grown so grave, the two men reproached the King, that repressive measures against the extremists were essential. Faisal must dissociate himself from the radicals and align himself squarely with the British camp. Begging him to agree, they asked permission to carry out the proper measures.

Faisal refused. If he did, he said, wincing in pain, the public would revolt. He knew how ill he was; he did not want to die with rebellion on his conscience. With that, the doctors took him away for the operation. It was none too soon. The appendix had abscessed; the King had been at the edge of death.

The extremists' stirrings had reached a danger point, bubbling too close to the sort of rebellion that had occurred in 1920. Sir Percy took no chances. With the King sick and ineffectual, the High Commissioner ordered the police to arrest the seven principal agitators, while he shut down the radical newspapers and outlawed their political parties. That evening he issued a communiqué: with no existing Cabinet, and the King severely ill, the High Commissioner was taking control of the government.

"It is Sir Percy at his best and you can't beat him," Gertrude cheered, noting that the effect was instantaneous. "Since the King couldn't summon up courage to come out into the open, his illness was beyond words fortunate. But Providence deserves comparatively little of the credit. Sir Percy has never made a mistake, either in resolution or in formulating his resolution."

The following week, when a visiting Arab writer came to her office and told her he had been to see the King, Gertrude unleashed her anger. Railing at Ameen Rihani, she spoke of the bitter mood between herself and Faisal. "I have worked very hard for King Faisal," she fumed, puffing furiously through her cigarette holder. "The tribes were against him, the chiefs would not vote for him. I argued with them. I persuaded them. I convinced them. I got them to vote for Faisal."

She rose from the white sofa and marched across the room, opening the casement windows to let in a breeze from the Tigris. Then, flopping down again on the couch, the Khatun continued. "Yes, indeed," she said. "I exerted every effort on his behalf. People said, 'This man is a Hejazi, a foreigner.' But I guaranteed him. I replied, '*Ana'l kafil*,' I am the sponsor. Believe me, Ameen Effendi," she implored, flattering her visitor by using the title Effendi, "I love Iraq almost as much as I love my own country. I'm an Iraqi, and I want to see the people of Iraq achieve their freedom and independence while helping us to promote at the same time the country's progress."

At a palace dinner a few nights later to welcome Faisal's brother Prince Zaid, who had just arrived from the Hejaz, the King tried to explain his own behavior. "Remember," he pleaded to Gertrude, "we have been slaves for six hundred years. The slave must protect himself by cunning. He is obliged to keep a foot in both camps—*hatta ana*: even I do it. We have not had centuries of liberty to train us to be free men."

When, at last, a promise came from Winston Churchill that he would do all he could to have Iraq admitted to the League of Nations, Faisal was joyous. He had received almost everything he had held out for. Admission to the League would mean the end of the mandate and recognition of Iraq as a sovereign state. On October 8, 1922, the treaty was finally signed. Now all that was needed was ratification by the national assembly.

∞ ∞ ∞

Early the same morning Gertrude joined the King and Cornwallis for a breakfast outing near Baquba. After picnicking at a long table under the fruit trees in Fakhri Bey's garden, she and Ken slipped off together to walk among the orchards, fertile grounds filled with vineyards and groves of oranges and dates. They watched the peasants gathering pomegranates, and they lay together on the river bank looking up at the poplar leaves against the sky. "As far as I was concerned, Fakhri's garden might well have been the gardens of paradise," she wrote later. They lunched with the King, nineteen regal courses, and in the afternoon she and Ken broke off from the others, just the two of them motoring home across the desert, putting up coveys of grouse and shooting them, laughing together when twice their tires were punctured. They returned to Baghdad just after sunset, "drunk with sun and air." It was years since she had described a day with a man so joyously. The languid pleasure of a picnic and the exuberant ride through the desert harked back to her youthful days with Henry Cadogan.

With more time now for socializing, she filled her calendar with dates with Ken Cornwallis and the King. Dinners and bridge games with Faisal (which he was always allowed to win), teas and tennis matches at the palace, races on Saturdays, rides through the palm gardens and, on Sundays, after a swim, intimate dinners at home with Ken.

There were her obligations as head of the Salam Library (she was, she noted, the only European ever elected); social calls on the Arab women, teaching them how to dress in fashionable French clothes; establishing an Iraqi branch of the Red Cross; and always more teas. Sati el Husari, chief aide to the Minister of Education, arrived with his wife and niece, and Gertrude welcomed them to her drawing room. Plopping a box of chocolates and some fashion magazines in front of her female guests, she quickly turned to talk to Sati. But after a while, his Turkish wife looked at her with disgust, and, to Gertrude's suprise, in fluent English announced, "The next time you want to talk to my husband, you don't need to invite me." With that, Gertrude apologized and turned more hospitable.

∞∞∞ ∞∞∞ ∞∞∞

Aside from her duties as the newly appointed honorary Director of Antiquities, her political workload declined. After a series of attacks by Kurdish rebels in the north, however, and counterattacks by the British air force, she set off to inspect the region. London was eager to solve the problem by creating a separate area of Kurdistan, but besides the fact that there was no defensible border between the two areas, "from the King downwards," she observed before she left, "we all know, as they know at home also, that the Arab state cannot exist without the northern province. Baghdad is too closely dependent on Mosul."

After investigating the situation among the local Armenians, Christians and Kurds, and after meeting with almost every important sheikh, holy man and notable, she returned to Baghdad on November 16, 1922, convinced that if the area was kept out of Turkish hands, the Kurds would become loyal citizens of Iraq.

The situation in Mosul was also of concern to Cox, but his long delayed border conference with Ibn Saud was about to take place, and by the time Gertrude came back to Baghdad, the High Commissioner was preparing to leave. She yearned to join him, but Ibn Saud had shown no fondness for her—too strong a woman for the chauvinist male—and for years Cox himself had nurtured the Arabian Sultan. Instead, it was Major Dickson and Major More, Sabih Bey, the Minister of the Interior, and Fahad Bey of the Anazeh who packed their dinner jackets and accompanied Cox as he set off on November 19 to sign a treaty.

Sir Percy had known Ibn Saud since the British official began his duties in the Gulf, and for eighteen years he had remained father figure, friend and financier to the Wahhabi leader. As Cox sailed toward Ojair, near Bahrain, Ibn Saud's slaves prepared for his arrival. Lavish white tents of various sizes were pitched in the sand for sleeping, bathing, dining and entertaining; thick carpets were laid, luxurious furnishings installed and ample supplies of fresh fruits, Perrier water, Cuban cigars and Johnny Walker Scotch were stocked for Kokus.

The negotiations over the boundary lines went on for five days and nights while Cox, dressed in his suit, bow tie and felt fedora, served as a mediator between the robed representatives of Iraq, Kuwait and Arabia. Ibn Saud demanded that the borders be based on tribes, not territory, and according to his scheme, two groups—Fahad Bey's Anazeh and part of the Shammar—would belong to Arabia, regardless of how far north they traveled. The two tribes would become a movable border, expanding and contracting, adjusting as they searched for grazing grounds; the border would change according to their nomadic needs. "East is East and West is West," Kipling had written, and the two were never farther apart. To Cox and the British, the notion of property revolved around territory, but for Ibn Saud and the Bedouin, the idea of property was tied to people.

No progress could possibly be made, and by the sixth day Sir Percy lost his temper. With only Major Dickson at the meeting, he berated Ibn Saud as if he were a schoolboy. At the rate that both sides were going, he told the perfumed Arabian ruler, nothing would be settled for a year. Ibn Saud was on the verge of tears; Sir Percy Cox was his father and mother, he cried, the one who had made him and raised him from nothing to the position he held. He would surrender "half his kingdom, nay the whole, if Sir Percy ordered."

With that, Sir Percy took hold of the map. Carefully drawing a red line across the face of it, he assigned a chunk of the Nejd to Iraq; then, to placate Ibn Saud, he took almost two thirds of the territory of Kuwait and gave it to Arabia. Last, drawing two zones, and declaring that they should be neutral, he called one the Kuwait Neutral Zone and the other the Iraq Neutral Zone. When a representative of Ibn Saud pressed Cox not to make a Kuwait Neutral Zone, Sir Percy asked him why. "Quite candidly," the man answered, "because we think oil exists there." "That," replied the High Commissioner, "is exactly why I have made it a neutral zone. Each side shall have a half-share." The agreement, signed by all three sides at the beginning of December 1922, confirmed the boundary lines drawn so carefully by Gertrude Bell. But for seventy years, up until and including the 1990 Gulf War involving Iraq and Kuwait, the dispute over the borders would continue.

∮ ∮ ∮

"Do you know," Gertrude wrote to Hugh toward the end of 1922, "a propos of nothing at all—that I've been four times mentioned in dispatches for my valuable and distinguished services in the files! It came to me as a suprise—indeed it is singularly preposterous—when I counted up the documents in order to fill up a Colonial Office Form. I hadn't realised there were so many." At a recent Arab ladies' tea party she had asked, "Who is the smartest lady in Baghdad?" "You, of course," the women replied, and her face beamed with pleasure. But as much recognition as she still received, Gertrude felt that her importance had already begun to diminish. By mid-December she had finished her yearly report for the Secretary of State, observing ruefully, "I seem to have done singularly little of interest." Her power lay in the strength of the British presence, and as the Arab Government took hold, her influence slipped even further. Although her friendship with the King continued, he no longer needed her as his liaison to the High Commissioner. Her role was changing from political counselor to personal companion.

A Christmas trip along the Euphrates with Ken Cornwallis and two other British officers served as a pleasant holiday respite, and, returning at the end of the month, she was not unhappy to find a pile of reports to write for Cox. "The fact remains," she stated, "that whatever I may do in the future, I shall never have a chief whom I serve more wholeheartedly than I serve him." Sir Percy was due to retire within a few months, but in preparation for that, he was returning to England to help conclude the government's peace with Turkey and its policy on Iraq. With the Turks threatening to invade, Cox was determined to see that Britain did not desert its friend. Britain had gone to Mesopotamia in 1914 to protect its oil fields, its trade and its interests in the Persian Gulf, Cox would remind the Cabinet committee, and if it withdrew from Iraq now, it might lose all that it had set out to preserve. "There is, remember, no defensible frontier between Mosul and Baghdad, and if the Turks take Baghdad will they not aim at taking Basrah too?" he would ask. "A bad peace will be more costly than our present responsiblities since it will compel us to take special military measures in our own defence."

∞ ∞ ∞

Before Cox left for England he appointed Henry Dobbs as his deputy, and in early January Gertrude gave a dinner at home to introduce Dobbs to her colleague Nigel Davidson, the Judiciary Adviser, and to her intimate friend Ken Cornwallis, the King's Adviser. The conversation focused on the Kurdish dilemma, which would continue long after the British left the scene. The Turks had denied the Kurdish claims for independence, while Faisal had indicated he would favor an autonomous Kurdish government within the boundaries of Iraq as long as the Kurds were tied economically and politically to Iraq (a position taken years later by Saddam Hussein). Faisal's words had served to quell the insurgents, but a few weeks later Dobbs, concerned about new attacks, sent troops to the northern border to discourage Turkish aggression, and the King sent his younger brother Zaid to set up a royal household in Mosul, hoping to win the Kurds to the Iraqi side. In the meantime, an international conference, convening in Lausanne, would take up the Kurdish claim to independence.

There was little that Gertrude could do about Mosul, and she turned her attention to archaeology. A group from Chicago's Field Museum had come to work at Kish, and a joint team had arrived from the British Museum and the University of Pennsylvania to excavate at Ur. As Honorary Director of Archaeology, Gertrude took great interest in inspecting the sites. The ancient Sumerian city of Ur, biblical birthplace of Abraham, had flourished nearly six thousand years earlier, and its mound would yield archaeological riches for years of digging to come. The excavation would produce every aspect of Sumerian life, from the ziggurats—the staggered staircased towers of 2000 B.C.—to the thin, curved canoes still being made to cross the marshes, to the most spectacular treasures in the Royal Tombs: golden statuettes, golden headdresses, golden daggers hilted in lapis lazuli, copper vases and cuneiform tablets. Seeing the excavation even in its early stages, she said, was the most thrilling sensation she had ever experienced in archaeology. Most important, under the law of excavation drawn up by Gertrude Bell, Iraq would be protected from being robbed of its ancient wealth.

In Baghdad that early spring, she busied herself with furnishings for the King's new palace and with receptions for Sir Percy Cox. He had pushed up his retirement to May, and although it was Ramadan, the month of April swirled with a rush of farewell parties. From Haji Naji to the King, from the Indian bazaar merchants to the Royal Air Force, everyone seemed eager to host an event for the High Commissioner. Finally, on May 1, 1923, the Coxes waved goodbye. It was a sad moment for Gertrude. "I'm rather overcome with departure," she confessed with a heavy heart. "Sir Percy left, a very moving farewell."

He had been the most significant figure in her life for nearly seven years; the Arabs thought the world of him and called him "foxy," but to her he was so much more; he was wise, caring and calm, a father figure and a friend, the one person in the East she could count on in troubled times. He understood her point of view, appreciated her tireless efforts, admired her abilities. He had accepted her when she first arrived in Basrah in 1916; welcomed her to join his office in Baghdad despite the objections of General Maude; relied completely on her Intelligence work with the Arabs during and after the war; defended her against A. T. Wilson's tirades; valued her knowledge of archaeology; and always, always treated her with respect. And she was devoted to him. "I think no Englishman has inspired more confidence in the East," she said. No Englishman except her father inspired more confidence in her. Her mentor had gone, and as Gertrude prepared warily for her own vacation at home, she felt unsure of the welcome she would receive when she returned to Baghdad in the fall.

CHAPTER THIRTY-FIVE

Troubles

∞

It was a smaller Rounton that Gertrude returned to in June 1923; not the omnipotent universe as viewed through a child's eyes, but the dwarfed and vulnerable world that an adult discerns. The shifting needs of twentieth-century industry, the great postwar Depression and the searing costs of labor strikes had taken their toll. The Bell family fortune was slipping away. In order to keep the costs down, part of the house had been closed off, some of the staff had been let go and a frugal accounting was being kept of all expenses. Gertrude's own world, too, was slipping away, and even as she sat for her portrait by John Singer Sargent or corresponded with T. E. Lawrence about the publication of *Seven Pillars of Wisdom*, she pondered her future. Percy Cox's retirement had left her feeling at loose ends. She had known his successor, Henry Dobbs, from the early days of the war when, as Revenue Commissioner at Basrah, he had shared her dislike for A. T. Wilson. But unlike Cox, Dobbs was neither her mentor nor a master statesman. Not that such a man was needed anymore in Iraq. The reins of government were resting more firmly in the hands of the Arabs.

Another matter also weighed on her mind. Her frequent dealings with Faisal had nudged her closer to his trusted adviser, Cornwallis. She and Ken sympathized with each other's frustrations and strategized over their plans. As they worked together in stride, pushing the King along the path to power, her admiration for Ken had begun to blossom into something more. His tall, lean frame, his moral strength, his gentle manner appealed to her sensibilities. She not only sought his advice; she yearned for his company and hungered for his love. At Rounton, strolling across the fields with a family friend, she compared Cornwallis to Doughty-Wylie. There would never be another man like Dick, she stressed, nor any correspondence that could ever soar to the level of passion theirs had attained. But Dick was gone; Ken was alive and vital. He was seventeen years her junior, and he had sparked the fire that lay in embers inside her.

∞ ∞ ∞

Henry Dobbs was pleasant and amiable, much easier to talk to than Percy Cox, Gertrude reported in September, soon after her plane touched down at Baghdad. "Yes, the atmosphere of the Residency has undergone a remarkable change," she noted. "If we haven't Sir Percy's wisdom, neither have we Lady Cox's folly and Sir Henry brings a geniality of his own. Sir Hon-ri, the Arabs call him."

Gertrude's life, too, was undergoing change. Instead of toiling for endless hours at the office, she fluttered around the palace arranging the English furniture she had ordered from London, despairing over the fake French antiques commissioned by someone else, still devising a heraldic coat of arms for the King. She hosted evenings for Ken or the King, fretted over Cornwallis's well-being and stood near Faisal as he cut the ribbon on the new train line leading to Karbala. She attended shooting parties and polo matches, engaged in tennis matches, bridge games, mah jong, chemin de fer, luncheons and teas, and shared dinners almost every evening with Ken. And when Ken moved into a new house, Gertrude spent the whole Sunday helping him arrange his belongings. "My existence is one of prolonged gaiety," she announced giddily at the end of November 1923.

Even Christmas, so often tinged with sadness, became a glorious time once again as she and Ken took off with friends for a week of hunting at Babylon. Before they left, the maid Marie, as she packed Gertrude's riding habits and evening clothes, insisted on including her prettiest pink crêpe de Chine nightgown. "But why?" Gertrude asked. "It's a shooting party." Yes, said her maid, but Ken's Sudanese servant would see them. Perhaps Marie thought he would describe the gown to Ken, or perhaps she thought there was something more; that not only his servant but Ken himself might see the nightgown. And then, after six days of relaxation and archaeological visits, Gertrude returned contentedly and announced, "I think no more delightful expedition has ever been made in Iraq."

Despite her cheerfulness, her waning power was evident, and indeed crudely described by a railway official. In a letter to St. John Philby, the functionary wrote: "Certain it is that the 'uncrowned queen' is no longer first and last in the land; just where she gets off is uncertain, unless in an advisory capacity of dishing out concessions to a bevy of tell-tale *tel* diggers from all continents and countries."

Unlike Cox, Dobbs neither asked for her advice nor allowed her to initiate actions on her own, and it wasn't long after her return from the trip that ennui set in. Her thoughts drifted back to the great civilizations of Mesopotamia and, daydreaming about a future empire ruled by Faisal, her attentions shifted again to antiquities. In early January 1924, when the dreaded cold weather had dampened her spirits even more, she sat in her office, shivering and wrapped in a fur coat, and fancied a visit to Kish and Ur. On the way down, she planned to take a jaunt by herself in the desert. "I want to feel savage and independent again," she declared.

The brief but adventurous journey revived her mood. She and her assistant, J. M. Wilson, had hardly driven very far when the front wheel of their car crossed over the edge of a narrow bridge and nearly fell into a canal. As they motored on, the car slid more out of control, and by the time they reached an open plain it spun around like a top. Her assistant refused to risk his life any further. It had started to rain, but she and Wilson pulled up their boots, plunged into the mud and, after trudging for more than an hour, reached the site of Kish. Mr. Mackay, the archaeologist, was waiting, and they spent the rest of the evening looking at his finds. With her baggage left behind in the car, she had only a cake of soap, a borrowed hairbrush and someone else's pyjamas. But it didn't matter. She went to bed in her tent and slept soundly, content to be in the desert.

The next day she set off on her own. Arriving at Warka, once the Sumerian city of Uruk, the Babylonian capital of the south, she found the archaeological mound thick with natives scavenging for treasure. Rounding up the Arabs, she asked sternly, amid their screams of fear, "Have you any *anticas*?"

"No," they answered, "by God, no."

"What are those spades and picks for?" she demanded to know. She would give them *baksheesh* for anything they had. The promise of money produced a marked change. One man discovered a cylinder hidden inside his shirt, another a seal, another a piece of terra cotta in his pocket. After paying a few *annas* for each, she took the objects for the museum.

∽   ∽   ∽

At her office, back in Baghdad, she marveled at a box from England delivered to her desk. There had been some difficult days, disagreements with Dobbs, who, she felt, had little understanding of the Arabs, and a package was a pleasant surprise. On slitting the cardboard open and sifting through the paper, she was delighted to find a silver frame with a photograph of Percy Cox. "To the best of comrades," it was signed. "Isn't that the nicest thing he could have written?" she asked. "I still miss him. We had worked together on and off for six years, and through difficult times. It had become a habit that he should always want to talk things over with me. Sir Henry doesn't always do that," she confessed; "there's no reason why he should. Often he does the thing first and then tells me about it." It was true that she lunched with Dobbs every day, but the conversation was light and frothy, hardly the meaty talks she had had with Cox.

∽   ∽   ∽

Just before she left again for Ur in March 1924, an American journalist came to meet her. Gertrude stood up from behind the mounds of papers piled on her desk, and with her willowy figure showing off a smart beige knitted dress, she reached out a manicured hand to say hello to Marguerite Harrison. Gesturing for the visitor to sit, she pushed away the stacks of documents covering the sofa and swept them onto the floor to join the overflow. Harrison looked around at the messy room, "the most untidy" office she had ever seen, its chairs, tables and sofa "littered with documents, maps, pamphlets and papers in English, French and Arabic." Yet Gertrude herself was as finely presented as a piece of Wedgwood china. "Her delicate oval face, with its firm mouth and chin and steel-blue eyes and with its aureole of soft gray hair, was the face of a grand dame. There was nothing of the weather-beaten explorer in her looks or bearing. 'Paris frocks, Mayfair manners.' And this was the woman who had made sheikhs tremble at the thought of the 'Anglez!'"

The writer had come for an interview, but Gertrude had her own agenda. Intent on extracting information, the Khatun fired one question after another to her about Turkey, from which Harrison had just returned after a six-month stay. Kemal Atatürk's intentions were still worrisome to Gertrude. What was Turkey's attitude about Iraq, Gertrude wanted to know. Officially? And unofficially? How did they feel about Mosul? What did they think about the internal situation in Iraq? What was the political situation like? Eager to hear more, Gertrude invited Harrison to dinner. Among the guests were Ken and a few officials, and as the hostess, in her blue velvet gown, presided over the elegant table with its linen cloth, its gleaming silver and sparkling crystal, the Baltimore woman told of her wild endeavors. "I never had such an uproarious dinner party," Gertrude wrote home happily; "extraordinarily amusing but the tales she told us . . . would make the hoariest official blush." She was glad to have good company, pleased to meet a female who equaled her in intellect and capacity for adventure.

Early the next morning Gertrude left for Ur. She was devoting more of her time now to her new museum, collecting ancient objects that gave credence to her dreams for a grand Iraq. The more proof she had of the achievements of the early Mesopotamians, the more she could substantiate her claims that Iraq would return to its former greatness. Archaeology meant tedious work, with hours spent in the broiling sun supervising the digs, examining even the most minuscule finds, but the ancient history of the country had captured her imagination. With the digging season at its end, she had, as Honorary Director of Antiquities, first rights to any treasures for the Iraqi Government. The process of dividing the finds began with the toss of a rupee, and Gertrude won a scarab, worth a thousand pounds. Among the larger pieces, she allotted the bronzes to the archaeologist Leonard Woolley but kept for herself an important bronze milking scene depicting early life in Mesopotamia.

She brought the booty to Baghdad and toiled with scholarly patience at the small museum—temporarily housed in a room at the palace—glueing fragments, cataloguing objects, identifying implements and overseeing people who had not the vaguest idea of what an archaeological institution was all about. On one occasion she found an old worker mending objects with plaster of Paris, drowning the ancient stone flower petals in the cement. Another morning, as she edited labels, she picked up a small marble fragment of a horse's neck and mane. Looking at the label she read: "This is a portion of a man's shoulder, marble object." She turned to the helper: "But does a man grow a mane on his shoulders?" she asked.

"True, by God," murmured the man.

Her eyes pierced him in disgust.

The museum was her creation, and she proudly brought anyone she could, from a former professor to visiting British officials to Arab Ministers, to admire it. When Woolley came to lecture on Ur in March 1924, she dragged along the King, translating for Faisal's uninterested ear every word the archaeologist uttered.

❧   ❧   ❧

The treaty with Britain still had to be ratified by the National Assembly, and the process was taking its toll. Sheikh by sheikh, sayid by sayid, the representatives of the entire country had to be persuaded to cast their approval. Tensions were running high, and the assassination of one representative in February did little to calm the air. Stormy debates continued through May 1924. At the start of the Id, the festival marking the end of Ramadan, Gertrude planned a holiday with the King's physician, Dr. Harry Sinderson; a colleague, Iltyd Clayton; and Ken. Their plan was to pitch tents near the stream at Qarashan, a junction point on the Diyala River, and for three days they would fish, swim, read poetry and play bridge. "The real reason for the scheme is Ken," Gertrude explained caringly, "so worn out and exhausted that I'm afraid if the acceptance of the treaty is delayed much longer he will break down." The respite was a success, but it took yet another month of arguing, until June, when, at the last possible moment, the treaty was ratified. "We beat Cinderella by half an hour," Gertrude announced.

She and Ken were almost always together now, he spending much of his time in her comfortable house, and the twosome celebrated the successful conclusion of their work, enjoying dinner and a quiet talk as they usually did before going to bed at ten. This was their last evening together before he took off for a difficult summer in England. His wife was filing for divorce and Gertrude shared his apprehension. Scrawling a hasty note to her sister Molly, she asked her to please look after Ken. "I have a very great affection for him and I think him one of the finest creatures I've known," she wrote. Would Molly invite him to lunch? she begged. "What a blessing it is to have a sister of whom one can ask anything. . . . I really think that except fathers, sisters can be the greatest gift in the world." She had omitted mothers from her list, but nonetheless she remembered to send off another shopping request to Florence. Among her recent needs: a tussore-covered sun helmet, a blue-ribboned straw hat for the morning, a dark-colored bathing dress, a few yards of lace and three pairs of brocade mules from the Galeries Lafayette—"not for riding, for wearing on the feet."

❧   ❧   ❧

The torpid heat of July smothered the city. Gertrude spent an "infernal" fifty-sixth birthday, suffering through wind that raged like a furnace, enduring loneliness that burned like acid. So many people had gone away—among them Henry Dobbs, her assistant J. M. Wilson and her friend Iltyd Clayton—"but Ken I miss most," she moaned; "we're so hand in glove over everything here and we work together so much. I never really know what is going on in the Palace and the Cabinet when he isn't here."

Rising each day before dawn, she exercised for fifteen minutes with a routine Ken had taught her, and then worked in her garden, pulling weeds, snipping zinnias, cutting great bunches of roses and double jasmine to fill her porcelain bowls. Dressed as lightly as possible, in stockings and a minimum of clothes—a silk chemise, a crêpe de Chine sheath and a loose muslin gown—she breakfasted on an egg and fruit, ordered dinner from her cook and, grabbing her hat, slipped into the waiting car for the five-minute drive to the office.

A pile of routine work awaited her, and at her desk, while the ceiling fan shifted the waves of heat, she scrawled memoranda to the ministries, made explanation notes for the acting High Commissioner, Nigel Davidson, translated the Arabic newspapers and handled the Arabs' petitions. By eleven o'clock beads of perspiration dotted her brow and a servant brought in a cup of iced broth on a tray. She continued working nervously, smoking one cigarette after another, careful not to make any errors as she wrote her reports for the Secretary of State. At lunch with Nigel Davidson she went over the pressing matters, and for the first time in months she felt like "a Person," if only because there was no one else around who knew the issues. Nevertheless, her confidence had slipped: "I hope I shall not make any dreadful mistakes," she noted anxiously, "but there's always Nigel to stop me. He is very cautious." It hardly made her feel better when he whipped out a copy of the *Westminster Gazette*; it contained a damning story about the 1921 arrest of Sayid Talib, leaked by Philby.

Instead of the ten-hour days she used to spend at the office, she now worked only three or four hours. After lunch she retreated to her house, but the empty rooms reverberated with loneliness; there was no Ken and little to do until teatime except to lie on the big sofa under the ceiling fan and write letters or read. Florence had sent her three new plays, *Saint Joan*, *Men and the Masses*, and *The Adding Machine*, but as she read Elmer Rice's account of Mr. Zero and his joyless existence, she could hardly help reflecting on her own.

There were few people around to talk to, and although once in a while she dined informally with the King, she almost always ate by herself. On Saturday evenings when the mail arrived, she sat at her table sipping cold soup or eating a bit of fish, reading the letters from England, lingering over the ones from Ken. At ten o'clock she climbed the stairs to the roof and went to sleep, numbed by the feeling that the next day would be much the same. "You know," she wrote, "I have grown into a very solitary person with all these months of living almost completely alone."

It had been "a trying summer"; besides the aching desolation, the *Westminster Gazette* had chafed at an open sore, charging her and Cox with conspiring against the Arabs, plotting the abduction of Sayid Talib and whisking him off. "It raked up the whole Talib story," she groaned, "accused us of having foisted Faisal on Iraq [and] of having intimidated the Assembly." The combination of hurtful accusations, loneliness and crushing heat brought her to the point of nervous exhaustion. She tried to slough it off when writing to her family, but by the end of August she was bedridden and seriously ill. Fearing for her life, Dr. Sinderson came twice a day to see her, and when Nigel Davidson paid a call, he was taken aback. Weak and thin, she lay under the covers in utter despair. Would he pray for her? she pleaded. Black depression, she told him, had settled over her like a dark cloud.

CHAPTER THIRTY-SIX

To Sleep

∞

In the autumn of 1924, after recuperating from her bout of depression, Gertrude was invited by the King to his new estate near Khanaqin. Only a short while before, with Ken still away, she and Faisal had spent an evening together at the theater in Baghdad. The occasion had perked up their spirits. "The King laughed and laughed," she reported, "and as we motored back (incidentally with the King's arm tightly enfolding my waist!) he observed that it had been like spending an evening in London."

Now, taking the overnight train, she arrived in the country early on Saturday morning and immediately joined the King for a partridge shoot; by noon it was too hot to do anything else but rest. She retired to her tent (his country house was not yet built), opened two of the side flaps and, undressing as much as she decently could, lay on her bed reading Thackeray's *Pendennis*. They were light years away from London's literary life, but after tea, riding with Faisal across miles of his empty land overlooking the Persian hills, hearing his dreams for the future, she felt part of an even more special world.

In the evening she dressed to dine with the King, and as they sat at the table under the stars, Faisal, a doleful look in his eyes, confessed that he was still unhappy. Baghdad could never replace Damascus, and though he left it unsaid, it was there, in that flowering desert capital of Greater Syria, that he yearned to rule. Patient and quiet, he kept his thoughts well hidden from most people and rarely exposed his emotions. But on this intimate evening he complained again to Gertrude of how lonely he felt; he had looked forward to coming up to this country place to escape the dull round of palace and office which was all that Baghdad offered. She realized how alone he would have been if she had not come. "He wanted someone to talk to about his plans, to say what fun it would be and how they would all come shooting with him and be keenly interested in what he was doing. I was glad I had come," she wrote. "Besides, I enjoyed it enormously; I too felt like a prisoner escaped."

∞ ∞ ∞

The following day they celebrated together as the city turned out to welcome the King's only son to Baghdad. Twelve-year-old Ghazi had arrived, the first of Faisal's family to flee from Mecca, where Ibn Saud and his Wahhabi warriors were about to attack on the way to conquering the Hejaz; even more people lined the streets than when Faisal had appeared in 1921. The boy seemed a miniature replica of his father, small and shy, with a long, sensitive face and a dignified air. Gertrude warmed to him at once. Taking him under her wing, she rushed to the palace to choose his clothes; suits and shirts had to be made, and she flitted around selecting stripes and tweeds from an English tailor called from Bombay, while, she said, the tailor behaved like a character in Thackeray, skipping about, pointing his toe, handing her patterns "with one hand on his heart." When Ghazi came in to be measured, he was "half shy and half pleased." The boy had been raised in the desert, barely educated but bright, and under her supervision, she had no doubt, he would learn fast. She found him a governess and a tutor to teach him English, and for Christmas she ordered a set of toy trains from Harrods. "He has been very much neglected in a household of slaves and ignorant women," she clucked. Still, she confessed, she could not do as much as she liked. She did not have the authority and would have to wait for Ken to come back.

Only recently Cornwallis had sent her a letter from England describing his divorce. The picture he gave of his wife and his in-laws revealed a painful relationship. "They must be inhuman people," she remarked. "He will be much better when he gets back to his work and to us who know him and love him." She could do a far better job of taking care of him than his wife had done, she felt sure, and in the deepest corner of her heart she hoped that she would become the new Mrs. Cornwallis.

For the moment, however, Gertrude had the company of her sister and brother-in-law. In November, Elsa and her husband, on their way to Ceylon, had stopped in Baghdad, but Gertrude was too ill with bronchitis to shower them with attention. Nevertheless, she begged her family not to bother about her health. The doctor had told her she had "the most surprising power of sudden recovery," and, indeed, by the time that Cornwallis returned at the end of the month, she was up and about, pronouncing herself "perfectly well again." Now it was Ken who needed attention.

The divorce had been a messy affair, with trumped-up charges for evidence and a decree that barred his legal rights to his children. "I'm dreadfully sorry for my dear Ken," she wrote; "[he] has been through a hell of a time and is miserable." Nevertheless, she was sure that he would soon be feeling better, now that he had returned to his work, his colleagues and his devoted friends, "of whom I am the chief. I do love and admire his salient, his almost aggressive integrity and I prize more than I can say the trust and affection he gives me in such full measure."

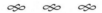

New Year's Eve came on the heels of a heavy snow, the first in fourteen years, and the holiday was one of the "nastiest" she could remember, followed by rains that mired the ground in mud and ice. As Gertrude made her way to the palace, she hardly felt cheered that she was about to meet the Queen. The arrival of Hazaima was as pleasing to her as the weather, but Gertrude slid across the slippery mush to see the royal consort and at once pronounced her "charming." Hazaima's two eldest girls, around eighteen years old, were just like their mother, she noted, "rather shy but eager to be outgoing," and within a matter of days she assigned Ghazi's governess, Miss Fairley, to teach them English, tennis and "European behavior." As for the Queen, Gertrude had few further comments; she was soon discovered to be a coarse, uneducated woman.

When, in the first week of January, it was decided that the Queen would hold her first tea, Gertrude drew up an A list, and invitations were sent to the most important Arab and British women. A few days before the event, she was called to the palace to arrange the tables for the King, and for the first time saw him interact with his family. "The girls were on very good terms with him but the Queen was mute in his presence," she observed, having noted that Faisal was none too pleased by Hazaima's arrival.

Gertrude had asked the wife of Ali Jawdat, chief of the royal household, to take on the job of Mistress of Ceremonies, but it was an uncomfortable role for the inexperienced young woman, and with the Arab ladies too intimidated to talk and the British ladies unable to speak in Arabic, a circle of silence surrounded the Queen. But, as always, Gertrude took things in hand, and, plumping down one guest after another, she managed to draw out the consort. She cringed, however, at the sight of the Queen and the two princesses, "abominably dressed," and announced she would "have to take their clothes in hand."

Her own wardrobe, despite its share of Worths and Molyneux, was suffering from a lack of financial underpinnings: the company with which her father had merged was holding back its dividends, and she was scrimping to save. "I have been very economical and I haven't had a new gown for eighteen months," she commended herself. "I am feeling a little dingy this winter but I hope my bankbook looks brighter." She had spent five hundred and sixty pounds above her salary for the year, much of that on housing, servants and food; the rest had gone for books and papers, seeds and bulbs, accessories, and fabrics for Marie to make into clothes. "On the whole I don't think it has been an extravagant year," she wrote to her father. "Do you?"

∞   ∞   ∞

The Frontier Commission, sent by the League of Nations to determine the borders between Iraq and Turkey, arrived in the middle of January 1925. Although the Turks still claimed the Mosul *vilayet* for themselves, the area was of vital strategic interest to Britain: the mountainous region provided defense against a Turkish invasion; the northern air bases offered protection for the oil fields in Persia and the refineries at Abadan; and the oil fields near Kirkuk not only would yield vast supplies of petroleum for Britain but they would fuel the Iraqi ecomony.

It was essential to present a show of Iraqi solidarity to the commission, and Gertrude was given the task of organizing the Arabs. There could be no sign of dissension within the Iraqi camp. Dobbs sent her to advise the King on his speech to the Commissioners, and a few days later she called on the Prime Minister to hear what he had told the Commission. She spent hours at the palace arranging the seating for the fifty-eight guests—all male except for her—and was decidedly pleased when, as a show of protest against the Turks, the Iraqis appeared, to a man, without a fez. "The Baghdadis are standing to their guns, Ministers, officials of all sorts, notables, all are testifying to the indivisibility of Iraq. Men of all parties have dropped their differences," she reported victoriously. Now all they needed was for those from Mosul to do the same and speak with one voice. "At any rate," she noted, "the Commission has realised that it's a struggle for life on the part of Iraq, not an effort on the part of the British Government to expand its dominions."

By early March, when the Commission announced its decision to give Mosul to Iraq, she busied herself in the negotiations over oil. The Turkish Petroleum Concession, a consortium of British, French and American interests, was the only group big enough and rich enough, she believed, to be able to build the pipelines from Iraq to the Mediterranean, but the local politicians were scurrying to support small local investment groups, and progress was being stymied. "If only the Iraq Cabinet wouldn't be so asinine," she complained. "I think there are better prospects before us than we have had for a long time. . . . The great thing from our point of view is that the development of the country should begin and foreign capital developed." On March 14, 1925 a seventy-five-year accord was granted to the Turkish Petroleum Concession.

∞   ∞   ∞

A few weeks later Gertrude finished a major report for the Secretary of State and left the office with a sense of satisfaction. But by the time she arrived at home, Ken was pacing the floor. Ibn Saud's two thousand Wahhabi raiders, who had already seized the Hejaz, had now attacked the Iraqi border: the King was extremely anxious, yet the High Commissioner, who spoke poor Arabic, refused to believe that the raid had even taken place. What were they to do? It was her job as liaison to explain the situation to Dobbs, and she and Ken agreed on the line she was to take; but troubled over the events, she spent a fitful night. By four in the morning she was up and about, writing a long letter home, arranging bowls of flowers, mulling over her usual breakfast. At last it was time to walk to work. At the office more reports had come in: in days she would learn that almost two hundred men, women and children had been killed; twenty-six thousand sheep and thirty-seven hundred donkeys had been captured; and floods of tribal refugees were rushing into Iraq. It didn't require much effort to convince Sir Henry that an attack had really occurred. But there was no way of avoiding the fact that the gap had begun to spread between Gertrude and the High Commissioner.

Edward DeGaury noticed it soon after he arrived as an army official in the spring of 1925. He had seen the Khatun riding out of a cloud of dust on the road to Kadhimain, sidesaddle on an Arabian mare. Next to her thumped the heavy black car of the High Commissioner waving its Union Jack, preceded by two Indian guards on horseback. As DeGaury approached the Ford, he saluted the passenger, Sir Henry Dobbs. Gertrude put up her riding whip and returned the salute, touching the whip to the brim of her tricorne. Then, her salukis beside her, she dug in her spurs and galloped off, leading the way for Dobbs. Her "very enthusiasm could be an embarrassment," DeGaury wrote later. "Dobbs did not always see eye-to-eye with Gertrude Bell."

He recalled another incident, a day when the King was inspecting the troops. Dressed in his khaki uniform and mounted on a white horse, Faisal was riding slowly out of the palm gardens to take his place for the military inspection. As he reached the saluting post, Gertrude appeared, wearing a white riding habit, galloping at full speed. As she reined in her black mare to his side, Faisal looked askance. She had made "an unforgettable sensation," wrote DeGaury, and behind her back the King complained to Dobbs that the Khatun was ubiquitous.

In truth, she had become almost irrelevant. Except for the death of two dogs—hers and Ken's—which had made her depressed, her days were "uneventful." In the evenings she went walking with Lionel Smith, the Education Adviser, or riding with Iltyd Clayton or motoring with Ken. Her letters, once fifteen pages long and brimming over with political news and anecdotes, were now merely brief notes home about duck shoots, picnics and bridge with the King, who, she was pleased to report, had improved enormously, "his only difficulty being that he can't remember which are clubs and which are spades." The highlight of the Easter season was a trip along the Euphrates, a "surprise," she wrote, adding dejectedly, "so many of my plans have come to nothing."

Packing the car with food, camp beds and baths, she and Ken and a few friends motored out to the Euphrates and indulged in a meal she had brought along: caviar, tongue and Stilton cheese. On the following day they drove to Karbala, and then it was off across the desert, passing lizards two feet long, to see the ruins she had first discovered at Ukhaidir. Her early find of the ancient palace had been one of the most thrilling events in her life, but, usurped and written about by French archaeologists before she had had a chance to publish her work, it had turned into one of her most painful memories. She had not been back since 1911. "It made me feel rather ghostlike to be in these places again, with such years between, and I was glad I wasn't there alone," she wrote to her father. "As for my plans, I'm thinking of coming home for a couple of months towards the end of July."

∞   ∞   ∞

She arrived in London after the season, deliberately wanting to avoid the rush, she said, in a state of mental and physical exhaustion. The family doctors advised a great deal of care and pronounced her unfit to return to the climate of Baghdad. Visitors came and went and saw her thinner and frailer than ever. Chilled even in the summer heat, she stood in the drawing room at Sloane Street, the windows closed, her back to a roaring fire, her long fox coat pulled closely around; smoking her Turkish cigarette through the long holder, she glared as she held forth on a range of subjects. Terrified young nephews and nieces were brought to meet her and remembered long after how "very fierce" she looked. Janet Hogarth came to dine, and Gertrude pulled her aside. "It's lovely out there," she told her wistfully. "What shall I do here, I wonder?" Run for Parliament, Janet suggested, and she toyed with the idea.

At Rounton, she watched her life being packed away. The house had become too expensive to maintain, and her parents were moving out. She knocked on the library door, as she did each morning, and found Florence at work at her desk. Over the years they had had their quarrels and their resentments, but now her mother put down her pen, and they talked about the family's financial crisis, Florence's playwrighting, Gertrude's work and her disappointment over never having married, about Doughty-Wylie and Ken Cornwallis, her father and her future. "I feel as if I had never known you *really* before, not in all these years," Gertrude wrote her later. "I feel certain that I have never loved you, so much, however much I may have loved you."

She took walks across the moors, ruminated over Janet Hogarth's suggestion and wrote a dejected note to her friend: "No, I'm afraid you will never see me in the House. I have an invincible hatred of that kind of politics and if you knew how little I should be fitted for it you would not give it another thought. . . . I have not, and I have never had the quickness of thought and speech which could fit the clash of parliament. I can do my own job in a way and explain why I think that the right way of doing it, but I don't cover a wide enough field and my natural desire is to slip back into the comfortable arena of archaeology and history and to take only an onlooker's interest in the contest over actual affairs."

She visited her sister Molly and confided in her about Ken. She was deeply in love with him, she revealed, and had hoped that after his divorce they would marry. But her dream was a fragile flower that he had crushed in his fist. He had refused to marry her, had flatly turned down her pleas. What would she do? she cried. How could she go back to Baghdad and face the humiliation? Yet how could she come back to England and face the emptiness? The talk with her sister was comforting. Molly made it all seem easy. "You have somehow given me my bearings and I feel as if I could steer straight," Gertrude wrote the next day; "you have taken all the bitterness out and encouraged me to feel that whatever I do it shall be fine and generous, and worthy of the people I belong to."

She tried to avoid Cornwallis, and when he arrived in London in August, escorting the King, she did not let him know that she would be in town. But her father offered to give a dinner for Faisal at the Automobile Club, and there was no way to escape from inviting Ken. When Gertrude took the train to London she found a note from Ken at her Sloane Street house. He would telephone the following morning. Might he come that afternoon? he asked when he phoned. They sipped tea and chatted lightly about his business affairs, his children, the King. Could he come again tomorrow? he asked in his slow, deep voice. No, she replied, her day would be full. She was meeting with Faisal, and besides, they would see each other that night at the club. At the dressmaker's the next day he came to pick her up, and after they lunched, he saw her off at Victoria Cross for Yorkshire. It had all gone well. But it was different. "Somehow," she explained to Molly after returning to Rounton, "I felt as if we had got into a new basis of friendship and I can't help hoping that as far as I am concerned the fire has burned out. Perhaps it was talking to you that did it. . . . Anyhow, Dearest, don't be afraid about us. . . . I leave England on the 30th."

A stream of turbaned visitors kissed her hand, called her "the light of our eyes" and welcomed her back to Baghdad. Ken came the first night for dinner, and at the office and at the museum her work continued. But Cornwallis refused to hear her continued pleas for marriage, and Dobbs refused to share her enthusiasm for the Arabs. Her influence was all but gone. "You must please remember that I am not a Person," she reminded Hugh, sadly. Nevertheless, her passion had not died out.

"The truth is," she wrote to Molly, "that I care for Ken as much as ever and for no one else in the world so much. Not like that, at any rate. After I came back we had some terribly bitter talks—I don't see him often alone—and I know that that only puts him at his most stony. . . . So now I'm bent on showing him what he really knows, that he can't do without me, and he *can't* any more than I can do without him." In their working together, she said, she had given him "inspiration after inspiration." If he did not marry her, she told him, she would leave Iraq.

"I know that if he will let me I can make him very happy and that he can make me happier than I could be any other way. For I want to stay here and do nothing but archaeology in my museum which is a full-time job and my passion; but I can't except on my own terms with him." If he couldn't return her love, she would go back to England "and try to make something of life. . . . But it cannot be any better than a half life." Not because she didn't love her family, she assured her sister, but because "the other sort of love is so overwhelming—It's that other love and the mother and the sister all combined. You understand, I know. I shant write this any more till I have something definite to tell you—whether I go or whether I stay. Ken will know what either means."

❧   ❧   ❧

Her friend Harold Nicolson, diplomat and author, came to visit in November 1925, and after he stayed a night in her house he remarked that she was "adorable . . . a rich generous mine of information about conditions in the Middle East." Nonetheless, at the office her relationship with Dobbs had not improved. They had spoken only recently about Syria, and it was a difficult talk. Their aims were diametrically opposed, and though she tried to be tactful and not antagonistic as she presented her point of view, she found a world of difference between Henry Dobbs and Sir Percy. She and Cox may have had contrasting thoughts about details, but their overall perspective was the same. "We were absolutely at one on the spirit of the thing we are doing. Sir Henry not only doesn't share that spirit, but thinks it nonsense."

The end of the year found her on her way to the King's country house, suffering from a head cold, bundled up in more clothes than she had ever worn, a hot water bottle resting between her knees. The following day, bedridden, with a high fever, she was diagnosed with pleurisy; but with nurses on call night and day, and with Ken at her side, she pulled through. And then, just one month later, only weeks before her parents moved out of Rounton, her brother Hugo succumbed to typhoid. His death came as a shock; his image clung to her mind. She had ridiculed him when they were young, had done what she could to stop him from joining the church, but in spite of her mockery, he had gained what she had wanted most in life and had never achieved. "The thing which comes uppermost," she reflected, "is that he had a complete life. His perfect marriage and the joy of his children."

∞   ∞   ∞

It was a Saturday morning in March 1926 when the writer Vita Sackville-West, Harold Nicolson's wife, came to Baghdad. She had struggled by train from Basrah, had bumped along the dusty roads in an old Ford, then skidded through the mud to Gertrude's house. Pushing the door in the blank wall, Vita limped along the path, past the pots of carnations lining the edge, past the white pony peeking out of the stable door, past the dogs—gray salukis and a little yellow cocker spaniel—and hobbled up to the verandah, where a peacock strutted about. Gertrude called out hello. They had known each other in Constantinople, had lunched in Paris and dined in England, but it was clear to Vita that it was here in Iraq that Gertrude was at home. Gertrude's spirits were up: she had been given a free-standing building for her museum, and her plans, she said, were to make it like the British Museum, "only a little smaller."

As soon as she spotted Vita she let flow a stream of questions; "Had it been very hot in the Gulf?" she asked. Did Vita have fever? Did she have a sprained ankle as well? "Too bad!" Would Vita like porridge first, or a bath?

"She had the gift of making every one feel suddenly eager; of making you feel that life was full and rich and exciting," Vita observed. When her guest expressed a wish for a saluki, Gertrude rushed to the telephone and ordered a selection of the slender, silky-haired dogs to be brought over at once. "Then she was back in her chair, pouring out information: the state of Iraq, the excavations at Ur, the need for a decent museum. What new books had come out? What was happening in England? The doctors had told her she ought not to go through another summer in Baghdad, but what should she do in England, eating out her heart for Iraq? Next year, perhaps . . . but I couldn't say she looked ill, could I? I could, and did. She laughed and brushed that aside. Then, jumping up—for all her movements were quick and impatient—if I had finished my breakfast wouldn't I like my bath? and she must go to her office but would be back for luncheon. Oh yes, and there were people to luncheon; and so, still talking, still laughing, she pinned on a hat without looking in the glass, and took her departure."

Later that day they went to visit the King, who looked, Vita said, "as though he were the prey to a romantic, an almost Byronic, melancholy." As Vita listened, Gertrude and Faisal discussed the kitchen lineoleum for his new country house and the virtues of his new cook and the latest troubles in the government. Then, driving back to Baghdad, Gertrude spoke of Faisal's loneliness. "He likes me to ring up and ask to go to tea," she told her friend.

    ∞   ∞   ∞

The news from England a few weeks later, that her father was deeply depressed over Hugo's death, and that Rounton had finally been abandoned, left Gertrude dazed. "All this sorrow," she wrote to Molly, "has made me feel very numb. . . . I don't think I have any other strong feelings left." Her romance with Ken had dissolved into companionship, a relationship she now called "comforting," and she clung to her quotidian work to keep her going. At least the new museum captured her thoughts.

When, in May 1926 her parents asked if she was coming to London, she refused to commit herself to any plans. Her finances had suffered as a result of a general strike in England, and a trip for just the summer was too expensive. She wanted to finish her work and then go away, she told Florence. Besides, she admitted, she was afraid to leave everything she had been doing to find herself "rather loose on the world. I don't see at all clearly what I shall do, but of course I can't stay here forever." Once in a while Ken stopped by, but for the most part she was alone, shunned by the younger and newer members of the male British staff. Mornings she worked at the museum, and every day Dobbs still kindly invited her to lunch, but, she confessed to her father, "The afternoons, after tea, hang rather heavy on my hands." She ached with loneliness, and the doctor had given her Dial, a sleeping potion, to help her fall asleep.

The new museum was nearly finished, and she hoped that she would be named its official director and put on the payroll of Iraq—just for six months, she said; she could not justify asking for more. Her job with the High Commissioner was almost over. "Politics are dropping out and giving place to big administrative questions in which I'm not concerned and at which I'm no good. On the other hand," she noted, "the Department of Antiquities is now a full time job."

In June there was cause for celebration. The treaty with the Turks, granting Mosul to Iraq, was finally signed. And the following day, at the opening of her new museum, the King helped out at the small ceremony. It pleased her that more than a dozen Baghdadis hurried to see the three thousand objects she had collected. But a letter from home brought more discouraging news. Her father was still depressed and hoped she would come back to England soon. "I don't see for the moment what I can do," she scrawled stubbornly. "You see I have undertaken this very grave responsibility of the Museum." She could not leave "except for the gravest reasons," she insisted; "it's a gigantic task." Nor could she resign from her post as Oriental Secretary. It would mean giving up a salary of a thousand pounds a year plus the greater part of her house rent. "Let us wait for a bit, don't you think, and see how things look."

To Florence she confided, "It is too lonely, my existence here; one can't go on forever living alone. At least I don't feel I can."

And to her former assistant J. M. Wilson, now living in England, she revealed the painful truth: "My horizon is not at all pleasant. The coal strike hits us very hard; I don't know where we shall be this year. I have been caught in the meshes of the museum (oh, for your help with it!) and I can't go away leaving it in its present chaos. So I shall probably stay here through the summer and when I come back, come back for good. Except for the museum, I am not enjoying life at all. One has the sharp sense of being near the end of things with no certainty as to what, if anything, one will do next. It is also very dull, but for the work. I don't know what to do with myself of an afternoon. . . . It is a very lonely business living here now."

An envelope arrived, the printed invitation announcing the state Banquet for the signing of the treaty with Turkey, to be held on the twenty-fifth of June 1926. Standing before the mirror, her slim figure even more fragile, her blue eyes even more piercing, Gertrude dressed for her final victory. Stepping carefully into her gown, with Marie's help, she attached her ribbons of honor to her dress and pinned her tiara to her hair, and then, with her cape over her shoulders, she motored off for the familiar drive to the palace. It was the last official function she would ever attend.

At the dinner, the King rose and expressed his profound thanks to the British Government and its representatives for all they had done for Iraq, and as he looked around the room, she knew he was speaking of her. But the glorious days were gone. Like the image she had drawn of snow, her power had melted away. Her reign of influence was over. Her family fortune had disappeared. Her last love had turned his back. Her health had declined. Physically tried and emotionally spent, she knew she had done all she could do for Iraq and all she could do for the British Empire. The future now lay in the hands of others.

∞ ∞ ∞

The July heat had forced most Baghdadis from the city: her assistant had gone, the King was taking the cures at Vichy, and the Sindersons were leaving for an around-the-world trip, not unlike the one she had taken with Hugo more than twenty years earlier. After seeing off her friends at the train station, Gertrude stood alone, small and frail, looking to Mrs. Sinderson "like a leaf that could be blown away by a breath." A few nights later she was invited by Henry Dobbs to a dinner for a visiting guest. Percy Lorraine, the British Ambassador to Teheran, was going home to report the news that Reza Pahlevi had established himself as Shah of Persia. It was thirty-five years since Gertrude had first met his predecessor, enveloped in his royal tents, attending a parade in Teheran. What memories she had of Persia! What hope she had held then, a young woman of twenty-three, visiting her uncle Frank Lascelles, the British Ambassador. What joy she had felt when she had met Henry Cadogan, handsome, attentive, well read and worldly. With what youthful exuberance she had breathed in the air of the East. Pomegranates and rose bushes, warm breezes drifting across the desert, languid hours by the river with Henry reading the Rubáiyát of Omar Khayyám:

> Oh, come with old Khayyám, and leave the wise
> To talk; one thing is certain, that life flies;
> One thing is certain, and the rest is lies;
> The flower that once hath blown for ever dies.

On Sunday July 11, 1926, three days before her fifty-eighth birthday, Gertrude lunched with Henry Dobbs and Lionel Smith and then went home alone to face the cloud of depression that hung over her every afternoon. Later, after a nap, she joined the Sunday swimming party, but the river current was strong, and she came back exhausted from the swim and the heat. She walked slowly through her garden, past her flowers and her animals, and went inside to ready herself for bed. Too tired to finish a letter to her parents, or even to leave a note, she asked only that Marie awaken her at six the next morning. But she had other plans. Wiping away the dreary future, she took an extra dose of the sleeping pills on her nightstand, turned out the light and went to sleep, a deep sleep from which she never awoke.

Epilogue

∞

Rumors raced through the city, denials of a suicide as strong as those of a natural death. But while acquaintances were shocked to hear that Miss Bell may have taken her own life, those who knew her well were not surprised at all. Her closest friends had known of her dark depression. The Political Officer in charge of organizing her papers called the next day at her house. Her servant admitted that Miss Bell had taken an extra dose of pills. In his public report, Colonel Frank Stafford declared that the Khatun had died of natural causes. But in his private account he concluded that the bulk of evidence pointed to suicide.

∞   ∞   ∞

The full military funeral for Miss Gertrude Bell C.B.E. took place two days before her fifty-eighth birthday. On the afternoon of July 12, 1926, hordes of Iraqis from near and far rushed to Baghdad to bid farewell to the British woman who had touched their lives in every way. Along the road lined with the uniformed troops of Defense Minister

Jafar Pasha's Iraqi army, scores of turbaned sheikhs and hundreds of ordinary citizens—peasants and landowners, merchants and bureaucrats—came to pay her homage. Standing solemnly alongside one another, the High Commissioner and the entire British staff, both civil and military, and the Prime Minister and all the members of his Arab Cabinet watched the group of young British Political Officers carry the Khatun's coffin from the gates of the British cemetery to the fresh place in the earth that marked her gravesite.

∞   ∞   ∞

Henry Dobbs issued an official announcement of her death: "She had for the last ten years of her life consecrated all the indomitable fervour of her spirit and all the astounding gifts of her mind to the service of the Arab cause, and especially to Iraq. At last her body, always frail, was broken by the energy of her soul. . . . Her bones rest where she had wished them to rest, in the soil of Iraq. Her friends are left desolate."

Indeed, her friend Haji Naji wrote touchingly to her parents, "It was my faith always to send Miss Bell the first of my fruits and vegetables and I know not now where I shall send them."

Newspapers throughout the world carried her obituary—not just in notices but in long articles complete with her photograph—and in England, King George sent a message to the Bells:

"The Queen and I are grieved to hear of the death of your distinguished and gifted daughter whom we held in high regard.

"The nation will with us mourn the loss of one who by her intellectual powers, force of character and personal courage rendered important and what I trust will prove lasting benefit to the country and to those regions where she worked with such devotion and self-sacrifice. We truly sympathise with you in your sorrow."

∞   ∞   ∞

When her will was read it was discovered that Gertrude Bell had left fifty thousand pounds to the Baghdad Museum, which she had created, from then until now one of the great antiquities museums of the world. "It is mainly owing to the wisdom and enthusiasm of the late Miss Gertrude Bell that archaeology in Iraq since the War has progressed on such efficient and able lines," wrote Percy Cox. "Thanks to her, too, Iraq has its Museum of antiquities." A plaque was inscribed and hung in the museum:

GERTRUDE BELL

Whose memory the Arabs will ever hold in reverence and affection
Created this Museum in 1923
Being then Honorary Director of Antiquities for the Iraq
With wonderful knowledge and devotion
She assembled the most precious objects in it
And through the heat of the Summer
Worked on them until the day of her death
On 12th July 1926
King Faisal and the Government of Iraq
In gratitude for her great deeds in this country
Have ordered that the Principal Wing shall bear her name
And that with their permission
Her friends have erected this Tablet.

Less than a year after her death, on April 4, 1927, at the meeting of the Royal Geographical Society, tributes were paid by Sir Percy Cox, Sir Gilbert Clayton and Hugh Bell. Sir Percy Goodenough declared, "Her life was an inspiration, her death a grievous loss; but if ever a man or woman left this world victorious it was Gertrude Bell."

Her former chief in the Arab Bureau, Sir Gilbert Clayton, assured the group that she was still well known throughout the length and breadth of the Arab world. The president of the society, her friend David Hogarth, added: "I do not think that any European has enjoyed quite the same reputation. She had all the charm of a woman combined with very many of the qualities that we associate with men. She was known in the East for those manly qualities. . . . I shall not serve any good purpose by trying to say how much I, and many others, have felt her loss. Hers was the brightest spirit that shone upon our labours in the East."

Even today in Baghdad, when old men speak about Miss Bell, their eyes light up and their hearts beat faster. One former official, now in his nineties and bedridden, boasts that when he was twenty years old (and she was fifty-six) he had a love affair with Miss Bell. It is most probably a figment of his imagination. But what matters is how proudly he tells the story. "I knew her," he says, with the pride of one who has known a queen. To him and to many others, the Khatun was the embodiment of the British Empire, the personification of British power. She overcame the obstacles and made her mark on history, and in the end, she was what she had wanted most to be: Miss Gertrude Bell was a Person.

∞ ∞ ∞

The constitutional monarchy that Gertrude Bell had worked so hard to create lasted only seventeen years. Some blamed its downfall on its being too pro-British; others said its defeat lay in the fact that a stranger from the Hejaz had been brought in to lead the distinct and dissimilar groups of people who made up Iraq. Nevertheless, as Gertrude had noted when she wrote about Ibn Saud, the Arabs needed a dynamic personality to unite them, and as long as Faisal was alive, the country survived. It was as much the weakness of his descendants as the attitude of its officials that let it fall into the hands of revolutionaries.

Iraq's economic ascent began in 1927, when the Iraq Petroleum Company struck its first oil wells in Kirkuk. In time it would be recognized that the country held, and continues to hold, the world's second largest oil reserves. But despite Iraq's wealth, the issues that had troubled the British continued to plague it. The clashing population of Shiites, Sunnis and Kurds never really congealed into a solid, unified group. The Kurds in the north still sought independence (as they do today, in Iraq, in Turkey and in Iran), while the Shiite tribes along the Euphrates repeatedly rose up to challenge Sunni rule in Baghdad. The Hashemite monarchy, although moderately successful as an Arab nationalist movement under King Faisal, represented an outside force and was not able to consolidate the various elements vying for control.

Under King Faisal's guidance, the Mandate was ended and Iraq was formally admitted into the League of Nations in 1932, securing the country's complete independence. The following year, on September 8, 1933, having at last made peace with his enemy Ibn Saud, but still feeling the discontent of the Shiite tribes in the middle and southern Euphrates, King Faisal died unexpectedly while on vacation in Switzerland. The country he had ruled, the first of the newly created Arab states to be accepted by the League of Nations, was considered a model for the other mandates.

Faisal was succeeded by his twenty-one-year-old son Ghazi, a popular but far less able leader. Despite his support for Arab nationalism, he lacked his father's political skills and could not maintain a hold on the country. Only six years later, in 1939, after a coup d'état by the Iraqi army and the brutal murder of the Minister of Defense, Jafar Pasha al Askari, King Ghazi was killed, some believe intentionally, in an automobile accident. His four-year-old son Prince Faisal II was proclaimed ruler under the regency of his uncle Abdullilah, the son of King Ali of the Hejaz. In 1953, at the same time that Faisal II reached the age of eighteen and assumed the throne in Iraq, his cousin Hussein was crowned the King of Jordan.

For several years Nuri Said served as Prime Minister and leader of Iraq, working in close alliance with the British, but his support of England in the Suez Crisis against the Egyptian leader Gamal Abdel Nasser helped bring him down. In a swift and bloody coup, on July 14, 1958, the king and his regent were assassinated at the palace, and the following day a mob of people murdered Nuri Said. The revolution marked the end of the Hashemite monarchy in Iraq.

A military junta, led by Abdul Karem Kassim, seized power and established Iraq as a republic. But in 1963 it too was overthrown; Kassim was assassinated and his government swept away by the clandestine Ba'ath Socialist Party. A number of coups and military juntas led to the rise of a young officer, Saddam Hussein. After a series of maneuvers beginning in 1971 and continuing throughout the 1970s, Saddam emerged in 1979 as President, Prime Minister, Chairman of the Revolutionary Council and Secretary-General of the Ba'ath Party.

Today, in Baghdad, in the center of the city, in a major traffic roundabout, atop a huge pedestal stands an imposing statue of King Faisal, slim and distinguished-looking, astride his horse. The giant monument, some thirty feet tall, is pointed in the direction of Damascus. In the basement of the Iraq Museum, on a forgotten shelf, a bronze bust of Miss Gertrude Bell waits to be dusted off.

The Hashemite Family of Sharif Hussein of Mecca

Sharif Hussein

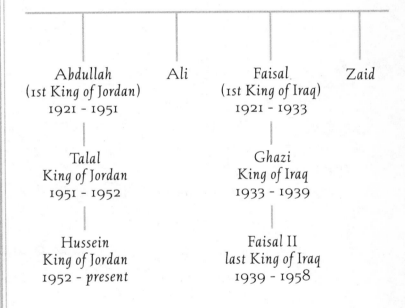

Abdullah
(1st King of Jordan)
1921 - 1951

Ali

Faisal
(1st King of Iraq)
1921 - 1933

Zaid

Talal
King of Jordan
1951 - 1952

Ghazi
King of Iraq
1933 - 1939

Hussein
King of Jordan
1952 - present

Faisal II
last King of Iraq
1939 - 1958

Glossary

∞

CALIPH
Spiritual leader. Considered to be the representative of God on earth.

GHAZU
A dangerous and often deadly raid staged by Bedouin in the desert, it can involve as few as a handful or as many as several thousand horsemen.

KAFEEYAH
A cloth, of cotton or silk, that is wrapped around the head as protection against the sun and the wind.

KHATUN
An important Lady, or the Lady of the Court, who keeps an open eye and ear for the benefit of the State.

RAMADAN
A holy month of fasting. Eating is permitted only between sundown and sunrise, and secular festivities are prohibited.

SAYID
A descendant of Muhammad through his daughter, Fatima, and her husband, Ali.

SHARIF

A descendant of either Hussein or Hassan, grandsons of Muhammad through his daughter Fatima and her husband, Ali. The Sharif Hussein was the guardian of the holy sites of Mecca and Medina.

SHEIKH

An elder statesman or the head of a village or tribe. One who has either political or religious authority.

SHIITE

Member of the Muslim sect that broke off from the Sunni branch of Islam. The political schism developed when the former group wanted to see Ali, a cousin and son-in-law of Muhammad, installed as Caliph and successor to the Prophet. Shiites also follow the doctrine of the Imams, or prayer leaders, who are descendants of the Prophet.

SUNNI

The Islamic branch that recognized Abu Bakr as Caliph and legitimate successor to Muhammad.

VILAYET

An Ottoman province (of which there were twenty-four in all). Administered by a governor but actually ruled from the imperial capital of Constantinople.

WAHHABI

A sect that follows a strict fundamentalist interpretation of Islamic law.

Endnotes

❦

PROLOGUE
❦

PAGE XXIII   *She had been, they seemed to agree* . . . Morris, James, *Farewell the Trumpets*, New York: Harcourt Brace Jovanovich, 1978, p. 408.

CHAPTER ONE
❦

PAGE 5   *"The smoke* . . *."* Quoted in Briggs, Asa, *Victorian Cities*, New York: Harper & Row, 1963, p. 269.

PAGE 9   *"a good wife* . . *."* Colls, Robert, and Philip Dodd, *Englishness: Politics and Culture 1800–1920*, London: Croom Helm, 1986, p. 196.

PAGE 10   *a world graced* . . . Ibid.

PAGE 14   *dead ravens* . . . Bell, Gertrude. Letters, University of Newcastle.

CHAPTER THREE
❧

PAGE 36   *"I write sensibly . . ."* Bell, Gertrude. Letters to Sir Valentine Chirol, University of Durham Library, Special Collections, Palace Green Section.

CHAPTER FIVE
❧

PAGE 44   *sixteenth-century German mapmakers . . . Koller, Teddy, and Moshe Pearlman, Jerusalem,* Jerusalem: Steimatsky's Agency, 1972, p. 12.

PAGE 45   *the British were chosen . . .* Morris, James, *Pax Britannica,* New York: Harcourt Brace Jovanovich, 1968, p. 502.

PAGE 46   *"Such a moon!"* Bell, Gertrude. Diaries, University of Newcastle.

PAGE 51   *"One has to walk . . ."* Ibid.

CHAPTER SIX
❧

PAGE 61   *"I am a Person . . ."* Bell, Gertrude. Diaries, University of Newcastle.

CHAPTER SEVEN
❧

PAGE 66   *The great meeting . . .* Morris, James, *Pax Britannica,* New York: Harcourt Brace Jovanovich, 1968, p. 507.

PAGE 72   *"The Oriental is like . . ."* Bell, Gertrude, *The Desert and the Sown,* London: W. Heinemann, 1907.

PAGE 73   *"It was a stormy morning . . ."* Ibid.

CHAPTER NINE
❧

PAGE 87   *"It's the greatest . . ."* Bell, Gertrude, Letters, University of Newcastle.

PAGE 88   *"I have seldom . . ."* Ibid.

CHAPTER THIRTEEN
∞

PAGE 133   *"damned fool thing . . ."* Tuchman, Barbara W., *The Guns of August*, New York: Ballantine Books, 1994, p. 71.

CHAPTER FOURTEEN
∞

PAGE 138   *"Is sex so much? . . ."* Bell, Gertrude, Private Papers, University of Newcastle.

PAGE 139   *"Someday I'll tell you . . ."* Ibid.

PAGE 140   *"I hated it . . ."* Ibid.

PAGE 140   *"And suppose . . ."* Ibid.

PAGE 141   *". . . there is an eternal . . ."* Ibid.

PAGE 142   *"I can't . . ."* Elizabeth Robins Collection, Series 2, Series 5, Bell Letters, Fales Library, New York University.

PAGE 143   *"speaking hopelessly . . ."* Ibid.

PAGE 143   *"I was falling . . ."* Ibid.

CHAPTER FIFTEEN
∞

PAGE 144   *"We saw nothing . . ."* Bell, Gertrude. Letters, University of Newcastle.

PAGE 144   *"It has ended . . ."* Bell, Molly. Diaries, University of Newcastle.

PAGE 147   *"The military people . . ."* Hogarth, David. Private Papers, St. Anthony's College, Oxford.

PAGE 147   *"Gertrude . . . is . . ."* Ibid.

PAGE 149   *"mostly writing notes . . ."* quoted in Garnett, David, *Letters of T. E. Lawrence*. London: Spring Books. 1964.

CHAPTER SIXTEEN
∞

PAGE 165   *"I get rather tired . . ."* Bell, Gertrude. Letters, University of Newcastle.

PAGE 166   *on March 9, 1916* . . . James, Laurence, *The Golden Warrior*, London: Weidenfeld & Nicolson, 1990, p. III.

CHAPTER SEVENTEEN
∞

PAGE 170   *"I am going away . . ."* Lawrence, M. R., *The Home Letters of T. E. Lawrence and His Brothers*, Oxford. 1954.

PAGE 171   *"Oh how glad . . ."* Bell, Gertrude. Letters, University of Newcastle.

PAGE 178   *"I want to express . . ."* F.O. 882/13 June 15, 1916. Public Records Office.

CHAPTER EIGHTEEN
∞

PAGE 183   *"a nice creature . . ."* Bell, Gertrude. Letters, University of Newcastle.

PAGE 185   *"Yes, it has been . . ."* Ibid.

PAGE 185   *"Rudolfe might be asked . . ."* Ibid.

PAGE 191   *"I hear from Gertrude . . ."* Hogarth, David. Private Papers, St. Anthony's College, Oxford.

CHAPTER NINETEEN
∞

PAGE 196   *"lady of the Court . . ."* Rihani, Ameen, *Ibn Sa'oud of Arabia*, London: Constable & Co., 1928, p. 7.

PAGE 196   *"A very shrewd . . ."* Author's interview with Abdul Razaq Hassani, Baghdad, 1994.

PAGE 202   *"Lawrence, relying on her reports . . ."* Speech by David Hogarth. Royal Geographical Society, April 4, 1927.

CHAPTER TWENTY
∞

PAGE 215   *"Your very affectionate . . ."* Bell, Gertrude. Letters, University of Newcastle.

CHAPTER TWENTY-ONE
∞

PAGE 220   *"Khatun . . . your nation is great . . ."* Interview by Gertrude Bell with the Naqib. Published in Wilson, Arnold T., *Mesopotamia 1917–1920, A Clash of Loyalties*, London, 1931.

PAGE 223   *"more affectionate . . ."* Hogarth, David. Private Papers, St. Anthony's College, Oxford.

PAGE 227   *"Miss Bell has . . ."* Haidar, Rustam, *Memoirs*, translated from the Arabic for the author by Suleiman Mousa, Amman, 1994.

PAGE 228   *"inverted megalomaniac,"* Burgoyne, Elizabeth. Private Papers, West Yorkshire Archives, Colverdale Central Library, Halifax, West Yorkshire.

PAGE 229   *"The Arabs would . . ."* Garnett, David, *Letters of T. E. Lawrence*, London: Spring Books, 1964.

PAGE 229   *"Mrs. Vita was over . . ."* Bell, Gertrude. Letters, University of Newcastle.

PAGE 231   *"I'm glad to be . . ."* Ibid.

CHAPTER TWENTY-TWO
∞

PAGE 235   *But Talib's methods . . .* Ireland, Philip, *Iraq*, London: Jonathan Cape, 1937.

PAGE 236   *"She is the only . . ."* Bell, Gertrude. Diaries, University of Newcastle.

PAGE 237   *"There is practically . . ."* Ibid.

PAGE 239   *"If the French . . ."* Ibid.

CHAPTER TWENTY-THREE
❧

PAGE 241   *"I'm very sorry . . ."* Bell, Gertrude. Letters, University of Newcastle.

PAGE 242   *"On any subject . . ."* quoted in *The Times of London,* obituary. July 21, 1926.

PAGE 243   *"An Arab State . . ."* quoted in Ireland, Philip, *Iraq,* London: Jonathan Cape, 1937, p. 197.

CHAPTER TWENTY-SIX
❧

PAGE 268   *"a sun-dried bureaucrat . . ."* Wilson, Arnold T., *Mesopotamia, 1917–1920, A Clash of Loyalties,* London: 1931, p. 320.

CHAPTER TWENTY-SEVEN
❧

PAGE 270   *"As he wants . . ."* Bell, Gertrude. Letters, University of Newcastle.

PAGE 273   *"I do hope . . ."* Ibid.

PAGE 278   *supporter of Adolf Hitler.* Marlowe, John, *Late Victorian: The Life of Sir Arnold Talbot Wilson,* London: 1967, p. 349.

CHAPTER TWENTY-EIGHT
❧

PAGE 287   *"there's the Jewish interest . . ."* Bell, Gertrude. Letters, University of Newcastle.

CHAPTER TWENTY-NINE
❧

PAGE 291   *"The wind is blowing . . ."* Ireland, Philip. Private Diary, Middle East Institute.

PAGE 293   *"A.T. stands convicted . . ."* Bell, Gertrude. Letters, University of Newcastle.

PAGE 296   *"a private laugh . . ."* quoted in Brown, Malcolm, *T. E. Lawrence, The Selected Letters.* New York: W. W. Norton, 1989, p. 352.

PAGE 297   *"The first ruler . . ."* Report on Middle East Conference held in Cairo and Jerusalem (secret) Cab 24/126, June 1921.

PAGE 299   *"You little* IMP! *. . ."* Quoted in Monroe, Elizabeth, "Gertrude Bell," *British Society for Middle East Studies Bulletin,* 1980.

PAGE 300   *"How easily . . ."* Quoted in Fishman, Jack, *My Darling Clementine.* New York: David McKay Co., 1963, p. 68.

CHAPTER THIRTY
∞

PAGE 303   *threats of intimidation . . .* Graves, Philip, *The Life of Sir Percy Cox,* London: Hutchinson, 1941.

PAGE 303   *gave away thousands . . .* Klieman, Aaron S., *Foundations of British Policy in the Arab World,* Baltimore: Johns Hopkins University Press, 1971.

CHAPTER THIRTY-ONE
∞

PAGE 314   *"There is no meaning . . ."* Quoted in Ireland, Philip, *Iraq,* London: Jonathan Cape, 1937, p. 466.

PAGE 316   *"Brothers! . . . my word is . . ."* Ibid.

CHAPTER THIRTY-TWO
∞

PAGE 325   *"Miss Bell . . ."* Private interview with Guzine Abdel Kadir Rashid, London, 1993.

PAGE 327   *"The notables here . . ."* Bell, Gertrude. Letters, University of Newcastle.

PAGE 328   *"outrageously low . . ."* Ibid.

PAGE 329   *"Muslim women . . ."* Ibid.

PAGE 330   *"since Kirkuk is . . ."* Ibid.

PAGE 332   *"I can't tell you . . ."* Ibid.

CHAPTER THIRTY-THREE
∞

PAGE 335   *"I'm an officer . . ."* Bell, Gertrude. Letters, University of Newcastle.

PAGE 339   *"I must form . . ."* Ibid.

PAGE 339   *"We betrayed him . . ."* Ibid.

CHAPTER THIRTY-FOUR
∞

PAGE 342   *"The King is . . ."* Bell, Gertrude. Letters, University of Newcastle.

PAGE 345   *"I have worked . . ."* Rihani, Ameen, *Ibn Sa'oud of Arabia*, London: Constable, 1928, p. 7.

PAGE 346   *"drunk with sun . . ."* Bell, Gertrude. Letters, University of Newcastle.

PAGE 346   *Sati El Husari . . .* Author's interview with Salma Sati El Husari, Amman, 1994.

PAGE 347   *Ibn Saud's slaves . . .* Rihani, Ameen, *Ibn Sa'oud of Arabia*, London: Constable, 1928.

PAGE 347   *The two tribes would become . . .* Author's interview with Amatzia Baram, Washington, D.C., 1994.

PAGE 347   *Ibn Saud was on the verge . . .* Rihani, Ameen, *Ibn Sa'oud of Arabia*, London: Constable, 1928.

PAGE 348   *When a representative . . .* Dickson, H. R. P., *Kuwait and Her Neighbors*, London, 1956.

PAGE 349   *"There is, remember . . ."* Graves, Philip, *The Life of Sir Percy Cox*, London: Hutchinson, 1941.

CHAPTER THIRTY-FIVE
∞

PAGE 352   *"Yes, the atmosphere . . ."* Bell, Gertrude. Letters, University of Newcastle.

PAGE 353   *"Certain it is that . . ."* quoted in Bell, Gertrude, *The Desert and the Sown*, Boston: Beacon Press, 1987, p. xiii.

PAGE 354   *an American journalist . . .* Harrison, Marguerite, *There's Always Tomorrow*, New York: Farrar & Rinehart, 1935, p. 591. Also Harrison, *New York Times*, July 18, 1926, obituary.

PAGE 355   *"I never had . . ."* Bell, Gertrude. Letters, University of Newcastle.

PAGE 355   *collecting ancient objects . . .* Author's interview with Amatzia Baram, Washington, D.C., 1994.

PAGE 356   *"I have a very great . . ."* Bell, Molly. Diaries, University of Newcastle.

CHAPTER THIRTY-SIX
∞

PAGE 359   *"The King laughed . . ."* Bell, Gertrude. Letters, University of Newcastle.

PAGE 360   *"They must be . . ."* Ibid.

PAGE 361   *"I'm dreadfully sorry . . ."* Ibid.

PAGE 362   *Worths and Molyneux* Author's interview with Mme. Rénée Kabir, London, 1994.

PAGE 362   *"I am feeling . . ."* Bell, Gertrude. Letters, University of Newcastle.

PAGE 363   *"If only the Iraq Cabinet . . ."* Ibid.

PAGE 364   *"his only difficulty . . ."* Ibid.

PAGE 364   *"so many of my plans . . ."* Ibid.

PAGE 366   *"You have somehow . . ."* Bell, Gertrude. Private Papers, University of Newcastle.

Page 366   *"Somehow, . . . I felt as if we had got . . ."* Ibid.

Page 366   *"The truth is . . ."* Ibid.

Page 367   *"We were absolutely . . ."* Bell, Gertrude. Letters, University of Newcastle.

Page 368   *It was a Saturday morning* . . . Sackville-West, Vita. *Passenger to Teheran*, New York: Moyerbell Ltd., 1990.

Page 370   *"I don't see for the moment . . ."* Bell, Gertrude. Letters, University of Newcastle.

Page 370   *"It is too lonely . . ."* Ibid.

EPILOGUE
∞

Page 373   *in his private account* . . . Author's interview with Ali Salah, Baghdad, 1994. See also, Burgoyne, Elizabeth. Private Papers. West Yorkshire Archives. Colverdale Central Library. Halifax, West Yorkshire. See also Ireland, Philip. Private Diary. Middle East Institute Library.

Bibliography

∞

PUBLISHED WORKS BY GERTRUDE BELL

Safar Nameh, Persian Pictures. Published anonymously, Bentley, London, 1894.

Persian Pictures. London: Benn, 1928, and Cape, 1937.

Poems from the Divan of Hafiz. Heinemann, London, 1897. Reprinted with foreword by Sr. E. Denison Ross, 1928.

"Islam in India," *Nineteenth Century and After*, vol. 60, 1906.

"Notes on a Journey through Cilicia and Lycaonia," *Revue Archélogique*, VII, 1906–7.

The Desert and the Sown. Beacon Press, 1987. Originally published in London by Heinemann, 1907.

The Thousand and One Churches (with Sir William Ramsay). Hodder and Stoughton, 1909.

"The Vaulting System at Ukhaidir," *Journal of Hellenic Studies*, XXX, 1910.

"Churches and Monasteries of the Tur Abdin and Neighbouring Districts," *Amida*. Heidelberg, 1910 (see Berchem and Strzygwski); included in *Zeitschrift für Geschichte der Architektur*, no. 9, Heidelberg, 1913.

Amurath to Amurath. London: Heinemann, 1911.

"Damascus," *Blackwood's Magazine*, vol. 189, 1911.

"Asiatic Turkey under the Constitution," *Blackwood's Magazine*, vol. 190, 1911.

"Postroad through the Syrian Desert," *Blackwood's Magazine*, vol. 190, 1911.

Palace and Mosque at Ukhaidir. Clarendon Press, 1914.

The Arabs of Mesopotamia. Published anonymously, Basra: Government Press, 1918.

Review of the Civil Administration of Mesopotamia. Cmd. 1061, HMSO, London, 1920.

"Great Britain and Iraq: An Experiment in Anglo-Asiatic Relations," published anonymously. *The Round Table,* London, 1924.

The Arab War. Confidential information for GHQ Cairo from Gertrude L. Bell. Dispatches for the *Arab Bulletin.* Introduction by Sir Kinahan Cornwallis. London: Golden Cockerel Press, 1940.

PRIVATE WORKS OF GERTRUDE BELL

Common Place Books

Gertrude Bell Diary, University of Newcastle Upon Tyne, U.K. The Robinson Library, Special Collections Department.

Gertrude Bell Diary for Doughty-Wylie, 1913–1914, University of Newcastle Upon Tyne, U.K. The Robinson Library, Special Collections Department.

Gertrude Bell Letters, University of Newcastle Upon Tyne, U.K. The Robinson Library, Special Collections Department.

Letters to Sir Valentine Chirol, University of Durham, University Library, Palace Green Section, Special Collections.

Gertrude Bell Papers, Royal Geographic Society, London, Nov. 1916.

Gertrude Bell Private Papers, University of Newcastle Upon Tyne, U.K. The Robinson Library, Special Collections Department.

Gertrude Bell Photography, University of Newcastle upon Tyne, Department of Archaeology, Photographic Collection.

OTHER PEOPLE'S PRIVATE PAPERS

Bell Letters, The Fales Library, N.Y.U. Library, Elizabeth Robins Collection, Series 2 and 5.

Bell, Molly, Diaries, University of Newcastle Upon Tyne, The Robinson Library, Special Collections.

Burgoyne, Elizabeth, Private Papers, West Yorkshire Archives, Colverdale Central Library, Halifax, West Yorkshire, U.K.

Hogarth, David, Private Papers, St. Anthony's at Oxford.

Ireland, Philip. *Private Diary.* Middle East Institute, Washington, D.C., 1934.

Lawrence, T. E., Letters, Karachi, 1927.

OFFICIAL PAPERS

Arab Bureau Papers, 1911–1919, (from Public Records Office, London). Library of Congress, Microfilm #05081

Arab Bureau Papers. Princeton University Library, Microfilm #06335.

Documents on British Foreign Policy, 1919–1939. Edited by E. L. Woodward and Rohan Butler, London, 1952. Middle East Institute, Washington, D.C.

Foreign Office Papers, FO 882/2 and 882/14. Official Papers, War Office. Whitehall, Sept. 9, 1914. Public Records Office, London.

Memo from Gertrude Bell. India Office Records (R/15/6/34), Office of the Civil Commission, Feb. 23, 1920.

Official Papers, War Office. Whitehall, Sept. 9, 1914.

Report on Middle East Conference in Cairo and Jerusalem (Secret). CAB 24/126, June 1921.

Telegrams (Secret) from Baghdad to India Office. From files of Philip Ireland, 1918–1919.

PERIODICALS AND NEWSPAPERS

Antiquity Magazine, Hill, Stephen, 1976.

Birmingham Gazette, July 14, 1926.

Daily Graphic, July 14, 1926.

Daily Mail, July 13, 1926.

Egyptian Gazette, March 1921.

Historical Series of the Reformed Church in America
    —Van Ess, Dorothy and John, "Pioneers in the Arab World," no.3, William B. Erdmans, Michigan, 1974.

Illustrated London News, George C. Leighton, London.

John O' London's Weekly, Sept. 12, 1931.

Journal of the Central Asian Society.
    —Curzon, Earl of Kedleston, Annual Dinner of CAS, Speech by President of Society, Oct. 12, 1920, vol. 8, part 1, 1921.
    —Sheppard, E. W., Capt., "Some Military Aspects of the Mesopotamia Problem," Oct. 21, 1920, vol. 8, part 1, 1921.
    —Wilson, Arnold, "Mesopotamia: 1914–21," April 15, 1921, vol. 8, part 3, 1921.

London Times
    —De Blowitz, Henri Stephan Opper. "Une Course a Constantinople," October, 1883.
    —August 1908
    —May 4, 1915
    —March 24, 1921

—July 13, 1926
—July 14, 1926
—July 21, 1926
—July 31, 1926

London Times Literary Supplement
   —Jan. 13, 1910
   —Jan. 12, 1911

Murray's Magazine,
   —Stewart, C. E., "Petroleum or Rock Oil," vol. 1, Jan.–June, 1889, London.

The New Yorker
   —Pfaff, William, "The Absence of Empire," August 10, 1992.

New York Times
   —Harrison, Marguerite, "Obituary regarding 1916–1917," July 18, 1926, also March 6, 1924.

New York University Journal of International Law and Politics
   —Khadduri, Majid, "Iraq's Claim to the Sovereignty of Kuwait," Fall 1990.

North American Review
   —Courtney, Janet

Observer
   —Raban, Johnathon, Oct. 15, 1978.
   —Nicolson, Harold, July 30, 1961.

Poetics Today
   —Baram, Amatzia, "A Case of An Imported Identity: The Modernizing Secular Ruling Elites of Iraq and the Conception of Mesopotamian-Inspired Territorial Nationalism 1922–1992," Summer 1994.

Saturday Evening Post
   —Lansing, Robert, "The Big Four of the Peace Conference," March 12, 1921.

United Empire
   —Cox, Sir Percy, Speech on Iraq, vol. 20, March 1929.

The World Today
   —MacMunn, George, Lt-General Sir, "Gertrude Bell and T. E. Lawrence: The Other Side of their Stories," November–December 1927.

GERTRUDE BELL BIOGRAPHIES

Bell, Florence. *Letters of Gertrude Bell*, vols. 1 and 2. London: Ernest Benn Ltd., 1927.

Burgoyne, Elizabeth. *Gertrude Bell*, vols. 1 and 2. London: Ernest Benn, 1961.

Goodman, Susan. *Gertrude Bell*. London: Berg Publishers, 1985.

Kamm, Josephine. *Daughter of the Desert: The Story of Gertrude Bell*. London: Bodley Head, 1956.

Marshall, Caroline. *Gertrude Bell: Her Work and Influence in the Near East 1914–1926*. University of Virginia Dissertation (unpublished), 1968.

Richmond, Elsa Lady. *The Earlier Letters of Gertrude Bell*. London: Benn, 1937.

Ridley, M. R. *Gertrude Bell*. London: Blackie, 1941.

Winstone, H. V. F., *Gertrude Bell*. New York: Quartet Books, 1978.

GENERAL

Aldington, Richard. *Lawrence of Arabia*. London: Collins, 1955.

Allison, Alexander W. *The Norton Anthology of Poetry*, 3rd ed. New York: W. W. Norton & Co., 1983.

Alsor, Susan Mary. *Lady Sackville*. New York: Doubleday, 1978.

Antonius, George. *The Arab Awakening*. New York: Putnam, 1946.

Askari, Jafar Al. *Memoirs of Jafar Al Askari*. Surrey, England: Laam Ltd., 1988.

Baedeker, Karl. *Palestine and Syria: Handbook for Travellers*. Leipzig: Karl Baedeker Publishers, 1912.

Baker, Randall. *King Hussein and the Kingdom of Hejaz*. Cambridge, England: Oleander Press, 1979.

Barker, A. J. *The Neglected War—Mesopotamia 1914–1918*. London: Faber & Faber, 1967.

Benjamin, S. G. W. *Persia and the Persians*. London: John Murray, 1987.

Benn, Ernest. *Happier Days*. London: Ernest Benn, 1949.

Black, Eugene C. *Victorian Culture and Society*. New York: Harper & Row, 1973.

Blunt, Lady Anne and Wilfred. *A Pilgrimage to Nejd, the Cradle of the Arab Race*. London: J. Murray, 1881.

Boucher, Francois. *20,000 Years of Fashion*. New York: Harry Abrams, 1966.

Bowman, Humphrey. *Middle East Window*. London: Longmans, Green, 1942.

Boyle, Andrew. *Trenchard*. London: Collins, 1962.

Bullard, Reader, Sir. *The Camels Must Go*. London: Faber & Faber, 1961.

Burton, Isabel. *The Inner Life of Syria, Palestine and the Holy Land*. London: H. S. King, 1875.

Busch, Briton Cooper. *Britain, India and The Arabs 1914–1921*. Berkeley: University of California Press, 1971.

Caldwell, Mark and Kendrick, Walter. *The Treasury of English Poetry*. New York: Doubleday, 1984.

Chambers, John. *The Devil's Horsemen*. New York: Atheneum, 1977.

Charmley, John. *Lord Lloyd and the Decline of the British Empire*. New York: St. Martin's Press, 1987.

Chirol, Valentine. *50 Years in a Changing World*. London: Jonathan Cape, 1927.

Collier, E. C. F. *A Victorian Diarist: Extracts from the Journals of Lady Mary Monkswell*. London: John Murray, 1944.

Collins, Robert O. *Sir Gilbert Clayton: An Arabian Diary*. Berkeley: University of California Press, 1969.

Colls, Robert and Dodd, Philip. *Englishness: Politics and Culture 1800–1920*. London: Croom Helm, 1986.

Cook, Roy J. *One Hundred and One Famous Poems*. Chicago: Contemporany Books, Inc., 1958.

Courtney, Janet. *Oxford Portrait Gallery*. London: Chapman and Hall, 1931.

———. *The Women of My Time*. London: L. Dickson, 1934.

De Gaury, Gerald. *Three Kings in Baghdad*. London: Hutchinson, 1961.

———. *Traces of Travel*. London: Quartet Books, 1983.

Dickson, H. R. P. *The Arab of the Desert*. London: Allen and Unwin, 1949.

———. *Kuwait and Her Neighbors*. London: Allen and Unwin, 1956.

Dickson, Violet. *Forty Years in Kuwait*. London: Allen and Unwin, 1971.

Edel, Leon. *Henry James: A Life*. New York: Harper & Row, 1985.

Egan, Eleanor Franklin. *The War in the Cradle of the World: Mesopotamia*. New York: Harper & Brothers, 1918.

Eliot, T. S. *A Choice of Kipling's Verse*. London: Faber & Faber Ltd., 1990.

Ffrench, Yvonne. *Six Great Englishwomen*. London: Hamilton, 1953.

Fishman, Jack. *My Darling Clementine*. New York: David McKay Co., 1963.

Fogg, Perry. *Arabistan or the Land of the Arabian Nights*. London: S. Low, Marston, Low and Serle, 1875.

Forbes, Rosita. *Appointment in the Sun*. London: Cassell, 1949.

———. *Forbidden Road: Kabul to Samarkand*. New York: E. P. Dutton, 1937.

———. *These Men I Knew*. New York: Dutton & Co., 1940.

Fromkin, David. *A Peace to End All Peace*. New York: Avon Books, 1989.

Garnett, David. *Letters of T. E. Lawrence*. London: Spring Books, 1964.

Gellhorn, E. Cowles. *McKay's Guide to the Far East and the Middle East*. New York: Van Rees Press, 1956.

George, David Lloyd. *The War Memoirs of David Lloyd George*, 2 vols., 1914–1915 and 1915–1916. Boston and New York: Little, Brown, 1933.

Gilbert, Martin. *Churchill: A Life*. New York: Henry Holt, 1991.

———. *Exile and Return*. Philadelphia: J. B. Lippincott, 1978.

———. *Winston S. Churchill*, vol. 4. London: Heinemann, 1966.

Glasse, Cyril. *The Concise Encyclopedia of Islam*. Harper San Francisco, 1991.

Grant, Christina Phelps. *The Syrian Desert*. London: A & C Black, 1937.

Graves, Philip. *Briton and Turk*. London: Hutchinson, 1941.

———. *The Life of Sir Percy Cox*. London: Hutchinson, 1941.

Graves, Robert. *Lawrence and The Arabs*. London: Jonathan Cape, 1927.

Greenfield, Ellen J. *One Hundred and One Classics of Victorian Verse*. Chicago: Contemporary Books, 1992.

Gwynn, Stephen. *The Letters and Friendships of Sir Cecil Spring Rice*. Boston: Houghton Mifflin, 1929.

Haddawy, Husain. *The Arabian Nights*. New York: W. W. Norton, 1990.

Hamilton, Charles. *Americans and Oil in the Middle East*. Houston: Gulf Publishing, 1962.

Harrison, Marguerite. *There's Always Tomorrow*. New York: Farrar & Rinehart, 1935.

Hogarth, David, Dr. Speech at the Royal Geographic Society, 1927.

Hopwood, Derek. *Tales of Empire*. London: I. B. Taruis, 1989.

Hourani, A. H. *Great Britain and the Arab World*. London: J. Murray, 1945.

————. *A History of the Arab People*. Cambridge, Mass.: Belknap Press of Harvard University Press, 1991.

House, Edward M., and Charles Seymour. *What Really Happened at Paris*. New York: Charles Scribner's, 1921.

Howell, Georgina. *In Vogue*. New York: Schocken, 1976.

Hudson, Michael. *Arab Politics: The Search for Legitimacy*. New Haven: Yale University Press, 1977.

Ireland, Philip. *Iraq*. London: Jonathan Cape, 1937.

Jalland, Pat. *Women, Marriage and Politics 1860–1914*. London: Clarendon Press, 1986.

James, Lawrence. *The Golden Warrior*. London: Weidenfeld & Nicolson, 1990.

Jolliffe, John. *Raymond Asquith: Life and Letters*. London: Century, 1980.

Kadourie, Elie. *England and the Middle East*. Hassocks, Sussex: Harvester Press, 1978.

Kaplan, Robert D. *The Arabist: The Romance of an American Elite*. New York: The Free Press, 1993.

Kemp, Geoffrey, and John Maurer. *Projection of Power, The Logistics of Pax Britannica, Lessons for America*. Hamden, Conn.: Archon Books, 1982.

Keyes, Roger, Sir. *The Fight for Gallipoli*. London: Eyre and Spottiswoode, 1941.

Khadduri, Majid. *Independent Iraq 1932–1958*. London: Oxford University Press, 1960.

Klieman, Aaron S. *Foundations of British Policy in the Arab World*. Baltimore: Johns Hopkins University Press, 1971.

Kollek, Teddy, and Moshe Pearlman. *Jerusalem*. Jerusalem: Steimatsky's Agency Limited, 1972.

Lawrence, A. W. *T. E. Lawrence by His Friends*. London: Jonathan Cape, 1937.

Lawrence, M. R. *The Home Letters of T. E. Lawrence and His Brothers*. Oxford: Blackwell, 1954.

Leary, Lewis G. *Syria, The Land of Lebanon*. New York: McBride Nast and Co., 1913.

Lees-Milne, James. *Harold Nicolson, A Biography, 1886–1929*. London: Chatto & Windus, 1980.

Lloyd, Seton. *Ruined Cities of Iraq*. London: Oxford University Press, 1942.

Locher, A. *With Star and Crescent*. Philadelphia: Aetna Publishing Co., 1889.

Longrigg, Stephen. *Oil in the Middle East*. London: Oxford University Press, 1968.

Lyell, Thomas. *The Ins and Outs of Mesopotamia*. London: A. M. Philpot, 1923.

Mack, John E. *A Prince of Our Disorder*. Boston and New York: Little, Brown, 1976.

Manchester, William. *The Last Lion: Winston Spencer Churchill—Visions of Glory, 1874–1932*. Boston and New York: Little, Brown, 1983.

Marlowe, John. *Arab Nationalism and British Imperialism*. London: Cresset Press, 1961.

Marlowe, John. *Late Victorian: The Life of Sir Arnold Talbot Wilson*. London: Cresset Press, 1967.

Mauger, Thierry. *The Ark of the Desert*. Paris: Interpublications, 1991.

Mee, Charles L., Jr. *The End of Order*. New York: Dutton, 1980.

Meinertzhagen, Colonel R. *Middle East Diary 1917–1956*. London: Cresset Press, 1959.

Mejcher, Helmut. *Imperial Quest for Oil: Iraq 1910–28*. London: Ithaca Press, 1976.

Melman, Billie. *Women's Orients: English Women and the Middle East, 1718–1918*. Ann Arbor: University of Michigan Press, 1992.

Monroe, Elizabeth. *Britain's Moment in the Middle East*. London: Chatto & Windus, 1963.

————. *Philby of Arabia*. London: Faber & Faber, 1973.

Moorehouse, Geoffrey. *India Britannica*. London: Paladin Books, 1984.

Morris, James. *Farewell the Trumpets*. New York: Harcourt Brace Jovanovich, 1978.

————. *The Hashemite Kings*. New York: Pantheon, 1959.

————. *Pax Britannica*. New York: Harcourt Brace Jovanovich, 1968.

Mustard, Sayid Ghulam. *Cross in the Subcontinent*. Karachi: Pakistan Publishing House, 1961.

Nicolson, Harold. *Diaries and Letters 1930–1939*, ed. by Nigel Nicolson. New York: Atheneum, 1966

Nochlin, Linda. *The Politics of Vision*. New York: Harper & Row, 1989.

Payne, Ronald. *Private Spies*. London: Arthur Barrer, Ltd.

Peterson, Jeanne M. *Family, Love, and Work in the Lives of Victorian Gentlewomen*. Bloomington: Indiana University Press, 1989.

Pettigren, Jane. *An Edwardian Childhood*. Boston and New York: Little, Brown, 1992.

Philby, H. St. J. B. *Arabian Days*. London, 1948.

————. *Arabian Oil Ventures*. Washington, D.C.: The Middle East Institute, 1964.

————. *Arabian Jubilee*. London: Robert Hale Ltd., 1954.

Raswan, Carl R. *Black Tents of Arabia*. New York: Creative Age Press, 1947.

Rich, Paul. *Arab War Lords and Iraqi Star Gazers*. Cambridge, England: Allborough Publishing, 1992.

Rihani, Ameen. *Ibn Sa'oud of Arabia*. London: Constable & Co., 1928.

Roosevelt, Kermit. *War in the Garden of Eden*. New York: Scribner's, 1920.

Rosen, Friedrich. *Oriental Memories of a German Diplomatist*. London: Methuen, 1930.

Rosenbaum, S. P. *Victorian Bloomsbury*, vol. 1. New York: St. Martin's Press, 1987.

Sachar, Howard. *The Emergence of the Middle East, 1914–1924*. New York: Knopf, 1969.

Sackville-West, Vita. *Passenger to Teheran*. New York: Moyerbell Ltd., 1990.

Said, Edward. *Orientalism*. New York: Random House, 1978.

Sanders, Ronald. *The High Walls of Jerusalem*. New York: Holt Rinehart & Winston, 1983.

Schulkind, Jeanne. *Virginia Woolf, Moments of Being*. New York: Harcourt Brace Jovanovich, 1976.

Seabrook, W. B. *Adventures in Arabia*. New York: Harcourt, Brace & Co., 1927.

Searight, Sarah. *The British in the Middle East*. London: East-West Publications, 1979.

Showker, Kay. *Fodor's Egypt*. New York: David McKay Co., 1979.

Sluglett, Peter. *Britain in Iraq, 1914–32*. London: Ithaca Press, 1962.

Stark, Freya. *The Arab Island*. New York: Knopf, 1945.

Stevenson, Frances. *Lloyd George: A Diary*. New York: Harper & Row, 1971.

Stewart, Desmond. *T. E. Lawrence*. New York: Hamish Hamilton, 1977.

Stocking, George W. *Middle East Oil*. Nashville: Vanderbilt University Press, 1970.

Storrs, Ronald. *Orientations*. London: Nicholson and Watson, 1943.

Tabachnick, Stephen. *The T. E. Lawrence Puzzle*. Athens: University of Georgia Press, 1984.

Tarbush, Mohammad. *The Role of the Military in Politics, A Case Study of Iraq to 1941*. London: KPI, 1982.

Thackeray, William Makepeace. *Cornhill to Grand Cairo*. Heathfield, East Sussex: Cockbird Press, 1991.

Thomas, Bertram. *Alarms and Excursions in Arabia*. London: Allen & Unwin, 1931.

Thomas, Lowell. *With Lawrence in Arabia*. Garden City: Garden City Publishing, 1924.

Thomas, Margaret. *Two Years in Palestine and Syria*. New York: Charles Scribner's Sons, 1899.

Thompson, Walter Henry. *Assignment: Churchill*. New York: Farrar, Straus and Young, 1955.

Trager, James. *The People's Chronology*. New York: Holt Rinehart Winston, 1979.

Tuchman, Barbara. *The Proud Tower*. New York: Macmillan, 1966.

Vaczek, Louis, and Gail Buckland. *Travelers in Ancient Lands*. Boston and New York: Little, Brown, 1981.

Van Der Mëulen and Von Wissmann. *Hadromout*. Leyden: E. J. Brill, 1932.

Villars, Jean Beraud. *T. E. Lawrence*. New York: Duell, Sloan & Pearce, 1959.

Ward, Philip. *Ha'il*. Cambridge, England: Oleander Press, 1983.

West, Rebecca. *1900*. New York: Viking Press, 1982.

Westrate, Bruce. *The Arab Bureau, British Policy in the Middle East, 1916–1920*. University Park: Pennsylvania State University Press, 1992.

Wilcox, R. Turner. *The Mode in Costume*. New York: Charles Scribner's Sons, 1958.

Wilson, Arnold T. *Loyalties, Mesopotamia, 1904–1917*. London: Oxford University Press, 1930.

———. *Mesopotamia, 1917–1920, A Clash of Loyalties*. London: Oxford University Press, 1931.

Wilson, Jeremy. *Lawrence of Arabia*. New York: Atheneum Press, 1990.

Winstone, H. V. F. *The Illicit Adventure*. London: Jonathan Cape, 1982.

———. *Leachman: OC Desert*. London: Quartet Books, 1982.

Yardley, Michael. *A Biography, T. E. Lawrence*. New York: Stein & Day, 1985.

Young, Gavin. *Iraq: Land of Two Rivers*. London, Collins, 1980.

———. *Return to the Marshes*. Harmondsworth: Penguin, 1989.

Young, Geoffrey Winthrop. Editor *Mountain Craft*. London, Methuen and Co., 1920.

Young, Hubert Sir, Major. *The Independent Arab*. London, J. Murray, 1933.

OTHER

The Grand Cause, Film made by Iraqi Government (courtesy Nizar Hamdoon, Iraqi Ambassador to United Nations). 1982

Karabel, Zachary. *The King Makers: Faisal and the Creation of Iraq 1918–1921*. St. Anthony's College, Oxford.

The Kingdom of Saudi Arabia. London: Stacey International, 1977.

Index